Lee Goldberg

HISTORY AND METHODOLOGY OF ECONOMETRICS

HISTORY AND METHODOLOGY OF ECONOMETRICS

Edited by

Neil de Marchi and Christopher Gilbert

CLARENDON PRESS · OXFORD
1989

Oxford University Press, Walton Street, Oxford OX2 6OR

Oxford   New York   Toronto
Delhi   Bombay   Calcutta   Madras   Karachi
Petaling Jaya   Singapore   Hong Kong   Tokyo
Nairobi   Dar es Salaam   Cape Town
Melbourne   Auckland
and associated companies in
Berlin   Ibadan

Oxford is a trade mark of Oxford University Press

Published in the United States
by Oxford University Press, New York

British Library Cataloguing in Publication Data

History and methodology of econometrics. (OEP special issue)
1. Econometrics, history
I. De Marchi, Neil   II. Gilbert, Christopher 1936–
III. Series
330'.028
ISBN 0-19-929311-3

Library of Congress Cataloging in Publication Data
History and methodology of econometrics / edited by Neil de Marchi and
Christopher Gilbert
p.   cm.
1. Econometrics.   I. De Marchi, Neil.   II. Gilbert, Christopher.
HB139.H57   1989   330'.01'5195--d 20   89-16188
ISBN 0-19-828311-3

Printed in Northern Ireland by The Universities Press (Belfast) Ltd

CONTENTS

SECTION 4. CRITICAL HISTORIES

NOTE

On page 2, lines 23 and 24 for 'tradition in economics: one, which' read 'tradition in economics, one which'.

On page 42, fig. 2 the dotted line at -1 should be at 0.86. The -1 refers to the end of the axis.

On page 46, line 25 for 'structural relations' read 'confluent relations'.

On page 105, equations (11) and (12) the x should be π in both cases.

On page 149, Table A1 under 'Function(s) fitted' line 8 should read i.e.

$$\log e = \alpha + \beta \log y + \gamma (\log y)^2$$

On page 182, equation (9c) should read

$$\log (\dot{W}/W + 0.90) = 9.638 - 1.394 \log U, \quad (R^2 = 0.96), \tag{9c}$$

On page 182, equation beginning 7a. should read

$$7a. \ \dot{W}/W + 1.0035 = 8.7339 \, U^{-1.2913} - 0.02529 \dot{U}/U^{1.1874}$$

On page 183, equation (11) should read

$$\dot{p}/p \equiv \alpha \dot{W}/W + (1-\alpha)\dot{p}_m/p_m - \dot{A}/A, \quad \dot{A}/A > 0, \tag{11}$$

Oxford Economic Papers 41 (1989), 1–11

INTRODUCTION

By NEIL DE MARCHI *and* CHRISTOPHER GILBERT[1]

1. Origins

THE ECONOMETRIC SOCIETY was founded on December 29, 1930. The enterprise of estimating economic-theoretic relations, however, is somewhat older; while formal solutions to the identification problem (in systems of equations) were derived only in the mid-1940s. In fact it is unimportant to date the birth of econometrics precisely, even if a criterion could be agreed. What matters is that econometricians can claim enough history and respect to permit some critical self-reflection without the attempt necessarily causing either angst or impatience. Critical reflection is in order just now because the momentum of the research programme carried out at the Cowles Commission in the 1940s has waned. This programme, which made structural estimation and methods to that end the core of standard econometrics, elevated simultaneity above other possible ways of portraying economic relations and placed economic theory above data and its characterization. These emphases are being re-evaluated and this volume is intended in part to facilitate the process of reassessment.

While dating the birth of econometrics is not crucial, it is important to note how the concept of econometrics has narrowed and altered over the past fifty years of so. We now understand the term 'econometrics' to mean statistical methods applied to economic data. The task to be undertaken, as conceived by the founders of the Econometric Society, was, however, both different from and broader than the merely technical. In 1930, there was seen to be:

(i) a need to gain acceptance by economists that statistical methods may validly be applied to economic data;
(ii) a need for agreement on how to apply these methods; and
(iii) a need for satisfactory data to allow the methods to be usefully brought to bear.

In addition, the econometricians of the 1930s had a strong sense that it was part of their mission to help make economics 'operational'. This meant showing how numbers could be put to economic-theoretic entities and relations; but before that could be done, verbal theories had to be checked for 'completeness', and expressed in terms of explicit and exact relations: that is, they had to be formulated mathematically.[2] 'Mathematicizing' economics thus was seen as a necessary part of the larger enterprise.

---

[1] This introduction has benefited from comments from Mary Morgan and Duo Qin. All views expressed are, however, our own. In addition, we wish to take this opportunity to thank Dr. Morgan for her very considerable assistance throughout the production of this volume.

[2] See Andvig [1985], ch. 2 on Frisch; and Tinbergen [1937], introduction; [1939] vol. 1, p. 13 and vol. 2, pp. 14–15; and [1940], pp. 80–81.

This last posed a distinct challenge to other economists. However, the extended conflict over the desirability of mathematical economics, while vociferous, probably involved philosophical prejudices less deep-seated than the proposition that statistical methods are applicable in economics. The attack on this position was led by Haavelmo.

2. Haavelmo

The paradigm for the research pursued at the Cowles Commission was laid down in Haavelmo's methodological manifesto (as it is correctly dubbed by Aldrich, below) *The Probability Approach in Econometrics* [1944].[3] Haavelmo supplied a framework to meet (ii), but his main purpose was to challenge the doctrine that statistics has little to contribute in economics. In particular, he insisted that economic theory is essentially "stochastic," not exact ([1944], pp. 2, 43, 51). He also confronted typical objections to applying probabilistic methods to economic time series, arguing that the difficulties of fulfilling the *ceteris paribus* condition, and of obtaining enough variation to extract from the whole underlying set of causes the separate relations responsible for the movements in the series, are neither peculiar to time series data nor insurmountable in practice (*ibid,* section 6). Finally, he urged that the fact that economic observations are not experimentally generated does not preclude treating them for practical purposes as if they were (*ibid,* pp. 43, 48).

This combined principled and pragmatic defence of probabilistic methods in economics defied a century-old methodological tradition in economics: one, which regarded economic theory as exact and true, although incomplete.[4] It defied too a more recent but equally heartfelt conviction that the reversibility problem—the non-constancy or non-homogeneity through time of economic data—precluded statistical methods. These two traditions had combined to limit the role of statistics in economics to verifying theory or to establishing just how large the gaps are between the predictions of (true) theory and the facts. The true theory, of course, embodied the main causes thought to be present and operating in a wide variety of cases; the supposedly minor, and irregular or 'disturbing causes' were put into the *ceteris paribus* pound.

Haavelmo suggested that these disturbing elements be incorporated as an error term; but he also suggested that this term be thought of as standing for the amalgam of all less than systematic influences, and as representable by a joint probability distribution. The parameters of this distribution then unavoidably enter into the formulation of the theory itself. But this was not at all consistent with the two traditions. As Marshall, here standing for those convinced about the non-constancy of economic data, put it in a letter to Bowley: "I regard the method of Least Squares as involving an

---

[3] Mimeo version circulated in 1941.
[4] i.e. true as far as it goes: Mill [1967] (first published 1844), pp. 326, 329.

assumption with regard to symmetry that vitiates all its applications to economic problems with which I am acquainted".[5] For such skeptics—and as Lawson reminds us below, one can invoke Keynes in this connection[6]— there was only a small class of problems (games of chance, actuarial problems, measurement problems in the natural sciences, perhaps heredity) where one can assume sufficient randomness to apply the law of large numbers. Elsewhere (including economics) statistics must eschew formal theory. Here the older tradition comes back in; for if a formal model of the disturbances is ruled out and economic theory is believed true as far as it goes, then the only role left for statistics is indeed to supply supplementary information about what is packed away in *ceteris paribus*. Marshall in fact shared both convictions. Referring in a veiled way to the sort of 'zero wind interference' assumption often put into *ceteris paribus* in the writings of economists, he made clear in the same letter to Bowley that "To study the wind and guess [on the basis of that study] how it will deflect the bullets is, in my opinion, the work of the statistician" (*ibid*).

Given these doubts on the part of influential economists, it is not surprising that many of the advances in applying statistical theory and methods in economics in ways that challenged the traditional views were made by individuals who were critical of accepted economic theory (Moore); or who pursued practical questions from a base in other disciplines or outside mainstream economics departments (the geneticist Sewall Wright; agricultural economists such as E.J. and Holbrook Working and Mordecai Ezekiel); or who came to economics from other disciplines (Tinbergen and Koopmans from physics—see Mirowski, below).

These early contributions are covered in Morgan (1989) and some are given extended treatment in various papers in this collection. We shall say no more here therefore, except to note that the problems these early workers dealt with, and their proposed solutions, were quite diverse. It was Haavelmo's achievement that, apart from posing a major challenge to traditional methodology, he also shaped for the first time a coherent framework for applying statistics to economics, thereby enabling agreement to be reached on methods.

3. Simultaneity

Simultaneity was the innovative unifying exemplar in Haavelmo's manifesto.[7] There are at least three points from which it may have entered his thinking. One is that he took seriously Frisch's longstanding concerns about how one can discriminate between alternative directions of regression (see Hendry and Morgan, below). A second likely influence from Frisch, to which Epstein has drawn attention (below) is his 1933 exploration of a

---

[5] Letter dated 21.ii.1901 (Pigou [1956], p. 419).
[6] Also Morgenstern, and even Frisch—see Morgan [1987b], p. 7.
[7] See Morgan [1987a], section 1.

simple (two equation) model in price and quantity, from which it emerged that the behaviour of these observables reflects information from the complete underlying system. A further result here was that least squares estimation applied to each equation separately would not guarantee consistent parameter estimates (*ibid*). Haavelmo generalized this insight and described simultaneity bias as "the statistical side of the problem of autonomous relations" ([1944], p. 84).[8]

This leads into a set of issues together amounting to a conceptual basis for preferring simultaneity. Frisch's early interest in identifying 'true' relationships had developed into his distinction between merely 'confluent' (derived, phenomenological) and 'autonomous' relations, which continue to hold when others in the larger complex of which they form a part alter (see Aldrich, and Hendry and Morgan, below). Autonomy was of importance because it meant that one could characterize the structure of a system in terms of the parameters of its autonomous relations; and the prevailing structure had to be known if one were to predict the effects of imposed policy changes. Frisch, but more particularly Tinbergen through his multi-equation models designed for policy simulation, pushed Haavelmo still farther in the direction of analyzing mutual dependence systems.

Now interdependence does not have to be characterized by simultaneity; recursive systems will also do (see the extended discussion in Morgan [1987b]). Haavelmo's 'theoretical' (non-statistical) justification for insisting on simultaneity seems to have been that structures are specific to time and place; they can and do change. Hence it is important to know, represent and understand the underlying (autonomous) system in such a way that various alternative structures may be considered and compared ([1944], pp. 26–28). A simultaneous system of relations both enables this comparison and "gives us an explanation of the fact that, out of . . . [the] enormous set of possibilities,only one very particular one actually emerges" (ibid, p. 27). This may still look like a justification of interdependence only; but again, structure, interpreted as interdependence at a point in time, seems to have been given precedence here over dynamic sequences because of the idea that policy is best viewed as imposed structural change. The connection with comparative statics and a starting position of (general) equilibrium, which also gives full place to the economic theory of optimization, is obvious.

4. The Cowles Programme

With Haavelmo's thoroughgoing concentration on simultaneity, identification and estimation too came to be defined as 'structural' problems in simultaneous systems. There was not much evidence then, or since, that simultaneous equations bias is in practice a serious problem (see Epstein and Fox, below). But Haavelmo's two-pronged methodological case—for the superiority of simultaneous and stochastic formulations—was very per-

---

[8] See also Epstein [1987].

suasive. His 1941 paper became the focus of discussion at the New York 'econometrics seminar' that year conducted by Jacob Marschak, Abraham Wald, Tjalling Koopmans and others (Epstein, below, and [1987], ch. 2) and his approach was soon adopted as the agenda for research at the Cowles Commission, where Marschak became director of research in January 1943. The new programme almost foundered because of the computational immensities associated with the maximum likelihood method chosen for use; but a simplified procedure (LIML) developed in 1945 by Girshik gave it renewed impetus (Epstein, below). This was an important justification of Haavelmo and those at Cowles who had placed their faith in structural estimation: the technique was their own, and LIML was significant because it was an application of statistical theory specifically developed for economics, an innovation almost made to order to silence those who had insisted for so long that economic data precluded any meaningful application of statistics in that discipline.

We have already characterized the Haavelmo–Cowles agenda as a programme, and it may even help to think of it as a Research Programme in the strict (Lakatosian) sense. In that vein, consider as elements of the hard core of the Programme the following:

(a) that the economy may be characterized as a set of autonomous and simultaneous behavioural (causal) relations with structural features captured by the parameters of these relations; and

(b) that these relations are essentially stochastic.

The stochastic nature of these relationships derives from the observation that, if each variable is determined by a composite of steadily acting (exact) plus stochastic influences, the variables themselves can be adequately described only by reference to the parameters of the joint probability distributions of these stochastic influences.[9] Given that the formulation of the structural system was thought to be crucially dependent on economic theory, and that of the general equilibrium sort, we may say that (a) embraces the particular claim that neo-Walrasian analysis enters essentially into the hard core of the Programme. Neo-Walrasian analysis is a Research Programme in its own right (see Weintraub [1985]), as is the theory of statistical inference which aims, in the words of one exponent, to arrive at a set of principles "to assess the strength of the evidence supplied by a trial or experiment for or against a hypothesis, or to assess the reliability of an estimate derived from the result of such a trial or experiment" (Pitman [1979], p. 1). So the Haavelmo-Cowles Programme was in effect the union of two independent programmes, one in economic theory and one in mathematical statistics.

We need to stress that there were restrictions implicitly or explicitly

_____

[9] This meant too, as Haavelmo himself saw ([1944], p. 85), that in statistical terms there is a common core to the problems of identification, estimation and testing.

placed by Haavelmo and the Cowles workers on this hard core. One was that, although the neo-Walrasian Programme does not exclude dynamics, and although the Cowles workers intended to make their inquiries dynamic, this never was accomplished; and in part this must be attributed to their prior commitment to simultaneity (see Morgan [1987b]). The commitment was reinforced by computational problems (forcing them to estimate at a high level of aggregation) and data limitations (most series were of annual observations), both of which tended to suppress the dynamic properties of the data. In contrast to the work of the early agricultural econometricians and of Tinbergen, therefore, it must be said that intimate knowledge of concrete problems and of the data themselves were not among the strengths of the Haavelmo–Cowles programme.[10]

We may note further that errors in measurement were more or less left off the Programme agenda.[11] Another compromise was that questions about the applicability of classical statistical inference to economic data were shelved. Haavelmo's approach was quite pragmatic. In one place he suggests "The question is not whether probabilities exist or not, but whether—if we proceed as if they existed—we are able to make statements about real phenomena that are 'correct for practical purposes'" ([1944], p. 43). Again, acknowledging that economic data do not repeat in the strict sense, he says that this means that "the theoretical notion of a probability distribution serves us chiefly as a tool for deriving statements that have a very high probability of being true" (*ibid*, p. 81). This sort of statement confirms the dominant role of economic theory—as carrier of accepted ('true') knowledge—indicated earlier.[12] Ironically, despite its appropriation of the language of statistical inference, the Programme was not far removed from that of traditional economic methodology, in which statistics serves merely to quantify prior knowledge (accepted economic theory).

The positive heuristic corresponding to this thus-softened hard core is simply stated: build, identify, estimate and assess the parameter estimates of structural models conforming to the theory of optimizing agent behavior, stochastically formulated.

5. Current worries

Have the probabilists won the day? Is economics now a scientific discipline conducted within a properly defined stochastic framework? Can we look back on the early Cowles work as providing the equivalent of the Quantum Theoretic revolution in economics?

[10] But see footnote 13, below.

[11] Following the work of Reiserøl [1945] and Geary [1949] it as known that measurement error problems could be resolved using instrumental variables, but work in this area remained peripheral.

[12] For a different reading, which stresses that Haavelmo was departing from an experimental (Gaussian) formulation of the error terms and deploying the Galton conditional expectation approach, thereby introducing *a priori* restrictions on admissible theoretical models stemming from both economic theory and the structure of the data, see Spanos [1988].

One answer to these questions is that, in fact, the Haavelmo agenda has been only partly implemented. It is true that econometrics, interpreted as 'statistical methods of econometrics', is now a compulsory component of almost every graduate programme in economics; and that it would be as reasonable to expect any professional economist to be familiar with basic econometric methods as with intermediate micro- and macroeconomic theory. It is also true that Keynes' [1939] well-known criticisms of Tinbergen and Robbins' [1932] caricature of Dr. Blank and his demand function for herrings would now generally be regarded as idiosyncratic; although they still attract some sympathy. It is also true that the journals carry a huge volume of regression-based empirical work; although this remains small relative to the volume of pure theory.

At the same time, most economic theory is developed as deterministic (game theory notwithstanding). Dr. Blank's contemporary counterpart derives his 'theoretical' relationship within the prescribed optimizing framework and then adds on disturbance terms which take into account errors in optimization, factors not taken into account in the model, etc. So at the theoretical level economics remains deterministic and deductive. It is also true that the role of data largely remains that of quantification of parameter values and corroboration or rejection of theoretical relationships. There is no role for discovery, least of all for data-instigated discovery, and no concept of modelling the data.[13]

These worries are reflected in contemporary disputes about econometric methodology. The issue in the eighties is not whether we should do econometrics, but how, and what conclusions it entitles us to draw. In particular, the claim that econometrics makes economics scientific is called into question by the growing chorus in favour of Bayesian inferential procedures in econometrics (Leamer [1978], Hill [1986], Zellner [1988]). We do not pursue those questions in this volume, but note here that the fact that they attract serious attention indicates that, after an optimistic period at mid-century when the profession simply got on with the job, some of the bothersome issues of the 1930s have reappeared. We have benefited from an accretion of experience, from longer time series and richer cross sections (even panels) of higher quality data, from enormous advances in computing power which have both facilitated and stimulated advances in estimation theory, and from developments in probability theory. Inevitably, therefore, the formulation of the questions and the character of the answers has changed; but the enduring methodological concerns with the relation-ship of theory to econometric estimates, of autonomy, of the comparison of competing hypotheses, and of the status of inference in econometrics remain.

[13] The role of knowledge of the data in setting up fruitful hypotheses to test is one of Haavelmo's neglected contributions (Haavelmo [1944], pp. 80–83). This role was formally acknowledged by Koopmans (see Spanos [1988b]) but somehow dropped out of view both within Cowles and in the standard textbook view of Cowles econometrics.

6. The History of Econometrics

The history of econometrics has only recently begun to be written. We now possess excellent studies of the pre-Haavelmo era (Christ [1985], Morgan [1989]), and of Frisch (Andvig [1985]); and our understanding of the Cowles contribution has been immensely furthered by the work of Hildreth [1986] and Epstein [1987]. But in a sense the light that has been thrown on large areas has also served to delineate more sharply the many dark corners that remain unexplored. We mention two, by way of illustration. Despite the best efforts of Karl Fox, there remains too little awareness of the contributions of the early agricultural econometricians. Second, apart from a superb treatment within the confines of one chapter in Morgan [1989], the work of Jan Tinbergen in the 1930s has somehow escaped serious notice.

In addition, a host of very concrete historical problems still await adequate investigation. To give just a sample: how are we to understand Frisch's obscure terminological distinctions, 'autonomous' and 'confluent' chief among them? How exactly did Haavelmo, Frisch's student, overcome his teacher's objections to statistical inference and come to write his plea for a stochastic economics? What, if anything, is relevant in the fact that Tinbergen and Koopmans (Marschak's successor as director of research at Cowles) came to their investigations with a training in modern physics? How did simultaneity come to dominate process (or recursive) analysis? What considerations led to the adoption of maximum likelihood, and the rejections of OLS at a time when maximum likelihood was scarcely feasible for computational reasons? Just what probelms were ignored in the Cowles Programme, and how did they come to resurface in recent years?

Some of these questions have been touched on in the first part of this introduction, but the sketchiness of our treatment attests to how little is actually known at this stage about the detailed history. To provide an inducement to qualified individuals to address some of these specific issues was the first of two reasons for our setting up this Special Issue of *Oxford Economic Papers*. The historical papers published here are selected from a larger set submitted. Even so, they are, to some extent, from the editors' point of view, passive observations: we did not try to accomplish the *Compleat History* at one go. Resources (space, and the availability of authors possessing the necessary interests and expertise) were, as usual, a constraint; and the selection offered here should be viewed as building blocks towards a more balanced or complete history. In terms of time span and focus, we decided to concentrate on the Haavelmo-Cowles econometrics paradigm, its ingredients, and immediately preceding and dissenting lines of work, and on the recovery of data-related (time series) interest; on an especially noteworthy tradition linking econometrics and policy analysis (the Tinbergen-Theil tradition); and on specific instances of applied econometrics (the Phillips Curve; the consumption function).

7. The Methodology of Econometrics

The second reason for setting up this Special Issue relates to methodological considerations. Methodology is, as everyone knows, a subject of formally acknowledged importance but carrying no weight. It is ignored by all but the young, the spent and those discontent. Partly this is because methodologists, like philosophers, are rarely practitioners, yet practitioners have a sneaky feeling that methodologists would like to tell them how they should be behaving. In fact methodology is inquiry into why the accepted is judged acceptable.

But standards alter; and while methodology can be suggestive, its suggestions are offered only on the basis of an understanding of past and current practice and the reasons for it. Methodology thus shades imperceptibly into historical inquiry, and indeed cannot do otherwise. To be self-aware, however, practitioners must look to methodology of this historically informed sort. This reason is valid at all times. However, since econometrics has now entered a new period of critical self-examination, it seems to us doubly appropriate to devote part of our space to papers which address history with methodological questions in mind.

8. A Guide

Turning to the papers themselves, section 1 contains three papers that fit into this mixed category. Autonomy is inextricably bound up with the nature of structure (hence of the Haavelmo-Cowles Programme; with how we come by a knowledge of structure; and with the relation between what we estimate and the true or underlying causal relations that we suppose to be there). John Aldrich addresses these issues in sketching the context and implications of Frisch's early work on autonomy. In a related paper, David Hendry and Mary Morgan offer an account of what lay behind Frisch's confluence analysis, explain his bunch map technique, suggest reasons why the technique and the underlying analysis fell into disuse, and discern renewed relevance for confluence analysis in the literature on cointegration. Karl Fox reminds us of the dangers of institutionalized mythology; in this case, the myths that outside the Cowles Commission there was general ignorance of the identification difficulty; and that to ignore single equation bias was of the utmost seriousness.

Section 2 includes two papers dealing with particular developments integral to the Haavelmo-Cowles Programme: Duo Qin on the evolution of formal treatments of identification, and Roy Epstein on how LIML came to supplant Ordinary Least Squares. Qin notes that in the search for formal solutions to the identification problem the methodological issues to do with the relation between theory on the one hand and data on the other were lost from view as the problem domain was made deliberately abstract and mathematical. Epstein indirectly alludes to another point touched on above, the loss of contact in this Programme with concrete problems and with data, by recalling the contributions of Sewall Wright; and might be read as implying that the institutional concentration of mathematical statistics talent among the Cowles Commission staff helps explain the change of problem domain noted by Qin. Finally, in this section, Christopher Gilbert shows how the Haavelmo-Cowles Programme both came to Great Britain and was transformed in its emphases, through the work of James Durbin, Bill Phillips and Denis Sargan, into a concern with the dynamic (time series) structure of data.

Section 3 contains four discussions of applied work. The econometric analysis of the consumption function was the first great success for econometrics. This was in part because the marginal propensity to consume played such an important role in Keynesian income-expenditure theory, so that economists now, like the physicists, had a universal constant to measure; and in part because the arguments for the 'new' consumption models of Friedman, Duesenberry and Ando and Modigliani were all based on econometric evidence. Jim Thomas traces the historical development of the econometric consumption function and Aris Spanos reevaluates some of the crucial 'evidence' using modern criteria.

The Phillips Curve became the second central pillar of the postwar orthodoxy and it too was econometrically based—indeed the theory was provided *ex post* by Lipsey and Archibald to underpin a relationship which Phillips saw as obvious. But as is well known, Phillips 'established' the Phillips Curve using statistical methods which are now seen as at best idiosyncratic. Nancy Wulwick looks at the context in which the Phillips Curve emerged, and traces the sources and the robustness of his estimates.

It was a widely shared conviction in the 1940s that scientific economics would lead to scientific policy. Nowhere was this taken more seriously than in the Netherlands, where under social democratic governments Jan Tinbergen and Henri Theil successively held senior posts in the Central Plan Bureau. In the final contribution to this section Andrew Hughes Hallett examines their impact on the development of policy analysis.

In section 4, Philip Mirowski takes up the theme that the Haavelmo-Cowles Programme, with its theory dominant stance, represents an attempt to save a neoclassical economics that had modelled itself on mid-nineteenth century deterministic physics, in an era when physicists themselves had adopted stochastic interpretations of their world. Tony Lawson offers an equally controversial reading of econometrics, using as a device for identifying what many (most?) econometricians believe about their world, the shibboleth: do you accept the concrete existence of the cause-effect relations modelled and estimated by you and your colleagues; or is their concrete existence of no serious importance in what you do? He does not examine what the consequences are of not believing, although he implies that the activity of an 'instrumentalist' econometrician is somehow akin to that of the blind leading the blind.

9. Evaluation

Econometrics is now a fully fledged and distinct discipline, lying between mathematical statistics and economics, drawing on the one and indispensable to the other. One can describe oneself as an econometrician in the same way that one might say one is an economic historian. There is a new professional self-awareness which has led to a consciousness of the history of the discipline and a realization that methodological problems posed as new in the current reflective period were, in many cases, anticipated in its formative years. We see this volume as a contribution to the re-evaluation both of our past and our present.

Duke University and University of Amsterdam
Institute of Economics and Statistics, Oxford, and CEPR.

SECTION 1

Conceptual Problems Before Cowles

Oxford Economic Papers 41 (1989), 15–34

AUTONOMY

By JOHN ALDRICH*

1. Introduction

KNOWLEDGE of structure is valuable and available—but only to those prepared to use both economic theory and statistical analysis. This has been one of the most powerful messages in twentieth century economics and, in microeconomics, field after field has fallen to it. Macroeconomics seemed to have succumbed long ago but, in the last decade or so, the matter has been reopened and the issue is in doubt.

One consequence of this questioning has been a revival of interest in the foundations of econometrics—especially in matters pertaining to structure. This paper tries to answer the obvious historical question: Where did those foundations come from?[1]

The short answer is that the concepts relating to structure were devised by Ragnar Frisch and they passed into classical econometrics through Trygve Haavelmo's *Probability Approach in Econometrics* (1944), the work that gave the subject its charter. At the centre of Frisch's network of concepts was "autonomy", or, as it is now more often called, "structural invariance". Before we embark on an elaborate account of the history of this and related concepts, it may be worth considering why the "most basic" question one can ask about a relation should be: How autonomous is it?[2]

A system of autonomous equations has the property "that it is possible that the parameters in any one of the equations could *in fact* change . . . *without* any change taking place in any of the parameters of the other equations."[3]

Autonomy is significant because an equation (or its parameters) in a system of autonomous relations will be "detachable" or "projectible".[4] Detachability matters both for interpretation and for "policy simulation", activities from which the structural econometrician would bar the "econo-mic barometrician", i.e. one who is interested only in finding empirical regularities.

The most familiar of structural equations is the demand equation. It describes how a consumer *would* respond to certain hypothetical

---

* I would like to thank Mary Morgan for many helpful suggestions and Janne Rayner for her comments on earlier drafts of this paper. The editors and referees and participants in seminars at Oxford and Southampton also made useful comments.

[1] This paper looks only at the structural side of classical econometrics. For the probability side see Morgan (1987a).

[2] Frisch (1948a) Preface.

[3] Girshick & Haavelmo (1947) p. 106.

[4] "Detachable" has been used in this sense by Professor T. J. Rothenberg. "Projectible" is taken from Goodman (1954) who uses it in something like the second sense. See also Cook and Campbell's (1979 p. 39) "external validity". Lawson (this volume) has an interesting discussion of "instrumentalism" in classical econometrics which is related to this issue, though on my reading classical econometrics was much more "realist" than "instrumentalist".

situations—not just to the price that is compatible with the conditions of supply but to any conceivable price. In particular, it should continue to describe the behaviour of the consumer when the supply function shifts, as a result, say, of the imposition of an excise tax.

To take a more elaborate example, consider the discussion of the Phillip's curve in Lucas's (1976) "critique of econometric policy evaluation", itself an analysis of the consequences of unwarranted projection.

The suppliers' optimal decision rule is assumed to be given by

$$y_t = \alpha(p_t - \bar{p}_t) \tag{1.1}$$

where $\bar{p}_t$ is expected price and p_t is actual price. It is assumed that prices follow a random walk

$$p_t = p_{t-1} + \varepsilon_t \tag{1.2}$$

where ε_t is $\mathbb{N}(\pi, \sigma^2)$. Suppliers form expectations rationally, i.e.

$$\bar{p}_t = E[p_t \mid p_{t-1}, \ldots,] \tag{1.3}$$

Thus expected price is given by

$$\bar{p}_t = p_{t-1} + \pi \tag{1.4}$$

From these relations we obtain the observable supply function

$$y_t = \alpha(p_t - p_{t-1}) - \alpha\pi. \tag{1.5}$$

If the observable supply function were estimated during a period of constant inflation, it might be interpreted as showing a trade-off between inflation and output. However, if policy makers decide on an inflationary policy to exploit this trade-off, the observable supply function would "shift" because of the change in π. The policy would not work.

Lucas argued that in much econometric policy analysis such cross-equation restrictions are ignored. In the Frisch–Haavelmo language, the problem is that (1.2) and (1.5) are *not* autonomous relations but they are being treated as though they were—what might be called a case of neglected heteronomy.

While Lucas claimed that much "structural" econometrics was disguised barometrics, Sims (1980, 1982) made the case for an honest barometrics. Reports of the existence of structure were exaggerated but also irrelevant, as economic policy was seldom so radical that knowledge of structure was needed to figure out its effects. The language of modern foundational debate, with terms like "structural invariance" and "deep parameters", is not that of Frisch and Haavelmo but they would recognise the concepts.[5]

The paper is arranged as follows. Section 2 examines how Frisch's thinking on structural concepts developed in the course of the pre-war debate over statistical macrodynamics. Section 3 considers how Frisch's

---

[5] From Engle *et al.* (1983) and Cooley and LeRoy (1985) respectively.

concepts were incorporated in the foundations of classical econometrics. Section 4 has some concluding comments.

2. Frisch and macrodynamics

Classical econometrics did not leap clean and complete from the pages of a philosopher-economist. The system of ideas developed slowly and its evolution was closely tied to the fortunes of particular empirical applications. Two fields of empirical research were especially significant in this respect—demand analysis and macrodynamics.

The role of demand analysis in the early history of econometrics ideas is very familiar.[6] The macrodynamics of the thirties was an attempt to apply the techniques of market analysis—both theoretical and empirical—to the economy as a whole. That attempt raised two questions: what was the nature of the techniques being applied and what could those techniques do that existing methods of business cycle analysis could not? What could remain implicit in demand analysis had to be made explicit here.

The main driving forces behind macrodynamics were Frisch and Tinbergen. They agreed about the general objectives of macrodynamics but came to disagree about the type of empirical analysis appropriate for the new field. While Tinbergen estimated structural models, Frisch advocated a form of non-structural analysis. While they agreed that it would be good to have structural models, Frisch was convinced that Tinbergen's models were *not* structural models.

Paradoxically, the conceptual foundations of structural econometrics were established by one who was sceptical of the possibility of structural econometrics. Frisch's arguments against Tinbergen were set out in the unpublished memorandum *Statistical versus Theoretical Relations in Economic Macrodynamics* (1938) which discussed Tinbergen's volumes on *The Statistical Testing of Business Cycle Theories*.

The key issue was the status of the equations that Tinbergen had estimated:

> The question of what connection there is between the relations we work with in theory and those we get by fitting curves to actual statistical data is a very delicate one. I think it has never been exhaustively and satisfactorily discussed. Tinbergen in his work hardly mentions it. He more or less takes it for granted that the relations he has found are in their nature the same as those of theory (pp. 2–3.)

When Frisch posed this question and argued that Tinbergen's relations were not the same as "those of theory" he was drawing on the results of a complex process of conceptual innovation. In this section we will try to identify the stages of that process.

Already in the twenties there had been discussion of whether statistical demand laws were actually demand laws and in the thirties both Frisch and

---

[6] For the demand side, see Christ (1985) and Morgan (1984) chapters 5 & 6.

Tinbergen contributed to this literature. However this discussion could proceed without any discussion of what constituted an economic law. Perhaps because everyone knew what a demand law was, there was no need to ask what a law was.

Frisch and Waugh (1933) introduced an appropriately general concept that would cover not only demand laws but the other functions of economic theory—"structural relation" or "structural equation". Frisch's structural terms could fill a volume but this is the only one still in use.

A "structural relation" is a "theoretical relation postulated a priori". In the case of a linear relation,

$$x_0 = \beta_{01,2...n}x_1 + \cdots + \beta_{0n,12...n-1}x_n$$

each of the constants in the equation is "conceived as to represent an independent influence on x_0, for instance, the constant $\beta_{0n1,2...n-1}$ represents the independent influence which time $[x_n]$ may exercise directly on x_0, regardless of the particular way in which the other variables $x_1,..., x_{n-1}$ happen to evolve", (pp. 389–90).

The problem of interpreting the coefficients in a single equation is perhaps the most primitive form of the problem of interpreting relations. The paper gives no indication of how it could happen that right hand side variables would *not* move independently of one another. Later Frisch would show how but for the present it remained an empty box.

Frisch and Waugh discussed a special case of the relationship between relations "postulated by theory" and relations "obtained by the classical statistical procedures". The question whether it was best to extract trends from variables prior to fitting or to include time as an explanatory variable in the regression had been hotly debated in the twenties. They settled the argument by showing that, under appropriate conditions, the two methods produced the same estimates.

Frisch and Waugh discuss the circumstances in which it would be better to use the structural relation and forecasts of the right-hand side variables (called a "composition forecast") instead of simply forecasting using the trend of x_0:

> The only reason ... is to make it possible to utilize some other information regarding the probable future trends of the variable $x_1 ... x_{n-1}$. Instead of assuming that all the variables will continue their growth at the average rate observed in the material, we may, for instance, assume that one of them is going to remain stationary at the level it had at the end of the period studied, or we may assume that its growth rate will become less, etc. (p. 400).

The point that the use of structural relations offered a chance of better forecasting when changes were contemplated elsewhere in the system had already been noted in demand analysis and would be prominent in the general case for structural analysis.

Meanwhile Frisch was working on two projects which emphasised, in very different ways, the importance of *systems* of relationships. In his search for improved techniques for understanding business cycles, he had been developing improved methods of periodogram analysis to incorporate the ideas of Slutsky and Yule.[7] Then he switched to a model-based treatment of the cycle.

His famous *Propagation and Impulse Problems in Dynamic Economics* (1933) was packed with important ideas—not least it launched the notion of a macroeconomic model! It emphasised the importance of having a complete structural model and criticised business cycle analysts for over-looking this requirement. It also explored the idea that the cycle was the result of random shocks applied to a damped mechanism.

Frisch wrote down a small model, inserted numerical values for the "structural coefficients" and calculated the trajectories of the variables. He proposed a complementary programme of structural estimation:

> I think, indeed, that the statistical determination of such structural parameters will be one of the main objectives of the economic cycle analysis of the future. If we ask for a real *explanation* of the movements, this type of work seems to be the indispensable complement needed in order to coordinate and give a significant interpretation to the huge mass of empirical descriptive facts that have been accumulated in cycle analysis for the past ten or twenty years. (p. 167).

While Tinbergen went ahead and estimated structural models, Frisch at first proceeded by using time series methods for uncovering periodicities in the data and then considering how these matched the simulations of theoretical models.

The other field, in which it was essential to recognise that a system of relations was involved, was in the type of statistical analysis he called "confluence analysis". We need to look at this work if we are to understand his reservations about structural estimation.

Statistical Confluence Analysis by Means of Complete Regression Systems (1934) developed from Frisch's dissatisfaction with conventional regression analysis. As a method of estimation and specification searching, regression analysis could be very misleading when the relation belonged to a *system* of relations, i.e. when there was "multicollinearity". A scheme of analysis for a system of exact relations with errors in variables had to be developed.[8]

Frisch emphasised a particular "pitfall" in regression analysis and most of the applications of confluence analysis were concerned with this problem. Consider the constructed example (p. 80): there are two exact relationships between the systematic parts of four variables.

$$x_1 - x_2 - x_4 = 0$$
$$x_1 + x_2 - x_3 = 0 \tag{2.1}$$

---

[7] For Frisch's time series work see Morgan (1984) Sections 3.2 and 3.3.

[8] Hendry and Morgan (this volume) explains how Frisch's "multicollinearity" changed into the modern notion and give a fuller account of confluence analysis.

The "danger of including too many variates" can be seen by multiplying the first equation by q and the second by p and adding to obtain an equation in all four variables:

$$(p + q)x_1 + (p - q)x_2 - px_3 - qx_4 = 0.$$

There are infinitely many choices of p and q and so there is no meaningful regression in all four variables. In practice, the indeterminateness of the coefficients may be concealed because the observations contain errors of observation—hence "fictitious determinateness created by random errors". The aim of "bunch map" analysis was to reveal this state of affairs, *if* it obtained.

Most of the applications of confluence analysis dealt with this problem of estimating a single equation with too many variables but many of the ideas developed for the analysis of this problem were to reappear in the simultaneous equations work of the forties. Frisch recognised that there were infinitely many ways of writing the basic relationships. In the section on the "amount of indeterminateness in regression slopes in multicollinear variates" (pp. 71–77) he takes two independent linear relations in n variables.

$$a_1x_1 + \cdots + a_nx_n = 0$$

$$b_1x_1 + \cdots + b_nx_n = 0$$

and shows how by taking a p/q combination a new equation can be obtained. "Of course in none of [these] situations has it a sense to speak of *the* regression equation connecting the variates, since no such determinate equation exists." (p. 73).

It may be that "some sort of *side condition* may be considered which will make the regression coefficients determinate." (p. 73). Frisch took seriously the point that the same equations can appear in different guises; thus if different variables were omitted from the equations, (2.1) could be written

$$\begin{aligned} 2x_1 - x_3 - x_4 &= 0 \\ 2x_2 - x_3 + x_4 &= 0 \end{aligned} \tag{2.2}$$

A technique is devised, "compatibility smoothing", to ensure that estimates are invariant to the form of parametrisation chosen. (pp. 111–120).

Frisch does not discuss the rationale of these conditions—in particular, he does not interpret them as part of the economic specification. To put Frisch's argument in modern terms: the mistake of including too many variables is in trying to estimate a relationship that is not identified while the equations with "determinate" coefficients are identified and can be sensibly estimated. While much of the *algebra* of the Cowles Commission identification theory is here, the point of view is different. The data is examined to see which relationships will be identified.

Frisch appears to have believed that his techniques—or refinements of them—would uncover all the linearly independent relations satisfied by the variables. Unfortunately he does not explain how we would choose between the "true regressions" of (2.1) and (2.2). His examples are no help: the constructed example is basically a factor analysis model where none of the relationships between the measured variables has a structural interpretation and in the main example using real data only one relationship is found!

The ultimate object of confluence analysis was to pick out a single relationship—or perhaps even a single parameter—from a number of relationships. It proceeded by finding all the relationships between a collection of variables. Then the relationships would be milked for information on the relationship or parameter of interest.

The statistical analysis was kept in a separate compartment from the interpretation. Like the regression analysis it was designed to replace, confluence analysis was non-structural. It seemed unrelated to his new model-based approach to the business cycle as well to his work (1933a) on identifying demand curves.

In September 1936 Frisch was outlining an "ideal programme" combining elements of confluence analysis and model-based stochastic business cycle analysis. According to the conference report (Econometrica (1937)):

Prof. Frisch developed an ideal programme for macrodynamic studies: A. *Theoretical inquiry*. (1) Define your variables. (2) State the structural relations which you suppose to exist between the variables. (3) Derive a number of confluent relations, which lead to confluent elasticities, showing the response of one variable in a certain sub-group to another when all the rest are held constant. (3a) Use these relations for reasoning about variations compatible with the subsystem. (3b) consider the response of the system to exogenous shocks: a dynamic analysis leading to criteria of stability. (3c) Consider how the whole system will evolve in time. B. *Statistical inquiry*. (4) Obtain some final equations. A final equation is a confluent relation which is reduced to its smallest degree of freedom, and in which the coefficients have a statistically uniquely determined meaning. Never try to fit to the data anything but a final equation. (5) One may also scrutinise the data, and derive empirical formulae by the statistical technique now known as "confluence analysis." In particular a final equation may be tested in this way. (6) If the final equation contains only one variable, and is linear, construct the corresponding characteristic equation and consider its roots. They will determine the time-shape of the evolution that would ensue if the system were left to itself. When we have found in this way how the system *would* proceed through time, we do not expect actual history to move like that, for the history is affected by a stream of erratic shocks. The actual time-shape will now be a weighted average extending over the shocks, the weights of the average being those given by the system as it would proceed in isolation. (7) Fundamental inversion problems: (a) to determine the system of weights from a given time-shape; (b) to determine the shocks. (8) attempt a forecast using the weights determined by the inversion, and assuming—in the absence of better information—the future shocks to be zero. (p. 365)

To understand the "ideal programme" and the reasoning behind it, it is useful to look at the paper presented to the conference by Frisch's assistant, Haavelmo (1938).

A "simplified macrodynamic picture of the whole economic system" consists of n dynamic structural equations in n variables. A structural equation was defined in the same way as in Frisch and Waugh. The reason such structural relations exist "may be certain technical conditions, psychological laws, etc." A "confluent relation" is a relation derived from two or more structural relations (p. 203). This use of "confluent" was an innovation for the term had not previously been applied to relations.

In the discussion of the paper Marschak observed that both structural and confluent relations were empirically determined. Frisch replied:

> (a) there was a difference in principle between the two kinds of relation, in that any coefficient in a structural relation might be changed *institutionally* without necessarily entailing a change in the other structural relations. A similar property did not belong to the confluent relations, whose coefficients are just consequences of the coefficients in the various structural equations, and therefore change with these. Another difference was (b) that in the case of confluent relations . . . one was asking: What *is* in fact the situation? While in the case of the structural relations one was asking: What *would* be the situation with regard to one variate *if* certain other variates, rates of change, etc. had such and such values? (Econometrica 1937, p. 374)

Only the word "autonomy" is missing.

The distinction between structural and confluent relations played a big part in Haavelmo's paper. Macrodynamics was a method of business cycle analysis in which a structural model was used to investigate cycles. But here, in contrast to demand analysis, the structural relations had to share the billing with a confluent relation, the *final equation,* the relation between a variable and its time derivatives. For the final equations carried information about the cyclical properties of the system and the cyclical properties were at least as interesting as the structural parameters. The final equation was seen as an important way of verifying the theory.

Not only was a particular confluent relation, viz. the final equation, a primary object of the statistical analysis but one of the paper's aims was to show how confluent relations could be used to complete a model. Completeness had been emphasised in *Propagation and Impulse.* Adherence to it presented a dilemma: only a part of the system was of direct interest and the remainder of the structure was likely to be misspecified *yet* some account had to be taken of it. Some variables could be treated as exogenous but "this would not permit a very profound analysis of the problem"—after all the problem was to explain the *cyclical* aspects of behaviour. For Haavelmo the solution to the missing equations problem was to use empirical relations of the kind used in the Harvard economic barometer. In principle, the structural model could be fully specified and the supplementary confluent relations derived algebraically. Instead they are simply postulated.

Haavelmo's system of mixed difference differential equations has a securely structural, a doubtfully structural and an avowedly confluent relation:

$$x_t = y_t + b\dot{x}_t$$
$$y_t = vq_t + \mu\dot{q}_t$$
$$q_t = kx_{t-\theta}.$$

x_t denotes an index of stock prices measured from its equilibrium position, q_t the general price level measured from its equilibrium position and y_t stock price appreciation (all measured in logs).

Evidently Haavelmo thought that confluence analysis methods could not be applied to the structural relations. There is "great danger of multi-collinearity" due to the existence of other relations in the system. ("Multicollinearity" covered "Simultaneity" as well as multicollinearity.) So the structural relations were not fitted.

Haavelmo explained why it was better to estimate the final equation directly rather than via the structural parameters. The indirect procedure would be "dangerous" because estimation of the structural parameters was hazardous and errors in the estimates of the structural coefficients would be transmitted to the coefficients of the final equations. It was also possible that some of the structural coefficients may refer to variables "for which it is impossible to have statistical observations".

So he followed Frisch's advice "never to fit anything but a final equation". There was no multicollinearity problem; the coefficients of the final equation have a "statistically uniquely determined meaning" or are identified.

Regarding the final equation,

$$x_t - b\dot{x}_t - kvx_{t-\theta} - k\mu\dot{x}_{t-\theta} = 0$$

Haavelmo noted that "we here have the special case of a structural coefficient, b, *entering isolated in the final confluent relation.*" As b is really the only structural parameter, the final equation(s) do not do too badly! It seems that Haavelmo and Frisch thought this the exceptional case and that, in general, structural coefficients could not be recovered from final equations. Profound anxiety about identification pervaded the "ideal programme" but the anxiety was not yet translated into rigorous analysis.

In the 1938 memorandum Frisch confonted the rival macrodynamic programme and gave an abstract account of what was involved in structural modelling. Frisch "models" Tinbergen in terms of a system of difference equations in the variables, $x_1, x_2, ..., x_n$:

$$\sum_{i,\theta} a_{ki\theta}x_i(t - \theta) = 0, \quad (k = 1, 2, ..., n)$$

He points out that a non-singular transformation of the system will yield equations of the same form but with changed coefficients; the original and the transformed systems of equations will have the same solution, i.e. the same functions of time satisfy both sets of equations. As we saw above, this was an insight from confluence analysis.

An equation is defined as "irreducible" with respect to a given set of functions if the set of functions satisfies this equation and no other with the same ij range. An equation which is irreducible with respect to the set of functions which forms the actual solution of the complete system is called a "coflux" equation. In the 1936 language, the coefficients of such an equation have a "statistically uniquely determined meaning".

Coflux equations were significant because they could be estimated (in the deterministic case, solved for) from the data—"they were discoverable through passive observations." In modern terms, coflux equations are the ones that are identified. One point that Frisch clears up is how an equation can hold yet fail to have the property emphasised in the Frisch and Waugh paper. The equation could merely demonstrate a "routine of change": the right hand side variables cannot be moved independently of each other for the changes that would make such movement possible would destroy the relationship expressing the routine of change.[9]

Coflux equations are estimable but they are not necessarily the most interesting equations. They may only be confluent relations. The important equations relate to autonomous features of the system:

> the most autonomous in the sense that they could be *maintained unaltered while other features of the structure were changed*. This investigation must use not only empirical but also abstract methods. So we are led to constructing a sort of *super-structure*, which helps us to pick out these particular equations in the main structure to which we can attribute a high degree of autonomy in the above sense. The higher this degree of autonomy, the more *fundamental* is the equation, the deeper is the insight which it gives us into the way in which the system functions, in short the nearer it comes to being a *real explanation*. Such relations are the essence of "theory". (p. 17).

Tinbergen (1938a) replied that he did use "abstract methods" as well as "empirical methods", that there was theoretical justification for his relationships. He could not understand why Frisch would accept as structural certain relationships but withold the status from others. (p. 23).

Frisch saw Tinbergen as arbitrarily imposing restrictions on his equations. The old insight from *Confluence Analysis* was given fresh life. His comment on Tinbergen's specification searching. "By a suitable choice of the variate and lag-numbers one can produce practically any coefficient one likes". (p. 19) echoed the statement in *Confluence Anaysis* (p. 71) "we may make the regression coefficient between any given set of two variates ... equal to any number we like." (cf. the discussion on p. 9 above). Of the consumption

---

[9] Frisch gives an example but the point can be made in terms of the Lucas example (p. 2 above).

equations that Tinbergen reviewed in the course of his specification searching, Frisch wrote *"In my opinion all these equations are acceptable* when interpreted as what they are: a number of coflux equations. But none of them can, I believe be, taken as an expression of *the* autonomous structural relation that will characterize demand." (p. 19).

Between them Frisch and Tinbergen had considerable insight into identification.[10] Tinbergen was aware that, provided there was sufficient variety in the included variables, the parameters in a model would be identified. Frisch developed a criterion for identifiability based on the characterstic roots of the dynamic model but more basically he realised that a model was not a correctly specified structural model just because it fitted well.

Frisch's position on the possible self-deception involved in macro-modelling anticipated that of Liu (1960). Structural models can achieve identification through the imposition of arbitrary restrictions. His own approach was to use time series modelling—fit final equations, a prescription that anticipates Sims (1980).

Though there was not structural information in the fitted relationships, thre was information! Tinbergen's results were important.

> They will have to be taken as starting point for any further investigation aiming at obtaining *limits* or other sorts of information concerning the structural coefficients. (p. 19).

Ten years after his critique of Tinbergen, Frisch (1948b) again considered macromodelling. He discussed the pitfalls in the estimation of economic relations and presented a revised version of the 1936 programme. He seemed even more pessimistic about the prospects of structural estimation than in 1938, or rather about the prospects when using time series observations alone:

> It is very seldom indeed that we have a clear case where the statistical data can actually determine numerically an autonomous structural equation. In most cases we only get a covariational equation with a low degree of autonomy... We must look for some other means of getting information about the numerical character of our structural equations. The only way possible seems to utilize to a much larger extent than we done so far the interview method i.e., we must ask persons or groups what they would do under such and such circumstances. (p. 370).

3. Haavelmo and the *Probability Approach*

The Probability Approach in Econometrics announced the arrival of classical econometrics, with its grand themes of structural analysis and the probability approach. The long term influence of the work of Haavelmo and

---

[10] See especially Tinbergen (1939, vol 1: pp. 62–4). Qin (this volume) traces the later history of identification. Rayner and Aldrich (1988) reconsider the identification issues involved in specification searching.

his associates at the Cowles Commission was profound for it did much to transform the economist's conception of empirical research.[11]

On technical issues Haavelmo's essay was soon surpassed but in its treatment of basic issues it stands as the deepest and most systematic account of the ideas of classical econometrics. Indeed, though rarely recognised as such, the *Probability Approach* is one of the masterpieces of twentieth century methodological writing in economics.

Many of the ideas came from Frisch but the atmosphere is not that of the macrodynamics programme. There was a new "ideal programme". A unified treatment of empirical economics is given: supply and demand and macroeconomics are treated in the same way. Econometrics was mirroring developments in business cycle analysis. Keynes had supplied a method that would do for macroeconomics what the Marshallian cross had done for microeconomics. With the new confidence in structural theory and in structural estimation, Frisch's 1936 programme was forgotten.

Tinbergen had actually been carrying out the "new" programme for years. The *Probability Approach* used many of the ideas from Frisch's memorandum but now they were used to justify Tinbergen, not to refute him. Of course, there was plenty of work to do. Though their aims were sound enough, the statistical analysis of Tinbergen and the demand analysts needed reconsideration.

Autonomy was absolutely central to the plan of econometrics set out in the *Probability Approach*. An econometric model tries to explain the behaviour of one set of variables in terms of the behaviour of another set of *autonomous* variables. "Parameters of interest" in the model are interesting because they are parameters of *autonomous* relations. The existence of such a privileged parametrisation creates the need for a theory of identification. Even when the distinctively econometric point of view recedes and "standard" statistical inference takes over, the statistical theory was distinctive. Confluence analysis had been data analysis—first find relations in the data and then make sense of them. Here the sequence was reversed: define the relations that made economic sense and estimate them.

We begin our account of autonomy with Haavelmo's formal definition:

> suppose that it be possible to define a class, Ω of *structures*, such that *one member or another* of this class, would, approximately, describe economic reality in *any practically conceivable situation*... Now consider a particular sub-class (of Ω), containing all those—and only those—that satisfy a certain relation "A". Let ω_A be this particular subclass. (E.g., ω_A might be the subclass of all those structures that satisfy a particular demand function "A.") We then say that the relation "A" is *autonomous* with respect to the subclass of structures ω_A. (p. 28.)

In terms of hypothetical changes in structure, the relation A would not be disturbed should the structure change from one point in ω_A to another.

---

[11] Christ (1952) and Hildreth (1986) give general accounts of the work of the Cowles Commission.

Autonomy is a "highly relative concept". To use a term that later became popular, autonomy is relative to a particular class of "interventions".

The bigger the class of interventions, the more autonomous the relation. This idea motivated the following definition:

> suppose that we define some non-negative *measure* of the "size" (or of the "importance" or "credibility") of any subclass ω in Ω... We say that "A" has a *degree* of autonomy which is greater the larger be the "size" of ω_A as compared with that of Ω. (pp. 28–29).

This is hardly an ideal definition—"size", "importance" and "credibility" are scarcely synonyms—but the basic idea is clear enough.[12]

Consider, for example, Lucas's Phillips curve analysis (p. 2 above). How autonomous is (1.5) compared to (1.1)? The degree of autonomy of a relationship depends on the "size" of the class of structures compatible with the relationship. There will be infinitely many structures which produce the same parameter values in (1.5), infinitely many combinations of α and π. There are also infinitely many structures compatible with (1.1). However while it is very unlikely that a change in α, say, will be exactly offset by the change in π which is needed to hold (1.5) unchanged, movements that leave (1.1) unchanged are much more likely. Haavelmo seems to expect an economic theory to include an understanding of the circumstances in which any of its structural relations would change and an appreciation of the probability of such changes.

Haavelmo gave three reasons for being concerned with autonomy: autonomous relations are likely to be more stable; they are more intelligible; they are useful for policy analysis. The first two considerations are brought out in the parable of the relationship between the speed of a car and the pressure on the accelerator:

> [I]f a man... wanted to understand how [automobiles] work, we should not advise him to spend time and effort in measuring a relationship like that. Why? Because (1) such a relation leaves the whole inner mechanism of a car in complete mystery, and (2) such a relation might break down at any time, as soon as there is some disorder or change in any working part of the car... We say that such a relation has very little *autonomy*, because its existence depends upon the simultaneous fulfilment of a great many other relations, some of which are of a transitory nature. On the other hand, the general laws of thermodynamics, the dynamics of friction, etc., etc., are highly autonomous relations with respect to the automobile mechanism, because these relations describe the functioning of some parts of the mechanism *irrespective* of what happens in some other parts. (pp. 27–28).

The parable was meant to show how statistical effort could be misdirected. The target was the Harvard economic barometer. After the barometer had closed down, the National Bureau method of business cycle analysis came to symbolise the wrong approach.

[12] A "deep parameter" for Cooley and LeRoy (1985) is a parameter—rather than a relation—with a high degree of autonomy.

In an earlier paper (1943b) Haavelmo had put more emphasis on the importance of autonomous relations for planning:

> If then the system... has worked in the past, [the economist] may be interested in knowing it as an aid in judging the effect of his intended future planning, because he thinks that certain elements of the old system will remain invariant. For example, he might think that consumers will continue to respond in the same way to income, no matter from what sources their income originates. Even if his future planning would change the investment relation..., the consumption relation... might remain true. (p. 10).

Where do these autonomous relations come from? "The principal task of economic theory is to establish such relations as might be expected to possess as high a degree of autonomy as possible." (p. 29). Haavelmo seemed to entertain few doubts that theory could deliver.

Haavelmo gave an abstract account of how economic theory works. He distinguished two kinds of variation: "hypothetical, *free* variations, and variations which are *restricted* by a system of simultaneous relations." (p. 26). It is essential that the hypothetical free variations be considered; these correspond to the "individual experiments" of economic theory.

> [Systems of theoretical relations] represent attempts to *reconstruct,* in a simplified way, the mechanisms which we think lie behind the phenomena we observe in the real world. In trying to rebuild these mechanisms we consider *one* relationship at a time. ... In constructing such a relation we reason in the following way: *If* x_2' be such and such, x_3' such and such, etc., *then* this implies a certain value of x_1'. In this process we do not question whether these "ifs" can actually occur or not. When we impose more relations upon the variables, a great many of these "ifs" which were possible for the relation $x_1' = f$ separately, may be impossible, because they violate the other relations. After having imposed a whole system of relations, there may not be very much left out of all the hypothetical variation with which we started out. (pp. 26–7).

Haavelmo was trying to capture in abstract terms the use of constructs such as demand functions for explaining behaviour. (Cf. the first sense of detachability on p. 2 above). The typical autonomous relation expresses a hypothetical "free" variation rather than a routine of change. A system of such relations constitutes a "structure". We saw above why he thought structures were more useful than descriptions of routines of change.

What was the connection between this analysis and Haavelmo's best known contribution to econometrics—the formulation and analysis of the simultaneous equations model? The connection seems clearer in his short 1943 paper than in the more elaborate *Probability Approach*.

The main point of the 1943 paper was that econometricians had failed to consider the "*statistical* implications of assuming a system of such stochastical equations to be *simultaneously fulfilled* by the data." (p. 2). The implications for statistical inference were large but we are less concerned with the implications than with the premise. What did it mean for several stochastical equations to hold simultaneously?

Haavelmo uses two examples, a multiplier-accelerator system and a simpler uninterpreted system. To keep things simple we will concentrate on the latter system. X and Y are random variables satisfying the equations:

$$Y = aX + \varepsilon_1,$$
$$X = bY + \varepsilon_2,$$

where ε_1 and ε_2 are independent random variables distributed as $N(0, \sigma_1^2)$ and $N(0, \sigma_2^2)$ respectively. Under these circumstances the conditional expectation of Y given X will be:

$$E(Y/X) = \frac{b\sigma_1^2 + a\sigma_2^2}{b^2\sigma_1^2 + \sigma_2^2} X$$

which is not equal to aX. This observation is the basis of the argument against estimating a by least squares.

If the structural equations of econometrics do *not* correspond to conditional distributions, what did they mean—what "experiments" did they represent? We must consider what the expected value of Y would be *if* X were fixed, if, in the consumption function example, the group of consumers in the society were "repeatedly furnished" with the same total income x. In a recent paper Pratt and Schlaifer (1984, p. 15) stressed the importance of this conception and, in their terminology, the experiment gives the "genetic distribution" of Y with parameter x. This is quite different from the conditional expectation of Y given $X = x$. Haavelmo's "experiment" gives the former not the latter.

Of course the experiment is never performed for income is a random variable rather than a fixed quantity. What is envisaged is that we suppress the second equation and ask how the agents whose behaviour is described by the first equation would react to different values of fixed x. This description, analysing the "hypothetical free variation", corresponds to the individual experiment underlying a structural equation.

Autonomy plays an essential part in this experiment because it is required that the consumption function remains unchanged when the other function is violated. Without autonomy there is no continuing existence of the consumption function. Of course, there should be nothing surprising about the role of autonomy as the simultaneous equations model was devised as a stochastic version of the systems of autonomous relations treated in economic theory.

There was also a "*statistical side* of the problem of *autonomous* relations." (p. 84). Corresponding to any system of autonomous relations there will always be infinitely many observationally equivalent confluent systems. From an inference point of view there is a serious problem when there are confluent relations of the same form as the autonomous relations but with different parameter values. This consideration motivated the development of a general identification theory.[13]

---

[13] See Qin (this volume) for a discussion of this theory.

The last major aspect of "autonomy" which we will consider is its connection with "causality" and "exogeneity", perhaps the two most contested concepts in econometrics. In their recent article, "Exogeneity", Engle *et al.* (1983) found a number of concepts relating to "exogeneity" in use amongst economists and proposed three new ones. The common theme of all these notions is that for some particular purpose an exogeneous variable can be taken as given.

One sign that Haavelmo took very seriously the connection between autonomy and exogeneity is that he called exogenous variables "autonomous variables"! Economic theorists sometimes used "independence" in the same way: independent relations *and* independent variables. However, "autonomous variable" did not establish itself and "exogenous variable" became the standard term.

For Haavelmo's account of thse concepts, we turn to the "General Formulation of the Problem of Estimating Parameters in Systems of Economic Relations" (pp. 85–88 of the *Probability Approach*). The formulation really is *general* and encompasses models with errors in variables as well as errors in equations. For our purposes, it is convenient to ignore the measurement error aspect and concentrate on the joint distribution of the "dependent" quantities x_{ij} (N observations on m variables):

$$\Phi_1[x_{11},\ldots,x_{mN} \mid \xi_{m+1,1},\ldots,\xi_{nN}; \alpha_1,\ldots,\alpha_k; \beta_1,\ldots,\beta_r; \gamma_1',\ldots,\gamma_q').$$

The α's, β's and γ's are unknown parameters. We are interested in the interpretation of the ξ's, the "autonomous" variables.

His treatment is very brief. The autonomous variables are treated as *"constants in repeated samples"*, an assumption which Haavelmo explained as follows:

> The economic meaning of this is that these variables are autonomous parameters fixed by forces external to the economic sector under consideration". (p. 86)

The "economic meaning" suggests that we are entitled to treat the ξ's as parameters just as the α's, β's and γ's are treated as parameters. There are differences: the ξ's vary from observation to observation while the others are constants and the ξ's are known while the others are not. The use of the qualifier "autonomous" and the phrase "forces external to the sector under consideration" suggest that were we to model the determination of the ξ's, the parameters of that model would be invariant to changes in the sectoral parameters, the α's, β's and γ's.

In "Measuring the Marginal Propensity to Consume" (1947) Haavelmo assumed that investment (z_t) is "autonomous in relation" to c_t and y_t:

> This condition is fulfilled if either the sequence z_t is a sequence of given numbers … or each z_t is a random variable which is stochastically independent of u_t [the consumption function disturbance].

What is the relationship between Haavelmo's two accounts—what relationship is intended between the economic assumption and the stochastic independence assumption? A plausible answer is provided by two later Cowles Commission works, Koopmans's "When is an Equation System Complete for Statistical Purposes?" (in Koopmans *et al.* (1950), though written in 1945) and Simon's "Causal Ordering and Identifiability" (1953).

There seem to be the same two considerations and the same gap in Koopmans's piece. He states a "causal principle" for determining which variable are exogenous: it "regards as exogenous those variables which influence the remaining (endogenous) variables but are not influenced thereby". (p. 394) Koopmans writes down a system of "structural equations" for *all* the variables with the properties: (a) some of the variables of the first set of equations (the "endogenous" variables) do not enter the second set of equations (determining the "exogenous" variables); (b) the disturbances between the two sets are independent; (c) the Jacobian of the transformation from the disturbances to the observables is nowhere zero. These properties, in effect, elaborate Haavelmo's stochastic independence assumption.

It is the assumption that it is a system of *structural* equations that ties together the "causal principle" and the "statistical point of view" embodied in assumptions (a) to (c). It is clear from the description of "structural equations" in Koopmans *et al.* (1950, p. 63) that they are autonomous relations, "they can, at least in theory, be changed one by one, independently". It is assumed that there is only one structural representation.[14] These ideas were further developed by Simon (1953).

Explication of the causal principle was the main point of Simon's paper. He identified a causal ordering with the existence of a recursive structure to the equations describing the generation of the exogenous and endogenous variables. This proposal faced the objection that "the same set of observations could be represented by different structures with different causal orderings of the variables" (p. 63).

Thus, because the different structures are "operationally" equivalent the definition of causal ordering is not operational. His solution was that only one recursive formulation will involve equations that remain unaltered when there are "interventions" (p. 65) in the rest of the system. Thus he appealed to autonomy as the way of operationalising the definition. He did not, however, use the word "autonomy".

"Exogeneity" is once again a topic of lively interest and it is worth considering what has become of the "Cowles" notion of exogeneity. The relevant literature is very large but the most ambitious recent account of exogeneity is the work of Engle *et al.* (1983). The only one of their exogeneity concepts that relates to structural invariance, or autonomy, is

---

[14] Engle *et al.* miss the significance of the equations being *structural* equations and find a lacuna in Koopmans's treatment that is not there. Thus in their Example 3.1 (pp. 287–8) Koopmans would not interpret *both* the observationally equivalent systems (27, 29) and (30, 31) as structural.

"super exogeneity". Is this the same concept as Haavelmo's "autonomy" and Koopmans's "exogeneity"?

The Koopmans/Simon recursiveness requirement reappears as the factorisation of the joint density for the random variables y and z into the conditional density for y given z and the marginal for z. If the density factorises

$$D(y, z \mid \lambda) = D(y \mid z, \lambda_1)D(z \mid \lambda_2)$$

[where $\lambda = (\lambda_1, \lambda_2)$ and λ_1 and λ_2 are variation free] with the conditional density $D(y \mid z, \lambda_1)$ invariant to changes in the marginal density $D(z \mid \lambda_2)$ then z is termed *super exogenous* for λ_1. Leamer (1985) develops a similar notion of exogeneity.

The concept of super-exogeneity seems to have been largely inspired by the Lucas disorder, discussed on p. 2 above, in which the transmission mechanism breaks down when the behaviour of the forcing function changes. In insuring only against this disorder, super-exogeneity appears to be less demanding than the Cowles notion of exogeneity. There is no requirement that the marginal density $D(z \mid \lambda_2)$ be invariant to changes in the conditional density $D(y \mid z, \lambda_1)$. If a change in the "transmission mechanism" induced a change in the way that the "forcing" variable were generated one could hardly say that the forcing variable is "generated by forces external to the sector under consideration."

One loose end to be tied: what was the status of assertions regarding autonomy, exogeneity, or structure in general? They were part of the a priori specification of the model—part of the contribution of economic theory to the econometric process. However that was not to say that they were not empirical propositions—indeed Simon saw the analysis of interventions as the way of "operationalising" his purely formal notion of a causal ordering. In the case of the weather and the market for wheat—Simon's leading example—one might accept that there were very good reasons for accepting the a priori specification but few cases are so clear-cut.

Although Haavelmo recognised that false autonomy assumptions would have observable consequences, testing assumptions about autonomy was not a problem emphasised by Haavelmo or his colleagues. Two methods of empirically assessing autonomy claims would fit into their framework: testing for structural stability of a relationship when another relationship changes and testing for neglected heteronomy as a prediction of another theory—cf. the discussion in Engle *et al.* (1983) of testing for super-exogeneity or in Sargent (1976) of testing for the invariance of "reduced forms".

In this section we have considered the significance of autonomy for the programme of classical econometrics. Although it is rarely cited, the *Probability Approach* was an extraordinarily influential work. Its programme was widely accepted and its insights were absorbed so thoroughly that it has become difficult to think of them as insights.

Two of its essential tenets—structural analysis and the probability approach itself—now appear commonplace. "Autonomy" belonged in this basic programme and has a place in any version of structural econometrics. Microeconometrics or rational expectations macroeconometrics may find little use for the simultaneous equations model but they rely on the general case for structural analysis made in the *Probability Approach.*

4. Conclusion

In the last section it was argued that "autonomy" was central to the whole conception of classical econometrics. Throughout the paper it has been insinuated that autonomy is essential to *any* structural econometrics, to any statistical analysis that aims to do more than find regularities in the data. If these views are correct, there seems to be a paradox: how could autonomy be so important and so neglected—how could "Hamlet" be played year after year without the Prince being noticed?

There are a number of reasons. Arguing about autonomy and related concepts is more like doing philosophy than doing economics or statistics.[15] The timing of all this "philosophical" activity is not at all surprising. The 1930s saw bigger changes in conceptions of how economics should be done than any decade since the 1870s. They were as much "years of high methodology" as "years of high theory".

Frisch was the highest of high methodologists. His ideas on structure were embodied in Haavelmo's *Probability Approach* and his ideas on dynamics clearly influenced Samuelson's 1947 *Foundations of Economic Analysis,* the works which above all others codified the methodological "discoveries" of those years.

However, once the codification was achieved, economists could settle down to "normal science" and discussion of "philosophical" issues was no longer appropriate. In applied econometrics, once the art of constructing structural systems had been learnt—or was believed to have been learnt—there was no need to consider rogue relations, to perplex oneself with concepts like autonomy or confluence. In the "normal science" of econometric theory Haavelmo's methods were quickly absorbed and his results on estimation and identification rapidly surpassed.

Autonomy also suffered from fashions in terminology. With his autonomous relations and autonomous variables Haavelmo "autonomised" the terminology of the subject. However the rest of the Cowles Commission never adopted "autonomy" in the same way. While Haavelmo avoided the term "structural relation" and wrote "autonomous relation", the others absorbed "autonomy" into their notion of structural relation: structural relations were autonomous by definition.

Nor did the usage, "autonomous variable", catch on. The use of the same

---

[15] There has been surprisingly little discussion of the close connection between structure and such basic concepts in the philosophy of science as laws and counterfactuals. See Simon's (1977) collection of essays and Hurwicz (1962).

term for variables and relations emphasised the "structuralness" of exogeneity and it is tempting to speculate that had "exogeneous" and
"structural" stayed tied to each other linguistically, much of the later
confusion surrounding the interpretation of exogeneity would have been
avoided.

The disappearance of the term "autonomy" appears to have cut Frisch
and Haavelmo off even from the later "philosophical" literature. Simon's
analysis of causality rests on the autonomy of the equations of his recursive
system. Hurwicz (1962) considered the connection between hypothetical
changes of structure and identification. Yet neither used the term
"autonomy".

Although methodological writing tends to be ephemeral, contributions
are sometimes preserved in textbooks. The concept of autonomy was given
some attention in the textbooks of Klein (1953) and Christ (1966),
econometricians who had been personally involved with the Cowles
Commission. Their books are much closer in design to Haavelmo's
monograph than are other standard works.

More often textbooks, e.g. Johnston (1963), told a different story than
the one about structure and ways of analysing it. Understanding of structure
was so much taken for granted that the emphasis could be on the
economist's requirements for specialised statistical techniques. The theme
was the threat to best linear unbiassedness and how to meet that threat. The
issue of *what* was being estimated was treated as settled. Discussions of
structure were confined to the technicalities of the simultaneous equation
model.

Recent discussions of "exogeneity" and "structure"—e.g. Engle *et al.*
(1983), Leamer (1985) and Cooley and LeRoy (1985)—have just about
established that there must be a Prince in there somewhere. What we have
tried to show in this paper is how the Prince was written into the original
play. Ironically—but perhaps inevitably—the Prince has only been found as
doubts about the viability of classical, or even any form of structural,
econometrics have multiplied.

The debates of recent years recall those of fifty years ago. Macroeconomic theory and macroeconometrics are both in question. There has been
advance in economic theory and in statistical theory but the conceptual
boxes for methodological debate have not changed. The old boxes have
been repainted and brought back into service. Structural econometrics
equals structure plus probability. If probability is not in doubt—and it does
not seem to be—debate about econometrics has to be debate about
structure.

University of Southampton

Oxford Economic Papers 41 (1989), 35–52

A RE-ANALYSIS OF CONFLUENCE ANALYSIS*

By DAVID F. HENDRY *and* MARY S. MORGAN

I. Introduction

CONFLUENCE analysis, developed by Ragnar Frisch in the 1930s, was the first general statistical method especially designed for econometric research. Frisch aimed to deal with two problems at the same time. First, the difficulty of unravelling the different linear relationships which might hold between any given set of observable variables; second, the difficulties caused for estimation when all variables are measured with error. In practice, Frisch also claimed that his method enabled econometricians to sort out the "true" relationships of interest in the data, so that, although conceived as a data analysing technique, confluence analysis also sought to deal with the problems of both variable choice and model selection. With hindsight, confluence analysis can be seen as an attempt to conjointly solve a variety of issues, some of which remain problematical.

The context of econometric ideas in the early 1930's is an essential prerequisite to understanding Frisch's confluence analysis. In the late 1920's, econometricians had become concerned about the question of "dimensionality" of the relationships of interest. This was the problem of several relationships holding simultaneously in the data. In Frisch's treatment, some of these relationships were recognised as spurious (due to characteristics of the particular data set used) whereas others were representative of the interdependencies of real economic relationships. In both cases, the dimensionality of the system collapses into less than the expected number because of the extra relationships holding between the variables. (For example, we can imagine demand and supply relationships giving two intersecting lines in the price/quantity data space but we can only observe a point where the lines intersect, instead of the two lines.) In Frisch's terms this was a problem of collinearity, the term *multicollinearity* applying when several linear dependencies existed. Unravelling the relationships of interest later became the problem of identification; unravelling those relationships which were a characteristic of the data set, but of no interest to the economist, became the modern problem of multicollinearity; note though, that for Frisch, this latter collinearity problem could involve the whole set of variables, not just the "independent" variables.

Frisch was actively investigating three different aspects of such confluent relations in the late 1920s and early 1930s. First, in a research programme begun in the mid-1920s, he was investigating the confluent components of time-series data. Secondly, he dealt with the problem of confluence as an

* We are grateful to the ESRC for finance under grant B00220012 for research on 'The Roles of Expectational Variables and Feedback Mechanisms in Econometric Models', and under grant HR6727 for 'A Study in the History of Econometrics'. We are pleased to acknowledge helpful comments from John Aldrich and the Editors and referees of *Oxford Economic Papers*.

identification problem in a 1933 paper on demand and supply analysis. In this he exhaustively analysed the variability in the economic variables and in the errors in trying to discover whether a measured relationship was a supply, a demand, or another (possibly nonsense) relationship. Thirdly, he analysed the degree of correlation and scatter in variables in a paper of 1929, and in a joint paper with Mudgett (1931). He developed this analytical framework in his main work on the subject of confluent relations in 1934. This version of confluence analysis is discussed in Section II.

It is also important to know that Frisch believed that the application of statistical reasoning based on probability ideas was often inappropriate to economic problems. In his view, Ordinary Least Squares (OLS) methods were frequently misapplied, for OLS assumed that there were measurement errors only in the dependent variable, while the independent variables were error free. He felt that this was not a reasonable assumption and indeed he was not alone in this view. Schultz (1938) for example, estimated both simple regressions in two-variable problems, and often worked out the orthogonal regression line as well. Frisch's views on probability went deeper than this. He believed that probability ideas (i.e. ideas concerning sampling distributions) were not the natural way to deal with economic data which were rarely the result of a sampling process, unlike for example the data of agricultural experiments. Other econometricians of the period were equally suspicious of probability reasoning, particularly for time-series data. They argued, as Morgan (1987a) shows, that the observations of economic data failed to satisfy the requirements of the probability calculus because successive observations are not generally independent and periods may not be homogeneous. With the rejection of probability reasoning, inference procedures in econometrics during the period were necessarily informal and this had obvious implications for model selection or finding the "true" model. Frisch preferred alternative methods of statistical analysis which depended neither on sampling ideas nor on probability reasoning; instead he adopted methods which explored data experimentally to see how they behaved under different circumstances.

The method which Frisch developed for discovering the confluent relations, and measuring the "true" relationships which held in the data, was called bunch map analysis. He suggested other methods of analysing the dimension of empirical relationships which included discussion of characteristic roots, principal components, clusters etc. (all of which eschewed the use of probability theory), but felt bunch maps were the most useful and the method came to be synonymous with confluence analysis. The bunch map method will be described in Section III, followed by a discussion of how Frisch thought it would work and the results he claimed for it. In Section IV, we discuss how bunch maps were used by others in the late 1930's and 1940's and in Section V, note some of the developments in confluence analysis and the reasons why the bunch map method went out of fashion. A more formal analysis of Frisch's bunch maps is presented in Section VI. The recent resurgence of interest in the confluence problem and its relationship with cointegration (see Engle and Granger (1987)) will be discussed in Section VII.

II. Analysis of the confluence problem

The assumptions in *Confluence Analysis* (denoted CA) are that: (i) all observables are measures of latent variables with errors of unknown variances; and (ii) there exists more than one exact linear relationship between these true or latent variables (though relationships need not involve all the variables in the data set). For example, consider a set of three observables, denoted x_{1t}, x_{2t}, x_{3t}. An exact linear relationship (i.e. a collinearity) is assumed to hold between the corresponding latent variables, ξ_{it} as in:

$$\xi_{1t} = \beta_{12}\xi_{2t} + \beta_{13}\xi_{3t} \tag{1}$$

The ξ_{1t} can be thought of as $E(x_{it})$ so that $x_{it} = \xi_{it} + v_{it}$ where v_{it} is the measurement error, a mean-zero random variable uncorrelated with ξ_{it} (i.e. $E(\xi_{it}v_{it}) = 0$). The existence of more than one exact linear dependence among the ξ_{it} would be a state of multicollinearity.

Either of the above assumptions, (i) or (ii), presented considerable problems for contemporary econometricians, and the joint assumption compounded the difficulties. The measurement errors both prevented any simple direct estimation of the relationships of interest, and their presence might well hide some other relationships lurking unknown in the data. Worst of all, their presence might lead you to think you could estimate the collinear relations, but the results would be nonsensical. (For example, imagine again the intersecting supply and demand curves; measurement errors here would cause a scatter of observations around the point of intersection, but any line fitted would reflect only the errors.) Further, Frisch argued that contemporaneous variables should be treated symmetrically, not only because of the general presence of measurement errors, but also because if there were interdependent relationships, there was no justification for selecting any particular observable as the dependent variable and estimating the associated conditional regression.

The absence of precise definitions of CA in Frisch's work makes any general formalisation hazardous. However, from Koopmans (1937) and Frisch's earlier critical appraisal of regression methods in cases where multiple relationships existed between the relevant latent variables and the observable counterparts were subject to measurement error, a reasonable attempt can be made at formulating the underlying model. Let $\mathbf{x}_t$, ξ_t and $\mathbf{v}_t$ denote the $n \times 1$ vectors of observed data, latent variables, and measurement errors at time t, so that $\mathbf{x}_t = \xi_t + \mathbf{v}_t$ (as above). There are assumed to be $k \leq n$ *constant* linear relationships connecting the ξ_t given by $\mathbf{A}\xi_t = \mathbf{0}$ where $\mathbf{A}$ is a $k \times n$ matrix of rank k. (For example, in (1), $\mathbf{A} = (1 : -\beta_{12} : -\beta_{13})$ and is 1×3 of rank 1.) It is assumed that $E(\xi_t\mathbf{v}_t') = \mathbf{0}$ and $E(\mathbf{v}_t\mathbf{v}_t') = \Sigma$

(constant, positive definite and diagonal), and that $E(\xi_t \xi_t') = \phi$ (the second moment matrix of the latent variables of rank $n - k$ since $\mathbf{A}\phi = \mathbf{0}$). Then, $\mathbf{A}\mathbf{x}_t = \mathbf{A}\xi_t + \mathbf{A}\mathbf{v}_t = \mathbf{A}\mathbf{v}_t = \mathbf{u}_t$ is the system of k stochastic equations connecting the n elements of $\mathbf{x}_t$, and if $E(\mathbf{x}_t \mathbf{x}_t') = \mathbf{M} = \phi + \Sigma$ is the population second moment matrix of $\mathbf{x}_t$, since $\mathbf{A}\phi = \mathbf{0}$, then $\mathbf{A}\mathbf{M}\mathbf{A}' = \mathbf{A}\Sigma\mathbf{A}'$, and $E(\mathbf{x}_t \mathbf{u}_t') = \mathbf{M}\mathbf{A}' = \Sigma\mathbf{A}' \neq \mathbf{0}$. Note that $\mathbf{A}$, ϕ and Σ are all implicitly taken to be independent of t.

The four issues with which Frisch was concerned can be seen from this formulation of his model.

(A) Normalising one x_{jt} to have a coefficient of unity in each equation and regressing that variable on any or all remaining x's will not consistently estimate the elements of $\mathbf{A}$ since $E(\mathbf{x}_t \mathbf{u}_t') \neq \mathbf{0}$. This is the measurement error or (now well known) simultaneous equations *inconsistency*: the former was formally analysed in Koopmans (1937) and the latter in Haavelmo (1943a). Frisch (1929) had earlier investigated this problem and discussed solutions based on orthogonal regression and on the eigenvalues of $\mathbf{M}$. He also discussed bounds on the elements of $\mathbf{A}$ obtained from minimising the residuals in all directions, which was the precursor of CA.

(B) Since rank $(\phi) = n - k$, the moment matrix $\mathbf{M}$ would be singular without the errors of measurement. Thus, regression estimates of $\mathbf{A}$ are determinate *only* because of observational errors (better data would make this worse!) and so Frisch regarded such estimates as being nonsense. The crime of using regression was compounded by the fact that the usual formulae for calculating the standard errors would *not* reveal the latent indeterminacy, since if Σ is small but positive definite, then $\mathbf{M}$ is non-singular.[1] For $k > 1$, Frisch regarded this problem as *multicollinearity* (due to the ξ_t satisfying k linear equations) *even though the x's themselves need not be very highly intercorrelated*.

(C) Since $\mathbf{A}\xi_t = \mathbf{0}$ then $\mathbf{D}\mathbf{A}\xi_t = \mathbf{A}^*\xi_t = \mathbf{0}$ for any non-singular $k \times k$ matrix $\mathbf{D}$. This is the problem of *identification*. Even if ϕ were known, distinguishing $\mathbf{A}$ (the economic theory parameters of interest) from $\mathbf{A}^*$ requires imposing restrictions on $\mathbf{A}$, and otherwise (for $k > 1$) is insoluble. When $k = 1$, $\mathbf{D}$ is a scalar and after normalisation, only one set of (population) coefficients can be obtained. For $k > 1$, we can learn the value of k from the rank of ϕ (i.e. how many linear equations exist among the ξ's) but not what $\mathbf{A}$ is. If ϕ is large relative to Σ, $\mathbf{M}$ will be "close" to rank $(n - k)$ and hence the observed data may throw light on k. This leads on to the topic of cointegration discussed in Section VII below.

(D) Finally, if k and the coefficients in $\mathbf{A}$ are not known *a priori*, then they have to be selected from the data. This is the *model selection* problem.

---

[1] This is the first example of a long list of situations in which estimated regression coefficient variances fail to reflect the underlying uncertainty: autocorrelated or heteroscedastic residuals, non-constant parameters, and integrated (non-stationary) time series are some other established cases.

Even if $k = 1$, which x_{it} (and hence which ξ_{it}) enter the relationship has to be established from the data.

One of Frisch's examples, used also by Koopmans (1937), serves as an excellent illustration of these problems.[2] Here, $n = 4$ and $k = 2$, and Frisch constructed $\mathbf{A}$ as:

$$\mathbf{A} = \begin{pmatrix} 1 & 1 & -1 & 0 \\ 1 & -1 & 0 & -1 \end{pmatrix} \text{ and so } \mathbf{AA}' = \begin{pmatrix} 3 & 0 \\ 0 & 3 \end{pmatrix}$$

implying that $\xi_{1t} + \xi_{2t} - \xi_{3t} = 0$ and $\xi_{1t} - \xi_{2t} - \xi_{4t} = 0$. Also, $\mathbf{\Sigma} = \alpha \mathbf{I}$ for a scalar $\alpha > 0$ and $\mathbf{v}_t \sim \text{IN}(\mathbf{0}, \mathbf{\Sigma})$ (meaning, distributed as Independent Normal variables) so that $\mathbf{Ax}_t \sim \text{IN}(\mathbf{0}, \alpha\mathbf{AA}')$. Finally, ϕ is 4×4 of rank 2, specified by letting $\phi_{33} = \phi_{44} = 2$, $\phi_{34} = 0$ and $\alpha = 0.01$, so that:

$$\phi = \begin{pmatrix} 1 & 0 & 1 & 1 \\ 0 & 1 & 1 & -1 \\ 1 & 1 & 2 & 0 \\ 1 & -1 & 0 & 2 \end{pmatrix} \text{ and hence } \mathbf{M} = \begin{pmatrix} 1.01 & 0 & 1 & 1 \\ 0 & 1.01 & 1 & -1 \\ 1 & 1 & 2.01 & 0 \\ 1 & -1 & 0 & 2.01 \end{pmatrix}$$

If the four zero and normalisation restrictions are *imposed* on $\mathbf{A}$, then the remaining parameters (which happen by scaling to be unity) are uniquely identifiable (the only admissible $\mathbf{D}$ is $\mathbf{D} = \mathbf{I}$); otherwise $\mathbf{A}$ is not identifiable. However, the two "structural" equations also imply the "reduced form": $\xi_{1t} = \frac{1}{2}(\xi_{3t} + \xi_{4t})$ and $\xi_{2t} = \frac{1}{2}(\xi_{3t} - \xi_{4t})$. It is clear that the fourfold set $(\xi_{1t}, \xi_{2t}, \xi_{3t}, \xi_{4t})$ is perfectly collinear, but so are *all of the following sets*: $(\xi_{1t}, \xi_{2t}, \xi_{3t})$, $(\xi_{1t}, \xi_{2t}, \xi_{4t})$, $(\xi_{1t}, \xi_{3t}, \xi_{4t})$, $(\xi_{2t}, \xi_{3t}, \xi_{4t})$. Consequently, regression estimates of the coefficients of $\mathbf{A}$ will be unidentified without the noted prior restrictions, and inconsistent otherwise, multicollinearity abounds among the ξ_t and without considerable prior knowledge, model selection looks hopeless. Nevertheless, for situations like this example, Frisch proposed a tool of analysis: Bunch Maps.

III. Bunch maps

It will be easiest to explain bunch maps with a numerical example. This example is, in part, taken from a mimeographed paper prepared by Staehle with Haavelmo's help to explain confluence analysis for students at Harvard in the early 1940's. Staehle's example concerned the demand equation for butter, where the observed variables x_{1t}, x_{2t}, x_{3t} and x_{4t} are the quantity purchased, the price of butter, income and the price of margarine all at time t. Using the observed data (x_{it}), and omitting x_4 for the present, β_{12} in (1) could be computed in three different ways by assuming in each case that the errors (of measurement) to be minimized occurred in only one of the

---

[2] The example is discussed in Sections 13, 23 and 33 of Frisch (1934) and pp. 33–38 of Koopmans (1937); the original data were constructed from ticket numbers drawn from the Norwegian State Lottery.

variables. This yields three different *elementary* regression equations (all re-normalised on x_{1t}):

$$\hat{x}_{1t} = b^1_{12.3} x_{2t} + b^1_{13.2} x_{3t} \tag{2}$$

$$\hat{x}_{1t} = b^2_{12.3} x_{2t} + b^2_{13.2} x_{3t} \tag{3}$$

$$\hat{x}_{1t} = b^3_{12.3} x_{2t} + b^3_{13.2} x_{3t} \tag{3}$$

where $b^h_{12.3}$ is a least squares estimate of β_{12} allowing for x_3, and the superscript h denotes the direction of minimisation.

The calculation of the *elementary* coefficients and the plotting of the associated bunch maps is made easier if the data are in deviations from means and have been normalised such that: $\sum_t x_{it}^2 = 1$ (for each i). Then the cross-moments of the normalised data are equal to the correlation coefficients, and the data covariance matrix $(\mathbf{X'X})$, where $\mathbf{X} = \{x_{it}\}$, is the same as the matrix $\mathbf{R}$ of correlation coefficients $\{r_{ij}\}$. The adjoint or cofactor matrix $\mathbf{R}^*$ plays a central role in the analysis, since the elements $\{\rho_{ij}\}$ of $\mathbf{R}^*$ are the cofactors of $\{r_{ji}\}$—equal to $(-1)^{i+j}$ times the determinant of the submatrix obtained by deleting the ith row and jth column (noting that transposition is irrelevant here). In Staehle's example, the observations yield:

$$\mathbf{R} = \begin{bmatrix} 1.0 & -0.875 & -0.373 \\ -0.875 & 1.0 & 0.637 \\ -0.373 & 0.637 & 1.0 \end{bmatrix} \text{ and } \mathbf{R}^* = \begin{bmatrix} 0.594 & 0.638 & -0.184 \\ 0.638 & 0.861 & -0.311 \\ -0.184 & -0.311 & 0.234 \end{bmatrix}$$

Using the conventional formulae for OLS estimates, after re-normalisation the *elementary* regression coefficients are given by:

$$b^h_{ij.r} = \frac{-\rho_{hj}}{\rho_{ih}}$$

and hence:

$$b^1_{12.3} = \frac{-\rho_{12}}{\rho_{11}}, \quad b^2_{12.3} = \frac{-\rho_{22}}{\rho_{12}}, \quad b^3_{12.3} = \frac{-\rho_{32}}{\rho_{13}}.$$

Thus, once $\mathbf{R}^* = \{\rho_{ij}\}$ is known, it is easy to calculate the $\{b^h_{ij.r}\}$. According to Frisch, the expressions for $b^h_{12.r}$ demonstrate the first advantage of confluence analysis. For 2 variables, b^1_{12} and b^2_{12} provide the limits (under extreme assumptions about the errors) of the coefficient β_{12} of the "true" relationship. Generalising suggests that β_{12} lies within the limits fixed by the three elementary coefficients, $b^h_{12.3}$ ($h = 1,2,3$).

The second and more important use of the technique claimed by Frisch is to uncover and disentangle the confluent relationships. This requires the calculation of all possible elementary regression coefficients, meaning both the coefficients in all two variable relationships, all three coefficients between those two variables in any three variable relationships and so on. These coefficients are then mapped into "bunch maps" for graphical analysis, which Frisch argued reveal an enormous amount about the relationships in the data, including the confluent relationships.

Each bunch map shows all the measurements for each of the coefficients between two variables (an intercoefficient) for a given set of other variables. By convention, the coefficient's numerator (e.g. ρ_{hj} for b_{ij}^h) is on the vertical axis, the denominator (ρ_{ih}) on the horizontal, and a 'beam' connects the origin to the point (ρ_{ih}, ρ_{hj}). Each beam on a map thus represents the slope of a coefficient when a different direction of minimisation is used—the beam being labelled with the direction (e.g. (1)). There is a set of maps for every selection of covariates (e.g. ignoring x_3 and x_4, including x_3 but not x_4 etc.).

Beginning with the two-variable relationships, the bunch maps are obtained from the two-variable cofactor matrices given by selecting the three relevant 2×2 blocks from **R** above and inverting these, so that:

$$\begin{bmatrix} \rho_{11} & \rho_{12} \\ \rho_{21} & \rho_{22} \end{bmatrix} = \begin{bmatrix} 1.0 & 0.875 \\ 0.875 & 1.0 \end{bmatrix}, \begin{bmatrix} \rho_{11} & \rho_{13} \\ \rho_{31} & \rho_{33} \end{bmatrix} = \begin{bmatrix} 1.0 & 0.373 \\ 0.373 & 1.0 \end{bmatrix}$$

$$\begin{bmatrix} \rho_{22} & \rho_{23} \\ \rho_{32} & \rho_{33} \end{bmatrix} = \begin{bmatrix} 1.0 & -0.637 \\ -0.637 & 1.0 \end{bmatrix}$$

In the two-variable case, the main points of interest are the directions of the beams and how close together the beams on the map are. The closer together the beams, the more precisely the coefficient is determined and the less the uncertainty about the true coefficient due to measurement error (the "first advantage" noted above): see Fig. 1.

Frisch felt it was important to analyse bunch maps starting from the smallest set of variables and adding more variables one by one to see if each additional variable was useful, superfluous or detrimental to the purpose of finding and fitting the true relationships. A new variable is useful if its addition draws the beams closer together and possibly changes the signs of the beams (as from a simple to a partial correlation). A new variable is superfluous if it neither changes the signs nor tightens the beams, and if the new beam is shorter and lies outside the original beams (indicating no improvement in fit). The cofactor matrix **R*** (reported above) yields the 'data' for the three (three-variable) bunch maps based on the $b_{ij.r}^h$ formulae.

Comparing Figures 1 and 2, suggests that adding income (x_3) to the relationship between price and quantity of butter is useful since the leading beams marked (1) and (2) on the $b_{12.3}$ map move a little closer together. Thus, x_3 adds to the precision with which the relationship between variables 1 and 2 is measured. The income coefficient b_{13} is not very accurately determined (the beams are "far apart" in Fig. 1) but in the three variable set, the coefficient does have the "correct" (i.e. expected theoretical) positive sign.

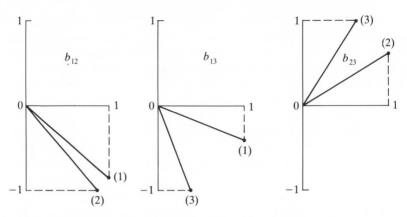

FIG. 1. Bunch maps for the two-variable regressions (x_1, x_2), (x_1, x_3) and (x_2, x_3)[3]

A new variable is to be considered detrimental if the bunch map explodes, for this is a sign of multicollinearity (in Frisch's sense). Suppose that several variables enter into a particular relationship and that there is an additional well-defined relationship between two of the variables. This could be either a previously neglected theoretical relationship involving the two variables or a characteristic of the sample of data. For example, theory suggests that the price of and demand for butter will be affected by the prices of other goods, in particular by the price x_4 of its substitute, margarine:

$$x_1 = b_{12.34}x_2 + b_{13.24}x_3 + b_{14.23}x_4.$$

Suppose that the latent prices of margarine and butter were jointly determined. This could cause collinearity in the data set since the bunch

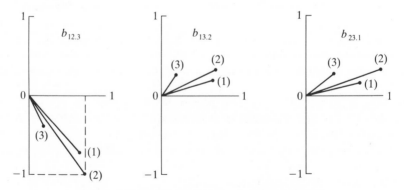

FIG. 2. Bunch maps for the three-variable regressions

[3] This and the following figure are adapted from the Staehle and Haavelmo (1941) paper.

maps have revealed the well-defined relationship $x_1 = b_{12.3}x_2 + b_{13.2}x_3$ and now we also have $x_2 = b_{24}x_4$.

In fact, the bunch map for the coefficient for $b_{12.34}$ does explode suggesting that x_4 is indeed a detrimental variable here:

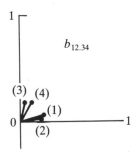

FIG. 3.

This is an example of our present day notion of multicollinearity, but in Frisch's bunch map technology, similar results would occur when two structural relationships linked the variables—such as the presence of both supply and demand relationships. The presence of both relationships together prevents us from distinguishing them separately. But despite the multicollinearity, the presence of measurement errors means that in practice the coefficients of the confluent relationship are determinate, though probably nonsense and these appear as the short, widely spaced beams of the exploded bunch map.

Frisch claimed that the great advantage of bunch maps over the usual methods adopted was that his analysis made no assumptions about the structural relationships (the theoretical relationships between the true variables) that were not thoroughly investigated in the data. The bunch map method helped to decide which variables, suggested by the theory, do actually enter in the relationship and which can be omitted. This was the model selection aspect of the method. The method also enabled one to see which relationships were "identified" (which ones could be found) and which other relationships held at the same time. By treating the variables symmetrically, the method also took into account measurement errors in each variable and helped to choose a well fitting equation closest to the true relationship. Frisch even claimed that, as far as computation was concerned, bunch maps were not much more burdensome than standard methods (he suggested that the complete confluence analysis of a six-variable problem—including checks and corrections—took about 13 hours). Frisch's own work had contained various applications, and he hoped that other econometricians would use the method so that it could be thoroughly tested and its usefulness appreciated.

IV. Practical applications

Frisch was one of the pre-eminent econometricians of the 1930's and consequently confluence analysis was well known,[4] if not well understood at the time. The bunch map method was used by econometricians, particularly in Europe, in the late 1930's and 1940's and even into the 1950's. A brief description follows of the ways in which two prominent econometricians used the bunch map technology.

Tinbergen, in his work for the League of Nations (1939), used bunch maps not as an investigation method to determine the models, but to check on the presence of multicollinearities in the data set. Bunch maps formed part of Tinbergen's battery of tests of the reliability and statistical significance of his results and were reported in a section along with tests of serial correlation of residuals and standard errors. He also computed tests due to Koopmans (1937), on the limits of the regression coefficients arising from the error of weighting.

Stone also used bunch maps extensively in his work on consumer demand and included them in his various reports on the subject between 1945 and 1954. In his first report in 1945, he was an enthusiastic proponent of the use of bunch maps. He chose his models using a combination of bunch map analysis and Tinbergen-style graphical methods (in which the components of the regression equation were selected and reported using more conventional time-series graphs). He used the bunch maps particularly to decide which variables to include and which to omit. Sometimes the evidence from the two methods seemed to him to conflict and he was obliged to try and pick groups of variables which appeared to perform best on the joint set of methods and tests. By 1954 he had calculated a huge number of bunch maps and these were reported in his massive study of consumer demand. He made little reference to the way these bunch maps were used in practice, a typical example being: "The bunch maps of these regressions are highly variable; some are excellent while others are bad, that is, exploded. On the whole they may be classed, subjectively, as fair" (Stone (1954) p. 320).

Stone's comment highlights one of the main practical problems of bunch map analysis. Much depended on an interpretation of results which could only be *subjective*. There were no precise rules of inference from the bunch maps such as were available in statistics based on probability theory, which for all their drawbacks did give some objective way of evaluating results and taking decisions. There were other practical problems which emerged as we shall see later.

---

[4] His book received at least two reviews; one of these, McIntyre (1936), pointed out that Frisch's model and method were similar to factor analysis, discussed independently by Thurstone (e.g. Thurstone (1935)) in psychometrics. Although Reiersøl worked with both models there were few other attempts to link the methods or exploit their similarities.

V. Advances in confluence analysis and the decline of bunch maps

Frisch had claimed that confluence analysis helped to solve the problem of collinearity, to find out what variables were in a relationship, what the true model was and what were the limits to the true regressions for the relationships. In modern parlance, Frisch's claims embraced multi-collinearity, identification, model choice and inference, and the estimation of errors-in-variables models. Griliches' (1974) assessment comes to roughly the same conclusion—that CA was developed to sort out a whole range of problems. Haavelmo has confirmed that confluence analysis was about identification, multicollinearity and how to find the "true" model when it was unknown (Interview 2.6.1982). Frisch therefore presented Bunch Maps (BM) as being a general analytical tool, yet both BM and CA are mainly remembered, if at all, as a tool for investigating multicollinearity. Why is this the case?

One reason is that by the 1950's, when the tool was last taught and used, all of these problems, apart from multicollinearity, had been subjected to other, more formal investigations and solutions than that offered by bunch maps. As we shall see, in important respects, Frisch and his associates were responsible for the developments in confluence analysis which made BM redundant.

Of all the individual problems addressed by confluence analysis, the errors-in-variables estimation problem was the one which seemed most immediately pressing during the 1930s. In the language of Section II problem (A), if Σ were known (or could be consistently estimated), then ϕ could be calculated from $M - \Sigma$ (i.e. by "purging" the data of measurement errors). The *estimation* problem in (A) would then vanish since if A were identifiable, it would be the solution to $A(M - \Sigma) = 0$. However, Koopmans' thesis (1937) criticised Frisch (1934) for ignoring sampling errors in his discussion of measurement errors. Koopmans extended Frisch's work to take into account both sorts of errors in determining the limits to the values of the true regression coefficients (although his extensions were not often used in practice—Tinbergen's work for the League of Nations being the obvious exception). Koopmans was not the only worker in this area. Allen (1939) proposed a method for estimating such models when the relative error variance was known. In 1940, Wald proposed a grouping method to bypass the unknown Σ matrix, and Tintner (1944 and 1950) suggested the use of the variate difference method for estimating the unknown Σ. The real breakthrough came with the development of instrumental variables estimators for the errors-in-variables problem, proposed separately by Reiersøl (1941 and 1945) and Geary (1943). Reiersøl's work[5] is particularly

---

[5] Reiersøl partly worked with Frisch on his method and although the general idea of instrumental variables was Reiersøl's, he has credited Frisch with the name (Interview 17.6.82).

interesting for it was a development of confluence analysis in which the
confluent variables were utilized (as instrumental variables) to provide a
better estimation method, whereas previously these variables had been a
bar to accurate estimation. Durbin's 1954 paper extends and generalises this
work on errors-in-variables, but by the 1950s, following Haavelmo's
reformulation of econometrics in 1944, errors-in-variables had been pushed
aside in favour of errors-in-equations (see Morgan (1984) for a general
historical account). With hindsight, estimators for the errors-in-variables
model from Allen to Tintner and the Instrumental Variables estimators
introduced by Reiersøl can all be viewed as attempts at obtaining ϕ (see
Hendry (1976) for a formulation).

The concept of confluent relations was developed further in papers
delivered by Frisch, and by (his then research assistant) Haavelmo, at the
1936 meeting of the Econometric Society. And, in a separate paper
criticising Tinbergen's work for the League of Nations, Frisch (1938)
introduced the important concept of autonomy. It seems clear from these
discussions that in Frisch's view, confluent relations were now to be defined
more narrowly and in opposition to both autonomous and structural
relations: confluent relations were those which emerged in the statistical
data, but which were not in themselves directly representative of underlying
economic forces.[6] It is indicative of this shift in meaning that the "true
regressions" which Frisch had sought in CA were relabelled "structural
equations" by Reiersøl (1941) with Frisch's approval. In the programme
which grew out of Haavelmo's 1944 reformulation of Frisch's ideas,
structural relations were marginalised, for by definition they were those not
of interest to the economist.

The redefinition of confluent relations did not make the problem of
collinearity disappear, but following Haavelmo's work the sorting out of
perfectly collinear structural relations became the question of the identification of simultaneous equations. Of course, in this guise, the identification
problem had been discussed earlier by Frisch (1933a) and Tinbergen (1930).
As a result of Frisch's (1938) autonomy paper and Haavelmo's probability
paper, the identification problem and its solution were formalised and
codified in a series of articles which came out of the Cowles Commission in
the late 1940s and early 1950s (see Qin this volume). Historically, the effect
of this change of meaning and separation out of the multicollinearity and
identification issues on the use of BM is seen in Stone's work. In his first
extended report, Stone (1945) interpreted the appearance of unexpected
relationships causing the confluence problem as due to the presence of other
relationships which held in the population or in the sample or in some

---

[6] This change of meaning of confluent relations is perhaps associated with Frisch abandoning
his time-series research programme but maintaining an interest in the study of confluence in
business cycle models. The subtle changes in the meaning of confluence and the development
of structural analysis and the autonomy concept are discussed in more detail by Aldrich (this
volume).

combination. By 1951, following the work of Haavelmo and the Cowles Commission on identification, Stone interpreted the presence of other relationships in the *population* as the question of identification. The confluence problem was interpreted more narrowly as a problem of the *sample*: (p. 69) "essentially the identification problem over again except that lack of identifiability may not be apparent from the formal study of a system of relationships [as in identification] since it may arise only as a sampling phenomenon". ([.]) denotes our insert).

The problem of which variables to include and inference and model choice issues generally (problem (D) of Section II), were attacked by Haavelmo (1944). His conversion to probabilistic reasoning and testing (which apparently followed from failure to persuade Jerzy Neyman of the benefits of CA) radically changed econometric practice (see Morgan (1987a). Probability reasoning did not in itself make BM redundant, but it provided a formal alternative to its informal and subjective inference procedures as Haavelmo (1950) himself remarked. The choice of variables and models became a subject for economic theory and statistical tests, and the probabilistic reasoning behind these tests was in contrast to Frisch's experimental and data-based approach to taking decisions on model content.

Thus the only aspect of the original confluence analysis which had not been developed by work of the 1940s was multicollinearity and this may in part explain the remembrance of the purpose of BM. There is some support for this view in the first generation of econometrics textbooks of the 1950s and 1960s. Tinbergen (1951a), Tintner (1952) and Valavanis (1959) all discuss BM in connection with the problem of multicollinearity in the independent variables, while both Beach (1957) and Valavanis portray BM as an extension of partial correlation analysis. These authors disagree as to the usefulness of bunch maps; Valavanis suggests that more can be learnt from a study of the correlation coefficients and finds BM to be of only "archaeological interest". Klein (1962) also discussed Frisch's work in connection with multicollinearity in time series data (because of the presence of trends and cycles). Malinvaud (1964) alone discusses BM as a systematic (though outdated) method for comparing different regressions, while multicollinearity is treated separately.

The separation out of the problems contained in CA by Frisch, Haavelmo and Reiersøl, and the change in paradigm due to Haavelmo's probability revolution in econometrics provide strong reasons for the fading out of BM. But we are left with a question raised implicitly in the previous section. Was BM analysis ever any use, either for understanding the problem of collinearities or uncovering confluent relations in empirical work, as Frisch claimed? The experiences of those who used BM in the 1930s and 1940s suggest that it was not a reliable tool, and this must also have contributed to its decline.

One reason for problems in BM lay in the behaviour of the measurement errors. Although Frisch made no assumptions about the structural relationships which he expected to find by his method, the same is not true for the errors in the variables. The BM method assumed that there were no correlations between any of the errors, and that there were no correlations between any error term and any true variable. At least one contemporary economist realised a possible source of problems here. Champernowne, in discussing Stone's confluence analysis of 1945, suggested that if each variable's errors were serially correlated, this was likely to result in high "spurious correlation" between the errors of different variables. This would, he claimed, cause a failure in the method because the bunch maps will not explode as they are supposed to do when there are collinear relationships in the set. Instead, the bunch maps will indicate that only one relationship holds and the shape of that relationship will depend on the correlation between the errors.

More recently Stone has also expressed dissatisfaction with the method (Interview 12.11.1980). He suggested that if the data moment matrix is nearly diagonal and the beams on the bunch maps lie close together, then almost anything can happen. After considerable experience working with the method in the late 1940's he concluded that you cannot discover multicollinearity from the bunch maps and they do not help to decide model content.

Even Frisch's own examples did not clearly prove the advantages of BM over conventional regression analysis (see Koopmans (1937, p. 33) and Frisch (pp. 190–191)). Consequently, we now formally analyse BM.

VI. A theoretical analysis of bunch maps

The CA model for which Bunch Map analysis was seen by Frisch as the relevant tool was set out in Section II above. The absence of distributional assumptions in the model's formulation is notable but there are three restrictive implicit assumptions: (i) in time series, even if ξ_t involves no lags, the $\mathbf{v}_t$ are taken to be serially uncorrelated (see Champernowne (1945)); (ii) as already recorded, both $\mathbf{A}$ and Σ are treated as constant; and (iii) both ϕ and $\mathbf{M}$ are assumed constant (so the data are weakly stationary). Moreover, Frisch's two explicit assumptions that $E(\xi_t \mathbf{v}_t') = \mathbf{0}$ and Σ is diagonal are highly questionable. The former will fail if additional "problems" occur (such as the simultaneous determination of the ξ_t in a world with errors in equations, or lags in responses when the $\mathbf{v}$'s are autocorrelated etc.). The latter will fail due to a result on which Frisch himself (in 1929) placed great emphasis, namely: *linear models are invariant to linear transformations*. The observable data used in any study will be $\mathbf{Dx}_t = \mathbf{x}_t^*$ rather than $\mathbf{x}_t$ (since we do not *know* the relevant ξ_t) with error variance $\mathbf{D}\Sigma\mathbf{D}'$ which will not be diagonal in general even if Σ is. For example, if the measurement errors in consumption and income are uncorrelated then those in savings (= income-consumption) and income will be correlated. Finally, to modern readers, a crucial *lacuna* is Frisch's unwillingness to make any weak exogeneity or conditioning assumptions (see Koopmans (1950) and Engle *et al.* (1983)); their introduction by Reiersøl in the guise of lagged information was an important development leading directly to Instrumental Variables techniques, and indirectly to a clear conception of exogeneity and the identification of parameters of interest.

However, even granting Frisch's assumptions, there seem to be serious difficulties in interpreting Bunch Maps, a point we illustrate by reconsidering the Frisch and Koopmans' example from Section II. The determinant of **M** is 0.000906, so $\mathbf{M}^{-1}$ is well defined with adjoint matrix;

$$\mathbf{M}^* = \begin{pmatrix} 0.0605 & 0 & -0.0301 & -0.0301 \\ 0 & 0.0605 & -0.0301 & 0.0301 \\ -0.0301 & -0.0301 & 0.0304 & 0 \\ -0.0301 & 0.0301 & 0 & 0.0304 \end{pmatrix}$$

Normalising any given column (j) by the element on the *j*th diagonal yields the negative of the regression coefficients of x_{jt} on the remaining **x**'s. Thus, from the first two columns:

$$x_{1t} \simeq 0.0x_{2t} + 0.4975(x_{3t} + x_{4t}) \quad \text{and} \quad x_{2t} \simeq 0.0x_{1t} + 0.4975(x_{3t} - x_{4t}).$$

These are almost precisely the *reduced form* equations noted above despite including perfectly collinear subsets of variables. Moreover, the coefficients are virtually identical to those in the regressions of x_{1t} and x_{2t} respectively on (x_{3t}, x_{4t}) *only*, which are the correctly specified reduced forms. However, the BM will indicate wild estimates, since regressing x_{2t} on x_{1t} and renormalising on the latter (or vice versa) will produce infinite results given that $m_{12}^* = m_{21}^* = 0$ (although sampling errors will hide that in any given data set).

If the zero restrictions on **A** are known and yet regression analysis is adopted, the two results correspond to:

$$E(x_{1t} \mid x_{2t}, x_{3t}) = -0.9708x_{2t} + 0.9805x_{3t}$$

and

$$E(x_{2t} \mid x_{1t}, x_{4t}) = 0.9708x_{1t} - 0.9805x_{4t}$$

which closely reproduce the actual *structural equations*, showing small inconsistencies in estimating the elements of **A**. However, given the results immediately above, adding x_{4t} to the former or x_{3t} to the latter will induce large changes in the parameter estimates as regression swings from estimating the structure to estimating the reduced form. These outcomes seem uninterpretable in terms of BM alone and yield little insight into what the "true" relationships are. Worse still, what occurs is highly dependent on the structure of ϕ, and on the sizes of the measurement errors. Since $\mathbf{M} = (\phi + \Sigma)$, when $\Sigma = \alpha\mathbf{I}$ (as above), $\mathbf{M}^{-1} = (\phi + \alpha\mathbf{I})^{-1}$ (i.e. ridge-regression!), and *increasing* α "stabilises" the estimates. Similarly, if we pick $\phi_{33} = 4$, $\phi_{44} = 2$ and $\phi_{34} = 0$, no infinite results are obtained although even for $\alpha = 1.0$ (one hundred times the original value), the ratio of b_{12}^1 to b_{12}^2 is still around 1600.

Overall, even if $\mathbf{A}$ is identifiable, it is difficult to see what can be learned from BM analysis and any attempts to dust it down and put it to use seem ill-advised.[7] However, to reject BM as a method does not herald the end of the confluence problem, and in fact, CA has attracted renewed recent interest.

VII. The recent history of confluence analysis

Kalman (1982a,b) closely links Frisch's CA model to systems analysis and argues for a symmetrical treatment of all variables (not ascribing "noise" to any particular subset), with k and $\mathbf{A}$ both unknown. He seeks to characterise the class of all solutions while determining k from the data, and discusses the case $k = 1$ in detail. Swann (1982) and (1985) investigates the consequences of, and measures for, the combination of multicollinearity and errors-in-variables which he views as far more serious than either alone. This naturally echoes several facets of CA, although Swann "inverts" the problem to try and establish critical levels (upper bounds) for measurement error variance such that $\mathbf{M} - \mathbf{\Sigma}$ is singular (for the special case $\mathbf{\Sigma} = \alpha \mathbf{I}$, α is the smallest eigenvalue of $\mathbf{M}$). These bounds can be related to the sizes of the conventional 't'-tests that regression parameters are zero. Klepper and Leamer (1982) formally analyse the properties of BM and relate their results to the set of possible maximum likelihood estimates (showing the latter to be bounded only if all sets of BM estimates are in the same orthant).

The final reason for renewed interest in CA is its intimate links to the literature on Cointegration (see Granger and Weiss (1983), Engle and Granger (1987), Granger (1986) and Hendry (1986)). First, some background. A weakly-stationary time series is integrated of order zero (denoted $I(0)$) since it needs to be differenced *zero* times to be stationary. An $I(l)$ series x_t is one which is $I(0)$ after lth order differencing:[8] i.e. $\Delta^l x_t \sim I(0)$. Note that an $I(0)$ plus or minus an $I(1)$ series is $I(1)$. An important issue is the degree to which linear combinations of x_{1t} and x_{2t} (say given by $z_t = [x_{1t} + \beta x_{2t}]$ need to be differenced to become $I(0)$. If $l = 1$ for both series, then x_{1t} and x_{2t} are *cointegrated* if z_t is $I(0)$. In the bivariate case, β must be unique (since adding δx_{it} to z_t would make it $I(1)$).

Consider the sample second moment matrix $\mathbf{M}$ of $\mathbf{x}_t$ where:

$$\mathbf{M} = \frac{1}{T} \sum \mathbf{x}_t \mathbf{x}_t' = m_{22} \begin{pmatrix} m_{11} m_{22}^{-1} & m_{12} m_{22}^{-1} \\ m_{12} m_{22}^{-1} & 1 \end{pmatrix}.$$

As $T \to \infty$, $\mathbf{M}$ diverges since $I(1)$ series have variances increasing faster than

---

[7] See, for example, Los (1986).

[8] Stationarity is convenient for expository purposes but is not necessary; similarly a special case of cointegration is considered below, covering only $I(1)$ variables.

T (e.g. as T^2 for a random walk, or T^3 for a random walk with non-zero drift). Nevertheless, if x_{1t} and x_{2t} are cointegrated then $\text{var}(z) = (m_{11} + \beta m_{12}) + \beta(m_{12} + \beta m_{22})$ is finite so that (e.g.) $m_{22}^{-1}\text{var}(z) \rightarrow 0$. Since:

$$(1:\beta)\mathbf{M}\binom{1}{\beta} = ((m_{11} + \beta m_{12}) : (m_{12} + \beta m_{22}))\binom{1}{\beta} = \text{var}(z),$$

then $m_{22}^{-1}\mathbf{M}$ becomes singular and $(1:\beta)$ is the linear combination that produces the singularity. Thus, when $\mathbf{M}$ is standardised to be finite, it is singular: cointegration reintroduces the confluence problem!

Since $x_{1t} = -\beta x_{2t} - z_t$, then z_t could be interpreted as "measurement error", but with *finite* variance σ^2. If x_{2t} is $I(1)$, $\sigma^2/m_{22} \rightarrow 0$ as $T \rightarrow \infty$, confirming that $\mathbf{M}$ has rank 1. Thus, the measurement error problem of CA becomes asymptotically trivial when $x_{it} \sim I(1)$ whereas $z_t \sim I(0)$: whichever direction of minimisation is selected, the same estimate of β results (i.e. the correlation between x_{1t} and x_{2t} tends to unity). Since it seems reasonable to assume a finite measurement error on *growth rates* of economic variables, the above will hold in practice.[9] Thus, we have come full circle. Long-run equilibrium relations of the form: $x_1^e + \beta x_2^e = 0$ can be interpreted as in CA with the latent variables $\mathbf{x}_t^e$ being the ξ_t and the equilibrium solutions being the equations $\mathbf{A}\xi_t = 0$ which hold exactly. Now z_t is the current disequilibrium (see Davidson *et al.* (1978)), differentiated from the $\mathbf{x}_t$ by being $I(0)$ when they are $I(1)$. Problems (A) and (B) of Section II cease to matter, despite an enormous weakening of the assumptions, and k is easy to determine asymptotically with $I(1)$ data. However, (C) and (D) remain: some "outside" source of information is needed to identify what the k cointegrating relationships actually are and to determine the "structural" rather than the "confluent" equations. Finally, the links to the "multi-collinearity" of the textbooks are now clear: adding a complete set of $I(1)$ *cointegrated* variables to a regression will both induce very high correlations and a near-singular data moment matrix.

VIII. Conclusion

It is important to maintain the distinction, proposed in this paper, between confluence analysis and bunch maps. Bunch maps, as a technique proposed by Frisch to uncover confluent relations, have faded out. There were good historical reasons for their demise and, as our analysis shows, there are good intellectual reasons why they should not be resurrected. Frisch's confluence analysis, on the other hand, played an important role in the development of econometric theory. Not only was it the first general theoretical treatment of econometric problems, but, as the historical analysis suggests, it prompted directly, or indirectly, the important changes

---

[9] Engle and Granger (1987) also show that autocorrelation in z_t does not affect their procedure for estimating β by regression, nor does simultaneity between the x_{it}. For other results see Phillips (1986a), Davidson (1987) and Johansen (1987).

in econometric ideas and techniques of the 1940s. These advances did not solve all of Frisch's difficulties. Confluent relations remain problematic for the modern econometrician, just as they did for Frisch and his contemporaries, and in view of recent research on cointegration, they once again deserve serious analysis.

Nuffield College, Oxford
London School of Economics

Oxford Economic Papers 41 (1989), 53–70

AGRICULTURAL ECONOMISTS IN THE ECONOMETRIC REVOLUTION: INSTITUTIONAL BACKGROUND, LITERATURE AND LEADING FIGURES

By KARL A. FOX*

U.S. AGRICULTURAL economists and their close associates were world leaders in applied econometrics during 1917–33 (Fox 1986). However, until recently few econometricians have been curious about history. An article by E. J. Working (1927), "What do statistical 'demand curves' show?" has been cited over and over again, but the rest of the extensive literature by agricultural econometricians has been ignored. Now that some younger scholars are preparing to specialize in the history of econometrics, we may hope for a more balanced coverage of that literature.

We begin with a description of the institutional framework within which agricultural economics developed up to and including the establishment of the U.S. Bureau of Agricultural Economics (BAE) in 1922.[1] As we have discussed the 1922–33 period in other articles (Fox 1986, 1988), we next comment on the Cowles Commission simultaneous equations approach as perceived by BAE agricultural economists during 1945–55. This is followed by a short section on the neglect of errors in variables by the simultaneous equations teaching tradition during the 1950s and 1960s, although the importance of such errors had been recognized in the agricultural econometrics literature since 1922 and by Frisch (1934) and Koopmans (1937). The final section introduces the econometric work of Mordecai Ezekiel and Frederick V. Waugh, the two most important of the agricultural econometricians. As Ezekiel joined the BAE in 1922 and both he and Waugh began publishing in 1923, their careers cast some additional light on the continuity of the agricultural econometrics tradition from 1922 to an arbitrary cutoff point in 1964.

The institutional background of agricultural economics in the United States

Before 1933, 'general' economics in the United States was primarily a teaching field. Economics departments in a few major universities encouraged research, but most of this was historical and/or descriptive and made no formal use of mathematics and statistics. The teaching of economic theory seldom went beyond Marshall and was often slighted in favour of courses on the history of economic thought. Publication took the forms of journal articles and books. The volume of publication was small and was intended mainly for fellow economists and students.

---

[1] For a broader historical perspective see Fox (1987).

In contrast, agricultural economics grew up in the land-grant colleges (now universities) and the U.S. Department of Agriculture, institutions created or authorized by acts of Congress in 1862. Their purpose was to promote agricultural development by helping farmers—directly by on-campus teaching and off-campus demonstrations and indirectly by research. The research function was strengthened in 1887 by an act to provide federal funds to the agricultural experiment stations which came to be associated with the land-grant colleges in the various states. Additional research funds were appropriated by state legislatures, and they implied a commitment to problem-solving and subject matter research on topics of current and near-future interest to farmers in the sponsoring states. Research programs were organized around soils, crops, and livestock species rather than physics, chemistry, botany, and zoology—the related 'pure' academic disciplines.

Research in the U.S. Department of Agriculture (USDA) was organized on a much larger scale than that of any one state agricultural experiment station but along similar subject matter lines. By 1905 the USDA included a Bureau of Animal Industry, a Bureau of Plant Industry, a Bureau of Soils, a Bureau of Statistics, a Bureau of Forestry, and several others. Rasmussen and Baker (1972, p. 15) assert that the USDA in the early 1900s was "the world's outstanding scientific research institution." As of 1912 it had 2,815 employees in Washington and 11,043 in other locations. Most of the Washington employees were engaged in research.

Agricultural scientists moved readily between the Washington bureaus and the state agricultural experiment stations. Most of their research was reported in technical bulletins published by the USDA or the stations. Many of these bulletins were too long, detailed, or specialized for journal publication; they circulated widely within the USDA and land-grant college system but rarely come to the attention of academicians devoted to 'pure' disciplinary research and teaching.

Agricultural scientists also established their own professional associations and journals along subject matter lines appropriate to their research activities. Scientific reputations, awards, and offices became coextensive with these professional associations and governed salary increases, promotions, and interinstitutional mobility. Sociologically speaking, each association became a relatively self-contained community providing all the usual satisfactions of a scientific career. Relations with 'pure' discipline-based associations were limited and one-sided: for example, soil scientists had to study chemistry but chemists did not have to study soil science.

Agricultural economics grew up in this research milieu. The first textbook entitled *Agricultural Economics* was published by Henry C. Taylor in 1905. Taylor held a Ph.D in Economics from the University of Wisconsin and sought to apply economic theory to the analysis of agricultural problems. At the same time, some agricultural scientists with backgrounds in crop production or horticulture were developing a highly eclectic and pragmatic field called 'farm management'. They established the American Farm Management Association in 1910. For a few years Taylor and others of like mind maintained a separate organization (the American Association of Agricultural Economists), but the two groups merged amicably in 1919 to form the American Farm Economic Association (with Taylor as its first president) and to establish the *Journal of Farm Economics*.

By 1919, the land-grant colleges in several states had created departments of agricultural economics, and the associated experiment stations were funding research in that field. In 1919, Taylor entered the USDA as chief of the Office of Farm Management. He successfully encouraged the consolidation of USDA's economic work into a single bureau. The Bureau of Agricultural Economics (BAE) was established in 1922 with Taylor as its chief.

Lowitt (1980, p. 6) says that the new BAE "became the economic research bureau of the department—conducting investigations in the costs of production and marketing, farm organization, farm financial relations, farm labor, agricultural geography and history, land economics, and the problems of rural life. The bureau also acquired and disseminated information concerning marketing and distribution of farm and nonmanufactured food products, and it was a storehouse for the collection and dissemination of statistical data relating to agricultural production. A publication program was inaugurated, making the results of its research easily available . . . . The bureau continually sought to improve methods of data gathering, reporting, and forecasting."

The BAE brought together by far the largest group of research-oriented economists that had ever been assembled in the United States and presumably in the world. It became the central institution of the agricultural economics profession, maintaining close ties with agricultural economists in the land-grant colleges and experiment stations and collecting, processing, and interpreting vast quantities of statistical data. Many BAE economists saw themselves as contributing to the well-being of 30,000,000 farm people—a fourth of the total U.S. population.

Some contributions of U.S. agricultural economists and their close associates to econometrics during 1917–33 were discussed in Fox (1986, 1988). From 1933 to 1941, many of those leaders became economic advisers, policy analysts, and administrators in the large action agencies of the Roosevelt New Deal administration. World War II and its aftermath further dispersed the early leaders. Ezekiel left Washington in 1946 and joined the Food and Agriculture Organization of the United Nations (FAO). Waugh left USDA in 1945 for the Office of War Mobilization and Reconversion and spent 1946–51 at the Council of Economic Advisers, returning to the BAE only in 1952.

I joined BAE's program appraisal and development staff in Washington in February 1945 and worked on fast-moving policy analyses and special assignments through June 1946. During that time M. A. Girshick was head of the Statistical Techniques section in BAE's Division of Statistical and Historical Research (S and HR), the traditional center of BAE's work on demand and price analysis. Girshick was greatly respected but I had little contact with him before he left BAE in July 1946. I occupied Girshick's former position very briefly before becoming Associate Head of S and HR, with *de facto* responsibility for innovative research on demand-supply-price structures for foods and farm products. I carried that responsibility from late 1946 through July 1954, and my comments on the simultaneous equations approach in the next section are written from that perspective.

Agricultural economists and the simultaneous equations approach, 1943–55

To motivate this section, I will attribute certain preconceptions to young 'general' economists who were thoroughly indoctrinated in the Cowles Commission simultaneous equations approach during the 1950s and 1960s but who did little empirical research themselves and had no contact with agricultural economists:

1. Single equation methods had no place in econometrics. Haavelmo had proved that all least squares estimates of demand functions were seriously biased.

2. E. J. Working's 1927 article proved that his contemporaries, and particularly the agricultural economists, were continually mistaking supply curves for demand curves and had no basis for deciding whether a least squares regression equation approximated one rather than the other.

3. The limited-information maximum likelihood (LIML) method immediately demonstrated its superiority to single equation methods in empirical research.

4. Agricultural econometricians were shadowy figures without names or faces. In fact, *all* econometricians writing before 1943 were shadowy figures without names or faces.

I encountered such preconceptions very frequently during 1955–71 as head of a joint department of 'general' and agricultural economics at Iowa State University. I did *not* encounter them among the actual creators of the simultaneous equations approach—Haavelmo, Marschak, Koopmans and others—during 1946–54.

Leo Rogin once said that the hottest arguments are based on different preconceptions as to what is self-evident. Arguments about the identification problem—the primary justification for the simultaneous equations approach—are a case in point.

In a recent article (Fox 1986) I asserted that, far from being baffled by E. J. Working's dilemma, leading agricultural econometricians in the 1920s never failed "to recognize and solve" the demand-supply identification problem. This statement surprised a 'general' economist who cited a 1941 or 1942 article by Jacob Marschak saying that the identification problem had not yet been solved.

The answer is that Marschak and I had different preconceptions as to what it means to "solve the identification problem." Our preconceptions reflected different ways of practicing science—by agricultural economists in the 1920s on one hand and the Cowles Commission group of the 1940s on the other. Agricultural economists regarded identification problems as potential obstacles, along with errors in variables and unavailability of data, to their success in estimating reliable demand functions for particular commodities at particular market levels. When I said that Ezekiel, Waugh, and the Workings never failed to "solve" the identification problem, I meant that, to the best of my knowledge, they never failed to recognize it in concrete instances and never seriously misinterpreted their results. The Cowles Commission group focused on "the" identification problem *as such,* isolated it from all concrete instances and from the question of errors in variables, and "solved" it at successively higher levels of abstraction and generality.[2] Each group was highly successful in accomplishing its own objectives.

To the best of my knowledge, economists working in the BAE and at the Cowles Commission during 1943–50 understood and respected these differences in objectives. During 1943–46 Girshick (BAE) was collaborating with Haavelmo (Cowles Commission) on a five-equation model of the demand for food in the United States as a nontrivial illustration of the limited-information maximum likelihood method. Girshick's two assistants went to the Cowles Commission (University of Chicago) for graduate study. James P. Cavin, Girshick's immediate supervisor, was strongly supportive of Girshick's collaboration with Haavelmo, and a Cowles Commission econo-mist told me enthusiastically that Girshick was "one of the few 'develop-mental statisticians' in Washington."

There was an extraordinary amount of personnel turnover throughout government during 1945–46. Girshick and his assistants all left BAE and I believe there was no further collaboration with the Cowles Commission until 1950 when Cavin negotiated a contract to support research by Clifford Hildreth and Frank Jarrett on an LIML model of the U.S. livestock economy. I visited the Cowles Commission a time or two in connection with that project.

I believe the Cowles Commission's intensely creative work on the simultaneous equations approach was completed by 1946.[3] Cowles Commis-sion Monograph 10 appeared in 1950 and the more expository Monograph 14 in 1953. My impression is that the authors of papers in the two monographs had long since moved on to other problems, leaving the books to be interpreted by young econometricians who had no part in their creation. A new paradigm had been gained, but the history of econometrics had been temporarily lost.

I will take up the four preconceptions in turn.

---

[2] See Qin (this volume).
[3] My impression seems to be supported by Epstein (this volume).

1. *The simultaneous equations theory recognized single equation complete models as a special case.* Koopmans (1945) had already pointed out a special case (the "uniequational complete model") in which an equation fitted by least squares would be identical with the maximum likelihood estimate indicated by the simultaneous equations approach. The "cobweb" or recursive demand-supply model fits this case. If the current year's supply, $q(t)$, is a strictly predetermined variable (i.e., if the current year's supply curve is a vertical line), then the demand curve $p(t) = f[q(t)]$ can be fitted appropriately by least squares with $p(t)$ as the dependent variable.

The cobweb model did indeed characterize many agricultural commodities and the agricultural econometricians' tradition of estimating their demand functions by least squares was well founded.

In principle, Haavelmo's method of reduced forms could have been used to explore the possibility that small elements of simultaneity in the supply functions might have been biasing the estimates of demand functions in not-quite-perfect cobweb models. I reported such an exercise in Fox (1954).

My least squares demand function for pork (p. 63) was

$$p = -1.16q + 0.90y + u; \qquad R^2 = 0.97 \tag{1}$$
$$(0.07) \quad (0.06)$$

My "structural" demand function derived by the method of reduced forms (p. 63) was

$$p = -1.1447q + 0.8974y + u \tag{2}$$

The coefficients of y, disposable personal income per capita, in the two equations are identical (within a fraction of one percent); the coefficients of q, per capita pork consumption, differ by only 1.3 percent, a small fraction of the standard error of the least squares coefficient; p is the retail price of pork. All variables are in first differences of logarithms, annual observations for the U.S. as a whole during 1922–41.

The figures in parentheses are standard errors of the least squares regression coefficients; the associated t-ratios would be 15 or greater in both cases. My judgement is that all or nearly all of the least squares demand functions estimated by Ezekiel, Waugh, the Workings, Henry Schultz (1938), and myself (Fox 1951, 1953, 1958) were so nearly free of the "simultaneous equations bias" that formal application of the method of reduced forms would not have yielded significant improvements.

2. *Agricultural economists rarely encountered E. J. Working's dilemma in its pure form.* The E. J. Working model of intersecting and shifting demand and supply curves is pedagogically effective. However, it grossly understates the amount of "identifying information" usually available to agricultural economists in the 1920s and later.

Figure 1 (from Fox 1953, p. 29) is a diagram of the demand and supply structure for pork in the United States during 1922–41; the directions of the

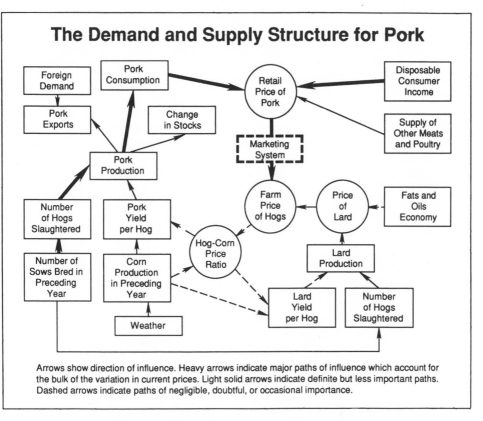

FIG. 1. The demand and supply structure for pork in the United States, 1922–41.

arrows are appropriate for annual observations. The diagram emphasizes considerations relevant to identification and estimation of demand functions at retail and farm price levels, and the heaviness of the arrows reflects their relative importances in contributing to variations in current prices. I drew the diagram in 1952, but I believe that Ezekiel, Waugh, and the Workings viewed the hog-and-pork economy in similar terms.

E. J. Working posed the identification problem in terms of paired observations on two variables; for concreteness, let's assume these are annual observations on pork production and the farm price of hogs. If we are completely ignorant of all other variables in Figure 1 and of their linkages and time lags, we have Working's dilemma. As a matter of fact, no U.S. agricultural economist in the 1920s could possibly have been ignorant of the time lags between the breeding of sows and the birth of pigs (nearly four months) and between birth and arrival at marketable weight (eight or nine months). They also knew a good deal about farmers' decision processes. They could not possibly have mistaken the supply curve

$q(t) = f[p(t-1)]$ for the demand curve $p(t) = f[q(t)]$ or some combination of the two.

Figure 1 also shows that a two-equation demand-supply model for pork is much too simplistic for many practical uses. The farmers' supply curve would include the farm price of hogs and pork production; the consumers' demand curve would include the retail price of pork and pork consumption. Additional links are needed (1) between the retail price of pork and the farm price of hogs and (2) between pork production and pork consumption. USDA economists in the 1930s therefore developed "supply and distribution tables," which put production, consumption, beginning inventories, imports, exports, and ending inventories into an accounting framework, and data on retail prices and "food marketing margins," which were also placed in an accounting framework.

USDA economists in the late 1920s also recognized the need for variables such as consumers' income as "demand curve shifters" and by 1933 they had developed proxies for, or approximations to, the desired measures.[4]

3. *In my personal experience, the LIML method did not surpass single-equation methods in the quality of its empirical results.* The best empirical applications of the LIML method through 1955 yielded equations much like those obtained by least squares. In my review article (Fox 1956) on the Klein-Goldberger 20-equation model of the United States, I concluded that the authors had "gained little or nothing of economic importance by using the limited-information method rather than least squares ... There is no evidence of significant difference between the Klein-Goldberger limited-information model and the least-squares counterpart which I had fitted." (p. 132). I strongly supported Klein's economic objectives and, at Klein's later invitation, I participated in constructing the Brookings quarterly econometric model of the United States.

In or shortly after October 1946 I had learned that the LIML method *could* give astonishing and unrealistic results. As a BAE staff member interested in statistical techniques, I received a copy of the prepublication version of Girshick and Haavelmo (1947) containing a five-equation model of the demand for food in the United States. I also received a copy of a modified version of the model done by one of Girshick's assistants, Lois Nelson Shores.

Shores had added a weather-related variable in the equation (number 4) determining farmers' production of food commodities and an industrial workers' average income variable in the farm price equation (number 5). The equation determining disposable income (number 3) was the same in both versions, being fitted separately from the others by least squares. The specifications of the equations determining consumers' demand for food (number 1) and dealers' supply of food (number 2) were unchanged.

The big surprise came in equation number 1 determining consumers'

---

[4] See Wells and Bean (1937).

demand for food:

	Elasticities of demand for food with respect to	
Model	This year's income	Last year's income
Girshick and Haavelmo (G–H)	0.247	0.051
Shores	0.037	0.469

The G–H elasticity with respect to this year's income is consistent with cross-section estimates from household expenditure studies. The Shores elasticity with respect to this year's income is incredibly small; that with respect to last year's income is incredibly large. Quite illogically, the modifications in two other equations had exploded the coefficients of the consumers' demand function. The results suggest a new and more virulent case of Frisch's old problem of multicollinearity, greatly aggravated by intercorrelations among variables and/or disturbances in different equations.

My own intensive work on statistical demand analysis was completed in 1952. I concentrated on farm products and foods to which the cobweb model had applied rather closely during 1922–41. These products had accounted for some 60 percent of farmers' cash receipts from crop and livestock marketings. Their peacetime demand-supply-price relationships had been badly disrupted from 1942 through about 1948 by price controls, rationing, food procurement for the U.S. armed forces and overseas allies, and other special circumstances. The outbreak of hostilities in Korea (June 1950) seemed to presage another period of price controls and other disturbances. It seemed imperative to estimate the 1922–41 demand-supply-price structures for these commodities without delay as a benchmark for policy decisions and analysis in the early 1950s. My empirical results were published in Fox (1951) and my methodology in Fox (1953). I used single-equation methods throughout.

From 1951 through 1957, Richard J. Foote supervised some young economists in BAE's S and HR Division who were able to spend their full time studying export crops, fats and oils, and other commodities with complex demand-supply-price structures. Foote had worked in the single-equation tradition since 1936 and had coauthored a book on agricultural price analysis. He and his group used both LIML and single-equation methods as indicated by model structures.[5] Foote (1955) gave a balanced view of the two methods. Friedman and Foote (1955) published a manual of

[5] In their introduction to Waugh (1984), Houck and Abel (p. xii) assert that "this work clearly set the pace for applied econometric work across the entire economics profession."

computing instructions for the LIML method which was widely circulated among agricultural economics professors and graduate students in the land-grant universities.

4. *Agricultural econometricians were real people.* I will try to establish Ezekiel and Waugh as such in a later section.

The neglect of errors in variables in the simultaneous equations approach

Holbrook Working (1922) and Waugh (1923) were aware of sizeable errors in some economic variables. Henry Schultz (1925) was so concerned that he experimented with a pure errors model in estimating the demand curve for sugar. In his later work, Schultz (1938) presented alternative least squares demand functions, one estimated with price and the other with quantity as the dependent variable. As a rule, he thought errors constituted a larger proportion of the observed variance in quantity than in price. Frisch (1934) and Koopmans (1937) also attached great importance to errors in variables.

Marschak (1950, pp. 20–21) said that the Cowles Commission group explicitly assumed away errors in variables, presumably to focus discussion on the revolutionary implications of disturbances in equations. Anderson and Hurwicz (1948) published an abstract on models containing both disturbances and errors, but it did not become part of the later teaching tradition. Computing instructions for the LIML method were based on the assumption of error-free variables; these instructions were followed, apparently without question, for two or three decades.

Griliches (1974) published a major article on "Errors in Variables and other Unobservables." He began by noting (p. 971) that Frisch's 1934 book "and the work of other early pioneers such as Sewall Wright" have "begun to be rediscovered by a generation to whom all of this was nothing more than obscure footnote references in Cowles Commission monographs." He offered some reasons why "by the late 1950s the simultaneous equations literature was developing rapidly without paying any more attention to the errors-in-variables problem" (p. 976).

Griliches was apologetic about this. On pages 974–975 he explained the neglect "based primarily on my own experience with what was taught to me in the fifties and what I was teaching to my students in the sixties." His excuses for ignoring Frisch and Koopmans were not impressive. On page 975 he implied that these and other works on errors in variables were "obscure, largely published abroad and inaccessible, both physically and intellectually. The work of Frisch and Koopmans was known only secondhand."

These are rationalizations rather than reasons! George Kuznets called these books to my attention in December 1940 or January 1941; I found them readily in the University of California (Berkeley) library. In subsequent years I found them whenever I needed them—in the U.S. Department of Agriculture library, the Library of Congress, and the Iowa

State University library. Waugh had spent several months with Frisch in Oslo during 1932–33; in 1950 when I wanted to experiment with orthogonal regression models Waugh directed me to the precise page (p. 66) in Frisch (1934) on which I would find a mathematical description of the required procedures.

Griliches further asserted that so long as econometricians worked only with aggregative data they could not have done much about errors in variables anyway. On the contrary, in the data-rich environment of BAE a good deal could be done, and occasionally was done, with knowledge about errors in variables.

Charles F. Sarle had published a USDA bulletin on the reliability and adequacy of the BAE's farm-price data in 1927 and another on the adequacy and reliability of its crop-yield estimates in 1932. BAE statisticians as of 1950 had a great deal of evidence concerning the approximate levels of measurement error in their estimates of year-to-year changes in price and quantity variables and I made some use of their judgments.

The results in Table 1 below were computed during 1950–51 but were reported most fully in Foote and Fox (1954). In the cases of eggs and turkeys, the estimated error variances in each of the three variables (price, consumption, and income) were subtracted from the observed variances; the remainders were used to compute the adjusted demand functions. The observed variances of year-to-year changes in production were small; the estimated error variances amounted to 15 percent of the observed for egg and 10 percent for turkey production. Estimated error variances in the price and income variables accounted for 0.2 percent to 1.5 percent of the observed. Hence, the adjusted price flexibilities were from 10 to 30 percent higher than the unadjusted. The adjusted R^2s were 0.06 to 0.07 larger than the unadjusted, but they still left 8 to 13 percent of the adjusted variances in prices to be explained by omitted variables or other "disturbances."

This type of error adjustment could have been made just as easily in computing the reduced form equations in the simultaneous equations approach.

TABLE 1

Price flexibilities and coefficients of determination (a) unadjusted and (b) adjusted for the estimated effects of errors in variables.[1]

Commodity and dependent variable	Price flexibility with respect to per capita production or consumption		R^2	R^2
	Unadjusted	Adjusted	Unadjusted	Adjusted
Eggs (retail price)	−1.83 (0.48)	−2.34 (0.44)	0.80	0.87
Turkeys (farm price)	−1.44 (0.26)	−1.58 (0.20)	0.86	0.92

[1] The figures in parentheses are standard errors.

An introduction to the econometric work of Mordecai Ezekiel and Frederick V. Waugh, 1922–64

In an earlier section we said that many BAE economists saw themselves as contributing to the well-being of 30,000,000 farm people. In 1922 many of these farm people were in economic trouble. Farm product prices had more than doubled during and immediately after World War I, but they dropped 50 percent from 1920 to 1921 while nonfarm prices remained high and it seemed clear that the agricultural sector would be depressed relative to the rest of the economy for several years at least (Fox 1987). Given this outlook, helping farmers impressed many USDA workers as a moral imperative.

Mordecai Ezekiel (1899–1974) joined the BAE at its moment of creation in 1922. He was 23. During the next eight years he did far more than any other person to establish applied econometrics as a highly prestigious field for agricultural economists. He had completed a B.S. degree at the University of Maryland in 1918 (at age 19) and had spent one year in military service and two or three at the Census Bureau. While working for the BAE, he picked up M.S. and Ph.D. degrees at the University of Minnesota (1924) and the Robert Brookings Graduate School of Economics and Government (1927) respectively, choosing thesis and dissertation topics of direct interest to the BAE. He moved to the newly-established Federal Farm Board in 1930 and became economic adviser to the Secretary of Agriculture, Henry A. Wallace, in 1933.

Frederick V. Waugh (1898–1974) delayed his education for two years to serve as an ambulance driver attached to the French army during World War I. He completed a B.S. degree at Massachusetts Agricultural College in 1922 and an M.S. at Rutgers in 1924. He worked successively for the New Jersey Department of Agriculture (1923–24), the Connecticut Agricultural Extension Service (1925–26), the Massachusetts Division of Markets (1926–28), and the New England Research Council (1928–32), taking courses intermittently at Harvard and Columbia. He completed a Ph.D. in Economics at Columbia in 1929 and spent 1932–33 studying in Europe before joining the USDA in 1933. Apart from a year as adviser to the Office of War Mobilization and Reconversion and five years at the Council of Economic Advisers, Waugh continued in the USDA until his retirement in 1965. In addition to his scientific publications, Waugh served as mentor and role model for several cohorts of young agricultural econometricians in the BAE and its successor agencies.

Ezekiel's contributions were concentrated between 1923 and 1933 and consisted mainly of the development of efficient and practical multiple regression techniques (linear and curvilinear, graphic and numerical), their rapid dissemination among agricultural economists, and their application to economic analysis and policy. Waugh also began publishing in 1923 but his work changed dramatically after his year of postdoctoral study spent mostly with Ragnar Frisch. From 1933 on, Waugh made explicit use of economic theory, mathematics, and statistics on the same levels as did the leading 'general' econometricians, but he surpassed most of them in the clarity and policy-relevance of his applications.

Between them, Ezekiel and Waugh represent two major aspects of the econometric revolution: the development of estimation techniques and the advancement of economic theory in its relation to statistics and mathematics. I hope this paper and the others cited in its opening paragraphs will encourage younger scholars to incorporate the work of Ezekiel, Waugh and other agricultural econometricians into the general history of econometrics.

The Professional Standings of Ezekiel and Waugh among Agricultural and 'General' Economists, Econometricians, and Statisticians

Although agricultural and 'general' economists constituted separate scientific communities, their prestige structures were related through dual citizenship (in some cases) and migration. In 1957 the American Farm Economic Association (AFEA) elected ten members to the newly-established rank of Fellow. Waugh was included in this group along with Henry C. Taylor and five former presidents of the American Economic Association: John D. Black (Harvard), Thomas N. Carver (Harvard), Joseph S. Davis (Stanford), Edwin G. Nourse (Brookings Institution), and Theodore W. Schultz (Chicago). The first four had also served as presidents of the AFEA, as had Waugh. Waugh and Schultz (b. 1902) were the two youngest among the ten. Ezekiel was the youngest of three Fellows elected in the following year (1958).

Evidently, Waugh and Ezekiel were ranked among the 13 most important living contributors to the agricultural economics profession; they were the only econometricians included. To the best of my knowledge, neither of the two held offices in the American Economic Association. However, Ezekiel was elected a vice-president of the American Statistical Association (ASA) in December 1928 (at age 29) and a Fellow in 1931; Waugh was elected a vice-president of ASA in 1940 and a Fellow in 1946. Ezekiel and Waugh were both charter members of the Econometric Society; Ezekiel became a Fellow in 1935 and Waugh in 1947. Ezekiel was first listed in *Who's Who in America* at age 35 and Waugh at age 38; few scientists in any field were included before age 40.

The Econometric Work of Mordecai Ezekiel, 1923–38

As of 1922, the BAE had vast accumulations of time series data and massive inflows of current reports and estimates. It was axiomatic to H. L. Moore (1917, p. 1) that "the most ample and trustworthy data of economic science" were "official statistics."

The elementary economic theory of demand curves, supply curves, and production functions was widely known among U.S. 'general' and agricultural economists as of 1922 but advanced statistical methods were not. It was logical for Ezekiel to emphasize the development and dissemination of efficient statistical methods for estimating economic relationships.

In the 1920s the desk-top calculating machines available to 'general' and agricultural economists were mechanical; most were operated by means of hand cranks, without electrical power. Even with electrically-powered machines, fitting a three or four-variable regression equation was a time-consuming process; research workers often skipped built-in checks on the accuracy of their computations and made serious numerical errors.

Tolley and Ezekiel (1923) presented the Doolittle method (including check-sums) for handling multiple correlation and regression problems. Its publication in the *Journal of the American Statistical Association* indicates that it was regarded as a significant contribution at the time.

In the following year, Ezekiel (1924) made a truly pathbreaking contribution with his method for handling curvilinear multiple regression problems in any number of variables. He developed it in connection with a classic study of agricultural production functions (Tolley, Black, and Ezekiel, 1924) which was not surpassed until after World War II. The other authors gave Ezekiel sole credit for developing the estimation technique used.

He first fitted the linear multiple regression of output upon the three inputs, $y = f(x_1, x_2, x_3)$. The residuals when plotted about the net regression of y on x_1 indicated some degree of curvilinearity, so a freehand curve was drawn with a shape consistent with production theory. The residuals from this curve were plotted about the net regression of y on x_2; if indicated the net regression line was replaced by a freehand curve with appropriate shape and the residuals from it plotted about the net regression of y on x_3. The cycle could be repeated, perhaps leading to further adjustments in the first set of curves.

Another BAE economist, Louis Bean (1929), invented a short-cut which substituted "drift lines" (approximations to the slopes of net regression curves) for Ezekiel's first-stage fitting of a linear multiple regression equation by least squares. One argument in favor of the Ezekiel–Bean approach was that economic theory did not require demand, supply, and production functions to be analytic; graphic curves could not be rejected on theoretical grounds. More important was the speed and economy of the graphic method.

The Ezekiel–Bean method was widely used by agricultural economists well into the 1950s. An excellent description of it is presented by Thomsen and Foote (1952, pp. 296–315).

Ezekiel was the central figure in a group of (mostly) USDA scientists that made many contributions to regression techniques. Ezekiel's *Methods of Correlation Analysis* (1930, pp. vi–vii) specifically cited Bradford B. Smith, Sewall Wright, Donald Bruce, Fred Waugh, Louis Bean, and Andrew Court in this connection. As of 1930, "correlation analysis" was a generic term covering all attempts to measure associations among two or more variables; despite its title, Ezekiel's book was exclusively devoted to *regression analysis*.

R. A. Fisher had only recently begun to make a clearcut distinction between the "regression model" appropriate to designed experiments and the "correlation model" appropriate to naturally-occurring bivariate or multivariate normal distributions found in some biological phenomena. H. L. Moore (1914, 1917) was one of the first economists, and by far the most influential, to use regression analysis to estimate demand and supply curves. Ezekiel and his young associates in the 1920s were pioneers developing the new territory only recently explored by Moore. Ezekiel's book was definitely on the frontier; most of the specific techniques reported and/or emphasized were first published between 1923 and 1930. I am reasonably sure that, at 427 pages, it was by far the most comprehensive work on applied regression analysis published up to that time.

Ezekiel published a second edition in 1941, substantially expanded and improved. Three chapters (80 pages) were devoted to graphic methods. On page vii Ezekiel thanks "two expert mathematical statisticians, W. Edwards Deming and Meyer A. Girshick," for advice in revising the more mathematical sections, especially those dealing with the sampling significance of results. This version remained a standard reference until it was replaced by the Ezekiel-Fox third edition in 1959. The title was then changed to *Methods of Correlation and Regression Analysis: Linear and Curvilinear.* The subtitle reflected Ezekiel's judgment that the third edition still contained a more satisfactory treatment of curvilinear regression than did any competing work. The third edition remained in print, without revision but with dwindling sales, until 1987, giving Ezekiel's 1930 classic a life span of 57 years.

When Ezekiel was elected a Fellow of the Econometric Society in 1935, he confined his list of publications to articles or bulletins with substantive economic content. Among these were Ezekiel (1927, 1928), Haas and Ezekiel (1926), and Ezekiel and Bean (1933). I surmise he had been advised that some of the Society's Fellows (whose votes would decide his election) were not enthusiastic about his work on graphic regression methods. Other Fellows elected in the same year were Jacob Marschak and R. G. D. Allen.

Several of Ezekiel's economic studies during 1924–33 were regarded as classics in their particular areas of application. However, in 1930 he became Assistant Chief Economist of the Federal Farm Board, an agency created in 1929 to encourage exports of certain crops with the help of a $500,000,000 revolving fund. As the economic depression deepened during 1930–32 the fund was soon exhausted. Meanwhile, Ezekiel had gained deep insight into the problems of agricultural adjustment and general economic recovery. He played a major role in drafting the Agricultural Adjustment Act of 1933, and in March of that year he became economic adviser to the new Secretary of Agriculture (Wallace).

Space does not permit a consideration of Ezekiel's influence on agricultural policies and on the research activities of the Industrial Committee of the National Resources Planning Board. Ezekiel became an excellent 'general' economist but most of his publications after 1933 represented spare-time activities. Waugh (1964a) wrote that Ezekiel's article on "The Cobweb Theorem" (1938) "still stands as a landmark in the theory of prices and production." With respect to his own 1964 article on "Cobweb Models," Waugh gratefully acknowledged suggestions "from four pioneers in this field: Mordecai Ezekiel, Wassily Leontief, Jan Tinbergen, and Herman Wold."

During 1943–46 Ezekiel assisted in planning for the Food and Agriculture Organization of the United Nations (FAO). He joined FAO in 1946 and devoted the rest of his career to research supervision and advising on the agricultural aspects of economic development.

The econometric work of Frederick V. Waugh, 1923–64

Twenty-nine of Waugh's most important publications have been edited by James Houck and Martin Abel and appear in Waugh (1984). The editors give an excellent summary of Waugh's career and an enthusiastic testimony to his personality and influence. Our own discussion can therefore be brief.

Waugh published his first econometric study in 1923, on factors influencing the price of New Jersey potatoes on the New York market. He thanks Holbrook Working for valuable suggestions. In appraising the limitations of his demand function, he notes the presence of errors of observation in three variables, errors (disturbances) caused by omitted variables, and errors (disturbances) due to "unsettled conditions" during the New Jersey shipping season. Here, near the very beginning of the agricultural econometrics tradition, we have the matter-of-fact recognition of both errors in variables and disturbances in equations.

Waugh's doctoral dissertation at Columbia University was published under the title *Quality as a Determinant of Vegetable Prices* (1929). In it Waugh used measurable attributes of fresh market vegetables to demonstrate that from 40 to 60 percent of the variance in prices among individual lots on any given day could be explained by factors generally lumped together as "quality."

Waugh's work changed decisively after his year in Europe on a social Science Research Council fellowship. He spent most of that year (1932–33) with Ragnar Frisch in Norway. He worked more briefly with Erich Schneider in Germany, Francois Divisia in France, and Jan Tinbergen in the Netherlands.

Frisch's influence was paramount. A joint article by Frisch and Waugh (1933) demonstrated that the common procedure of computing multiple regressions using residuals from linear trends in all variables gave the same results as if the original values had been used and "time" added as a separate linear independent variable. Waugh became intensely interested in Frisch's use of matrices and published a matrix method for determining multiple regression constants in 1935. Also in 1935, Waugh followed Frisch in attempting statistical estimates of the marginal utility of money.

Waugh's 1938 article on market prorates and social welfare provided the theoretical rationale for the Food Stamp Plan which was tried in several U.S. cities on a pilot basis during 1939–42 and became a nationwide program in the early 1960s. It was still in effect as of 1988.

Waugh was convinced that economic theory should be tested by empirical applications and that innovative statistical methods should be illustrated with nontrivial examples. Waugh (1942) was the first economist to apply Hotelling's method of canonical correlation. In 1950 Waugh presented a practical method for inverting Leontief input-output matrices of order 100 to 200 by means of power series. Waugh (1951) published the first application of linear programming to agricultural data; it was also the first article on linear programming specifically directed to agricultural economists. In 1956 he estimated a "partial indifference surface" for beef and pork using U.S. aggregate data.

Despite his proficiency in mathematics and statistics, Waugh was a vigorous proponent of graphic methods in the exploratory stage of research. He wrote three popular USDA handbooks on graphic analysis in 1955, 1957, and 1966.

Waugh received three awards from the American Farm Economic Association (now the American Agricultural Economics Association) for best article of the year in the Association's journal, a record equaled during his lifetime only by T. W. Schultz and Harold Breimyer. Waugh's USDA Technical Bulletin No. 1316, *Demand and Price Analysis*: *Some Examples from Agriculture* (1964b), brought him the Association's award for "Publication of Enduring Quality" in 1974, the first year this award was given. Appropriately, the inside front cover carried a quotation from H. L. Moore (1917, p. 11): "The seal of the true science is the confirmation of its forecasts; its value is measured by the control it enables us to exercise over ourselves and our environment."

Concluding Remarks

Stigler (1962, p. 1) wrote that "if one seeks distinctive traits of modern economics . . . he will find only one: the development of statistical estimation of economic relationships." He named Henry L. Moore as the founder of this development.

Two of Moore's books, published in 1914 and 1917, presented statistical demand functions for corn, oats, hay, potatoes, and cotton. Ezekiel and Waugh were still in their teens when these books were published, but in and after 1922 they and other young agricultural economists took up Moore's methods and objectives with great enthusiasm. They established a tradition of applied econometrics which antedated the first theoretical articles on the simultaneous equations approach by two decades and the first serious empirical applications of it by almost three.

We have illustrated the continuity of the agricultural econometrics tradition during 1922–64 with comments on the careers of Ezekiel and Waugh and on contacts between BAE and Cowles Commission economists during 1943–55. A great deal more should be known, and written, about the history of agricultural econometrics as a major segment of the field as a whole.

Iowa State University, USA

SECTION 2

Structural Econometrics

Oxford Economic Papers 41 (1989), 73–93

FORMALIZATION OF IDENTIFICATION THEORY

By DUO QIN*

Introduction

IN present-day econometrics textbooks, identification theory is commonly taught in relation to the conditions under which a certain structure (often represented by a set of values of parameters) can be identified among all the permissible structures embodied in a mathematically complete theoretical model. Since the model usually takes a linear form, such conditions are frequently referred to as the order and rank conditions. However, identification theory actually has a much wider scope, as may be appreciated through the history of its formalization. Identification problems appeared in the economic literature as early as the second decade of this century. They were dealt with and solved under particular conditions and in particular forms of model forms with *ad hoc* methods around the '20s (See e.g., (Fox, this volume)). A general theory took shape in the 1930s, but much of the systematic work was completed in the 1940s with some extensions into the '50s and onwards. This paper will concentrate on the formative period of the theory.[1] We observe that the formalization undergoes a process from concreteness to abstraction and then again towards concreteness, i.e. the theory starts from very concrete applied work, is generalized in line with the formalization of modern econometric theory and further develops to meet the requirements of econometric practice. From the standpoint of the development of mathematical methods employed in identification theory, the process can also be viewed as one from content to form and then towards content. As is often the case, a theory is formally established once it has passed the abstract stage and moved towards concreteness.

1. Taking shape

Identification theory evolved originally from discussion about correspondence problems, i.e. "the correspondence between economic activity, the data that activity generates, the theoretical economic model and the estimated relationship" (p. 182, Morgan, 1984). Discussion of identification soon became focused on the possibility of uniquely determining an *a priori*

---

* The first draft was prepared in April of 1987. I wish to thank David Hendry and Christopher Gilbert for their indefatigable guidance and encouragement. My thanks should also go to Mary Morgan, Neil de Marchi, John Aldrich, Neil R. Ericsson, Karl Fox, Wu Wei and Bill Farebrother for their invaluable help, comments and suggestions.

[1] There is a chapter on the early development of identification problems in M. Morgan's Ph.D. thesis (1984). This paper can be viewed as its sequel. It bears frequent references to Morgan's work in respect to those very early facts. Only a very succinct picture of the early period is provided here as the necessary background.

theoretical model from a statistical estimation.[2] Nevertheless, identification problems in the early days were in a muddled state. They were intermingled with other modelling problems and dealt with by methods which were *ad hoc* and not specialised. Terminologies varied in different econometricians' discussions and this made their works harder to understand. To avoid possible confusion, the commonly accepted terms are used here to restate what was the essence of the identification problem in those days.

Identification problems first came to notice in the second decade of the century, when some early pioneers in applying statistics to economics examined estimated demand curves.[3] It was noticed that sometimes mistakes occurred and estimation intended to yield demand curves of certain goods turned out to result in the supply curves instead. The phenomenon became more conspicuous if estimation was carried out in a model of interdependent supply and demand equations using a single set of quantity and price data. The simplest case would be:

$$D = \alpha_0 + \alpha_1 P + u$$
$$S = \beta_0 + \beta_1 P + v$$

under the assumption of constant elasticities. As denoted commonly, D (demand), S (supply) and P were the (usual) log forms of the actual quantities and price. At the time, it was realized generally that this phenomenon resulted from discrepancies between theory and practice—a problem of identifying "statistically determined demand curves" "with theoretical demand curves" (Working, H., 1925). Many saw it as an estimation problem arising from inaccurate data, because it seemed from the above equations that only one set of parameters (either α_0 and α_1 or β_0 and β_1) could be estimated if the data showed a much greater shift or "variability" in the other (i.e. $\text{Var}(u) \gg \text{Var}(v)$ or vice versa). So discussions centred on classifying and handling the data, as in the works of the Working brothers and Wright. Wright suggested clearly that additional information should be used when the data were not sufficient.[4] However, there was also an opinion that the trouble arose from model misspecification rather than estimation. The demand and supply curves could be determined if the model was specified, say, as:[5]

$$D_t = \alpha_0 + \alpha_1 P_t + u_t$$
$$S_t = \beta_0 + \beta_1 P_{t-1} + v_t$$
$$S_t = S_t$$

---

[2] The aspect of locating true theoretical relations (with respect to reality) in the correspondence problem was reduced to the issue of model specification later. Identification discussion in economic time series analysis, which emerged much later, has tried to recover that aspect (see (Box and Jenkins, 1970)). However, that development falls outside the period of examination here.

[3] For example, the works of Lehfeldt, Lenoir and Moore as described in Morgan (1984; Chapter 6).

[4] For detailed descriptions, see Morgan (1984; Chapter 6).

[5] As in the works of Ezekiel and Moore, see (Morgan, 1984; Ch. 6). The model later became known as the "cobweb" model.

Identification theory began to take shape in the thirties, as econometricians tried to develop suitable methods and useful rules or patterns for modelling, especially for model estimation. The first major contributor was Tinbergen. In a study of supply curves (Tinbergen, 1930), Tinbergen introduced the reduced-form method into the two-equation demand-and-supply model to separate (perhaps subconsciously) estimation of statistical relations from that of theoretical relations.[6] By doing this, Tinbergen was able to illustrate how additional information was required on the demand and supply functions respectively, if estimation (identification) of the original (structural) relations was to be achieved. He adopted the approach of adding new variables separately to the two equations so as to enable the unique evaluation of all the parameters.

Frisch also played an important role in the formalization of identification theory and of the whole system of modern econometrics during those early days. He was among the first to become aware that the identification problem stemmed from the desire to "approach a statistical material with the object of determining numerically the constants of certain theoretical laws that we have worked out a priori" (Frisch, 1933a, p. 8). Frisch endeavoured to set up a new system of analysis, and in doing so he tackled the identification problem in a more systematic way than ever before. But unfortunately, in his effort to eliminate "spurious correlations" in meaningless regressions to get at the true theoretical relations, Frisch included identification problems in the category of "multicollinearity" (Frisch, 1934). His approach to identification of demand and supply elasticities was to make assumptions (as a kind of precondition) about the values of the variances and covariances (the shifts) of the error terms (Frisch, 1933a). In essence, this approach formalised the *ad hoc* methods of case studies about different shifts developed by E. J. Working *et al.*

In his influential "Statistical Confluence Analysis by Means of Complete Regression Systems" (1934), Frisch extended the discussion from the demand-and-supply context to the general two-variable model form and based the estimation of a "true" regression equation on the method outlined above—on additional information or assumed knowledge about the disturbances. This led to a series of discussions of identification conditions in a single equation with errors in variables. The simplest form with two variables was:

$$Y_t = \alpha X_t + \beta$$
$$X_t = x_t - \varepsilon_t \quad t = 1, \ldots, T$$
$$Y_t = y_t - \partial_t$$

where X, Y were true values of two random variables, x, y their observed values and ε, ∂ their errors; α and β were parameters to be estimated. Koopmans both criticized and then extended Frisch's approach to a more

---

[6] Tinbergen's mathematical deduction is fully represented in (Morgan, 1984; Ch. 6).

general form based on probability theory (Koopmans, 1937). He assumed in his model (quite reluctantly because he recognised its unreality) that the ratios of the variances and covariances of the disturbances were "a priori given" (p. 61), so as to ensure that the parameters could be estimable. It is also interesing to observe that Koopmans put the above discussion in a section on "specification". Allen reiterated that the condition for consistent estimation of a two-variable linear regression equation was to take the values of two of the three parameters—standard derivations of the two variables' errors and their correlation coefficient—as given a priori (Allen, 1939).

From the late 1930s, discussion of identification ceased to be confined to the particular demand-supply context and began to appear in non-empirical studies on general modelling problems. It was already a recognised "common feature" that "the fitted straight line (of variables subject to errors)* cannot be determined without a priori assumptions (independent of the observations) regarding the weights of the errors" (Wald, 1940; p. 285). Efforts were made to replace unrealistic assumptions with more realistic ones. Wald made use of the geometric method of a generalized two-point form, by dividing the sample of observations into two groups, to guarantee the existence of consistent estimates of the parameters, in a rather limited framework of a two-variable model under the assumptions of no correlation in the error series and between errors, etc. (Wald, 1940). In a rather technical paper, Reisersøl used the method of confluence analysis to develop under certain assumptions, a number of less arbitrary theorems relating the determinability of structural coefficients to the rank condition of the matrix of second moments of the disturbances (Reiersøl, 1941).

Another major step forward was taken again by Frisch, somewhat earlier, in a memorandum concerning Tinbergen's business cycle model for the League of Nations (Frisch, 1938). Although the term "identification" was never mentioned and the problem was not completely isolated, the ideas conveyed by Frisch contained many of the basic principles of identification theory and pointed to its formal emegence.[7] These ideas can be summed up as follows: First, Frisch advocated thorough inquiry into the "delicate" connection between "the relations we work with in theory and those we get by fitting curves to actual statistical data" (p. 2). He set forth a number of definitions to facilitate the inquiry. The most prominent of them was "structure": a quantifiable set of "all the characteristics" described by means of functional equations to explain the phenomena of a system. Next, Frisch examined the mathematical property of coefficient determinability in the general linear equations model with lags. He designated "irreducibility" as the case in which coefficients could be uniquely determined and

---

* Words in brackets are added by the present author.

[7] Koopmans, Rubin and Leipnik acknowledged that "the first systematic discussion of the problem of identification was given by Frisch" in his 1938's paper (Koopmans, Rubin & Leipnik, 1950, p. 69).

"reducibility" as the converse. He chose the exponential function to specify the x's (variables) of the lag-equations and worked out a general criterion for reducibility in terms of the rank condition of a matrix whose elements were deduced from the exponential function. Then he classified all equations into "coflux" equations and "superflux" equations according to the irreducibility or reducibility of their coefficients with respect to the set of x's involved. Finally, Frisch put forward a very important notion about the nature of passive observations, i.e. "the investigator is restricted to observing what happens *when all equations in a large determinate system are actually fulfilled simultaneously*". He recognised clearly that such passive observation prevented the investigator from discovering these equations "unless they happen to be coflux equations" (p. 15).

It is remarkable that, on the one hand, Frisch had brought together the chief points about identification: the general setting of statistical versus theoretical relations, the mathematical nature of the coefficient determinability (reducible or irreducible) and the basic rank method, as well as the cause of the problem—passive observations; but, on the other hand, he was still quite vague in certain respects about the whole concept. The problem seems to result from the lack of consistency between his non-mathematical analysis and his mathematical treatment. While he emphasized the difference between statistical relations and theoretical relations, he failed to make a corresponding distinction between them when he discussed the mathematical property of reducibility/irreducibility of the set of equations (structural and statistical alike). In other words, Frisch was able to view econometric modelling from a multi-dimensional perspective (i.e. he regarded theory, economic models and estimated relations as being at different layers of abstraction). He was correct in observing that statistically discovered equations should be coflux equations (implying that reduced forms are always identifiable) and that coflux equations were not always the desired structural equations, but he lost this perspective when he came to mathematical discussion of these issues.

A formal identification theory for a system of general equations was on the verge of being realised at the beginning of the 1940's. This was best shown in an article "Economic Interdependence and Statistical Analysis" by Marschak (written in March, 1940) in memory of Henry Schultz (Marschak, 1942). Marschak encountered the identification problem in his acceptance of the relative importance of interdependent economic relations, or in his words, "the single empirical equations are less useful or necessary for the empirical analysis of the system" (p. 136). He observed "that complete clarity on the subject is certainly still far from universal and that a systematic and elementary treatment may be some use if only to point out where the unsolved questions seem to lie" (p. 140). Drawing upon the analyses of both the a priori information approach and the reducibility approach due to previous econometricians, Marschak asked two questions concerning the identification of a system of m equations with unrestricted functional forms: 1) Which equations in a system of equations "had the relatively stable parameters" (or were "identifiable")? 2) What were the conditions making possible the "evaluation" of the parameters in those identifiable equations? He discussed these questions under two separate headings: "Variate Parameters" and "Lost Dimensions" to distinguish additional restrictions from the model feature. He maintained that the answer to the first question depended on additional sources of information that were neither embodied in the statistics nor derivable from them; and that the answer to the second question was based on "the nature of the theoretical system itself" (pp. 140–141), because "whatever the number of observations as compared with the number of parameters", it was possible that "some of the sets of the observation equations become dependent and therefore indeterminate" (p. 144). He employed the condition of a vanishing Jacobian determinant (each element of which was a partial derivative of one of the equations with respect to one of its parameters) to examine this indeterminacy.

Evidently, Marschak came quite close to the heart of the identification problem despite his obscure view of the whole concept. He narrowed down the range of inquiry set by Frisch and outlined the subject more explicitly. But, unable to escape from the existing modelling procedure (specification and then estimation) he simply further divided identification problems into two separate issues: one, which he took as identification and was assigned to model specification, was essentially about the order criterion of identification; the other, assigned to estimation, was the rank criterion. In his view, while information additional to the statistics was needed irrespective of the number of observations, it was insufficient only to possess such information for parameter identification, without imposing certain conditions on the system itself. Nevertheless, he had stated by far the clearest view about the cause of the problem—the limits in the economic statistics available. His analysis continued in embryo the idea of formalizing two separate (necessary and sufficient) identification conditions (in terms of orders and rank), as in the now standard identification theory, which was about to emerge.

II. Systematization

The early forties saw the formalization of basic, modern econometric theory. As the simultaneous-equations system with random components became the most widely adopted model, various methods were devised to solve the problems involving the system which went beyond the power of traditional statistical methods. The systematisation of identification theory was part of that movement.

One of the earliest attempts to generalize identification conditions using explicit mathematical terms was made by Haavelmo in his epoch-marking paper "The Probability Approach in Econometrics" (mimeographed in

1941) (Haavelmo, 1944). In Chapter V "Problems of Estimation", Haavelmo described the identification problem as the "problem of confluent relations (or the problem of arbitrary parameters)", which formed one of "the two fundamental problems of estimation in economic research" (the other one was the problem of best estimates) (p. 91).[8] In his view, identification was "a problem of pure mathematics", and "of particular significance in the field of econometrics, and relevant to the very construction of economic models" (p. 92). He undertook "a very general discussion of one central problem in identification: the formulation of conditions under which all structural relations of the system can be identified" (Koopmans, Rubin and Leipnik, 1950; p. 70). Haavelmo's discussion proceeded from a very general (i.e. no particular functional form) real functions of s real indepenent (i.e. not functionally related) variables involving k parameters:

$$y = f(x_1, x_2,..., x_s; \theta_1, \theta_2,..., \theta_k)$$

He then put the problem as one of seeking the least number $(k - v(v \geqslant 0))$ of parameters, the values of which could be uniquely determined. Under certain assumptions to ensure local solvability, Haavelmo used the theorem of existence of inverse functions to determine this number, which was transformed into the condition that a corresponding Jacobian determinant should be non-vanishing in order to obtain a non-singular mapping from the parametric space onto the state space. Determination of this condition was then related to that of the number of linearly independent functions by an extension of the Gramian criterion, which was thought to be a common and feasible method in practice. By doing this, Haavelmo established a general theoretical framework for identification in terms of rigorous mathematical theorems. His results fostered the eventual systematization of identification theory as an issue separate from estimation and specification by Koopmans *et al.*, who regarded their own work "as a specialization of Haavelmo's results" (Koopmans, Rubin and Leipnik 1950; p. 70).

Haavelmo concluded his discussion with an illustration of his theorems by a simple supply-demand model, which, unfortunately, was misleading. He first transformed his structural model into a reduced form (without calling it such) and then set up indirect estimation equations for the structural parameters and the joint probability density function of the endogenous variables' all in terms of the reduced-form parameters. Without checking, he inferred that there existed a one-to-one correspondence between the old parameters (those of the structural model) and the new ones (those of the reduced form), and hence the former would be identifiable if the latter were shown to possess unique values. So he applied his method to the

---

[8] A preliminary mathematical deduction of the problem was made by Haavelmo in a paper called "The Problem of Testing Economic Theories by Means of Passive Observations", which was delivered at the 1940's Cowles Commission conference (Cowles Commission, 1940).

reduced-form parameters and verified that in general all of them were determinable. Actually, Haavelmo could have applied his theorems directly to the structural parameters, the actual object of identification, instead of the reduced-form parameters, which are always identifiable.[9] Haavelmo's slip shows that the nature of identification—investigation of different types of correspondence between economic theory embodied in the latent structures and the statistical relations embodied in the reduced forms—was not yet totally within his grasp. It is only because his original model happened to have been specified in a uniquely identifiable way that he obtained the right result.

Of equal, if not greater, importance, is Haavelmo's non-mathematical discussion in the first two chapters about the relationship of theoretical models and economic reality, and the degree of permanence of economic laws. The analysis implied some very basic ideas about the origins of the identification problem and the need to build a formal identification theory. His descriptions of the differences between true variables, theoretical variables and observational variables, or between facts, theoretical models and observed relations, and of the passive position of economists with respect to economic phenomena and to the generating processes of economic data indicated the main reasons for the emergence of identification theory. Haavelmo maintained that in order to test whether observed variables correspond to theoretical variables, a theory (embodied in a model) was needed, with which "a corresponding system of quantities or objects in real economic life" must be identified through observed relations, to define "one particular theoretical structure of the economy" (Haavelmo, 1944; p. 8). But he realized that economists did not have the power to control and manipulate economic performance so as to get the desired or even sufficient observational results to enable this. He observed furthermore that a structure was not always invariant due to different degrees of permanence in the underlying economic relations, and that it was therefore necessary to know and understand the structure in order to explain the causes of movements and in order to predict the future. All this anticipated the emergence of a formal identification theory independent of theories of model specification and estimation.

It is worth noting that many ideas developed here by Haavelmo are rooted in Frisch's works, especially in "Statistical versus Theoretical Relations in Economic Macrodynamics" (Frisch, 1938). Haavelmo's systematic exposition of the theoretical base for econometric modelling is an extension of Frisch's memorandum. More specifically, Haavelmo retained some of Frisch's ideas and methods in solving the identification problem, such as attributing the problem to the rule about the reducibility of the

---

[9] Haavelmo knew of the relationship between parameters of the structural equations and their reduced forms, and referred to Mann and Wald's paper on this issue (See the footnote on p. 91 (Haavelmo, 1944)).

parameters; and also improved upon his methods, e.g. in generalising the functional equations and by moving from assuming specific functional forms to discussion in terms of inverse functions. But like Frisch, Haavelmo failed completely to clarify identification problems (e.g. he used "confluent relations" to denote the phenomena). Furthermore, his mathematical formalizations did not always correspond to with the economics (e.g. he treated structural equations and their reduced forms indiscriminately).

In another important paper "On the Statistical Treatment of Linear Stochastic Difference Equations", Mann and Wald provided a clearer view of the relation between structural forms and reduced forms with respect to identification (they still considered the problem under the category of estimation) in a general system of linear simultaneous equations. They noticed that reduced-form parameters could be evaluated uniquely, while problems arose in determining parameters of the "original" (structural) equations. They found it "impossible to have consistent estimates for all the unknown parameters" when two (structural) systems were not distinguishable in form from each other on the basis of empirical observations. In such cases, they suggested that reduced forms should be used because the reduced form parameters were always estimable from the observations (Mann and Wald, 1943; pp. 201–202). To demonstrate the advantages of the reduced-form method, they gave examples using two models discussed a little earlier by Haavelmo (1943).[10] The first model, they showed, was unidentifiable unless additional knowledge was available or assumed, such that the variances of the errors were identical, because there were four unknown structural parameters with only three reduced-form parameters estimable. On the other hand, in the second model, they deduced that seven reduced-form parameters could be estimated against only five structural parameters. Additional restrictions were needed in this case to prevent excess information being arbitrarily discarded in the process of moving from the reduced form to the original (structural) system (pp 215–216). *Remarkably*, These examples provide a remarkably clear view of the differences between what is known now as under, exact and over identification.

---

[10] Haavelmo' first model was a general stochastical system:

$$Y = \alpha X + \varepsilon_1$$
$$X = \beta Y + \varepsilon_2$$

His second model was an investment and consumption system:

$$u_t = \alpha r_t + \beta + \varepsilon_{1t}$$
$$v_t = k(u_t - u_{t-1}) + \varepsilon_{2t}$$
$$r_t = u_t + v_t$$

(u: consumption, v: investment and r: total income). Haavelmo used the models only to demonstrate the inconsistency of the least-squares estimates in contrast to the consistent maximum-likelihood estimates. He neglected the identification aspect of the models.

The first successful attempt to systematize identification theory as an integral part of econometrics was carried out by the Cowles Commission for Research in Economics and reported in the Commission Monograph 10 (ed. Koopmans, 1950).[11] The major work was completed around 1945 by Koopmans, Rubin, Hurwicz and Wald. The initiation of such a systematic study as a separate issue was attributed to Koopmans, who, together with Rubin and Leipnik, set up criteria using *a priori* information to "determine the identifiability of equations in linear sytems." "Hurwicz and Wald further clarified the identification problem in logical and mathematical terms" (Cowles Commission, 1952; pp 36–37).

Koopmans *et al.* made the first explicit statement of the nature of the identification problem. They argued that if a linear system of difference equations "is viewed only as a mathematical specification of the joint probability distribution of the observable variables, it can be written in many different ways" which would be mathematically equivalent, and which they called different "representations". If representations had the same probability distributions for all variables, they were "observationally equivalent" and could not be distinguished even employing "the best that can be expected from statistical methods". "The distribution of the variables can be looked upon as determining the set of all observationally equivalent representations of it, and is completely defined by any of these representations. From a mathematical point of view, it is immaterial which representation is employed, except that it will be desirable to choose a simple one. In terms of economics, however, different representations of the same system are not at all equivalent". From the economic point of view, it was "important" to have the equation system "in a form in which the greatest possible number of its equations can be identified and recognized as structural equations", because any one of them, according to theory, could be changed independently [Koopmans, Rubin & Leipnik, 1950; pp 62–63]. They argued further that since identification theory dealt with the unique determination of structural equations or the "unambiguous definition" of the parameters of these equations to be estimated, identification in fact was "a logical problem that precedes estimation. It is therefore not a problem in statistical inference, but a prior problem arising in the specification and interpretation of the probability distribution of the variables. As such it deserves separate classification" (p. 70).

Koopmans *et al.* translated the above ideas into formal mathematical terms and discussed the imposition of various restrictions, according to *a priori* knowledge and information, on the system in order to achieve

[11] Carl F. Christ has provided a detailed historical account about the research activities of Cowles Commission during that period [Cowles Commission, 1952; see pp. 36–37 about the identification problem]. He also emphasizes the importance of Monograph 10: "the volume sets a new standard in adapting statistical methods to econometric analysis" (p. 38). C. Hildreth (1986) gives an account of the technical developments in the Commission.

identification. The discussion was limited by the general assumption of linear independence between endogenous variables and between predetermined variables and error terms (only in the context of the errors-in-equations model). They first established a number of theorems on the necessary and sufficient conditions for identifiability of one structural equation in the system under linear restrictions (i.e. zero restrictions on single parameters and restrictions of linear dependence on two or more parameters in the same equations). The necessary and sufficient condition for a single equation was formulated in terms of the rank condition of a submatrix of parameters (obtained by deleting from the parametric matrix of the system the row of the one equation to be identified) which corresponded to the absent variables in that one equation. A derived necessary condition was connected to the number of independent restrictions imposed on parameters of that equation. These conditions are now standard in econometric textbooks as the rank and order conditions for identification. Next, they examined the situation in which not all equations of the system could be identified. They used linear dummy restrictions to supplement the insufficient number of independent a priori restrictions to produce identifiability, provided that these dummy restrictions did not eliminate the observed variables from the original probability distribution. They then extended their anayses to other types of restrictions, such as bilinear restrictions and linear dependence restrictions on the distributions of disturbances. However, they could not derive any general condition for these circumstances. Finally, they set out a number of problems requiring further discussion.

Koopmans *et al.* also classified three types of identification as "unique," "multiple" and "incomplete" identification in terms of a transformation matrix (which represented relations among observably equivalent structures), with respect to part of a model. When the matrix was a unit matrix, the identification was defined as unique in that there were no other structures equivalent to the one identified. The label of multiple identification was applied to cases where there were a finite number of different transformation matrices (to represent a finite number of observational equations). When the number became infinite, identification was said to be incomplete. Both unique and multiple identification were called complete identification. This classification corresponds to exact, over- and under-identification respectively in the present terminology.

Although their paper relied mainly on linear algebra, it is not very easy to read since it used many complicated symbols, often using several subscripts and superscripts. Wald made an effort to generalize Koopmans, Rubin and Leipnik's results. In his very succinct note, Wald went straight to the mathematical nature of the identification problem bypassing all its econometric content. He turned the problem directly into one of the existence of an inverse function, as Haavelmo had done, and attained a general solution for the identifiability of every parameter by making an ingenious use of a statistical property concerning the change of values of the moments in linear transformations. In other words when an admissable transformation (i.e. a transformation that left the *a priori* restrictions intact) was performed on the coefficient matrix of the structural parameters A by a nonsingular matrix γ, or when the vector of all variables was multiplied by γ, the corresponding transformation on the covariance matrix Σ (the matrix of the second moments) should be in the form of $\gamma\Sigma\gamma'$. He deduced further, in the form of two lemmas, that such transformations had the property of keeping a set of composite coefficients ξ_{ij} of A and Σ invariant during the process [Wald, 1950; pp. 240–241].[12] Meanwhile, he rearranged the elements of A and Σ in one vector θ, denoting its transformation form by $\theta(\gamma)$. He summed up the identification problem in a very general form $F\{\theta(\gamma)\} = F(\theta)$ ($F(\theta)$ was a function of θ) (p. 242), and then gave the vital proof that $F(\theta)$ was a function of $\xi_{ij}(\theta)$ (or a composite function of θ: $F(\theta) = F\{\xi(\theta)\}$) and all the functions $\xi_{ij}(\theta)$ formed a fundamental set of $F(\theta) = F\{\theta(\gamma)\}$. Reducing the number of unknown parameters by a priori restrictions and assuming that the restrictions admit continuous first-order partial derivatives on the parameters, Wald established an identification condition in terms of the rank condition of the Jacobian matrix concerned, in a similar approach to that of Marschak and Haavelmo.[13]

Unlike Koopmans and Wald, Hurwicz concentrated his attention on the concept of identification and expressed it in formal mathematical language, to help in "clarifying the logic of the identification problems" (Hurwicz, 1950; p. 246). His clarification covered three aspects: the general concept of identification in relation to models, the classification of different degrees of identification, and the function of *a priori* conditions. Hurwicz maintained that identifiability was an intrinsic attribute of a model "entirely independent of any sampling aspects of structural estimation" (p. 257). He used the term "identification power" to denote the attribute (p. 245). He defined a

---

[12] Roughly, Wald's lemmas can be expressed in the following matrix operations:

$$(\gamma Ax)'(\gamma\Sigma\gamma')(\gamma Ax) = x'A'\gamma'\gamma'^{-1}\Sigma^{-1}\gamma^{-1}\gamma Ax = x'A'\Sigma^{-1}Ax$$

x is a column vector of variables. Let a matrix of composite coefficients ξs be $\Xi = A'\Sigma^{-1}A$, and

$$\Xi(\gamma) = A'\gamma'\gamma'^{-1}\Sigma^{-1}\gamma^{-1}\gamma A,$$

then

$$x'\Xi x = x'\Xi(\gamma)x, \quad \text{i.e.} \quad \Xi = \Xi(\gamma).$$

[13] Wald wrote the *a priori* restrictions, say R restrictions, as:

$$\varphi_r(\theta) = 0 \quad (r = 1,\ldots, R)$$

and changed it into:

$$\theta_p = \psi_p(\theta_1,\ldots, \theta_{p-r}) \quad (p = P - R + 1,\ldots, P)$$

P denoted the number of total parameters. He assumed that ψ_p admit continuous first-order partial derivatives so as to ensure the existence of Jacobian of the functions $\bar{\xi}(\theta)$ (reduced from $\xi(\theta)$ by taking ψ_p into account).

model $\mathfrak{G}_0$ as "an *a priori* postulated class of structures S that is a proper subset of the class $\mathfrak{G}$ of all structures", generating the cumulative probability distribution G of the observed variables. Structures, which were not directly observable, were represented by "the distribution F of the (nonobservable) disturbance" and "an operation (usually a transformation) $\mathfrak{T}$", from the nonobservable distribution G into the observable one $F: S = (F, \mathfrak{T})$ (pp. 247–248). However, since in general, G might be generated by more than one structure, structural estimation through G to obtain S depended on the identification power of the particular model formulated.

This approach to explain identification in terms of the identification power of a model has two immediate implications. It is essential to build an identifying model for the purpose of prediction when the structure is subject to change; and it is important to distinguish identification from estimation: the former is concerned with the possibility of getting a unique S from a G and the latter deals with the problem of how to get the best value of G from a given sample.

Similarly to Koopmans, Hurwicz classified the identification power of a model into the three categories of "unique", "multiple" and "incomplete". But instead of distinguishing them from the transformation matrix, he directly used the number of structures for the definition, which was closer to the heart of the problem. He described as "uniquely identifying" models that possessed "the property that for any element G_1" in the class of all G's generated by the elements of the model, "there exists *one and only one* S_1" in the model "such that S_1 generates G_1" (p. 249). If there existed more than one such structures S_1 generating the same G_1 in the model, but the number was "finite or denumerably infinite", the model was multiply identifying (p. 249). When the number of such structures became "nondenumerable infinity" (256), the model was incompletely identifying. As before, uniquely and multiply identifying models were grouped as models with "complete identification power" (p. 248).

A priori conditions comprising "identifying restrictions" and criteria were regarded as provisional means to help originally incompletely identifying models to achieve identification. Identifying restrictions were "additional assumptions" "with regard to S" for the purpose of narrowing down the model $\mathfrak{G}_0$ to "a proper subset" of it (p. 248). Criteria established *a priori* facilitated the originally observably indistinguishable structures in a model to become distinguishable, by partitioning the class of "all structures into a system of nonoverlapping subclasses" (p. 253).

In sum, these three classical papers in Monograph 10 solved the identification problem both in form and in content: the problem was separated out from model specification and estimation, basic criteria were worked out in the form of order and rank conditions for econometric practice within the framework of linear stochastic equation systems, a mathematical presentation of the problem and a general method for solving it were set out, and the whole concept was put into formal, logical terms. It can therefore be said that identification theory by then had been formally established as part of econometric theory.

III. Further developments

Identification theory underwent further expansion both in breadth and in depth around 1950, on the basis of the groundwork laid down by Monograph 10. The development helped to solidify the integral position of the identification theory in econometrics and in the process generalized further the theory itself.

One direction of expansion is the explicit formulation of identification theory in the context of errors-in-variables models. Research on this issue was led in the late 1940's by Reiersøl, who developed the necessary and sufficient conditions for identification of a linear equation with two variables subject to errors [Reiersøl, 1950 (written in 1948)]. Reiersøl's model ran like this:

$$y_2 = \beta y_1 + \beta_0$$
$$x_1 = y_1 + v_1 \qquad v_1 \sim N^2(0, \sigma_1)$$
$$x_2 = y_2 + v_2 \qquad v_2 \sim N^2(0, \sigma_2)$$

x_i were observed values of the true variables y_i. A structure was represented by a set of values β, β_0, σ_1 and σ_2 were the standard variances of v_1 and v_2 respectively, $\sigma_{12} = \mathrm{cov}(v_1, v_2)$, and the logarithm of the characteristic function of y_1: $\Psi_y(t)$. Reiersøl deduced the distribution functions of the variables and their moments by means of characteristic functions, and determined the identification conditions in four theorems under the assumptions of joint normal distribution of the errors and of independent error distributions respectively. The conditions were found to be closely connected with the distribution form (normal or otherwise) of y_1 and y_2 and hence x_1 and x_2, and the conditions of v_1, v_2.

There has been little subsequent research on identification in the errors-in-variables model and this is associated with the eclipse of this model form in mainstream econometrics (the reason of the eclipse goes beyond the present topic). However, the analysis of identification problems in this model form seems to have called the econometricians' attention to the identifiability of the parameters of the disturbances' distribution (i.e. their moments) and hence to the influence of the stochastic elements embodied in probability models on the commonly-accepted order and rank conditions for identification.

A more important development came in Koopmans and Reiersøl's rather compact paper "The Identification of Structural Characteristics" (1950), in which the identification concept and theory were further generalized. Koopmans and Reiersøl emphasized the identification concept in connection with statistical inference, a fact that had been obscured to a certain degree by the stress on the distinction of identification from estimation and by the rank and order conditions concerning only the coefficients of variables, in the framework of simultaneous-equation systems (in fact, Wald was the only one who employed statistical methods in solving the identification problem in Monograph 10, but implicitly). They redefined identification as "the problem of drawing inferences from the probability distribution of the observed variables to the very underlying structure". They observed that identification was a "general and fundamental problem arising, in many fields of inquiry, as a concomitant of the scientific procedure that postulates the existence of a structure" (p. 165). In their formulation of the identification problem, they adopted the basic concepts set out by Hurwicz and further expressed the probability distribution of the observed variables y conditional on the structure S: $H(y \mid S)$ (equivalent to G in Hurwicz's paper). They also reformulated the concept of specification, according to Hurwicz's model concept, as "specifying a model which by hypothesis contains the structure S generating the distribution H of the observed variables" (p. 168). In this context, it became clear where the identification problem had stemmed from. The cause was two-fold: on the one hand, what statistical inference could do at best was to attain, as closely as possible, "an exact knowledge" of the distribution function $H(y \mid S)$ from the available sample—"Anything not implied in this distribution is not a possible object of statistical inference" (p. 169); but on the other hand, while "a given structure S generates one and only one probability distribution $H(y \mid S)$", the inverse was not true, i.e. there might be one-to-many correspondence from H to S, e.g. $H(y \mid S) = H(y \mid S^*)$, $S \neq S^*$ for all y. Furthermore, the criteria for model specification excluded "the desire for identifiability" in general. Thus identification theory came into its own right. In other words, "identification problems are not problems of statistical inference in a strict sense" (the former $H \rightarrow S$ and the latter: a sample of $y \rightarrow H$); but the identification theory was to "explore the limitations of statistical inference" (p. 170).

Having thrashed out the relations between identification and statistical inference, Koopmans and Reiersøl put forward their general themes of the identification theory with major stress on (unique) identifiability subject to statistical tests. In their formulation, identifiability of (or part of) a model was reduced to identifiability of (or some of) its structural characteristics $x(S)$ which encompassed structural parameters and nonparametric functional forms (following Hurwicz). A characteristic structure was defined as identifiable by a model if it maintained the same value in all structures equivalent to that structure. Each characteristic x thus divided all the structures of a model into "two mutually exclusive subsets": one uniquely identifiable and the other not. Correspondingly, all the distribution functions $H(y \mid S)$ were divided in the same way (p. 170). So in principle, identifiability of the characteristics could, in some cases, be achieved through tests of the distribution of the observations, e.g. to test the hypothesis that $H(y \mid S)$ belonged to the subset of identifiable distribution functions against the maintained hypothesis: $H(y) \in$ all S. Particularly, tests could be made of *a priori* restrictions (termed "particular specifications") which further narrowed down the set of distribution functions generated by S. The applicability of statistical tests to "the pre-statistical analysis of identifiability" (p. 170) manifested the close link of identification with statistical inference, in that identification of the characteristics depends not only on the model (necessary condition), but also on the components of the structures (sufficient condition), the evaluation of which depended totally on statistical estimation of observed data.

Another point worth mentioning in Koopmans and Reiersøl's paper was that their discussion extended beyond the econometric context. The knowledge that the same problem had arisen in fields other than econometrics such as factor analysis and biometrics, enabled them to explore the nature of the problem more thoroughly and to generalize the theory further (Koopmans & Reiersøl, 1950, p. 167).

In 1949, another Monograph, "Studies in Econometric Method", was compiled by the Cowles Commission to explain and extend "some of the problems treated more technically in Cowles Commission Monograph 10" (Hood and Koopmans, eds., 1953; preface p. xvi). The identification problem was dealt with in several papers (chapters) of the book, including Koopmans' comprehensive exposition (Chapter 2), Marschak's general introduction (in Chapter 1), Simon's logical extension of the idea with respect to the concept of causation (in Chapter 3) and Koopmans and Hoods' practical description (in Chapter 6). Basically, identification theory had been refined in this book to the extent that its function of moving from observable statistical relations to theoretical models had been formally established. A full and clear explanation was given about the cause and core of the identification discussion.[14] Identification theory was further extended in both applied and theoretical directions on the basis of this insight. From the viewpoint of statistical inference, the identifiability of any parameter was regarded as "a property of the distribution of the observations" (Koopmans, 1953; p. 39), which implied that all the parameters were viewed as parameters of statistical functions obeying certain distributional laws, instead of simply as parameters of the simultaneous-equation system. Accordingly, the identifiability of these parameters was "subject to some suitable statistical test" (p. 39). Such tests discussed in the book included tests of *a priori* restrictions on one structural equation and tests of the identifiability of the equation using the χ^2 distribution (Chapter 6 by Koopmans and Hood, pp. 178–185). An interesting extension in the theoretical aspect discussed in Chapter 3 by H. A. Simon (1953) related identifiability of a structural model to its causal ordering (i.e. asymmetrical relations in the structural equations such as those between exogenous and

---

[14] See Marschak's introduction (Marschak, 1953).

endogenous variables).[15] The discussion further clarified the identifiability concept with respect to its "epistemological" implications: it was the desire to search for the logical cause or the strucural relationship behind the empirical or nonstructutal relationship and to make a distinction between the two, "that lies at the root of the identifiability concept" (p. 66); and, this desire was aroused by the recognition that accurate prediction depended on the status of the latent structures, possible changes in which made identification theory meaningful.[16] Furthermore, the concept of causal ordering helped make theoretical insight of identification concepts tangible in mathematical forms—especially in the order conditions: the *a priori* specification that certain coefficients in any one equation must be zero meant that the corresponding variables did not appear in that equation and hence determined the whole causal ordering of the model. In other words, the fulfilment of exact identification conditions amounted to an unambiguous causal ordering of the variables of the structural model.

Identification conditions were also expanded in this book. Order and rank conditions were formulated with respect to reduced-form equations in support of the application of the indirect least-squares estimation method in empirical studies. Other methods of identification, such as model disaggregation and the introduction of specific explanatory variables, were also examined (Section 6, Chapter 2 by Koopmans).

By this time, the work to set up the basic identification theory in the context of the stochastic simultaneous-equation system had, on the whole, been completed. Incorporating econometric content with mathematical formulation and logical thinking, the theory was ready to serve the later theoretical research and empirical studies in econometrics. In addition, simplified expositions of the theory were becoming available. Tintner's textbook (1952) was especially important in that it is pehaps the earliest text to explain identification theory under a separate heading. Further developments afterwards up to the 1960s were mainly extensions concerning different forms of *a priori* restrictions.[17] Discussion on these developments exceeds the scope of this paper.

IV. Review

Having surveyed the historical process of the formalization of identification theory, I would like to re-examine now, from the viewpoint of the evolution of econometric thought, the issue of identification in the process

---

[15] K. Fox has pointed out to me in a letter that Wright had anticipated much of Simon's work in the 1920's. However, Wright's work did not seem to have received much attention from econometricians of the 1940's and Simon was apparently ignorant of Wright's work when he developed his own results.

[16] Note, similar views on the usefulness of identification theory with respect to econometric prediction were explicitly expressed before by Hurwicz in Monograph 10 [ed. Koopmans, 1950].

[17] Later results in this area have been summarized into a book by F. M. Fisher [1966].

in which the theory was elaborated and in relation to other developments in econometric theory during the same period.

Methodologically, the formalization of identification theory can be said to have gone through a three-stage process: from concreteness to abstraction and then back towards concreteness. Generally at the first concrete stage, miscellaneous phenomena abound displaying a collection of disparate and entangled problems. The journey from concreteness to abstraction begins as the problem become focused and the non-essential features are discarded. The cause and nature of the problem becomes clear in isolation once the abstract stage is reached. Often, a basic theory is formalized at this stage. Practice calls for further development of the basic theory to suit various circumstances. That leads to the shift from abstraction to concreteness, during which detailed methods or more generalized theories entailed by these methods are worked out. It should be emphasized that this latter phase is by no means a simple inverse of the previous one. It requires that the previously discarded relations be reconsidered and connected to the now established theoretical base. The resulting extended theory should provide a "panorama" of the whole problem (its origin, nature and methods thereof) in a clear relationship with other relevant issues within a well-ordered logical space. The new concreteness should encompass the abstraction of the previous stage. Therefore, it usually takes a longer time and greater effort to cover this second phase. The present examination of identification theory actually ends when this last phase had just started.

Identification problems first appeared in demand-curve estimation. At this very concrete stage, the problem was entangled with the problems of specification and estimation and was perceived from a very pragmatic angle by most of the applied workers whose main concern was how to handle the bulk of their data in the light of the almost indubitable economic theory.[18] Accordingly, only *ad hoc* methods were developed. The theoretical disarray began to be cleared up once the distinctions between structural relations and reduced-form relations were worked out in applied work (as by Tinbergen) and between economic laws and statistical regressions in theoretical studies (as by Frisch). These distinctions extended the scope of econometric modeling into one with many layers of abstraction (or with a multi-dimensional perspective) and hence helped to locate the origin of identification problems in a kind of logical space. Meanwhile, econometricians observed more and more clearly that the identification problem was by no means exclusive to demand-supply models. It was a general feature in econometric modelling and had a close link with the form of model specified. This led to an examination of the problem for more general solutions in generalized model forms. The 'taking-shape period' forms just such a stage of going from concreteness to more and more abstraction by

[18] A clear description of how empirical econometricians used to view and approach the identification problem is given in [Klein, 1943].

rejecting, step by step, the nonessential components in the mixture of the problems.

Abstraction has reached its height when the identification problem is explicitly separated from the problems of specification and estimation. The issue then looks so distinct that it can be easily studied for what it is. Thus, a formal identification theory comes into being. The systematization work concerning identification undertaken by the Cowles Commission in the mid 1940's and reported in Monograph 10 [ed. Koopmans, 1950] forms the main element of this stage.

The third stage is caused by the natural motive to apply and try out the theory just established in econometric practice. It was eventually realized that the identifiability of a model cannot be totally separated from the whole process of econometric modelling. The distinction of identification from specification and estimation, for instance, is only relative, and the factual relations existing in between ask for improvement of the theory which has been simplified by abstraction. A recombination of the related but nonessential contents with the essence of identification constitutes the theoretical task for the phase from abstraction to concreteness. The paper by Koopmans and Reiersøl was a remarkable contribution to this end. Particular efforts are embodied in the development of new statistics for testing the identifiabilities of structual equations in Hood & Koopmans (1953). Another aspect of concretization is in detailing the basic identification conditions corresponding to various *a priori* conditions that may exist in reality. The work carried out towards the end of the period under consideration as well as afterwards contain contributions to this aspect.

Mathematics (including statistics) has played an indispensable part in the formalization of identification theory. To a large extent, it has promoted the process of understanding of the issue, in both the concrete-abstract phase and the abstract-concrete phase. In view of this mathematical application, it may be more helpful to regard the whole process as one from content to form and towards content again, corresponding to the concrete-abstract-concrete description. Econometricians turned to mathematics (mainly using linear algebra) as they were fumbling after the core of the identification problem during the initial phase. Mathematics then helped them at least in two ways to abstract the "skeleton" (form) of the problem out of the particular contents: it helped to pinpoint the crux of identification—the determinability of the structural parameters from statistically estimable parameters (of the reduced forms) and to generalize this determinability by extending the particular model form into more generalized forms used in econometric modelling. The former especially is crucial here. This is shown in the works of Frisch (1938), Marschak (1942) and Haavelmo (1944). They all fell short of success mainly because they could not make a correct mathematical presentation of what they had clearly perceived about the economic significance of distinguishing structural relations from statistical relations, even though their approach to solving the parametric deter- minability by means of rank conditions was correct. In Haavelmo's case especially, his failure to reconcile the available mathematical knowledge about the reduced forms with the econometric theory he developed resulted in a small slip at the final step of his attempt of systematization. The basic abstract theory for identification did not become fully formed until the problem was finally translated correctly into mathematical language (as by Hurwicz (1950)) and solved by rigorous mathematical deduction (as by Wald [1950]). As for the phase from abstraction towards concreteness, any progress would be impossible without resort to mathematical tools. Only by encompassing the linear algebra method within probability and statistical theory, could identification be restored to its proper relation with other issues in the general framework of econometric theory. Identification criteria embedded in mathematical statistics have facilitated the substantia- tion of the theory. In addition, various mathematical methods have assisted the solutions of identification conditions under alternative kinds of *a priori* restrictions, which have also enriched and concretized the whole theory.

It is interesting to note that mathematics and statistics not only serve as forceful tools during the concrete–abstract–concrete (or content–form– content) movements, but also undergo a similar process in their application: traditional statistical methods were used when identification problems first came about; linear algebra served as the main tool in establishing basic identification theory, and eventually modern mathematical statistics (backed by probability theory) came into use again in the extension of a more generalized and more complicated identification theory.

It should be emphasized that the application of mathematical methods could not have been successful without the background development of econometric thinking in general. The growing interest in formalizing econometric modelling procedure in the 1940's provided the essential hotbed for the formation of identification theory, which, with respect to the general development of econometric thinking, shows the following three main features:

First, the formalization of identification theory is synchronous with that of modern econometric theory. Econometrics before Haavelmo lacked a generalized and consistent theoretical foundation. It was designed largely for applied purposes and tended to cure all the econometric problems together in an *ad hoc* way. Meanwhile, the identification problem was only looked at intermingled with other econometric problems and was dealt with on a superficial and pragmatical level. A formal identification theory was coming into being in the 40's, as an integral econometric theory base (founded on probability theory, based on simultaneous-equations systems and employing maximum-likelihood estimation methods) was abstracted, mainly the work of Cowles Commission, from the previous piecemeal analyses oriented heavily to the applied field. The basic identification theory was not brought to (relative) completion until the basic econometric theory had fallen, into configuration, into a working pattern of model specification, identification, estimation, testing and prediction.

Second, the formalization of identification theory has played an important role in undertaking the central task of econometrics—building a "bridge" between "economic theory" and "actual measurement" (Haavelmo, 1944; preface, p. iii). Actually, the formalization itself can serve as an epitome of the bridge construction. From a general point of view, the acceptance of probability theory in econometrics has accomplished a vital job of joining the two ends of the bridge. Similarly, the formalization can also be regarded as having done the same thing on a smaller scale: it has developed methods for determining "the possibility of drawing inferences from observed samples to an underlying theoretical structure" (Rothenberg, 1971; p. 577); and it has rectified the logical procedure of econometric practice by better bridging model specification and estimation.

Third, the formalization marks the beginning of econometrics as an independent subdiscipline of economics. Although the identification problem is not limited to econometrics, its solution developed in a general theoretical form first took place in econometric studies. Before that, econometricians carried out their research work mainly with mathematical and statistical methods directly borrowed from other fields. Studies of the identification problem are the first attempt by econometricians to devise some tools of their own by blending economic thinking with mathematics and statistics, for the purpose of solving economic problems. The resulting identification theory becomes the first major indigenous product of (theoretical) econometrics. Furthermore, identification theory embodies the purpose, object and methods of econometrics of bridging economic theories with actual measurement to advance economic analysis on a more scientific base with the help of mathematics and statistics.

Nuffield College, Oxford

Oxford Economic Papers 41 (1989), 94–107

THE FALL OF OLS IN STRUCTURAL ESTIMATION

By Roy J. EPSTEIN

Introduction

A recurrent debate in the history of econometrics is the extent to which ordinary least squares (OLS) estimation can yield valid information about economic structure. This debate started well before the work of the Cowles Commission in the 1940's on simultaneity bias. For example, in 1912 Marshall was strongly condemning Henry Ludwell Moore, the first American econometrician, as a "nightmare." The problem of interpreting econometric results has not diminished with time. This article discusses early developments in the analysis of identification and single equation estimation which do not seem to be widely known among modern economists, despite the insight they provide into econometric practice.[1]

Economists such as Marshall became more tolerant of econometric work when multiple correlation was explained as a technique that could embody the ceteris paribus clause of pure theory. Nevertheless, the early experience of estimating demand and supply curves showed that econometricians faced unique difficulties. Statistical models in other fields used the logic of cause and effect to specify relationships with one dependent variable and several explanatory factors. It was apparent from the outset, however, that a scatter of simultaneous price and quantity observations could not directly reveal either demand or supply schedules without additional information.

Substantial progress on what was later called the identification problem was achieved by the end of the 1920's. One result of this work was to suggest that OLS might be an inappropriate estimator for simultaneous systems. A form of instrumental variables estimation appeared in the literature as early as 1928 and an example of indirect least squares was given in 1929.

The paper is organized as follows. The first section discusses the work of Sewall Wright in the 1920's as a kind of instrumental variables solution to the "market equilibrium" problem. The second section discusses an early discovery by Tinbergen of identification and estimation using exogenous variables in an indirect least squares setting. The third section discusses the work of Haavelmo and Koopmans in the emergence of structural estima-

I would like to thank Mary Morgan, Chris Gilbert, and the referees for very valuable criticisms and suggestions and for pointing out several significant errors in the original version of this paper. I have also benefitted from conversations with Peter Phillips. Many improvements are due to their collective scrutiny, especially Morgan's. Responsibility for errors that may yet remain is my own.

[1] Epstein (1987, chapter 1), Morgan (1987), and Fox (this volume) provide additional discussion on approaches to identification and estimation that pre-dated the Cowles Commission.

tion. The fourth section presents some little known material on the origins of limited information maximum likelihood (LIML) estimation in the early work of the Cowles Commission. With the work of the Cowles Commission and the later development of instrumental variables methods the theoretical case against OLS seemed overwhelming for any general equilibrium, simultaneous, economic model. The last section offers some observations on recent work on regressions with "integrated" variables and its relevance to the use of OLS with economic time series.

Sewall Wright and instrumental variables

Some of the most interesting econometric work of the entire era before the Cowles Commission was actually carried out by a brilliant geneticist named Sewall Wright. Wright had developed a general method that he called "path analysis" that was intended to impose a causal structure on a matrix of correlation coefficients. He had made an initial foray into economics during World War I, when he estimated the relationship between corn prices and hog production for the U.S. Department of Agriculture. His father, economist Philip Wright, was a prominent authority on the tariff who mistrusted econometrics and did battle on many occasions with Henry Schultz, the leading American econometrician and a protege of Moore (see Epstein (1987)). Sewall Wright saw the estimation of elasticities for the tariff problem as a natural use of path analysis, which he demonstrated in an anonymous appendix B to Philip Wright (1928). Path analysis in this case amounted to a variant of instrumental variables estimation.

Sewall Wright reasoned in this appendix that market equilibrium could only be disturbed by either a demand shock (D) or a supply shock (S). Path analysis normalized each variable by its standard deviation. For economic data Wright removed trends by expressing the data as annual percentage changes. His model could then be written simply as:

$$P = p_1 D \sigma_P / \sigma_D + p_2 S \sigma_P / \sigma_S$$
$$Q = q_1 D \sigma_Q / \sigma_D + q_2 S \sigma_Q / \sigma_S \tag{1}$$

where p_i and q_i were the path coefficients (known later as beta coefficients). In essence, this was an error components model without exogenous variables. To estimate demand elasticity η, he assumed a *zero* demand shock to find $\eta = Q/P = q_2/p_2 \sigma_Q / \sigma_P$. Of course, the path coefficients could not be estimated directly because D and S were assumed to be unobservable.

Wright assumed that it was possible to find an additional factor A that was correlated with S but not with D (e.g. lagged price). Then it followed that his solution could be written as $\eta = (\rho_{AQ}/\rho_{AP}) \sigma_Q / \sigma_P$, which evidently was quite different from an OLS estimate of the demand curve. Supply elasticity could be estimated similarly. The assertion made above that the method was akin to instrumental variables is based on Wright's evident, perhaps intuitive, understanding of orthogonality conditions to impose structure on observed variables and unobserved disturbances. His approach perhaps was motivated by Philip Wright (1915), who made the point that when an equation was part of a simultaneous system, information about the shifts in all equations was relevant when evaluating least squares estimates of its parameters. A notable consequence was the clear implication that OLS simply did not lead to correct, i.e. consistent, estimates of the coefficients of simultaneous equations.

Wright (1934) restated these results in more detail. His discussion clearly brought out how estimation of the system (1) involved 3 equations (for $\Sigma P^2, \Sigma Q^2, \Sigma PQ$) in five unknowns (the path coefficients and ρ_{DS}, the correlation between the two shocks). The instrumental variables in effect raised the number of equations faster than the number of unknowns, which made a unique solution possible in a manner analogous to indirect least squares (see next section). He perceived the phenomenon of overidentification insofar as the existence of multiple "additional factors" implied multiple estimates of the structural parameters in finite samples. Wright attempted to address the issue within the limits established by his overall approach. He experimented with repeatedly solving the system using different instruments and then averaging the results. He stressed that such a procedure, when sufficient instruments were available, would lead to increased efficiency for the structural estimates. In other situations, of course, it was clear that a lack of instruments could make estimation of a particular equation impossible.[2]

Mainstream econometricians in the late 1920's were also developing new analyses of market equilibrium that did not rely on the recursive (lagged price) supply function in use since Moore. Like Wright, they focused on the structure of the shocks. It is worth comparing Wright's work to Frisch (1933a), the first algebraic analysis of the stochastic, simultaneous equilibrium model originally presented by Working (1927). Frisch studied how the behavior of the (logged and demeaned) observables P and Q in the system:

$$Q - \alpha P = u$$
$$Q - \beta P = v \tag{2}$$

depended on the underlying parameterization in terms of α, β, σ_u/σ_v (the "variability ratio") and ρ (the correlation between the two disturbances). He clearly analyzed the identifiability of α and β in this context and his key result also showed directly that OLS applied to each equation would not generally lead to a consistent estimate of either slope. Letting ρ equal zero for simplicity, Frisch demonstrated that:

$$\alpha - \hat{\alpha}_{\text{ols}} = \pm (\sigma_u/\sigma_v)\sqrt{(1 - \rho^2)}$$
$$\beta - \hat{\beta}_{\text{ols}} = \pm (\sigma_v/\sigma_u)\sqrt{(1 - \rho^2)} \tag{3}$$

---

[2] See P. Wright (1928, p. 314) and S. Wright (1934, p. 210).

where the right hand sides in each case depended on information from the entire system. Frisch wrote:

> Even if the shifts are uncorrelated, the absolute value of the slope of the (Q,P) regression does not tell us *anything* about the elasticities α and β. (p. 27, emphasis added)

However, Frisch did not stress this insight into OLS which, incidentally, disproved a conjecture by Working (1927). His major concern was a broader critique of identification that Frisch (1934) called "confluence analysis." Frisch did not seem very interested in the estimation problem at this juncture, perhaps because knowledge of the variability ratio in (3) could not often be expected in practice.

Wright himself soon gave up his econometric sideline. He was acquainted with Henry Schultz, since both were at the University of Chicago, but his efforts to interest Schultz in path analysis met with little response. From the viewpoint of demand analysis, Wright's examples merely confirmed directly the standard assumption that agricultural supply had little sensitivity to current price (although Wright was also able to compute long run supply elasticities that often exceeded 0.5). European researchers were turning to macroeconomic models where such analysis did not seem very applicable. In the early 1930's simultaneity bias appeared to be a minor curiosity of empirical work on market demand.[3]

Jan Tinbergen and indirect least squares

A somewhat different approach to the estimation of simultaneous relations was derived in one of the first publications by Jan Tinbergen. Tinbergen's specification assumed that each demand and supply equation contained an observable and economically relevant variable that acted to shift the curve in price-quantity space. The shift variables were preferable to assuming a known variability ratio in assessing identification but the idea of a stochastic shock was altogether eliminated in his treatment. Statistically, the model seemed in the tradition of exact relationships perturbed only by measurement errors.

Tinbergen (1930) wrote a simultaneous structural model for the Dutch potato flour market as:

$$
\begin{aligned}
Q &= a_0 + a_1 P + a_2 A \quad \text{(supply)} \\
Q &= n_0 + n_1 P + n_2 N \quad \text{(demand)}
\end{aligned}
\tag{4}
$$

where N was foreign flour production and A was an inventory variable. He apparently was the first economist to explicitly derive a reduced form in terms of the structural parameters and the exogenous variables. He recognized, analogously to Wright, that the estimated reduced form

---

[3] See also Epstein (1987, chapter 1) and the informative discussion in Goldberger (1972). My views have been influenced by a personal communication from Wright, who was still at work in 1986 at the age of 96.

coefficients themselves comprised six equations in the six unknown parameters that could be solved to obtain the structural estimates.

Tinbergen called this method the "indirect" approach but he did not attach great importance to it for purposes of estimation. He clearly realized from an analysis of the reduced form that for an equation to be estimated with the method it was necessary for the other equation not to shift *more,* as Working (1927) believed, but to shift *uniquely* via an exogenous variable. With the identification issue resolved in this way, Tinbergen decided that OLS could as well be used on the individual equations once an adequate number of shifts was introduced. His approach appeared to imply asymptotic differences with OLS estimates of the structural parameters but he did not pursue this question. In fact, the differences between OLS and the new procedure were small in his sample and Tinbergen was satisfied to average the two sets of estimates without further discussion

Another reason may be advanced for why "indirect" estimation was not studied further at that time. Advances in economic theory and data collection were beginning to justify models with larger numbers of variables. For example, a minimal addition to (4) would be an income variable in the demand equation. Tinbergen's method for this case could not be solved uniquely for the structural parameters. OLS had the advantage at least of providing unambiguous estimates of the (presumably identified) structural equations. Without a stochastic error term, "indirect" estimation raised no interesting questions. In particular, the possibility of OLS bias (apart from measurement errors) in estimating a system of equations could not even arise.

The rise of the 'Probability Approach'

The two volume macroeconomic project of Tinbergen (1939) epitomized the aspirations of young econometricians in the 1930's to become "social engineers" who would set prices, taxes, public investment, and other variables to maintain full employment and otherwise improve the welfare of society. The sheer scale of his undertaking, and his audacious claims for his approach, were sufficient to generate an enormous debate over the proper *economic* interpretation of newly evolving econometric methodology. An international conference held at Cambridge, England in 1938 was devoted to a critical analysis of his 'structural' paradigm for estimating complete, i.e. closed, models of the business cycle. Tinbergen strove to defend a view of the data as being generated by an economically meaningful system of difference equations, where each equation represented the behaviour of a particular sector of the economy. Moreover, he conceived of 'structural' economic policies to alter the coefficients of the system so as to eliminate unwanted cycles and drive target variables along any desired and feasible path.[4] I wish to focus on the responses to Tinbergen's work by Tjalling

---

[4] For discussion and references on the critical reaction to Tinbergen see Hendry (1980) and Epstein (1987).

Koopmans and Trygve Haavelmo, two other members of the small community of European econometricians.

Unlike almost all other economists in that era, Koopmans had received considerable training in mathematical statistics and R. A. Fisher's (1925) maximum likelihood theory. He was scheduled to succeed Tinbergen at the League of Nations to carry out his own business cycle studies for Great Britain. The outbreak of war ended the League's activities and Koopmans soon found refuge in the United States. He never produced a large empirical model but his methodological essay, Koopmans (1941), indicated little substantive difference with Tinbergen's overall approach. It is plain, however, that Koopmans was more concerned about the power of inference in large models. Tinbergen's 1939 study had estimated dozens of alternative equations with only 14 annual observations. Koopmans sought to further develop the likelihood theory as a coherent framework for more precise inferences in econometrics.

Koopmans was something of a lone wolf among his peers: Tinbergen avoided highly technical theoretical statistics and Frisch (1934) and elsewhere explicitly rejected the use of sampling theory. His thesis, published as Koopmans (1937), had already unified the likelihood (or "shock") method with Frisch's interpretation of the errors in variables model. Koopmans (1942) began to address the extremely complicated question of the exact distribution of finite sample estimators of residual serial correlation and coefficients of lagged dependent variables. Although he was no doubt familiar with Frisch's (1938) memorandum, he still had not formulated a response to its fundamental (though rather obscure) argument that the coefficients in Tinbergen's models did not necessarily sustain any "structural" interpretation. His statistical work seemed intended to yield better estimates of the coefficients of difference equations to predict their dynamic behavior. He did not suspect any problems with the behavior of OLS in simple multi-equation systems like (4) above.

Haavelmo began his study of econometrics under Frisch and was deeply influenced by his teacher's emerging analysis of "autonomy". Frisch's (1938) memorandum summarized his two main points about using time series data for inference about the parameters of a system of equations. First, a non-singular linear transformation of the coefficient matrix of a (non-stochastic) difference equation system yielded a new system but one with the identical solution for the paths of the endogenous variables. This fact, which later would motivate Koopmans's analysis of the order condition for identification, meant that researchers like Tinbergen had not proved that their estimated 'structural' coefficients in fact represented the elasticities, multipliers, and lag patterns of underlying economic behavior. Second, if a given equation was actually just a combination of other, perhaps unsuspected, structural relations it became much less clear how to gauge the effects of proposed structural policies. "Autonomy" referred to the extent to which an equation's coefficients depended on coefficients elsewhere in the system. The less autonomy there was, the less an equation could sustain a structural interpretation.[5] Haavelmo found himself a thesis topic in a further analysis of these ideas, which threatened in the first place to destroy confidence in econometrics as a policy tool.

Unlike Frisch, Haavelmo also became quite interested in explicit probability models of the "shock" term in an econometric model. One suspects this was due in part to the influence of the great statistician and mathematical economist Abraham Wald. After leaving Vienna to avoid the Nazis, Wald became affiliated with an unusual private institute in Chicago called the Cowles Commission for Research in Economics. The Commission ran a well known summer seminar which, in 1939 and 1940, became happy reunions of refugee economists, with Wald and Haavelmo among them. Haavelmo was receptive to much of Wald's thinking, which was already extending the basic maximum likelihood approach by introducing an explicit notion of a loss function. Wald also departed somewhat from the likelihood principle by investigating estimation methods that demonstrated consistency without necessarily maximizing the likelihood in finite samples. Haavelmo's brilliant stroke was to see a fruitful application of these ideas in the context of the economic models he had been studying with Frisch.

Haavelmo apparently was the first econometrician to see a common logical structure of the stochastic market equilibrium models and Tinbergen's "macrodynamic" systems. This, of course, was the discovery of statistical simultaneity. In so doing, he actually combined two separate strands in Frisch's work. Haavelmo readily found not only that both equations in a system like (2) were unidentified in the absence of additional information but also that OLS could be an inconsistent estimator even when a "structural" equation in fact was identified and did not omit any relevant variables. In one sense, of course, this merely replicated Frisch's (1933a) result. But the generality of Haavelmo's analysis had an enormously greater impact. In a 1941 Harvard essay, published as Haavelmo (1944), he argued brilliantly for the use of probabilistic models in econometrics, illustrated the identification problem, and showed that the inconsistency of OLS was endemic to *any* stochastic simultaneous equation system.

His results were intensely studied in a so-called "econometrics seminar" that was conducted in New York City during 1941 by Jacob Marschak, Wald, Koopmans, and others (see Epstein (1987)). His discussion of identification in one sense was very broad, in that he discussed systems that were highly nonlinear in the variables and the parameters. However, his analytical machinery left open how to determine the identifiability of individual parameters in cases where identification failed for the system as a whole. Haavelmo (1944, p. 92) regarded estimation of a simultaneous system as "straightforward" once the identification problem was solved but he did not indicate how to incorporate overidentifying information in an estimation procedure. His own examples used ML to estimate exactly

---

[5] See Qin (this volume) for a discussion of Frisch and the general problem of identification.

identified models. In this respect his work left unclear a significant question that, as argued above, had emerged from the earlier work of Tinbergen and Wright. Furthermore, despite his lengthy presentation of the Neyman-Pearson theory, Haavelmo did not address the problem of finding confidence intervals for structural estimates. Haavelmo was not primarily a statistician and it seems doubtful that he was prepared to solve the new technical problems implied by the paradigm of simultaneity. Other members of the seminar were eager to generalize his work. But his own theoretical econometric research appears to have reached its limits with the publication of his Harvard paper.[6]

Almost immediately, Mann and Wald (1943) showed in a classic article that linear, stochastic difference equation models could be estimated consistently in a manner analogous to ML under normality but using much weaker assumptions about the distribution of the error terms, where only the existence of moments up to the fourth order was needed. They also proved the asymptotic normality of their estimators, which justified construction of standard confidence intervals. Moreover, their analysis allowed for the imposition of overidentifying restrictions on the estimates and they emphasized, much more so than Haavelmo, that this step should lead to increased statistical efficiency. Although they did not make reference to Frisch (1938), it seems very likely that their purpose was also to interpret Frisch's. extremely compressed discussion of identification. Parallelling Frisch's notion of a "reducible" equation, Mann and Wald used the term "reduced form" for a particular linear transformation of the structural equations and showed that only it was identified without additional information. Such information would allow one to "solve back" for the structure in much the same way as Wright and Tinbergen had done informally fifteen years earlier. Their setup was *economically* incomplete, however, in that no distinction was made between endogenous and exogenous variables. Indeed, it was not clear how this distinction should be made.

Koopmans had far greater mathematical ability than Haavelmo and, once put on the trail, he quickly outlined a remarkably general treatise on the identification of linear models. He also adapted the Mann and Wald results for (quasi) FIML estimation to permit the use of exogenous variables. It appears that the fundamental work eventually published as Koopmans, Rubin, and Leipnik (1950) already existed in crude form in a paper that Koopmans delivered at a Cowles Commission seminar in 1943 and was largely complete by January 1945.[7] His examination of the likelihood function yielded the straightforward checks for identification that he termed

[6] Peter Phillips has informed me that Haavelmo worked with little success for many years to find the exact distribution of simultaneous equations estimators in finite samples. I have no further information on Haavelmo's activities in this area.

[7] See Epstein (1987, p. 62).

the rank and order conditions. Koopmans also saw from Mann and Wald that overidentification implied restrictions on the likelihood function, so that a ratio test could evaluate the tenability of such information. This sort of analysis lay completely beyond investigators who did not adopt the likelihood framework. For comparison, Koopmans devised examples where OLS applied to a structural equation resulted in estimators with asymptotic biases that exceeded the true coefficients by orders of magnitude. Koopmans devoted all of his energies to the rigorous development of these ideas, which he expected would be the groundwork for all future work in econometrics.

Koopmans was recruited to complete his research at the Cowles Commission in Chicago, where Jacob Marschak had become research director in 1943. By 1945 Marschak assembled an extraordinary group of people, with T. W. Anderson, Leonid Hurwicz, Lawrence Klein, Herman Rubin, and many other occasional visitors and "associates," including Haavelmo, as members of the staff. Collectively, their sophistication in mathematical statistics reached an entirely new level for econometricians. Koopmans and Marschak, amplifying Haavelmo (1944), were especially insistent that econometricians who did not adopt their research program were hindering the scientific advance of the subject.

They were doubtless surprised, and perhaps disappointed, that simultaneity bias in their early empirical work did not appear to be the major problem originally heralded by Haavelmo and Koopmans. Still, the likelihood framework had the great advantage of being able to critically test a far greater variety of statistical hypotheses with proper allowance, at least in principle, for the uncertainties caused by small sample sizes. The new theory was already being applied in the course of 1945 when work commenced at Cowles on a Keynesian structural model that was expected to lead to a new era of planning and control of economic fluctuations. Their pride and expectations were running very high.

The origin of LIML

As massive in Tinbergen's (1939) computational job had been, it appeared small in comparison to the iterative and nonlinear matrix equations that the Cowles research assistants had to solve to maximize the likelihood function for the structural system. This bottleneck threatened to destroy hope for practical application of the estimation theory that was presented as indispensable for meaningful inferences with economic data.

A possible resolution of this dilemma was offered by M. A. "Abe" Girshick, a gifted statistician himself who was collaborating with Haavelmo on a wartime project to estimate the demand for food using the new methods. In a letter to the Cowles Commission in December 1945, Girshick proposed a radically simplified estimation method for simultaneous models.[8] Girshick's letter showed that when a model was exactly identified it would be possible to estimate the structural coefficients directly from the reduced form. The example he used was formally identical to Tinbergen (1930) but this earlier work, oddly enough, was never referenced by the Cowles researchers. He worked with the structure:

$$x_1 + \alpha_2 x_2 + \alpha_3 x_3 + \alpha_0 = u \tag{5}$$

$$x_1 + \beta_2 x_2 + \beta_4 x_4 + \beta_0 = v \tag{6}$$

and presented the structural estimators in the form:

$$\hat{\alpha}_2 = \frac{\begin{vmatrix} M_{33} & M_{13} \\ M_{34} & M_{14} \end{vmatrix}}{\begin{vmatrix} M_{33} & M_{23} \\ M_{34} & M_{24} \end{vmatrix}} \qquad \hat{\beta}_2 = \frac{\begin{vmatrix} M_{13} & M_{34} \\ M_{14} & M_{44} \end{vmatrix}}{\begin{vmatrix} M_{23} & M_{43} \\ M_{24} & M_{44} \end{vmatrix}} \tag{7}$$

where M_{ij} is cov (x_i, x_j). However, Girshick did not include the details of his derivation. He simply described the results as "non-maximum likelihood estimates which are consistent and for which exact fiducial limits are available."

Girshick further argued:

Consider the variate $z = x_1 + \alpha_2 x_2$. By assumption, $E(z) = -\alpha_3 x_3 - \alpha_0$. Hence if we were to write a regression of z on x_3 and x_4, the least square estimate of the coefficient of x_4 would have zero expectation in the population.

Using this observation, he constructed a confidence interval for α_2 by considering the standard error of the variable:

$$w_1 = b_4(\hat{\alpha}_2 - \alpha_2) \tag{8}$$

where b_4 is the regression coefficient of x_2 on x_4 in the reduced form. Moreover, he discovered a statistical test of identification. Applied to (5), for example, this amounted to t test on b_4, which indicated the reliability of x_4 in shifting (6) to trace out the structural equation of interest. Girshick closed his letter on a somewhat mysterious note by mentioning that he was experimenting further with a 'black magic' method of structural estimation that could also be used for incomplete equation systems.

My examination of unpublished material in the Cowles Commission archive suggests that Koopmans had two main reservations about this method, which was soon called indirect least squares (ILS). The first was that large systems might still require an amount of computational labor that was comparable to that needed for FIML. More importantly, it appears from my research that Koopmans interpreted a practical use of Girshick's

[8] Girshick to Marschak, 24 December 1945. The original is in the Jacob Marschak papers that are stored at the University of California at Los Angeles. This remarkable letter was uncovered after nearly forty years through the inspired detective work of Mary Morgan.

method to imply abandoning the available overidentifying restrictions and that this was too high a price to pay for the convenience gained. Small data sets were still a fact of life for econometricians and the overidentifying restrictions were essential to get significance tests with any power. Moreover, these restrictions could be said to form the empirically refutable core of an economic theory since they were the elements of the structural equations that were in principle subject to test.[9]

Another possible reading of Girshick's letter, and the reference to black magic, leads one to speculate further on Girshick's place in the development of econometrics. In particular, did Girshick see his method as applicable only to an exactly identified equation? This argument raises the question, however, of why he specifically described his results as *non-maximum* likelihood estimates. Since it is obvious that MLE (assuming normality) and indirect least squares estimates coincide under exact identification, perhaps he in fact meant only that ignoring any extra restrictions would yield less efficient estimators. But Phillips (1986b) offered the striking observation that the setup in Girshick's letter verges upon an instrumental variables formulation. Furthermore, Malinvaud (1964) showed in hardly more than a line how ILS can be extended to handle overidentification. The open question becomes whether "black magic" was actually the discovery of some variant of two-stage least squares by Girshick in late 1944. It appears that Girshick lost interest in econometrics rather quickly after his wartime research and the details of the "black magic" were never discussed in his published papers or known correspondence. Unfortunately, nothing more is known about this possible sequel to indirect least squares.

Anderson indicated in his interview with Phillips (1986b) that the idea of first estimating the reduced form and then solving back for the structure was a new one for the Cowles group. It also appears from the Cowles Commission archive material that the problem of estimating only part of a structural system, including just a single equation, was emerging as an important research topic at that time. Girshick's method was of interest here as well. Anderson and Rubin undertook the problem of generalizing it to estimate a single equation while preserving the overidentifying information.

Anderson discovered a solution almost immediately. Extending Girshick's observation, he wrote down the reduced form as:

$$Y_t = \pi^* x_t^* + \pi^{**} x_t^{**} \tag{9}$$

where Y was the vector of length g of the included endogenous variables and x^* and x^{**} were matrices of the included and excluded predetermined

---

[9] The basis for this paragraph is the Minutes of Staff Meeting, 28 January 1946, Cowles Commission Archive, Cowles Foundation Library, Yale University. Additional discussion is contained in Epstein (1987, chapter 2).

variables, respectively. It then followed that:

$$\beta\pi^* = \gamma \tag{10}$$

$$\beta x^{**} = 0 \tag{11}$$

where β was the structural coefficient vector and γ was the coefficient vector for the exogenous variables in the equation. He immediately saw that a necessary condition for a unique solution for β in (11) (subject to a normalization) was that the rank of the reduced form coefficient matrix π^{**} be $g - 1$. This matrix could always be estimated but in a sample it would have full rank with probability one, leading to an estimate of β equal to zero. Anderson proposed instead simply finding an estimate b in (11) that was small in a least squares sense by minimizing the quadratic form:

$$b\pi^{**}Mx^{**\prime}b' = 0 \tag{12}$$

subject to a suggested normalization $bWb' = 1$ (where M was the inverse of the estimated covariance matrix of π^{**} and W was the estimated covariance matrix of Y). The first order condition took the form:

$$(\pi^{**}M\pi^{**\prime} - \lambda W)b' = 0 \tag{13}$$

where λ was a Lagrange multiplier. It then followed that the solution should set b equal to the eigenvector associated with the smallest eigenvalue of the matrix $W^{-1}\pi^{**}M\pi^{**\prime}$, after which the normalization could be imposed.

Progress was extremely rapid. Anderson, working with Rubin, worked out the algebra of their so-called "reduced form method" by early February 1946.[10] Girshick was quite impressed with these results. He sent his congratulations in a letter to Marschak and urged immediate publication, saying that "Anderson and Rubin obtained all the results I have and more" and that "they [might] simply acknowledge my contribution in a footnote to a paper which they write under their own names".[11] Anderson and Rubin proceeded to derive the estimator in a rigorous maximum likelihood setup, where the condition (11) was imposed directly, and developed an associated distribution theory for the estimates. Fortuitously, Anderson had examined a version of this problem in a more general setting as part of his dissertation.[12] The results that now comprise the LIML estimator were largely in hand by April 1946 and of course were eventually published as Anderson and Rubin (1949).

[10] The early drafts of this work are preserved in the Cowles archive.
[11] Girshick to Marschak, 19 Februray 1946, Marschak Papers, UCLA. Mary Morgan also discovered this letter. Malinvaud (1983) gave more credit to Girshick for the discovery of LIML than seems justified by this evidence.
[12] See Phillips (1986b). The relevant material from the dissertation is very tersely presented in Anderson (1958, chapter 14).

OLS and structural estimators

The experience with early uses of LIML by Lawrence Klein and others has been analyzed elsewhere (see Epstein [1987]). The introduction of two-stage least squares in the 1950's was motivated as an even more simple method for consistent estimation of an overidentified structural equation. Perhaps the most striking empirical result, however, is how seldom these estimators differed meaningfully from OLS, especially in the large macro-economic models that grew out of the Tinbergen and Cowles traditions. This phenomenon suggests that few models have been truly overidentified through the use of simple exclusion restrictions. The identifiability test statistic, known since the development of LIML yet very seldom reported, has tended to confirm this judgment. Moreover, simultaneity bias will vary directly with the magnitude of the contemporaneous coefficients of en-dogenous variables. Economic theory may justify small current values when the variables enter the equation as distributed lags. The future relevance of LIML and 2SLS for applied research will depend in large part on the degree to which economic theories can successfully impose exclusion restrictions on structure.

OLS has proven to be much more durable than Haavelmo and the Cowles Commission had expected in estimating a single equation. However, it is currently an open question how OLS will fare against full information methods in the presence of the cross equation restrictions implied by rational expectations models. Koopmans had never pursued a detailed analysis of such restrictions, terming it "pretty hopeless".[13] Indeed, the Cowles Commission did not see a significant economic rationale for cross equation restraints. Rational expectations models in fact have had a salutory effect on the Cowles paradigm. They have restored the analysis of structure to a central place but in a new framework which does not hinge upon simultaneity in the variables. This remarkable advance in economic theory, vitally facilitated by the advent of great computing power at near zero cost, has served to reopen the fundamental economic and statistical questions that essentially motivated the development of modern econometrics.

Conclusion

The econometric problems caused by simultaneous equations had already received significant theoretical analysis during the 1920's. Rudimentary solutions to identification and estimation took the form of recursive structures, restrictions on the ratios of the structural variances, instrumental variables, and indirect least squares. The use of OLS in this context was shown to yield results that fundamentally differed with these alternative procedures. Nevertheless, this discovery appeared to be a minor curiosity that failed to generate further research.

[13] Quoted in Epstein (1987, p. 196).

The study of simultaneity became a dominant research program when Haavelmo (1944) recognized it as a unified approach to demand studies, Tinbergen's macroeconomic models, and Frisch's confluent systems. The Cowles Commission further developed the theory as a multi-equation problem in Fisher's likelihood framework. The basic statistical premise of this research was that OLS was likely to be fundamentally unsuitable for structural estimation.

A great variety of structural estimators soon followed the initial development of FIML and LIML. The research program has been remarkably successful in solving extremely complicated problem of theoretical statistics. Yet the empirical experience has been very different from what Haavelmo and the Cowles Commission originally expected. OLS was rarely shown to be grossly inferior to other estimators when used with real world data, especially in macroeconomics. Rational expectations models have revived interest in FIML but for reasons of efficiency and hypothesis testing, not for consistency of the estimates.

OLS has received striking new justification in recent work on inference with integrated processes. This work turns back the clock, as it were, to re-open data oriented modeling questions that have been dormant since the early 1930's.[14] An integrated process is of the form

$$x_t = x_{t-1} + u_t \tag{14}$$

where u_t may be a serially correlated and even *nonstationary* disturbance. Phillips and Park (1986) have shown under general conditions that regressions involving integrated variables can be estimated consistently by OLS, regardless of the correlation between regressors and the equation error. Since many economic time series appear to be integrated processes, their results suggest that biases due to simultaneity and measurement error may have only second-order effects in practice.

This rehabilitation of OLS is part of a broader change in our understanding of econometrics. Structural estimation, including rational expectations models, is based ultimately on the cause and effect logic of a laboratory experiment. However, the current literature on cointegrated processes, viz. Engle and Granger (1987), seems more in the tradition of Frisch's (1934) confluence analysis, where linear dependence among variables indicates co-movement without imputing a specific causal structure. Cointegration can also be viewed as a new type of time series restriction on the reduced form of a complete system which, like (11), also involves the rank of a matrix of reduced form coefficients. Such a reduced form can be estimated consistently by OLS and efficiently by constrained multivariate regression. It remains to be seen whether OLS can remain a competitive estimator in this new modeling context.

University of Illinois at Chicago, USA.

[14] See Hendry and Morgan (this volume).

Oxford Economic Papers 41 (1989), 108–128

LSE AND THE BRITISH APPROACH TO TIME SERIES ECONOMETRICS*

By CHRISTOPHER L. GILBERT

1. Introduction

BRITISH economists adopt an approach to time series econometrics which is noticeably different from that prevalent in the United States. There is an emphasis on relatively free ('databased') dynamic specification in conjunction with a commitment to extensive specification tests. The error correction dynamic adjustment specification is frequently adopted, and found acceptable. And there is a tendency to identify residual autocorrelation with equation misspecification. Elsewhere (Gilbert (1987)), I have referred to this approach to econometrics as the LSE approach and contrasted it with two very different American methodologies; and in Gilbert (1986a) I attempted to codify a particular exemplar of the British approach. In this paper I shall be concerned with the origins of this approach to econometrics.

I argue (Section 4) that the British approach arises from the successful marriage of traditional structural methods, deriving from the Cowles tradition, with the methods of the statistical theory of time series analysis most familiar in the analysis of business statistics. In the United States these disciplines have remained largely distinct.

An important historical question is why this cross-fertilization took place in Britain and not in the United States. One possible answer[1] is that the British were relatively strong in statistics and less strong in economic theory, while the reverse was true in North America. I find it difficult to see evidence for the premise of this argument. I claim that the British tradition in applied econometrics is an LSE (London School of Economics) tradition that has to some extent colonized and to some extent been infiltrated into the remainder of the British university system. I suggest that the evolution of the British approach to econometrics arose from the unique position of statistics at the LSE, and from the particular individuals who were involved in econometrics at the LSE in the postwar decades.

In Section 2 I attempt an account of the development of the teaching of econometrics at the LSE from the early fifties to the mid sixties. At the

* This paper is based in part on Gilbert (1986b) which was prepared for a joint session of the American Economic Association and the History of Economics Society in New York, December 1985. I am grateful for comments from Manuel Arellano, Neil de Marchi, Jim Durbin, Bill Farebrother, Zvi Griliches, Andrew Harvey, David Hendry, James MacKinnon, Grayham Mizon, Mary Morgan, Sir Claus Moser, Sir Henry Phelps Brown, Peter Phillips, Denis Sargan, Jim Thomas, Ken Wallis, Nancy Wulwick and to the referees of an earlier version of the paper. I have not been able to accommodate all their comments. I remain responsible for all errors, both of omission and commission.
[1] Suggested by a referee of an earlier version of this paper.

beginning of that period there was no econometrics; by the end of the period, one had what was essentially a modern economics teaching programme with econometrics provided for undergraduate economics degrees and with advanced courses for graduates. These developments are due to Jim Durbin's fostering of econometrics in the LSE statistics department and to Bill Phillips' promotion of econometrics in the economics department. The result has been the pre-eminence of LSE certainly in British and arguably in international econometrics.[2]

In Section 3 of the paper I switch to methodology and discuss Denis Sargan's formative Colston paper (Sargan (1964)) which anticipates, both substantively and stylistically, the direction that econometrics would take at the LSE over the next two decades under his direction. Then, in Section 4, I revert to history, and look at the interface between time series econometrics and that branch of statistics known as time series analysis which took place at LSE during the sixties and seventies. This is the source of the LSE approach to dynamic modelling, formalized in the General to Simple approach which I discuss in Section 5.

The best known product of LSE econometrics is probably the Davidson *et al.* [1978] (DHSY) consumption function model, and in Section 6 I consider that paper. This paper serves to illustrate the development of British time series econometrics over the fourteen years since Sargan's Colston paper but also indicates new directions. One of its most important features is the insistence that competing models should be systematically compared on identical datasets. This anticipates the development of non-nested testing and the associated concept of encompassing. The argument is summarized and drawn together in Section 7.

2. Econometrics teaching at the LSE

Although academic appointments are made largely on the basis of research achievement and promise, the number (and even the existence) of posts in particular disciplines and areas of disciplines is almost entirely justified by teaching requirements. If we are to understand the timing and location of the growth of research in econometrics we therefore need to look at the growth of econometrics teaching.

The 'A' level ('Advanced' level) school examination system in England requires school children to specialize very much more than their counterparts in other Anglo-Saxon countries (even Scotland). Partly as consequence and partly as cause, undergraduate degrees at English universities are also shorter (typically three years to honours) and more specialized than those elsewhere. Again partly as consequence and partly as cause, histori-

---

[2] The LSE was ranked first internationally in terms of theoretical econometric articles in leading journals over the period 1980–85, second (after Chicago) in all econometrics, and fourth in all economics. The next highest British university in this ranking was Cambridge (16 in theoretical econometrics, 19 in all econometrics and 37 in all economics). Source: Hall (1987).

cally there has been much less provision for graduate tuition at English universities than at universities elsewhere in the English-speaking world. In looking at the growth of instruction in econometrics, we must therefore concentrate on undergraduate degrees.

Economics teaching in British universities in the fifties and sixties, as elsewhere in the world, was predominantly non-mathematical. Courses in Economic Statistics had become standard at least since the war. These courses covered concepts and methods of national income accounting, the use of index numbers, methods of trend fitting and, usually also some elementary statistical theory. However, in general it was not until the sixties or even the seventies that modern econometrics courses were provided. This is neither surprising nor scandalous: it was not until the mid-fifties that multiple regression became the standard statistical tool employed by economists, and it was only around that time that econometrics was distinguished from mathematical economics and was equated with what had previously been known as 'Statistical Methods of Economics'. Furthermore, courses spread as texts become available and both the growth in the number of texts and the narrowing of the concept of econometrics were phenomena of the sixties.[3]

For example, at Cambridge undergraduates reading the Economics tripos in their final year could take as their optional paper either a standard Economic Statistics paper or a more advanced paper in the Theory of Statistics. The content of the Economic Statistics paper in the late fifties and early sixties is evident from Blyth (1960). The Theory of Statistics paper was an advanced paper in mathematical statistics with a small regression content, but a rubric change in 1970 substantially increased the econometric component. The paper remains in that form today. In Oxford there has never been a single honours degree in Economics, and the vast majority of students reading Economics do so as part of the degree in Philosophy, Politics and Economics (PPE). An option combining economic statistics and elementary statistical theory has been offered since the forties and a specific paper in econometrics was introduced in 1971. The Oxbridge pattern of provision was standard throughout the British university system.[4]

The LSE, Manchester and (later) Essex and Warwick, constitute the major exceptions to this pattern. Of these four, LSE had the largest Economics department, and has had the greatest influence. At LSE, econometrics was taught to undergraduates reading for the B.Sc.(Econ.) degree in Statistics almost from the beginning of the fifties, but by members of the School's Statistics department. The first session in which an undergraduate course bearing the name 'Econometrics' (as distinct from economic statistics) was offered was 1951–52 when the government statis-

[3] Tintner (1952), Klein (1953), Fox (1958), Valavanis (1959), Johnston (1963), Malinvaud (1964), Goldberger (1964), Christ (1966).

[4] Sources: Cambridge degrees, *Cambridge University Student Handbook* (various issues); Oxford degrees, *Examination Decrees* (various issues).

tician Geoff Penrice gave a 10 lecture course.[5] Penrice also gave a new 10 lecture course on the 'Analysis of Time Series' that year. In the following year, after Penrice's departure to the Government Statistical Service, the econometrics course was taken over and expanded to 24 lectures by Harold Booker, whose main interests were in national accounting, and game theorist George Morton. Wilfred Corlett, whose affiliation was to University College, joined the team to strengthen the estimation and modelling component. Maurice (later Sir Maurice) Kendall took on the time series course, and from 1958 it was given by M. H. Quenouille, who had been appointed to the LSE from the Oxford Institute of Statistics. The Booker–Corlett–Morton course remained the sole econometrics course offered at the School until the 1961–62 session.

At a formal level, this teaching all took place entirely in the Statistics Department and was specifically for students reading for the B.Sc. (Econ.) in Statistics. Students reading for the Economics degree were able to do courses in economic statistics or in elementary statistical theory. In this respect an LSE Economics degree was, at that time, no different from the Cambridge Economics tripos or even from the Oxford PPE degree. The major advocate of econometrics within the Statistics Department was Jim Durbin who had been involved with economists during his relatively brief initial appointment at the Cambridge Department of Applied Economics which had given rise to his important work on the diagnosis of residual serial correlation with G. S. Watson (Durbin and Watson (1950)). In the Economics department, the impetus for econometrics came from Bill Phillips, a New Zealander whose background was in engineering. Phillips is now chiefly remembered for the Phillips Curve (Phillips (1958a)) but his reputation at LSE in the fifties was not due to published articles but to the famous Phillips machine, a hydraulic model of the circular flow of income. "He thought the interest theory was muddled with confusion between stocks and flows. Setting it out in mathematical form he realized he had the model of a hydraulic system, and he proceeded to build a real model." (Blyth (1978)). The initial machine was built in a friend's garage in Surrey in conjunction with Walter Newlyn of Leeds University and this was subsequently used for teaching at Leeds (Newlyn (1950)). An improved design was used for an LSE machine (Phillips (1950)). Subsequently, Phillips machines were employed in Oxford, Cambridge, Birmingham, Manchester and Melbourne (Blyth (1978)).

It is important to recall that this was the pre-computer era. Digital computing machines were becoming available, but as Klein (1987) notes,

[5] LSE *Calendar* (various issues). The course syllabus reads: "Scope of Econometrics. Derivation of supply and demand curves by regression analysis and simultaneous probability equations. Production and Consumption functions. Problems of identification and aggregation. Connection between micro-economic and macro-economic models. Problems of obtaining suitable statistical data." *LSE Calendar*, 1951–52. Roy (later Sir Roy) Allen had given a graduate course entitled "Problems of Econometrics" in both the 1946–47 and 1947–48 sessions. This was probably the first course in econometrics in a British university.

early macroeconometric models such as the Klein *et al.* (1961) model of the
UK economy, were estimated in a mixed manner, the tedious moments
calculations being undertaken by electronic computer leaving the subsequent equation solutions to be done on desktop calculating machines. No
one could foresee the extraordinary advance in digital computer technology
that was to take place over the next thirty years. The rival technology,
which offered equal promise, was that of analogue computing. The
advantage of analogue machines is that they can deal with nonlinear
equations, which was simply not possible with early digital machines.
Phillips' hydraulic model was a water-powered analogue computer—"a
calculating machine for solving differential equations" (Phillips (1950)). The
major purpose of the machine was to aid teaching and it was for this reason
that coloured water flows within a perspex apparatus were used in
preference to electronic currents. It was this machine which established
Phillips' reputation. James Meade, who in 1950 offered Phillips his first job
at the LSE as an Assistant Lecturer (the most junior appointment in British
universities at that time) despite a very poor first degree in sociology and no
subsequent training, was a particular enthusiast and linked two Phillips
machines to exhibit trade flows between two countries (Blyth (1978)).

Lionel (later Lord) Robbins was head of the Economics Department
throughout the fifties. Robbins had a certain respect for statistics in the
sense of the marshalling of available quantitative evidence as practiced by
traditional economic historians, but on the whole he regarded the activity as
a form of drudgery, an intellectually unimportant activity suitable perhaps
for the second XI.[6] His views on econometrics were even more negative and
the famous caricature of the imaginary economist Blank and his estimated
demand function for herrings (Robbins (1932)) is notorious.[7] However,
Robbins was also won over by Phillips who was promoted to Reader in 1954
and Tooke Professor in 1958. There is some evidence that under the joint
influence of Phillips and philosopher Sir Karl Popper, Robbins moderated
his position in his later years—see Peston (1981, pp. 185–186). But in any
case, there was no 'departmental view' and Robbins was happy to allow
faculty members to research on whatever they chose.

Phillips' enduring concern was with modelling disequilibrium adjustment
processes. This is evident in the Phillips machine, in his two stabilization
articles (Phillips (1954, 1957)) and in the Phillips Curve itself (Phillips

---

[6] Although he had considerable respect for certain statisticians, in particular A. L. Bowley.
See also his comments on the statistical appendices to the Robbins Report—Robbins (1971),
pp. 274–275.
[7] The crucial sentence is quite carefully hedged: "Important as such investigations may
be—and nothing that is here said on their methodological status should be regarded as
derogating from their very considerable practical value—there is no justification for claiming
for their results the status of the so called 'statistical' laws of the natural sciences." (pp.
109–110 in the 1948 edition.) One response to the quoted passage might be to agree but to ask
whether the statistical laws of the natural sciences correspond to Robbins' paradigm—see
Cartwright (1983).

(1958a)). He was the dominant force in the establishment of econometrics in the Economics Department at the LSE. An optional paper in 'Statistical Methods in Economics' was first offered in the B.Sc. (Econ.) in Economics for students registering in the autumn of 1961 and, at the same time, an Econometrics paper was offered in the B.Sc. (Econ.) in Statistics. Phillips and Jim Thomas[8] gave a major lecture course in conjunction with the Statistical Methods paper, and this was the first course in econometrics offered within the Economics Department. The econometrics course for the Statistics degree was now given by Thomas and Corlett and a separate set of lectures was offered on game theory. Durbin and Phillips worked together to obtain the appointment of Denis Sargan as Reader in Econometrics in the Statistics department in 1963. And in 1965, after Rex Bergstrom's departure to the new University of Essex, Sargan's readership was converted into a chair in econometrics in the Department of Economics, and a lectureship in econometrics was created in the Department of Statistics which was filled, after a short delay, by Ken Wallis. From this point, the teaching of econometrics nominally became the responsibility of the Economics Department while the teaching of time series analysis remained with Statistics; but in practice the whole enterprise was cooperative.

Econometrics provision at the LSE exploded in 1964–65 with the inception of the new M.Sc. degree in Economics and Econometrics. It had been traditional in the humanities and social sciences in British universities to appoint graduates with top first class honours degrees directly into assistant lectureships or college fellowships without expecting either a doctorate or attendance at any taught graduate courses (which, in any case, were not widely offered). The LSE took the view that this tradition was no longer tenable, and taught M.Sc. courses were introduced across a range of subjects. One of these was the M.Sc. in Economics and Econometrics.[9] It is not too far-fetched to view these taught M.Sc. courses as an attempt to infiltrate a trained cadre of technically equipped young lecturers into a largely amateur academic community. In the case of econometrics this mission was heightened by the fact that, outside the LSE, the teaching of economics remained largely hostile to the use of mathematics. A large proportion of econometrics lecturers in Britain in the late seventies were graduates of this M.Sc. programme.

In the initial year of the new M.Sc. Jim Durbin gave a course on 'Advanced Statistical Methods for Econometrics' covering LIML, FIML, 2SLS, 3SLS and time series regression models, and Phillips and Sargan jointly gave courses in Quantitative Economics. Phillips and Sargan also jointly gave the major Statistical Methods in Economics course for the Economics B.Sc. From the 1965–66 session Sargan dropped out of the

[8] From 1962. In the 1961–62 session a shorter course was given by Thomas.
[9] With the subsequent introduction of an M.Sc. in Economics, it became simply Econometrics and then Econometrics and Mathematical Economics.

undergraduate course, which was now advertised as given by Professor Phillips and others, to concentrate on graduate teaching. From that year until his retirement he gave the M.Sc. "Advanced Statistical Methods for Econometrics" course previously given by Durbin.[10]

It was from this course that the rising generation of British econometricians learnt their econometrics. The first half of the course was based around least squares and instrumental variables (IV) estimation of both single equations and systems; and the second half, which closely followed the Cowles monographs, was devoted to Maximum Likelihood (ML) estimation. Throughout both components there was an emphasis on testing—F tests in least squares models, likelihood ratio tests in ML models, and also, by virtue of the asymptotic equivalence of IV and ML estimation, in IV models.[11]

There were very few separate statistics departments in British universities in the immediate postwar period. The LSE Statistics Department was in the tradition of the nineteenth century statistical movement and, from the time of the first professor (A. L. Bowley), had been directed towards social and economic statistics. This is in contrast to the Sir Karl Pearson's department at University College, the largest and longest established department in Britain, which was associated with the biometric movement. I have shown that econometrics teaching at LSE was initially developed by the Statistics Department and it was the presence of this independent economics-oriented group of statisticians, and not any feature of the LSE Ecomomics Department, which is responsible for LSE taking the lead in the teaching of econometrics in Britain. In the remainder of this paper I shall attempt to show how the collaboration between the statisticians and the econometricians determined the direction in which British time series econometrics would develop.

3. Sargan's Colston paper

In April 1964 the Department of Economics at the University of Bristol organized a symposium on "Econometric Analysis for National Economic Planning" under the aegis of the Colston Research Society. The subject was timely since a general election was imminent and it seemed probable that a Labour government, sympathetic to this approach to economic management, would be returned. One contribution to this symposium is still widely cited: Denis Sargan's paper "Wages and prices in the United Kingdom: a

---

[10] In the 1965–66 session, when Durbin was on leave, Sargan also gave an M.Sc. course introduced the previous year on "Time Series Analysis". The rubric for this course was "Stationarity, autocorrelation, time series models including autoregressive and moving average models, the fitting of time series models, trend and periodic components, the periodogram and spectral analysis." (*LSE Calendar*, 1965–66.) Durbin reassumed this course on his return the following session. Phillips left the LSE in 1967 for Australia.

[11] Rowley (1973) is highly correlated with the course given by Sargan in the late sixties.

study in econometric methodology" (Sargan (1964)),[12] often referred to as Sargan's Colston paper. This is somewhat ironic since the paper attracted relatively little contemporary interest—even if a policy-maker were prepared to plough through four sections of mathematics before reaching the section entitled "The econometric model", he might have been dissuaded from doing so by Sargan's opening declaration that the primary motivation of the contribution was methodological.

However, the paper did have substantial implications for policy. A major question was whether a new government should devalue sterling. The Wilson government, elected in October 1964, ducked this issue until devaluation was forced in November 1967. It is arguable that an immediate devaluation would have allowed export-led growth in a much healthier international environment than was present in 1968–69. Sargan's policy discussion focussed explicitly on the devaluation issue. He concluded that, although the impact of sterling devaluation would only be temporary,[13] real wages might be depressed for a sufficiently long period to make the devaluation worthwhile.

Policy was very little influenced by econometric studies at that time, and it is doubtful that any of the Labour government's economic advisers were aware of Sargan's work. By contrast, the paper had enormous influence on the development of time series econometrics in Britain over the subsequent two decades. Sargan had just arrived at the LSE and the Colston paper may be seen as an inaugural manifesto for the direction in which he was to take econometrics teaching. Moreover, it anticipated a large number of developments in theoretical approach and applied practice. Perhaps of greatest importance, it embodied a concern with time series dynamics and an approach to dynamic modelling which set a style for British time series econometrics in the seventies and eighties.

The principal methodological objective of the Colston paper was to demonstrate the practicality of autoregressive least squares (ALS) and autoregressive instrumental variables (AIV) estimation of econometric equations. Suppose we are interested in estimating the standard regression model

$$y_t = \beta' x_t + u_t \tag{1}$$

but that we suspect that the disturbance term u follows the first order autoregression

$$u_t = \rho u_{t-1} + \epsilon_t \tag{2}$$

where $\{\epsilon_t\}$ is a white noise process. The traditional iterative approach is that due to Cochrane and Orcutt (1949) where ordinary least squares (OLS) is applied to the equation quasi-differenced by the operator $1 - \rho L$ (where L is the lag operator) and where the autoregressive coefficient ρ is estimated

---

[12] Reprinted in Hendry and Wallis (1984).
[13] Since eventual restoration of the equilibrium real wage is entailed by the error correction specification—see below.

from the residuals at the previous iteration. Thus one estimates

$$y_t^* = \beta' x_t^* + v_t \tag{3}$$

where $y_t^* = y_t - \hat{\rho} y_{t-1}$ and $x_t^* = x_t - \hat{\rho} x_{t-1}$. This remains the standard estimation procedure in many regression packages. It suffers from the drawbacks
that estimated coefficient standard errors are conditional upon the estimated
value of ρ and the possibility of convergence to a local but not global
minimum of the residual sum of squares.

Sargan (1959) and Durbin (1960a) had shown that the full ALS estimators
could be obtained as the restricted least squares estimator of an expanded
regression, and Sargan (1959) had demonstrated that this approach generalizes to IV estimation. (1) and (2) imply

$$y_t = \alpha y_{t-1} + \beta' x_t + \gamma x_{t-1} + \epsilon_t \tag{4}$$

with

$$\alpha\beta + \gamma = 0. \tag{5}$$

Sargan's ALS procedure consisted of the restricted least squares estimation
of (4) subject to (5). Since the ALS estimates are asymptotically maximum
likelihood, coefficient standard errors may be obtained from the sample
information matrix inverse. The theory of this estimation method was
developed by 1958 and is discussed in Sargan (1959) but it took Sargan until
the end of 1962 to develop the AIV computer programs. The paper was
then written up for the Colston conference in the spring of 1964.

Ironically, the discussion of autoregression is almost irrelevant to understanding the applied part of the paper since none of Sargan's estimates of
the post-war wage relationship demonstrate significant serial correlation[14]
and the AIV estimates of this equation are very poorly determined. The
same policy conclusions could have been obtained through OLS estimation
and this would certainly have resulted in a more accessible paper. But this is
to overlook the methodological agenda implicit in Sargan's theoretical
discussion:

(i) Interpretation of ALS as a restricted least squares estimator allows the
restriction (5) to be tested. Sargan suggests that rejection "can often be
interpreted to mean that a more complicated structure of lags, or a longer
lag is required in the structural equations on at least one of the variables".
This anticipates Hendry and Mizon (1978), but at this stage the analysis is
simple to general—see section 5 (below).

(ii) Sargan develops a residual-based test for higher order serial correlation, anticipating the Lagrange Multiplier (LM) test of Godfrey (1978).

(iii) The paper contains a discussion of numerical maximization methods
which would become standard in ML estimation.

(iv) There is a section on choice between linear and logarithmic
functional specifications. As Sargan noted, this choice had previously been

---

[14] There is significant serial correlation in the estimated price equations.

made on an *a priori* basis. Development of a statistical test for this problem is difficult, but Sargan initiated the subsequent literature (Pesaran and Deaton (1978), Godfrey and Wickens (1981)) by proposing a choice criterion.

(v) The paper contains an important argument that the specification of the dependent variable in a regression equation should be such as to result in independent residuals. Using quarterly data, Klein *et al.* (1961) had used the annual change in wage rates $w_t - w_{t-4}$ as the dependent variable in their wage equation on the argument that wage changes reflect an annual wage round. Sargan noted that if the quarterly changes $w_t - w_{t-1}$ are independent the Klein equation will be subject to moving average errors. This argument recurs in Wallis's (1971) criticism of the Lipsey and Parkin (1970) analysis of the effects of incomes policy.

However, the feature for which Sargan's Colston paper is now best known is that it contains the first application of the error correction specification (ECS) which we now know may be rationalized by the theory of cointegration (Granger (1986), Engle and Granger (1987)). In obvious notation, the basic specification is[15]

$$w_t - w_{t-1} = \beta_0 + \beta_1(p_{t-1} - p_{t-4}) - \beta_2 U_{t-1} - \beta_3(w_{t-1} - p_{t-1}) + \beta_4 t \quad (6)$$

The error correction term is $w_{t-1} - p_{t-1}$ which (if the variables are in logarithms) may be interpreted as the log of the real wage. Equation (6) implies that the higher the real wage, the less the rate of nominal wage inflation *ceteris paribus*. Equation (6) implies an equilibrium real wage ω given as

$$\omega_t = [\beta_0 + \beta_1(p_t - p_{t-3}) - \beta_2 U_t + \beta_4(t+1)]/\beta_3 \quad (7)$$

allowing (6) to be summarized as an adjustment of real wages to their equilibrium level:

$$w_t - w_{t-1} = -\beta_3(w_{t-1} - p_{t-1} - \omega_{t-1}) \quad (8)$$

A standard model in classical control, used in the study of servomechanisms such as thermostats, is the PID (Proportional, Integral, Derivative) model discussed in Phillips (1954, 1957). In (6), the term $\beta_1(p_{t-1} - p_{t-4})$ is a derivative control since it forces the wage to react to the derivative of the price level. Workers are interested, however, in their real wage (this is the 'temperature' that the wage bargaining thermostat is required to control). If β_1 differs from unity, then in the absence of the proportional control $\beta_3(w_{t-1} - p_{t-1})$, price inflation would result in permanent erosion of the real wage. As Sargan notes, the equation would be non-homogeneous in money prices: ". . . unions are very conscious of the effects of price rises, and it is possible that if past changes have unfavourably affected the level of real wages, they will increase their pressure so as to correct the level of real

---

[15] A political trend shift variable has been omitted to simplify the exposition.

wages again. It is possible to test this possibility by introducing one extra variable ..." (op. cit., p. 37). It is clear from this discussion that Sargan's wage model should be seen as anticipating modern NAIRU models of wage determination.

In Section 2 I noted Phillips' involvement in Sargan's move to LSE and documented the close links in teaching between the two men. This prompts the question of whether Phillips directly influenced Sargan's work, a link suggested in Gilbert (1986a). Sargan does not refer to the PID model in his discussion of error correction and the single reference to Phillips is to his more famous Phillips Curve article (Phillips (1958a)) where only proportional control is present. Sargan notes[16] that he had the idea of the ECS worked out before his 1958 visit to Minnesota and Chicago, but that he saw error correction as a natural set of restrictions of a general autoregressive model. He was aware of Phillips' feedback models and had read the two stabilization articles (Phillips (1954, 1957)) but did not "really make any connection between the optimal control problem ... and the rather arbitrary lags in the adjustment of wage negotiators to changes in the real wage".

This relates to the subtle issue of modelling style. The dominant paradigm in post-war economic theory has been of agents optimizing subject to constraints. The modeller is required to accurately specify the constraint set. He can then solve the optimization problem and is in a position to compare the predicted time paths of the choice variables with actual realizations. For Phillips, the ECS was justified by a more or less formal optimization exercise, and this rationale has recently been made explicit under rational expectations in Nickell (1985). Sargan was sceptical about the applicability of optimizing models to wage bargaining and was more impressed by institutional features of the labour market—in particular the annual 'wage round' and the prevalence of pricing based on mark-up of historical costs, both of which featured prominently in Dicks–Mireaux and Dow (1959) and in Klein *et al.* (1961). These give the "rather arbitrary lags" referred to above.

So for Sargan, the ECS arises as an economically plausible set of restrictions on a general distributed lag model. But if the lag distribution is theoretically arbitrary, what restrictions are plausible? Sargan experimented with a large number of alternative lag specifications (in a way which has now become common) with the objective of obtaining an interpretable and parsimonious specification of this arbitrary dynamic relationship linking wages to lagged prices and unemployment. However, at that time he lacked a formal framework in which the simplification of distributed lag models could be discussed. I shall argue that this framework would be provided by time series analysis.

---

[16] Letter to the author, February 1988.

4. Time series econometrics and time series analysis

Time series econometrics is the application of econometric methods to structural models of economic time series, typically using multiple regression of ML methods. Time series analysis is the branch of statistics which is concerned with the identification and estimation of relationships governing the evolution of data series over time. In general, series are considered in isolation, although in principle virtually all the techniques employed generalize to multivariate time series. The problems analyzed include trend identification and extraction, seasonality and deseasonalization, serial dependence and the representation of periodicity.

An important part of time series analysis is concerned with stochastic difference equations. It is apparent that many natural and socio-economic phenomena are cyclical. Typically, however, economic time series cannot be well represented by simple trigonometric functions of constant amplitude and periodicity. Although we can always use Fourier analysis to analyze a (stationary) series into a sum of sine waves of different periodicities

$$y_t = \sum_{i=0}^{n} (a_1 \sin (w_i t) + b_i \cos (w_i t)) \tag{9}$$

(where $w_i = 2i/T$, T (odd for convenience) is the sample size and $n = (T-1)/2$ gives the highest frequency one can detect with sample size T—see e.g. Gottman (1981, pp. 212–213)). These models imply non-decaying serial correlation patterns. For example, if (9) is dominated by a four year cycle one would expect high serial correlations at eight, twelve, sixteen etc. years. In fact, serial correlations in economic time series tend to decay over time. An alternative class of model, introduced by the English statistician Sir George Udny Yule (Yule (1937)) in the context of sunspot cycles and extensively discussed in Wold (1938), posited an autoregressive stochastic difference equation

$$\alpha(L)y_t = \epsilon_t$$

(where the $\{\epsilon_t\}$ process is independent). This will result in cyclical behaviour so long as the autoregressive polynomial has complex roots, but, provided these roots all lie within the unit circle, the cycles will be damped. So the random shocks ϵ provide the source of the cyclical variation but its periodicity is determined by the autoregressive structure.[17] Mann and Wald (1943) proved consistency of least squares estimation of equations of this form.

Slutsky (1927, English translation 1927), had shown that cyclical behaviour could also result from the averaging of independent disturbances and this remarkable observation underlies what we now refer to as moving

[17] See Frisch (1933b) who attributes the idea to Wicksell.

average models. The important class of autoregressive-moving average (ARMA) models

$$\alpha(L)y_t = \beta(L)\epsilon_t \qquad (10)$$

was introduced by Quenouille (1957) as a natural generalization of the pure autoregressive and moving average models. This class was to form the basis of the Box–Jenkins methodology (Box and Jenkins (1970)).

Box and Jenkins' major contribution was the popularization of the ARMA model with the result that it became the major time series forecasting methodology employed in business. In part this was through the provision of computer programs, but it was also important that they suggested a solution to the endemic problems of trend and seasonality by noting that the filter Δ_s, where s is the number of periods in the year (four on quarterly data), would eliminate a constant seasonal pattern. This is no more than the old technique of 'variate differencing'.[18] It generalizes (10) to the ARIMA (autoregressive integrated moving average) model[19]

$$\alpha(L)\Delta_s x_t = \beta(L)\epsilon_t. \qquad (11)$$

Box and Jenkins advocated parsimonious specification of the lag polynomials $\alpha(L)$ and $\beta(L)$. Thus, the opening sentences of the introductory section "Basic ideas in model building" of Box and Jenkins (1970) read:

"We have seen that the mathematical models ... contain certain constants or parameters whose values must be estimated from the data. It is important, in practice, that we employ the *smallest possible* number of parameters for adequate representation." (*op. cit.*, p. 17, emphasis in original.)

In particular Box and Jenkins' famous 'airline model', which on monthly data sets $\alpha(L) = 1$ and $\beta(L) = (1 + \beta_1 L)(1 + \beta_{12}L^{12})$ in (11), has been found to 'fit' large classes of data (see Anderson (1980, p. 7), and Harvey and Durbin (1986)).

There have always been arguments for parsimonious specification in statistics. At the most simple level, one might believe that the processes being modelled have an inherently simple structure, but it is difficult to see any general basis for this belief. A more secure argument is that we always have a finite number of observations and this must limit the degree of complexity of our models—in particular short time series will frequently force very simple structures. In such cases one will need to content oneself with modelling the salient features of the data generating process. Furthermore, although the higher the parameterization (i.e. the more variables or lags included) the better the 'fit' on standard criteria (residual sum of squares, likelihood), it may be shown that after a certain point forecasting performance (expected mean square forecast error) deteriorates (Mallows (1973); see also Judge *et al.* (1980), pp. 417–423 and Akaike (1985)).

---

[18] See Yule (1921) on the origins of this technique.
[19] More generally $\alpha(L)\Delta^r\Delta_s x_t = \beta(L)\epsilon_t.$

These arguments are not in Box and Jenkins (1970). An argument which is implicit in their account (see e.g. *op. cit.,* p. 12) is that the ARMA formulation permits a very general serial correlation pattern to be modelled with a small number of parameters. This is exactly the same argument as Jorgenson's (1967) characterization of rational distributed lags. Furthermore, parsimony was important for Box-Jenkins analysis since the widespread use of monthly data in business implied a need for long lag lengths. But it may also have been forced on them.[20] If the original disturbance term on the undifferenced counterpart of (11) is more or less serially independent, differencing will induce a moving average error of exactly the sort implied by the airline model. Hence the need for the ARMA specification. But it is well known (see e.g. Harvey (1981b, p. 41)) that the presence of common factors in $\alpha(L)$ and $\beta(L)$ will give rise to identification problems ('model multiplicity' in Box and Jenkins (1970)) and this requires that either $\alpha(L)$ or $\beta(L)$ or both be specified parsimoniously. The problem of parsimonious model selection is central to time series analysis and, indeed, this is what time series analysts imply by their use of the term 'identification'. For a time series analyst, identification has been achieved if a suitably parsimonious statistical representation of the series in question is found which meets accepted fit criteria. The principal method identification was inspection of the correlogram of the differenced series.

I have already noted (section 2) that there had been a long tradition of time series analysis in the LSE Statistics Department initially through the presence of Durbin and Kendall. M.H. Quenouille's book on multiple time series (Quenouille (1957)) introduced the ARMA model, further discussed in Durbin (1960b). In the Economics Department, Phillips made a significant contribution to the time series literature (Phillips (1966, published 1978)). And I noted (section 2) that Sargan lectured on time series analysis. This LSE background of cooperation between the time series analysts and the time series econometricians is important since it allowed the development of a fruitful dialogue in a controversy between the two disciplines which erupted in the early seventies. Box–Jenkins methods had become widely used in business forecasting and, at the same time, economists were developing structural macroeconometric models. There was clearly some interest in asking whether these 'white box' models could out-perform the 'black box' Box–Jenkins models. Nelson (1972) showed that Box–Jenkins models had superior out-of-sample forecasting performance relative to the major United States macroeconometric models, and Cooper (1972) obtained the same result for purely autoregressive models.[21] There was no reason to suppose that different results would be obtained for the British models.

[20] This argument is due to Andrew Harvey.

[21] Cooper emphasized the structural instability of the econometric models. This emphasized the importance of subjecting estimated equations to extra- (in addition to intra-) sample tests. Use of the Chow (1960) test is standard in work in the LSE tradition—see Harvey (1981a).

If time series models beat structural models it must follow that the structural models do not, in fact, adequately represent the dynamic inter-relationships between the variables of interest, however well they may represent the simultaneous interactions.[22] The LSE response to the time series analysts' challenge was therefore to ask what the econometrician can learn from time series methods. This concern is first clearly in evidence in Hendry and Anderson (1977) where the authors insist that both simultaneous and dynamic aspects of economic interactions be considered *ab initio* and in the context of "an appropriate economic theory" (*ibid*, p. 362).[23] This programme resulted in the evolution of an approach to modelling that allowed data-based dynamics within an overall structural framework. I consider these developments in the next two sections.

5. General to simple modelling

It is widely believed that classical statistical testing procedures are invalidated if the specification to be tested is selected on the basis of preliminary regressions or other data-related procedures. Any data based choice of specification gives rise to 'pretest bias' in subsequent tests. One cannot, for example, pick the single specification out of 100 trials that gives all coefficients 'correctly' and significantly signed, and then claim that this regression supports the theory with which it is necessarily consistent.

A number of articles by Ed Leamer emphasizing the role of specification search in econometrics attracted the attention of British econometricians (Leamer (1974, 1975)), and the publication of Leamer (1978) brought these issues to a wider audience. Leamer has argued[24] that classical testing of equations selected by preliminary regressions requires the assertion of the 'Axiom of Correct Specification' (ACS), and implies that there is no basis for asserting this axiom. He has therefore preferred to adopt a Bayesian approach to model selection. The classically-trained British profession was generally unwilling to follow in this direction and preferred to look for an extension of classical methods. This extension took the form of 'general to simple' (GtoS) methodology.

For time series analysts, forecasting is the only criterion of success, and the 'structure' of the model used is entirely instrumental. Inference is therefore not an issue. However, the LSE econometricians were engaged in structural modelling and therefore needed to be able to argue for the validity of inference on parsimoniously simplified equations.

[22] But see Zellner and Palm (1974) on ARMA models as the final form of structural models. It nevertheless follows that structural models generally exhibited dynamic misspecification.

[23] An immediate product of this concern was the research programme into dynamic models of multiple time series directed by Ken Wallis—see Prothero and Wallis (1976) and Wallis (1977).

[24] See in particular Leamer (1983). I discuss the ACS at greater length in Gilbert (1987).

Identification in time series analysis has two components: discovery of an appropriate simplification, and testing that the proposed simplification is acceptable. The modelling power of GtoS arises from allowing the discovery component to be largely databased. Its acceptability or lack of acceptability as a scientific as distinct from descriptive technique depends on whether or not it can provide a valid basis for statistical inference. The claim that GtoS is valid rests on the fact that unrestricted general hypotheses which contain unrestricted distributed lags on all variables of interest (subject to degrees of freedom constraints) uncontroversially allow valid inference, which however lacks power. Simple models, which if valid will permit more powerful inference, are validated as acceptable simplifications of the unrestricted general model.

Traditional econometrics may be caricatured (as in Gilbert (1986a)) as Simple to General (StoG). One starts with a specification which one hopes will be acceptable, performs (a limited number of) tests on the basis of the estimated simple specification (coefficient signs, magnitudes and significance, Durbin–Watson near two) and, if these tests are unsatisfactory, one complicates the model to correct these deficiencies (additional or alternative lags, autoregressive estimation etc.). The estimated equations reported in Sargan's Colston paper resulted from a search of this sort, and this lack of test structure is still apparent in Hendry (1974).

The stimulus which prompted the LSE econometricians to move to GtoS was Ted Anderson's demonstration that procedures which test sequentially hypotheses in increasing order of restrictiveness are uniformly most powerful (relative to the relevant class—Anderson (1971)). This sequential testing methodology was first applied among the LSE econometricians by Mizon (1977) who looked at three factor CES cross section production function specifications (Cobb–Douglas did best). In this application, the simplifications were suggested by theory. It was less obvious how one would proceed in the time series context of distributed lag estimation once one had decided on the overall lag length by sequential truncation.

Sargan suggested a solution through the COMFAC (common factor) procedure which in principle allows one both to discover and test valid simplifications using information from the unrestricted estimates (Sargan (1980)). Thus both discovery and testing go downward. By contrast, 'standard econometrics' both discovers and tests upwards. Sargan himself described COMFAC as[25]

"... a procedure which starts from a more general specification and tests downward rather than a diagnostic procedure in which having started from the most simple specification one then finds, 'this will not do' and then adds

---

[25] Sargan interviewed in P. C. B. Phillips (1985), p. 132. He also notes (*ibid*, p. 130) that the procedure has not been used to the extent that he "might have hoped".

autoregressive error structures to cure the problem. It always seemed to me that it was worthwhile to start from an unconstrained type of model in order to get the advantages of having simple Wald-type tests for constraints, the kind of constraints that are involved in the common factor specifications."

The Cowles likelihood approach to econometrics suggested the use of likelihood ratio (LR) tests, and Sargan always put great emphasis on the use of the LR to test the overidentifying restrictions in simultaneous models. The difficulty with LR tests is that they require ML (or equivalent) estimation of both null (simple) and alternative (general) models. This may be burdensome if a number of alternative simple hypotheses are to be considered. Wald (1943) had derived an asymptotically equivalent test, now known as the Wald test, which only requires estimates under the alternative hypothesis. The econometric theory of the use of Wald tests to discover the extent to which common factors may be extracted from an unrestricted equation specification was given in Sargan (1980), and it is this theory that underlies the COMFAC procedure.

Consider a general distributed lag relationship between a scalar y_t and a vector x_t:

$$\alpha(L)y_t = \beta(L)'x_t + \epsilon_t \tag{12}$$

where $\alpha(L)$ and $\beta(L)$ are lag polynomials of order m and n respectively and $\{\epsilon_t\}$ is a white noise process. A scalar lag polynomial common factor $\gamma(L)$ of order p ($p \leqslant \min(m, n)$) may be extracted if we can write

$$\alpha(L) = \gamma(L)\alpha^*(L)$$

and

$$\beta(L) = \gamma(L)\beta^*(L)$$

where $\alpha^*(L)$ and $\beta^*(L)$ are lag polynomials of order $m - p$ and $n - p$ respectively. If this is the case we may rewrite (12) as

$$\alpha^*(L)y_t = \beta^*(L)'x_t + \gamma^{-1}(L)\epsilon_t \tag{13}$$

simplifying the structural relationship at the expense of obtaining a serially correlated error. The COMFAC procedure tells one the extent to which simplifications of this sort are possible on the basis solely of estimates of the unrestricted equation (12). The most simple application of this arises if (13) is (1) and $\gamma(L) = 1 - \rho L$. This is the test that apparent residual correlation does in fact represent an autoregressive error and not dynamic misspecification formalized in Hendry (1974) and Hendry and Mizon (1978) but anticipated in Sargan's Colston paper (Sargan (1964)) discussed in section 3 above.

The difficulty with the COMFAC approach is that Wald tests indicate at best the extent to which simplification is possible but do not reveal the form that these simplifications will take. Moreover, Monte Carlo evidence suggests that the tests will have low power in samples of the size normally encountered (Mizon and Hendry (1980)). This motivates a rival approach to

GtoS, associated with David Hendry, in which one discovers upwards (as in standard econometrics) but tests downward (i.e. relative to the unrestricted hypothesis). In this approach no prescription is given for model discovery.

Use of GtoS will eliminate a large number of candidate specifications as being incompatible with the data.[26] Nevertheless, this still leaves the econometrician following this route open to the objection of arbitrariness since in general there will be a large number of false simple specifications which cannot be rejected on this criterion. A further component is required if one is to have some hope of identifying (in the time series sense) the 'true' model. This would be provided by the concept of encompassing anticipated in the important Davidson et al. (1978) consumption function paper.

6. The DHSY consumption function

Sargan's Colston paper provided a paradigm of applied economic practice for the new generation of LSE econometricians. The Davidson et al. (1978) consumption function paper, generally referred to as DHSY, was seized upon by a much wider group of young econometricians, many LSE-trained, throughout the British university system and in the Government Economic Service as defining new standards of best econometric practice.

In many respects DHSY may be seen as a continuation of the programme foreshadowed in Sargan's Colston paper. Like Sargan, DHSY tested (using Sargan's criterion) between the log and the linear specifications. Second, the DHSY model is specified in error correction form. Neglecting the important inflation terms (and a dummy variable) for simplicity of exposition, their model was specified as[27]

$$\Delta_4 \ln C_t = \beta_1 \Delta_4 \ln Y_t - \beta_2 \Delta_1 \Delta_4 \ln Y_t - \beta_3 \ln (C/Y)_{t-4} \qquad (14)$$

It was DHSY which introduced the ECS to a wide audience of potential imitators. And again, DHSY followed Sargan in solving for the steady state of their model. Finally, it is true of DHSY as it was of Sargan's Colston model, that there is very little discussion of economic theory. Indeed, the only economic content of (14) is the long run homogeneity of consumption and income and (for $\beta_1 < 1$ and β_2 small) the implication that consumption will be less variable than income. These observations are consistent with both the Life Cycle and Permanent Income hypotheses.

What of the points of departure? There are two features of DHSY which derive directly from the time series tradition. First note that the paper contains a long introductory section reviewing the data. This is only remarkable in that it had become standard in econometrics to proceed from model to estimates with at most a brief discussion of the data. The view that

---

[26] This is sufficient to make Leamer's extreme bounds (Leamer (1983)) uninteresting, since these bounds are likely to relate to rejectable models—see McAleer et al. (1985).

[27] The intercept was omitted because of collinearity with the (near constant) error correction term in $\ln (C/Y)_{t-4}$.

inspection of the data is useful, even essential, in framing the model to be estimated comes from the time series and not the econometric tradition. Indeed, for Leamer, inspection of the data would generate a form of pretest bias. Second, there is an interesting discussion of differencing. The use of Box–Jenkins equations (9), which are specified entirely in terms of differenced variables, had become widespread. DHSY note that these may either be interpreted as equations which had been filtered by the Δ operator, or as a particular set of restrictions on the undifferenced equation. DHSY were particularly interested in the annual difference filter Δ_4 which removes (or simplifies) seasonal effects. Consider for example the regression on quarterly data given by

$$y_t = \alpha + \beta' x_t + \gamma' q_t + u_t \tag{15}$$

where q_t is a vector of three quarterly dummies. Annual differencing simplifies this to

$$\Delta_4 y_t = \beta' \Delta_4 x_t + v_t \tag{16}$$

where $v_t = \Delta_4 u_t$. Alternatively, if one considers the expanded regression

$$y_t = \alpha + \sum_{i=1}^{4} \delta_i y_{t-i} + \sum_{i=0}^{4} \beta_i' x_{t-i} + \gamma' q_t + u_t \tag{17}$$

(16) requires $\delta_i = 0 (i = 1, 2, 3)$, $\delta_4 = 1$, $\beta_0 + \beta_4 = 0$, $\beta_i = 0$ $(i = 1, 2, 3)$ and (although this is not necessary for the interpretation to be sustained) $\gamma = 0$. The two interpretations are not equivalent since in the latter case ((16) as a restriction of (17)) both $\{u_t\}$ and $\{v_t\}$ should be white noise processes, whilst in the former (annual filter) case, only one of $\{u_t\}$ and $\{v_t\}$ can be white noise. DHSY preferred the former interpretation and set a brief fashion for the annual difference specification. Again the influence of time series methods is apparent.

However, the most novel and, I would argue the most important, feature of the DHSY paper is its insistence that a valid model must not only be able to explain the data to hand, but also why competing models cannot do so.[28] They argued (*ibid*, p. 662) that it is

"... an essential (if minimal) requirement that any new model should be related to existing 'explanations' in a constructive research strategy such that previous models are only supplanted if new proposals account (so far as possible) for previously understood results, and also explain some new phenomena".

This view is very similar to Imre Lakatos' requirement that a new scientific theory should have 'excess empirical content' (Lakatos (1970)). To this end, they related their proposed specification to specifications previously prop-

---

[28] A further important difference between DHSY and Sargan (1964) is DHSY's revision to OLS. The emphasis on least squares estimation of conditional relationships and the requirement that these should have white noise residuals is a particular feature of Hendry's approach to econometrics (Gilbert (1986a)) and raises somewhat different questions to those discussed here.

osed in three earlier papers. The three 'old' models were respecified in terms of the DHSY dataset, and then re-estimated over the DHSY sample allowing an effective comparison—an attempt at "encompassing previous findings" (*ibid*).

The subsequently developed theory of non-nested hypothesis testing, and the associated concept of encompassing, is both one of the most important but also one of the most straightforward developments in econometrics over the past two decades. The initial statistical theory was provided by Cox (1961, 1962). The Cox test was first applied to regression models by Pesaran (1974) working in the Cambridge DAE, and generalized in Pesaran and Deaton (1978). Subsequently, other tests were discovered and there appeared to be an embarrassingly large number of alternative ways of comparing competing hypotheses. The confusion was dispersed by Mizon (1984) and Mizon and Richard (1986) who provided in encompassing theory a unifying framework for these tests.

Consider two rival hypotheses A and B. If $A \subset B$ then A is nested within B and conversely if $B \subset A$. This is the situation to which classical procedures relate. Suppose that neither of these-conditions hold. A and B are then said to be non-nested. We say that A encompasses B if (i) A fits the data better than B and (ii) A can explain the way in which B fails to fit the data. (If B is nested within A then A encompasses B trivially.) Mizon and Richard show that in the non-nested case, the most general test that A encompasses B is provided by the classical F test of B against the encompassing regression implied by $A \cup B$ (i.e. of the common dependent variable against all the regressors in both A and B). This is coefficient encompassing.

This relates crucially to the discussion of whether econometrics needs the ACS. The objection made by Leamer and others to the GtoS regression methodology rests on the arbitrariness of the simplification derived. For Leamer, these simplifications are merely convenient ways of summarizing the data and have no scientific status. If used for inference, they will be positively misleading since the estimated standard errors are relative to the arbitrary simplifying restrictions. For Hendry, by contrast, they are hypotheses that (i) summarize the data, (ii) accord with theory, and (iii) are able to explain why other proposed theoretically sound simplifications are inadequate. Encompassing forms a major plank in the LSE defence against the arbitrariness charge.

7. Conclusions

The LSE was the major centre for econometrics in Britain from the beginning of the fifties. In the fifties, the teaching of econometrics was fostered by the Statistics department. Jim Durbin was particularly enthusiastic. There has always been a close relationship between the Statistics and Economics departments at LSE, and cooperation between the two was encouraged by Bill Phillips. The rapid expansion of econometrics at the

LSE in the early sixties, and its introduction into the teaching of Economics degrees, was due to Phillips more than to any other individual. The latter half of the sixties and the seventies were a period in which econometrics teaching and research rapidly expanded at the LSE under the direction of Denis Sargan who held the econometrics chair. Many of the directions in which this expansion was to take place were mapped out in Sargan's 1964 Colston paper.

A new challenge, perceived in the seventies, was the failure of structural econometric models to 'beat' black box time series models. Both because of the continuing cooperation between the LSE Economics and Statistics departments, and because the LSE econometricians were involved in teaching time series analysis, it was natural that the LSE response would involve combining structural econometrics and time series analysis. The result is the LSE tradition in time series econometrics, which is now the dominant British tradition. The paper with which this tradition is most closely associated in the 1978 DHSY consumption function analysis. It combines a relatively free approach to the specification of distributed lags deriving from time series statistics with a commitment to testing which comes from the structural econometric tradition, and which anticipates the development of encompassing.

This British approach differs markedly from the standard approaches to econometrics in the United States. In part, this is to be explained by the personalities and interests of Durbin, Phillips and Sargan. But it is also an LSE story. LSE statisticians automatically become involved in econometrics because, at LSE, there were no departments of mathematics, biology or medicine which, elsewhere, resulted in probability theory, biometrics and medical statistics proving greater attractions. The reason econometrics developed at LSE and not elsewhere in Britain was because of the close links between the Economics Department and an independent but economics-oriented Statistics Department, links which did not exist elsewhere. These close links promoted a fertilization process in which the LSE econometricians took over elements from time series analysis. The intellectual problem was how to benefit from the data-instigated time series approach to specification (identification) while at the same time being able to make structural inferences in the Cowles tradition. The answer came through the General to Simple procedure, and, latterly, through encompassing.

Institute of Economics and Statistics, Oxford and CEPR

SECTION 3
Applied Studies

Oxford Economic Papers 41 (1989), 131–149

THE EARLY ECONOMETRIC HISTORY OF THE CONSUMPTION FUNCTION

By J. J. THOMAS*

I. Introduction

DESPITE the existence of surveys of early empirical studies of the consumption function, such as Orcutt and Roy (1949) and Ferber (1953), the stylised history of the early econometrics of the consumption function that has become a fashionable feature of many macroeconomic textbooks and survey articles is far from the historical truth.[1] According to this stylised history, in the earliest studies, short periods of time series data were used to estimate a linear consumption function, often referred to now as the 'Keynesian' consumption function, in which real consumption is a linear function of real income

$$(C/P)_t = \alpha + \beta(Y/P)_t + u_t, \qquad 0 < \beta < 1. \tag{1}$$

At first the results obtained supported the specification proposed in equation (1), but as new information appeared doubts were cast on the 'Keynesian' consumption function. Thus, analysis of averages by decade over the long run of US data published by Kuznets (1942) suggested a proportionate relationship between consumption and income, and while it

* I am grateful to Vicky Chick, Meghnad Desai, Mary Morgan, and Robin Rowley for helpful comments on an earlier version of this paper and to the participants in a Workshop in Econometrics at Nuffield College, Oxford in June 1987 for many useful suggestions. I am also very grateful to Coleman Bazelon for assistance with the computation. Finally, I received valuable comments through correspondence with Colin Clark, Karl Fox, Sue Howson, Sir Richard Stone and Jan Tinbergen and from two anonymous referees. None of the aforementioned are responsible for any remaining errors in this paper.

[1] See, for example, Ackley (1961), Evans (1969), Timbrell (1976), Sargent (1979), Parkin and Bade (1982), Evans (1984), Leighton Thomas (1984) and Dornbusch and Fischer (1987).

The earliest version of the stylised history I have found is Friedman (1957). While too long to quote in full, Friedman presents the following account of early empirical studies "Numerical consumption functions were estimated from two kinds of data: first, time series on consumption, savings, income, prices, and similar variables available mostly for the period after World War I; second, budget data on the consumption, savings, and income of individuals and families available from numerous sample surveys made during the past century and a half. Both sources of data seemed at first to confirm Keynes' hypothesis. Current consumption expenditure was highly correlated with income, the marginal propensity to consume was less than unity, and the marginal propensity was less than the average propensity to consume, so the percentage of income saved increased with income. But then a serious conflict of evidence arose. Estimates of savings in the United States by Kuznets for the period since 1899 revealed no rise in the percentage of income saved during the past half century despite a substantial rise in real income. . . . Examination of budget studies for earlier periods strengthens the appearance of conflict." (Friedman (1957), pp. 3–4.)

It is interesting to note how selective is the evidence presented. Thus most of the authors cited above refer to Kuznets (1942), Smithies (1945), Haavelmo (1947) and Duesenberry (1948), although Sargent merely cites Ackley. In contrast, Ferber (1953) contains a very full account of the early empirical studies of the consumption function. See also the survey in Suits (1963).

was possible to fit equation (1) to short sub-periods, it appeared that the intercept moved up over time, the so-called "ratchet" effect. In contrast, the cumulation over time of data obtained in family budget studies (many of them carried out in the 1930s) suggested that the ratio of consumption to income fluctuated cyclically. In response to this new evidence, the specification of the consumption function was modified in a number of ways. For example, to capture the "ratchet" effect, Smithies (1945) introduced a trend term into the consumption function (in per capita terms) estimated from annual US data, 1923–40, as

$$(C/NP)_t = \alpha + \beta(Y/NP)_t + \gamma(\text{Time} - 1922) + u_t, \qquad (2)$$

while Brown (1952) introduced lagged consumption to capture the "ratchet" effect and proposed

$$(C/P)_t = \alpha + \beta(Y/P)_t + \gamma(C/P)_{t-1} + u_t. \qquad (3)$$

The cyclical variations in the relationship were analysed by Duesenberry (1949), who proposed the Relative Income Hypothesis (RIH), in which the ratio of current saving to current income depended on the ratio of current income to past peak income, Y_0, so that

$$(S/Y)_t = \alpha + \beta\{(Y/NP)_t/(Y/NP)_0\} + u_t. \qquad (4)$$

With further work, more satisfactory theories emerged in the form of the Permanent Income Hypothesis (PIH) in Friedman (1957) and the Life Cycle Hypothesis (LCH) in Modigliani and Brumberg (1954).[2]

While the details differ, in outline the stylised history consists of the following four propositions:

(i) Early empirical studies of the consumption function were based on the analysis of short periods of time series data.

(ii) The 'Keynesian' consumption function was the dominant functional form in the early studies.

(iii) Evidence against the 'Keynesian' consumption function cumulated in the mid to late 1940s.

(iv) The theoretical breakthrough came with the work of Friedman and Modigliani.

Evidence will be presented in this paper to show that this stylisation distorts the reality of the early econometric history of the consumption function in three important respects. First, while the simple consumption function of equation (1) may have come to dominate much of the estimation in the 1950s and 1960s, it was neither the first consumption function fitted

---

[2] According to Duesenberry (1949), p. 56, n.1, Modigliani presented his Saving-Income relationship at the Econometric Society Meetings in January 1947. He also published a *verbal* account of the relationship in Modigliani (1947), but the earliest study containing numerical estimates is Modigliani (1949). See Modigliani (1975) for an account of the early work on this hypothesis and further references.

nor the dominant functional form used in the early econometrics of the consumption function. For example, it would appear that the first consumption function to be estimated by conventional regression techniques in response to the publication of Keynes' *General Theory*[3] was that published by Staehle (1937b), in which quarterly time series data for Germany for the period 1928(1) to 1934(4) were used to estimate a non-linear consumption function that also included a variable to measure the effects of changing income distribution. Secondly, and perhaps more seriously, concentrating on the time series studies of the late 1940s and the 1950s and ignoring earlier work gives the false impression that estimation of the consumption function represented the beginning of a new era of macroeconometrics. In reality, the earliest studies of the consumption function in the 1930s and early 1940s show a continuity with a tradition of cross-sectional studies of family expenditure that goes back, via William Ogburn and Carroll Wright in the United States, to the original work of Engel. This explains why the earliest studies demonstrate a concern with the effects of income distribution on consumption behaviour that disappeared with the concentration on aggregate time series data in later studies. Finally, if the wide variety of consumption (and saving) functions that were fitted from the outset is taken as evidence that equation (1) was not generally accepted, it suggests that dissatisfaction with (1) occurred much earlier than is suggested by the stylised history outlined above.

The structure of the paper is as follows. A survey of the functional forms and data used in estimating consumption (or saving) functions in studies published between 1937 and 1950 is presented in Table A1 of Appendix 1. The main features of this table will be discussed in the next section, where the major discrepancies between the stylised history and what really

---

[3] Patinkin (1976) discusses Keynes' use of Kuznets' data to calculate the multiplier for the United States for 1925–33, from which Keynes then deduced the corresponding estimate of the marginal propensity to consume. "Let me at this point note that, to the best of my knowledge, this was the first estimate of the marginal propensity to consume that was based on an examination of statistical time series. And, in any event, . . . , by virtue of his having derived his estimate of the marginal propensity to consume from an estimate of the multiplier, Keynes might be said to have been the first person to have made use (even if unintentionally) of a reduced-form equation to derive an unbiased estimate of a structural parameter!" (Patinkin (1976), p. 234).

One important pre-Keynesian consumption function was produced by Tinbergen as part of a model of the Dutch economy in 1936. This was an interesting model, since as Hansen (1969), p. 331 points out "Money wage changes are explained by a neat Phillips-relation! The rate of change of the money wage rate is a linear function of the rate of change of consumer prices lagged one period, and the level of unemployment." In addition, aggregate consumption and saving were modelled separately as functions of income and a linear time trend, using annual data from 1923 to 1935. However, this study was originally published in Dutch and an English translation was not available until Tinbergen (1959). It is not referred to in the consumption function literature and has been omitted from Table A1.

One other early study that has been omitted from Table A1 is Radice (1939). This article, which is referred to in Clark (1940) p. 472, has been omitted because, although Radice reports a numerical estimate for dS/dY and states that there is some evidence that $\log S = \alpha + \beta \log Y$ would have given a better fit, it is unclear whether he estimated dS/dY from $S = \alpha + \beta Y$ or $S = \beta Y$.

happened are examined. Section III contains an evaluation of the econometric standards of the early work. Section IV presents some conclusions.

II. Early econometric estimates of the consumption function

A survey of the functional forms and data used in estimating consumption functions from 1937 to 1950 is presented in Appendix 1, Table A1, and the main characteristics with respect to Propositions (i) and (ii) of the stylised history are summarised in Tables 1 and 2.[4]

Proposition (i): Early studies of the consumption function were based on the analysis of short periods of time series data.

To evaluate this proposition, the studies reported in Table A1 have been classified in Table 1 by period and the type of data used. It is clear that Proposition (i) is not consistent with the facts, since in the earliest period, from 1937 to 1940, cross-sectional data were used in almost half of the studies reported. While the proportion of studies using time series data rises sharply over the period, overall the number of studies using cross-sectional data represent about 25% of those covered in Table A1.

At first sight, the fact that five of the first ten studies make use of cross-sectional data, may seem odd, but in the historical context this should be expected for two reasons. First, by the time the *General Theory* was published, a considerable amount of statistical work had been undertaken in

TABLE 1

Data used in early consumption function studies

Period	Data used [XS]	[TS]	Total
1937–40	5	6	11
1941–45	2	10	12
1946–50	3	15	18
Total	10	31	41*

Note. [XS] = cross-sectional data, [TS] = time series data. (*The total in Table 1 is 41 compared with 40 in Table A1 because one study used both [XS] and [TS].)

---

[4] The table is based on Orcutt and Roy (1949); Ferber (1953), a detailed survey of Volumes I to IV of the *AEA Index of Economic Journals* and references obtained through background reading. I am grateful to Andrew Roy for providing me with a copy of Orcutt and Roy. The decision to terminate Table A1 in 1950 is obviously arbitrary, but after that date the number of empirical studies of consumption or saving rises very rapidly. Thus a scan of article titles in the volumes of the *AEA Index* for 1951–54 and 1954–59 suggests totals of 22 and 26 articles respectively related to these topics, quite apart from the empirical results published in monographs and other sources not covered by the *AEA Index*.

a number of microeconomic areas (for example, the estimation of demand and supply functions for individual markets and commodities, production functions for individual industries and budget studies of expenditures for individuals or households[5]). Among budget studies, as early as 1919, W. F. Ogburn (1919b) had submitted sample data on the incomes and expenditure of 200 families in Washington D.C. in 1916 to regression analysis.[6] Defining y as annual family income, s as 'saving' (i.e. the deficit or surplus, defined as income minus total expenditure) and f as family size in standardised male units, Ogburn reported the following estimated 'saving' functions[7]

$$s = -166.45 + 0.144y \tag{5}$$

$$s = -82.70 + 0.149y - 26.31f. \tag{6}$$

Ogburn's work was quoted extensively in Zimmerman (1936), as well as by Kaplan (1938), who used sample data on total expenditure (e) and family

[5] Paul Douglas's work on production functions is discussed in Douglas (1948, 1976) and Samuelson (1979). Stigler (1954) provides an historical account of early demand studies and budget studies.

[6] William Fielding Ogburn (1886–1959) was a graduate student at Columbia University, where, as a student of Henry Moore, he developed his interests in quantitative techniques. He obtained his Ph.D in 1912 and taught economics, political science, history and sociology at Princeton, Reed College and the University of Washington between 1911 and 1918, before becoming Chairman of the Department of Economics and Sociology at Barnard College from 1919 to 1927. In 1927 he became a senior Professor in the Department of Sociology at the University of Chicago, where he remained until his retirement in 1951. For an account of Ogburn's influence on the development of quantitative methods at Chicago, where he was a friend of another student of Henry Moore, the economist Henry Schultz, see Bulmer (1984).

During World War I, Ogburn had a period of service in Washington D.C. as the Director of the Cost of Living Division of the National War Labor Board and in the Bureau of Labor Statistics and it was here that he pioneered methods of analysing family budgets and constructing index numbers in the course of many studies of the standard of living, for example, Ogburn (1919a, c and d). His major economic preoccupation was with the role of living standards in the determination of wages and he was a strong advocate of minimum wage legislation, Ogburn (1923). See Duncan (1964) for further information and a bibliography.

[7] One intriguing feature of this article is that in the text on p. 378 Ogburn describes Diagram I, showing the plot of actual 'saving' against income with the estimated simple regression line (5) superimposed. However, Diagram I does not appear in the article and a footnote reports that "This diagram was not available for the Quarterly, but will be published in another edition of the Author's work–ED". A search of Ogburn's publications of around this time has failed to reveal the missing diagram and the noted Ogburn scholar, Professor Barbara Laslett, has been unable to clarify the mystery. This diagram, had it appeared, would have been the first representation of an estimated cross-sectional 'Keynesian' saving function known to this author.

Another pre-Keynesian pioneer was Jessica B. Peixotto of the University of California, Berkeley. Cookingham (1987) notes that in several budget studies (Peixotto 1927, 1929), Peixotto "found and described a relative-income theory of consumption. Families strived to reach the level of consumption achieved by others with similar educational backgrounds. College professors, for instance, tried to live as physicians, lawyers, and other well-paid professionals did. Since their incomes were markedly lower, academics had difficulty saving and struggled to make ends meet, while doctors lived comfortably and accumulated wealth. Typographers, on the other hand, were reasonably content with their economic position, given their income and peer group. Peixotto concluded that acceptable minimum consumption standards varied by occupational group, and consumer preferences were not independent." (Cookingham, 1987, p. 53.)

income (y) for families in Chicago in 1935–6 to estimate separate total expenditure functions for Wage Earner Families (WEF) and Salaried Business Families (SBF), obtaining

$$\text{(WEF)} \quad e = 357 + 0.747y \tag{7}$$

$$\text{(SBF)} \quad e = 1145 + 0.538y. \tag{8}$$

A number of the authors of the early studies listed in Table A1 had experience of working with cross-section data.. For example, Staehle, who had worked at the International Labour Office in Geneva, had published an *Econometrica* survey article on family budgets (Staehle 1934b) and articles on income distribution (Staehle 1934a, 1937b). Gilboy, in addition to her distinguished work in economic history, had also published a number of empirical articles on demand analysis (Gilboy (1931, 1932a, b, 1934) and by 1937 was one of a group of Harvard professors co-operating with the Massachusetts Emergency Relief Agency in a study of the unemployed in Cambridge, Mass. (Gilboy 1937, 1938(b), Sorenson and Gilboy 1937). Polak was assistant to Tinbergen at the League of Nations in Geneva (see Tinbergen (1939), p. 5) and both were aware of Staehle's study and its concern with income distribution, while Mendershausen, formerly of the University of Geneva, was appointed as a Fellow by the Cowles Commission in 1938, where he worked (among other things) on the inequality of income distribution.[8] Since in Chapters 8 and 9 of the *General Theory*, Keynes had formulated his theory of consumer behaviour in microeconomic terms, it was to be expected that attempts would be made to examine his theory in the light of family sample data, particularly by those who felt that Keynes had not placed sufficient emphasis on the distribution of income in determining consumers' expenditure.[9] Thus, it is possible to view the early econometric studies of the consumption function as a continuation of the long tradition of budget studies in economics and a gradual move towards the estimation of macroeconomic relationships, rather than the sudden dawn of a new era.

A second reason for the relative importance of cross-sectional data in the

[8] Polak's article is a direct outcome of this work, since Tinbergen (1939), p. 37 contains identical functional forms and similar numerical results to those of Polak. For this reason Tinbergen's study has not been listed separately in Table A1.

I wrote to Professor Tinbergen in order to clarify the degree of interaction among the group of economists working in Geneva in the 1930s and received the following reply: "The people you mention [Polak, Staehle, Mendershausen and Woytinsky] often met and were friends, except for Woytinsky, whom I only knew from his publications . . . Staehle, Polak, Mendershausen and I were members of the Econometric Society and participated in the European meetings, once a year between 1931 (Lausanne) and 1938; but saw each other frequently in Geneva." (Letter from Jan Tinbergen to the author, dated 10 July 1987.)

[9] Two of the earliest empirical studies of the consumption function, Staehle (1937) and Gilboy (1938a), were direct criticisms of Keynes for failing to take account of changes in income distribution in his theory of consumption. This topic and Keynes' reaction to the early econometric work on the consumption function will not be discussed here. See Thomas (1985).

early studies reported in Table A1 was the shortage of readily available national income data in a suitable form for estimating consumption functions. Patinkin points out that ". . . as far as I can judge . . . the pre-World War I estimates of all countries were of national income by factor shares (wages, profits) or by industrial origin (agriculture, manufacturing). They were not of national income—or, rather, product—by final use (viz., consumption and investment, respectively)." (Patinkin, 1976, p. 241.)

The fact that some of the earliest studies, even including the first one listed in Table A1, made use of time series data may seem to cast doubt on the shortage of national income data, but before drawing this conclusion one should look carefully at the data and the authors concerned. For example, the quarterly data on labour income and its distribution for Germany used by Staehle were "available as a by-product of the German invalidity-insurance scheme .. (which incidentally is compulsory for all wage earners) . . ." (Staehle, 1937b, pp. 135–6). The total number of individuals covered by this scheme in 1928 was about 18 million and the official publication of such detailed information seems unusual for the time. Among other early contributors should be noted the presence of such pioneers in the collection and construction of national income data as Colin Clark and one of his students, Richard Stone.[10] Thus, it would be inaccurate to conclude that suitable national income data did not exist. Rather, where these data did exist, they were generally not easily available. The days of routinely published national income data available to any economist with an econometric turn of mind were yet to come, though many of the studies published towards the end of the period covered in Table A1, after US Department of Commerce annual data for 1923–1940 became available in 1945, might be described in this way.[11]

Proposition (ii): Equation (1) was the dominant functional form.

In order to investigate the functional form of the equations used in early studies of the consumption function, the detailed results presented in Table A1 are summarised in Table 2.

From this summary it is clear that while equation (1) does appear among the early empirical studies of the consumption function, it is mainly conspicuous by its absence among a wide variety of functional forms and array of additional variables. Overall, the results summarised in Table 2 would suggest that equation (1) never dominated the early estimation of the consumption function in the way that is suggested in the stylised history outlined above.

---

[10] See Clark (1985), p. 63.
[11] Thus the emphasis in the stylised history on the use of short time series to estimate the consumption function does describe studies carried out towards the end of the period covered in Table A1, but still fails to take note of the wide variety of functional forms being fitted.

TABLE 2
Functional forms used in early consumption function studies

Period	Equation (1)			Other functional forms			Total
	[XS]	[TS]	Total	[XS]	[TS]	Total	
1937–40	1	1	2	4	8	12	14
1941–45	1	5	6	1	8	9	15
1946–50	2	7	9	4	24	28	37
Total	4	13	17	9	40	49	66*

Notes. Equation (1) includes *both* $C = \alpha + \beta Y$ and $S = \gamma + \delta Y$. "Other functional forms" includes $\log c = \alpha + \beta \log y$ and $\log s = \gamma + \delta \log y$, as well as all other formulations. (*The total number of cases in Table 2 exceeds the totals in Table A1 and Table 1 since many studies used a number of alternative formulations of the consumption or savings function.)

The next feature of Table A1 to be discussed in this section is the wide range of functional forms and explanatory variables. Functional forms range from logarithmic to linear, with the variables in the linear model being variously defined in current, constant or per capita terms, while in some studies the dependent variable is the consumption (or saving)/income ratio. Additional variables used in the analysis of consumption or saving include measures of income distribution, time trends, lagged values of income, changes in income, the highest value of income attained in earlier years, the disaggregation of national income into its labour and non-labour components, non-linear terms (such as the square of income) and inter-active terms (such as the product of income and time), as well as variables to measure the effects of changes in the distribution of income.[12]

Functional form. The choice of the log-log relationship in the cross-sectional studies of Gilboy (1938a, 1941) represents the influence of earlier budget studies and an interest in computing elasticities, since plotting expenditure against income on a double logarithmic scale provided a simple method of estimating elasticities.[13] In the case of Stone and Stone (1938), the choice seems to have been determined by an examination of the data.

The use of the consumption (or saving)/income ratio reflected a number of factors. For example, Staehle (1937b) chose the expenditure/income ratio in order to test what he understood to be Keynes's hypothesis that the marginal propensity to consume declined with increasing income. In the case of Mendershausen (1939, 1940), the saving/income ratio was used partly to deal with the problem of heteroscedasticity, though as Mack (1952), p. 54, n.16, points out, these studies present an early formulation of the hypothesis that ". . . the higher the community's income level the lower

[12] The role of income distribution in the consumption function is discussed in Thomas (1985).
[13] Gilboy (1939), while still concerned with the need to test Keynes' psychological law, admitted there were advantages to splitting the expenditure elasticity, $\eta = (dc/dy)/(c/y) = (mpc)/(apc)$ into its components of *mpc* and *apc*.

its disposition to save." (Mendershausen (1940), p. 134), which was later taken up by Modigliani and others.

Definition of the variables. Despite Keynes' argument for real income, rather than nominal income, as the appropriate variable in the consumption function (Keynes (1971), VII p. 91), real income was used in only ten of the 24 studies using aggregate data, as compared with fourteen using nominal data. Whereas the case for using real income was restated in a number of the studies using this variable, the question of choice is generally ignored in the studies that use nominal income. Per capita data in real terms, first used in Samuelson (1941) on the grounds that "The same real income divided up among more people cannot be expected to yield the same real consumption expenditure." (Samuelson (1941), p. 252), was used in a total of six of the studies reported in Table A1.

Additional explanatory variables. There is no simple way to account for the choice of additional explanatory variables in the consumption/saving functions that appear in Table A1. In some cases they reflect the availability of disaggregate income data (Polak (1939), Tinbergen (1942b) and Klein (1947b)), while in others they represent attempts to deal with awkward features of the empirical data. In the latter case, there are some studies that introduce time trends, the square or first difference of income, as well as the product of income and time, presumably as the outcome of an exercise in data mining, since there is no attempt to provide a theoretical justification for the specification chosen. In other studies, the introduction of lagged income (for example, Clark (1938), Stone and Stone (1938) and Tinbergen (1942b)) represented an attempt to model a dynamic adjustment process, while the appearance of past peak income (Clark (1948), Duesenberry (1949) and Modigliani (1949)) reflected the increasing influence of the RIH, already referred to in the stylised history of the consumption function.

Proposition (iii): The evidence against equation (1) appeared in the mid-1940s.

What is clear from the summary given above is that the modifications to the consumption function, which were alleged to have been a response to the failure of equation (1) in the mid-1940s, in fact occurred much earlier at a time when it was *not* the dominant form of the consumption function. For example, a linear time trend was introduced into the consumption function by Stone and Stone (1938) and used widely in other studies long before its inclusion in the article by Smithies (1945) cited in the stylised history. Similarly, in an article that acknowledged the assistance of Milton Friedman, Mendershausen (1940), p. 131 compared graphically for 1935–36 "... the income-savings relationships for all whites and all negroes. The difference is quite striking." Finally, as Tobin (1968), p. 364 notes, Samuelson (1943), pp. 34–5 proposed a "ratchet" model of the consumption function.

Even a casual reading of the early literature shows that many authors were aware of the complexities of consumers' behaviour.[14] For example, the concept of the life cycle, first described in Rowntree (1902), was used by rural sociologists in the United States to investigate the standard of living of farm families during the Depression. Not only was expenditure related to the stage in the family life cycle, but the stage in the life cycle, for example the number of children and their ages, also determined the degree to which the farm family could reduce cash expenditures by using more unpaid family labour (Kirkpatrick (1934)). In a comment on the family classification used in the Survey of Consumer Purchases it was suggested that "A further break-down of the family types used would be highly desirable, not only to shed more light upon changes in consumption with changes in the family life cycle, but also for many other purposes." (Monroe (1937), p. 38.)[15]

The relevance of relative income positions and the time needed for adjustment were also known. Thus

> In the absence of further information we have, therefore, to *assume* that when a £1,000 a year family gets £900 a year it spends and saves like a £900 a year family. From a realistic point of view this may not seem satisfactory. It may be thought that as incomes fall an attempt will be made to preserve the old standard of life, and so expenditure will not fall to the level of a £900 a year family. . . . Expenditure would no longer depend on income, but on a conventional standard of living to which our imaginary families cling tenaciously. (Stone and Stone (1938), p. 2.)

> A farmer's disposition to save is due primarily to two causes: first, the irregularity and variability of his income; second, the fact that he is continually tempted to reinvest for the purpose of improving his own farm business. Owing to the irregularity and variability of his income, he is inclined to set his scale of living according to what he can count on regularly, his egg and butter money, say, and

[14] For example, Tebbutt (1933), having carried out a detailed analysis of consumers' expenditure during the early years of the depression concludes that "Any of the present measures of business conditions shows a sharp decline from the prosperity period of 1928 and the boom period of 1929 to the depressed conditions existing in 1931 and 1932. Consumption of goods by the mass of the people, on the other hand, has held up remarkably well considering the extreme severity of the business depression. . . . Consumption, then, does not fluctuate entirely with business conditions; only in cases of severe adversity in business, such as the prevailing conditions in 1932, does consumption appear to decline at all substantially, and even then not in the same proportion as the decline which takes place in business as a whole."

[15] For further discussion of the concept of the life-cycle in rural sociology, see Loomis and Beegle (1950). Woytinsky (1943) discusses the concept and, as an example of its application, cites Sydenstricker, King and Wiehl (1924). This study, which was made in connection with an epidemiological investigation of pellagra, examined the economic status of about 4,000 worker families in 24 South Carolina cotton-mill villages in 1924.

One of the anonymous referees suggested that Joseph S. Davis might also have been aware of the life cycle concept. This is borne out to some extent, since in his Presidential Address to the American Economic Association (Davis 1945) we find the following passage: "Standards of living most obviously change for individuals, as they progress from infancy through childhood, adolescence, youth, maturity, family life in its successive phases, and old age. Needs, preferences, and priorities alter through this human cycle. For the family groups in which most individuals live, moreover, standards of living change as the group's composition undergoes successive alterations." (Davis, 1945, p. 12.) I am grateful to the referee for suggesting this reference.

except for rather unusual consumption expenditure, to save and reinvest the rest. (Hoyt (1938), p. 309.)[16]

It must be assumed that individuals in one income group will on the average act in the same way as individuals in the higher (or lower) income groups, should they be moved to those groups, in the time interval studied. Obviously it will take time before this is the case. It is well known that a period of adjustment occurs when individuals find themselves suddenly with greater or lesser income. (Gilboy (1939), p. 71)

Studies of families on work relief indicated that, with their incomes cut in half or more, they made every attempt to maintain their previous level of living. They were not able to do so, but they went into debt in the attempt, and the pattern of their expenditures was more nearly related to that of the employed group from which they had come than to the suggested and more economical budgets of relief families. (Gilboy (1941), p. 163.)

While the authors quoted above are describing something very close to the permanent income hypothesis, this concept did not appear until somewhat later.[17] Thus, while familiarity with the cross-sectional data had

[16] The important role of Iowa State College in the early development of consumption studies should be recorded. As Hoyt (1938) acknowledged, "In the days when home economics meant to most people only cooking and sewing, Dean Anna E. Richardson of Iowa State College perceived that home economics must take account of the principles of economics as they relate to the use of goods and services, that home economics itself is, to a large degree, applied consumption." (Hoyt, p. vi.) The work at Iowa State College began under Hazel Kyrk (see Kyrk (1923)), who later moved to the University of Chicago, where she supervised Margaret Reid's doctoral thesis (1931). Reid taught at Iowa State College from 1930 to 1943. See Reid (1934, 1938).

The early emphasis on consumption studies at Iowa State College may be seen in connection with the heavy emphasis in early research in Home Economics on studies of the rural cost of living and farmers' living standards (see, for example Zimmerman (1927) and Waite (1929). In commenting on Waite, Kyrk argues that "those of us who are interested in research in consumption should seek avowedly the laws or uniformities of consumer's behavior through the analysis of data on expenditures and not make 'cost of living' studies." (Kyrk (1929), p. 576.) Hoyt and Meints (1932) is also of interest in discussing the importance of conspicuous consumption as an explanation of differences in expenditure patterns of faculty at the University of California and at Iowa State College.

[17] There can be little doubt that Friedman was aware of the cross-sectional studies, since he was employed by the National Resources Committee from 1935 to 1937, where he was involved in planning a major analysis of family budget data in the Study of Consumer Expenditure in the United States (see Kneeland, Schoenberg and Friedman (1936)). The importance of his knowledge of these data is shown by the number of acknowledgements to his assistance in published studies. See, for example Gilboy (1939), p. 638, n.1, Mendershausen (1940), p. 122, n.1 and Wallis (1942) p. 180, n.6. In the Preface to Friedman (1957), having noted that he had not done any empirical work on consumption since 1935–37, the auther states "I nonetheless kept in close touch with empirical research on consumption, thanks to the combined accident of my wife's occasional interest in the field and of our joint friendship with Dorothy Brady. Mrs. Brady's unrivaled knowledge of the empirical evidence from family budget data, penetrating insights into their explanation, and deep understanding of the scientific problems involved in their analysis occasioned a series of conversations on the interpretation of consumption data, in which discussions Margaret Reid subsequently joined. Miss Reid, with characteristic enthusiasm, persistence, and ingenuity proceeded to put to a crucial test the hypothesis that had been evolving out of these conversations. When it seemed to be passing the

(continued overleaf)

revealed many empirical regularities, what was missing from the early studies was any *theoretical* model for incorporating the information into the study of the consumption function. The provision of such a model involved a considerable period of gestation[18] and in the United States these problems were largely ignored by economists working with the consumption function, who increasingly turned their attention to the problem of predicting the course the US economy was likely to follow in the recovery period after World War II.[19]

III. An econometric evaluation of early studies of the consumption function

Many of the early studies of the consumption function reported in Table A1 are unsophisticated by modern econometric standards, since the majority involve single equation estimation by ordinary least squares and usually only parameter estimates are reported without standard errors or other supporting statistical information.[20] However, a more detailed examination of the studies suggests that they may be classified into two periods. During the first, which lasted up to 1942, some of the studies show a concern for the statistical properties of the estimates and problems of estimation that predates later, better known developments. The second

---

(*footnote 17 continued*)
test with flying colors, she pressed me to write up the underlying theory so that she could refer to it in a paper presenting her conclusions." (p. ix.) He also notes that "The earliest written version of the hypothesis I can find in my files is in a four page typescript dated June 8, 1951." (p. ix, n,1).

However, Brady (1951), p. 22 n. 29 and Reid (1952), p. 172 both credit Friedman and Kuznets (1945) with the introduction of the concept of the permanent component of income. Friedman (1957), p. 6 also refers to the development of the concept in the 1945 paper.

[18] There are probably many reasons for the long period of gestation, but a careful chronological analysis of the evolution of Friedman's economic thought would suggest that within his programme for the development of monetarist economics, the restatement of the Quantity Theory of Money was of great importance and that it was not until his empirical studies on the stability of the demand for money function that it was necessary to turn his attention to the theory of the consumption function. See Butler (1985).

Franco Modigliani, who emigrated to the United States from Italy at the outbreak of World War II, was a part-time Instructor in Economic Statistics at Barnard College of Columbia University from 1942–1944 and Assistant Professor of Mathematical Economics at the New School of Social Research from 1943–1948, where he was working on macroeconomic theory. He seems to have become aware of the problems of estimating the saving function with the work published in Modigliani (1947) was probably unaware of the earlier literature.

Both Friedman and Modigliani stress the importance of the work of Dorothy Brady for their studies, and she provides an important link with the early cross-sectional studies discussed above, having published an analysis of data collected in the Study of Consumer Purchases in Brady (1938). Faith Williams, Brady's co-author in the survey article Brady and Williams (1945), had also published an early analysis of family expenditure, Williams (1937), in which she cited the earlier work of Ogburn (1919a, b).

[19] This is typified by the group of articles in the January 1945 issue of *Econometrica* and the articles in the November 1946 issue of the *Review of Economic Statistics* responding to Woytinsky (1946).

[20] In this context one may note that the early study by Ogburn (1919a, b) provided considerable information on goodness-of-fit and standard errors of the parameter estimates.

period contains two conflicting elements since, while the general level of econometric competence declines, the work of the Cowles Commission was beginning to have a strong, positive influence on the estimation of the consumption function.

The first period reflects one of the main theoretical interests of the 1930s, the problem of multicollinearity, but reactions to the problem differed. For example, Staehle and Polak use confluence analysis and report the results of bunch map analysis, but for some, the possibility of multicollinearity seems to have provided a good reason for not running additional multiple regressions, perhaps an understandable reaction given the computing facilities of the period![21]

There are some interesting individual contributions. For example, among a number of suggestions for dealing with the problem of multicollinearity, both Polak (1939) and Tinbergen (1939) proposed using cross-sectional estimates of some of the parameters combined with time series data, or the possibility of eliminating a variable by minimising the residual sum of squares (RSS) while conducting a grid search over one of the parameters. Mendershausen (1939) used weighted regression to deal with the problem of heteroscedasticity and used analysis of variance to test for differences between cities and Ezekiel (1942) carried out informal stability tests. Tinbergen (1942b) discussed testing for serial correlation, but the first study in Table A1 to report a formal test for serial correlation is Modigliani (1949), which uses the von Neumann ratio. In a comment on this paper, Leontief had plotted Modigliani's residuals against time and, having demonstrated graphically the presence of a cycle, argued for the introduction of lagged income into the consumption function. However, that well known applied economist, Paul Samuelson, had already in 1941 used the fact that the plotted residuals from his estimated consumption function appeared non-random to argue for the need to respecify his model and thus presented the first published diagnostic use of residual analysis in the econometrics of the consumption function.[22]

With a few exceptions the second period shows a decline in econometric standards, with a large number of studies mining the short time series of US

[21] With respect to the problems of computation, I received the following comment from Professor Sir Richard Stone: "I also like your emphasis on the limitations set by the computing facilities of those days. When my 1938 paper appeared I was a clerk in an insurance office and all the calculations had to be done at home on a Monroe hand calculator by my wife or myself. We thought the distribution of income should be important but since the only measure we had, Pareto's alpha for postwar United States didn't seem to do much good we gave it up." (Letter from Sir Richard Stone to the author, dated 14 October 1987.)

[22] It appears that Samuelson was taught the importance of examining regression residuals by his teacher, Paul Douglas. Douglas had examined the residuals from estimated production functions to provide further economic evidence on the 'fit' of the function. For example, positive residuals would be expected in industries characterised by monopoly or highly imperfect competition. See Douglas (1976), p. 909, where it is claimed that the study by Bronfenbrenner and Douglas (1939) "first introduced an analysis of the deviations of the actual from the theoretical as measured in the standard errors of estimate." I am grateful to Robin Rowley of McGill University for bringing this Samuelson–Douglas connection to my attention.

annual data from 1920 to 1940, or subperiods thereof. OLS parameter estimates are reported and there is some graphical discussion of the fitted relations, but in the debate between Woytinsky (1946) and his critics over the questions of whether the consumption function varied between prosperous and depressed years, one finds Bennion (1946) reporting the results of fitting equation (1) separately to eight prosperous, five semi-prosperous and five depression years.[23]

At the same time, one also finds the first signs of the work of the Cowles Commission on the problems of simultaneous equation estimation. This began with Klein's comprehensive criticism of Ezekiel's failure to recognise the problem of identifying the savings and investment functions in Ezekiel (1942)[24] and is reflected in the use of Limited-Information Maximum-Likelihood estimation in the econometric work of Klein and Haavelmo.

The reason for the decline in econometric standards during this time may well reflect the fact that since the relevant US annual data were now readily available and, thanks to the Doolittle technique, the computation of regression parameter estimates was not difficult, the way was open for many economists who were not statistically trained to enter the important policy debates by estimating consumption functions. More generally, this state of affairs continued long after the period covered in this survey and has only gradually been improved by the increased training of economists in econometrics and the need felt by non-quantitative economists to understand the output of the more sophisticated diagnostic tests of computer software packages.

IV. Conclusions

This paper has outlined the stylised history of the early econometric history of the consumption function that has become widely used in many macroeconomic textbooks and surveys. This claims that the dominant functional form in early work on the consumption function was the 'Keynesian' consumption function of equation (1) and that it was only after this function had failed to explain the long-run time series data provided in Kuznets (1942) and the results of cross-section studies for the United States that it was modified. After various attempts, such as those by Smithies (1945) and Brown (1952) with time series data and Duesenberry (1949) based on cross-sectional data, the consumption function was finally able to explain these data with the development during the mid-1950s of Friedman's Permanent Income Hypothesis and Modigliani and Brumberg's Life Cycle Hypothesis. It has been shown that this stylised history is a travesty of what actually happened and that the early work on the consumption function was

---

[23] With hindsight it is clear that this debate might have reached more conclusive results if dummy variables had been in use at this time.

[24] Since this represents the first discussion of the identification problem in the context of a simple macroeconomic model, it seems strangely neglected in the econometric literature. I am grateful to Meghnad Desai for bringing this reference to my attention.

both much richer, in terms of the insights into consumers' behaviour it produced, and superior econometrically to much of the work that followed.

A more accurate stylised history of the early econometric studies of the consumption function would be as follows. The early response to Keynes' theory of the consumption function did not represent a sudden blossoming of applied macroeconometrics, since neither economists trained in macro-economic theory nor the relevant time series data were generally available. Instead, much of the early work was conducted by economists who had experience working with cross-sectional data on family expenditure studies. Their awareness of the complexities of family expenditure meant that equation (1) never dominated these studies and many of the puzzles that were to be answered by theoretical developments in the mid-1950s were well known in the 1930s. By the mid-1940s, when annual US time series data from 1923 to 1940 became available, there were more studies using equation (1), though it never dominated in the way the stylised history suggests, and the standard of the econometric work declined. While the publication a long run time series data for the US in Kuznets (1942) did raise serious questions regarding the adequacy of equation (1) and its considerable importance should not be underestimated, the developments in the theory of the consumption function associated with Friedman and Modigliani, being both essentially *microeconomic* theories, were more affected by the results of the cross-sectional studies that had been carried out in the 1930s, with the work of Dorothy Brady being particularly important.

Econometrics is a relatively youthful subject and has made remarkable progress in terms of its theoretical and computational development, if not in terms of the average quality of its applications. The result of this rapid progress is that econometricians have been too busy doing econometrics to spend much time considering the history of the subject. The result is that it has been left to others to construct a history of econometrics, with distorted results in the case of the consumption function. It could be argued that now is the time for econometricians to write their own history of the subject, particularly while some of the pioneers are still available to contribute to an accurate account of the early work.[25] If we miss this opportunity, we may deserve the old maxim that 'history is merely a pack of tricks we play on the dead'.

APPENDIX 1

Key to the notation in Table A1

General: Lower case letters refer to cross-sectional [XS] data on individual or household consumption (c), saving (s), expenditure (e) or income (y), while upper case letters refer to

---

[25] The writings of Karl Fox on the work of Ezekiel and other United States agricultural economists in the 1930s (Fox 1986, 1987) and the *Econometric Theory* interview with Jan Tinbergen (Magnus and Morgan 1987) represent important contributions to such a history of econometrics.

time series [TS] data on aggregate variables. The subscript $-n$ indicates a variable lagged by the corresponding proportion of a time period. A = annual and Q = quarterly data. (Data published) indicates data given in original study.

Specific symbols:

ALPHA	Pareto's α, taken without regard for sign.
B	A measure of income inequality, defined as follows: Let CMI = Cumulative Median Income and OMI = Ordinary Median Income. Then $B = (\text{CMI} - \text{OMI})/\text{CMI}$.
C	Aggregate consumption in nominal terms.
M	Narrow definition of money stock in nominal terms.
N	Population.
P	Price index.
P_f	Index of farm prices.
P_w	Index of wage rates.
r	Interest rate.
R	Index of retail sales in nominal terms.
S	Aggregate saving in nominal terms.
S_E	Aggregate enterprise saving in nominal terms.
t	Linear time trend.
Y	Aggregate income in nominal terms.
Y_f	Aggregate farm income in nominal terms.
Y_g	Aggregate speculative income in nominal terms.
Y_h	Aggregate highest incomes in nominal terms.
Y_l	Aggregate lowest incomes in nominal terms.
Y_L	Aggregate labour income in nominal terms.
Y_{NL}	Aggregate non-labour income in nominal terms.
Y_0	Highest income attained in earlier years.

TABLE A1

A summary of consumption functions published 1937–1950

Author and date Data	Function(s) fitted
(1) Staehle (August 1937) [TS] Germany (Q) 1928(1)–1934(4) (Data published.)	$(R/Y_L) = \alpha + \beta(Y_L/P_w) + \gamma B$
(2) Kaplan (March 1938) [XS] US 1918 and 1935 Data on families in Chicago and Denver.	$e = \alpha + \beta y$
(3) Dirks (August 1938) [TS] Germany (Q) 1925(3)–1934(4)	$\Delta R = \alpha + \beta\{(\Delta Y_L)^\gamma\}_{-\frac{1}{2}}$
(4) Staehle (August 1938) [As in (1) above, in mean deviation form.]	$(R/P_w) = \beta(Y_L/P_w)$ $(R/P_w) = \beta(Y_L/P_w) + \gamma B$
(5) Clark (September 1938) [TS] UK (Q) 1929(1)–1937(4)	$(C/P) = \alpha + \beta(Y/P) + \gamma(Y/P)_{-5}$

TABLE A1 *(continued)*

Author and date Data	Function(s) fitted
(6) Stone and Stone (October 1938) (i) [XS] Japan 1925–6, US non-farm families 1929	$\log c = \alpha + \beta \log y$
Germany 1926–7, US farm families 1929	$\log c = \alpha + \beta \log y + \gamma (\log y)^2$
(II) [TS] Germany 1932–36, Sweden 1896–1916 & 1923–30	$C = \alpha + \beta Y$
Germany 1925–32, Holland 1923–32	$C = \alpha + \beta Y + \gamma t$
US 1919–35, UK 1929(3)–1935(3), Poland 1928–36 (Data published.)	$C = \alpha + \beta(0.75\gamma + 0.25Y_{-1})$
(7) Gilboy (November 1938) [XS] US 1935–6. Data on Families in various cities	$\log e = \alpha + \beta \log y$
and also by occupation.	$\log s = \gamma + \delta \log y$
(8) Polak (February 1939) [XS] US (A) 1919–32 (Data published.)	$(C - Y_f) = \beta_0 + \beta_1 Y_1 + \beta_2 Y_h + \beta_3 Y_g + \beta_4 \Delta P_f$ $+ \beta_5 \text{ALPHA} + \beta_6 t$
(9) & (10) Mendershausen (September 1939 & August 1940) [XS] US 1935–36	$(s/y) = \alpha + \beta y + \gamma(1/y)$
(11) Samuelson (1941) [TS] US (A) 1921–39	$(C/NP) = \alpha + \beta(Y/NP)$
	$(C/NP) = \alpha + \beta(Y/NP) + \gamma t$
	$(C/NP) = \alpha + \beta(Y/NP) + \delta(S_E/NP)$
(12) Gilboy (November 1941) [XS] US 1935–36	$\log e = \alpha + \beta \log y$
(13) Tinbergen (February 1942) [TS] UK 1874–1910 (Data published.)	$C = \beta_0 + \beta_1 Y_L + \beta_2 Y_{NL(-1)} + \beta_3 Y_{NL(-2)} + \beta_4 P + \beta_5 P_{-1}$ $+ \beta_6 \Delta C + \beta_7 t$
(14) Ezekiel (March 1942) [TS] US (A) 1920–39	$C = \beta_0 + \beta_1 Y + \beta_2 \Delta Y + \beta_3 t + \beta_4 t^2$
(15) Bangs (April 1942) [TS] US (A) 1929–40	$C = \alpha + \beta Y$
(16) Wallis (August 1942) [XS] US Families in various Minnesota cities, 1918 and 1935.	$s = \alpha + \beta y$
(17) Stone (Winter 1942) [TS] US (A) 1929–41	$C = \alpha + \beta Y + \gamma(t - 1935)$
	$C = \alpha + \beta Y + \gamma(t - 1935) + \delta Y^2$

(continued)

TABLE A1   (*continued*)

Author and date Data	Function(s) fitted
(18) Steindl (September 1944) [TS] US (*A*) 1929–40	$(S/P) = \alpha + \beta(Y/P)$
(19) Smithies (January 1945) [TS] US (*A*) 1923–40	$(C/NP) = \alpha + \beta(Y/NP) + \gamma(t - 1922)$
(20) Livingstone (January 1945) [TS] US (*A*) 1920–40	$C = \alpha + \beta Y$
(21) Mosak (January 1945) [TS] US (*A*) 1929–40 (Data published.)	$C = \alpha + \beta Y$
(22) Paradiso (1945) [TS] US (*A*) 1923–40 (Data published.)	$C = \alpha + \beta Y + \gamma(t - 1935)$
(23) Woytinsky (February 1946) [TS] US (*A*) 1923–40 (Data published.)	$100(S/Y) = \alpha + \beta Y$ $100(S/Y) = \gamma + \delta(Y/P)$ $100(S/Y) = \gamma + \delta(Y/P) + \lambda(Y/P)^2$
(24) Klein (April 1946) [TS] US (*A*) 1921–41	$(C/P) = \alpha + \beta(Y/P) + \gamma(Y/P) \cdot t + \delta t$
(25) Bassie (August 1946) [TS] US (*A*) 1910–16	$(C/P) = \alpha + \beta(Y/P) + \gamma N$
(26) Friend (November 1946) [TS] US (*A*) 1923–40	$(C/NP) = \alpha + \beta(Y/NP) + \gamma(t - 1930)$ $(C/NP) = \alpha + \beta(Y/NP) + \gamma(t - 1930) + \delta\Delta(Y/NP)$
(27) Bennion (November 1946) [TS] US (*A*) 1923–40 (Data published.)	$(C/P) = \beta(Y/P)$ $(C/P) = \alpha + \beta(Y/P)$ $(C/P) = \alpha + \beta(Y/P) + \gamma t$ $(C/P) = \alpha + \beta(Y/P) + \delta(Y/P)^2$
(28) Haavelmo (March 1947) [TS] US (*A*) 1922–41 (Data published.)	$(C/NP) = \alpha + \beta(Y/NP)$ $(C/NP) = \alpha + \beta(Y/NP) + \gamma(Y/NP)_{-1}$
(29) Klein (April 1947) [TS] US (*A*) 1922–41 (Data published.)	$(C/NP) = \alpha + \beta(Y/NP) + \gamma(Y/NP)_{-1}$ $(C/NP) = \alpha + \beta(Y/NP) + \delta(M/NP)_{-1}$ $(C/NP) = \alpha + \beta(Y/NP) + \lambda(t - 1931)$

TABLE A1   (*continued*)

Author and date Data	Function(s) fitted
(30) Klein (1947) [TS] US (*A*) 1921–41	$(C/P) = \alpha + \beta(Y/P)$
	$(C/P) = \alpha + \beta(Y/P) + \gamma(Y/P)\cdot t + \delta t$
	$(C/p) = \alpha + \beta(Y_L/P) + \gamma(Y_{NL}/P)$
	$(C/P) = \alpha + \beta(Y_L/P) + \gamma(Y_{NL}/P) + \delta(Y_{NL}/P)_{-1}$
(31) Lewis and Douglas (October 1947) [XS] US 1901, 1918–19 and 1922–24	$e = \alpha + \beta y$
	$e = \alpha + \beta y + \gamma y^2$
	$\log e = \alpha + \beta \log y$
	$\log e = \alpha + \beta \log y(\log y)^2$
(32) Brady and Friedman (1947) [XS] US, various years	$(s/y) = \alpha + \beta \log y$
(33) Clark (1948) [TS]US (*Q*) 1921(1)–1941(4)	$(C/P) = \alpha + \beta(Y/P) + \gamma(Y/P)_0$
(34) Koffsky (February 1948) [XS] US family data 1941	$c = \alpha + \beta y$
(35) Rosa (May 1948) [TS] US (*A*) 1920–40	$C = \alpha + \beta Y$
(36) Duesenberry (1948) [TS] US (*A*) 1923–40	$(S/Y) = \alpha + \beta(Y/NP)/(Y/NP)_0$
(37) Winston and Smith (October 1948) [TS] US (*A*) 1929, 1933, 1935–41	$C = \alpha + \beta Y$
(38) Mack (November 1948) [TS] US (*A*) 1929–40	$C = \alpha + \beta Y$
	$C = \alpha + \beta Y + \gamma \Delta Y$
	$C = \alpha + \beta Y + \delta(Y_{-1} - Y_{-3})/2$
(39) Modigliani (1949) [TS] US (*A*) 1921–40	$(C/NP) = \alpha + \beta(Y/NP) + \gamma(Y/NP)_0$
	$(S/Y) = \alpha + \beta(Y - Y_0)/Y$
	$S = \alpha + \beta Y + \gamma Y_{-1} + \delta Y_0$
(40) Klein (1950) [TS] US (*A*) 1921–41	$(C/P) = \alpha + \beta(Y/P) + \gamma(t - 1931) + \delta(Y/P)(t - 1931)$

Oxford Economic Papers 41 (1989), 150–169

EARLY EMPIRICAL FINDINGS ON THE CONSUMPTION FUNCTION, STYLIZED FACTS OR FICTION: A RETROSPECTIVE VIEW

By ARIS SPANOS*

1. Introduction

THE EMPIRICAL consumption function, referring to the relationship between consumers' expenditure and income, is undoubtedly one of the first and most intensively researched topics in macro-econometrics. However, despite the extensive research effort there seems to have been relatively little progress on the question of relevant and irrelevant empirical evidence and its bearing on the various theories postulated since Keynes' absolute income hypothesis (AIH). Reading any applied econometrics text (see Wallis (1979), Thomas (1985) *inter alia*) one is left with the impression that a plethora of disparate and often contradictory empirical results coexist happily. Indeed, very few empirical results have been superseded or discarded (see Hadjimatheou (1987) for an excellent recent survey). This situation reflects the state of affairs in empirical modelling in general; this is despite the considerable progress in econometric techniques.

The main aim of the paper is to take a retrospective view at the early literature on the consumption function in order to show that the current state of the empirical literature is largely due to the inadequacy of the textbook methodology. In particular, the inadequate attention paid to the question of statistical adequacy is largely responsible for the proliferation of often misspecified empirical models which are used to draw misleading conclusions. Such conclusions permeate both macroeconomic and applied econometrics textbooks. A case in point is the early stylized history of the empirical consumption function.

According to this stylized history the Keynesian consumption function:

$$C = \alpha + \beta Y, \qquad \alpha > 0, \qquad 0 < \beta < 1 \tag{1}$$

dominated the early empirical literature of the late 1930s and 1940s. When (1) was estimated using annual data for the period 1929–40 it turned out to be a reasonable characterization of the observed data but run into several difficulties in the late 1940s and early 1950s. First, it consistently under-predicted when used to predict consumption for the after the war period. Second, evidence provided by Kuznets showed that the average propensity to consume (APC) for the period 1869–1938 was constant in contrast to the implication from (1) that it's a decreasing function of Y. Third, evidence

* Thanks are due to Jim Thomas, Chris Gilbert, Hashem Pesaran, Ed Leamer and Arnold Zellner for a number of valuable comments. I am particularly grateful to an anonymous referee who went out of his way to be constructive. The usual disclaimer applies.

form cross-section data seemed to suggest a lower estimate of β and an upward shifting α. These two findings were interpreted as suggesting that there was a conflict between short-run and long-run evidence. The subsequent literature relating to the relative income, permanent income and life-cycle hypotheses is then viewed as attempts to resolve these apparent paradoxes and their success or failure is judged by how well they achieve this goal (see Evans (1969), Ferber (1973), Dornbusch and Fischer (1987), Hall and Taylor (1986), Wallis (1979)).

In this paper is it argued that the above interpretation of the empirical evidence is very misleading because the empirical models based on (1) are seriously misspecified (statistically) and thus any conclusions based on such models were invariably erroneous.[1] The main argument is that *statistical adequacy* is a necessary condition for structural modeling and theory testing. On closer examination the apparent paradoxes of the "stylized history" turn out to be either erroneous interpretations of the evidence or they are easily explainable on statistical grounds. In a nutshell the argument is that the textbook methodology led to a search for theory solutions to problems largely statistical in nature. The same methodology which still occupies a central position in econometrics testbooks.

In Section 2 the concept of statistical adequacy and related methodological issues are discussed as a prelude to the subsequent discussion. The early literature on the empirical consumption function is briefly reviewed in Section 3. No attempt is made to provide a thorough discussion of this literature. Instead we concentrate on a number of key papers in order to raise the issues of interest. In Section 4 the literature is re-evaluated calling into question the so-called "stylized facts". It is shown that the under-prediction for the post-war period can be easily explained as symptomatic of the serious dynamic misspecification the early empirical consumption functions suffered from. A re-appraisal of Kuznet's findings, using the original data, reveals that the average propensity to consume (APC) is not constant but growing steadily over the period in question. Section 5 concludes the argument and briefly considers its implications for econometric modelling in general.

2. Statistical adequacy and related issues

A *statistical model* constitutes a set of probabilistic assumptions related to the random variables giving rise to the data chosen by a theory. Such a model is said to be *statistically adequate* when the underlying assumptions are tested and not rejected by the data in question. The principle of statistical adequacy is generally accepted as the cornerstone of modern statistical inference (see Hinkley (1984)). The extensive discussion of error

---

[1] In a related paper Thomas (this volume) questions the historical accuracy of the early domination of the AIH and the subsequent developments related to the life-cycle and permanent income hypotheses.

autocorrelation, heteroskedasticity and collinearity in econometric text-books (see Intriligator (1978), Johnston (1963) *inter alia*) attest to the fact that the statistical adequacy principle is implicitly accepted by the textbook methodology. The problem, however, is that it has not been fully integrated within it because the probabilistic structure of the data is treated as an afterthought. Statistical models within the textbook approach are specified by attaching an error term to the theoretical relationships before any data is even chosen. As shown in Spanos (forthcoming) the statistical model can be very different for different data sets[2]. The parameters of this model are then estimated and various formal and informal tests are performed in order to judge to what extent the data conform to the theory in question. If problems such as incorrect signs or/and size of estimated coefficients, serial correlation or/and non-linearities are encountered, a variety of "solutions" are undertaken which are often beyond the formal scope of the approach. In practice these "solutions" take the form of ad hoc adjustments to the original model such as postulating an error-autocorrelation process. The problem of treating the data and its structure as an afterthought begins with the implicit assumption that the model exists and is known to the modeler before any data, whose analysis is required, is chosen. Such an assumption leaves no room for implementing the statistical adequacy principle and leads to the use of ad hoc statistical and theoretical adjustments to the original model. An alternative approach to econometric modelling formalized in Spanos (1986, 1988a) was designed explicitly to accommodate the principle of statistical adequacy within a coherent framework where both the theory and the data have important roles to play. This approach has its roots in the seminal work of Haavelmo (1944) (see Spanos (1988b)) and can be viewed as a formalization/extension of the LSE tradition in econometric modelling (see Gilbert (1986b, this volume)).

In order to integrate the principle of statistical adequacy within a coherent framework we need to ensure that the structure of the data is taken into consideration at the statistical model specification stage. This is achieved by adopting a more elaborate structure for the transition from the *theoretical* to the *econometric model*. The first step in this direction is to distinguish between the theoretical model and the statistical model in the context of which the former is embedded. In the case of the AIH this entails distinguishing between (1) and the linear regression model by interpreting the latter as a set of assumptions related to the stochastic process $\{y_t/X_t, t \in \mathcal{T}\}$ giving rise to the observed data chosen. The statistical model is separated from the theory by viewing it in purely statistical terms as:

$$y_t = b_0 + b_1 x_t + u_t, \qquad t \in \mathcal{T} \tag{2}$$

[2] For example if data on intentions are available, the statistical model appropriate for the demand-supply schedules model is the fixed regressor linear model. On the other hand if the data refer to quantities transacted and the corresponding prices problems of identification and simultaneity arise.

with the following probabilistic assumptions:

[1] $D(y_t/X_t; \theta)$ is normal,
[2] $E(y_t/X_t = x_t) = b_0 + b_1 x_t$, linear in x_t,
[3] $\mathrm{Var}\,(y_t/X_t = x_t) = \sigma^2$, homoskedastic,
[4] $\theta \equiv (b_0, b_1, \sigma^2)$ are time invariant,
[5] $y_1, y_2, \ldots, y_T$ is an independent sample sequentially drawn from $D(y_t/X_t; \theta)$.

In addition, the parameters θ are given statistical interpretations as follows:

$$b_0 = E(y_t) - b_1 E(X_t), \qquad b_1 = [\mathrm{Cov}\,(y_t, X_t)/\mathrm{Var}\,(X_t)], \qquad (2a)$$

$$\sigma^2 = \mathrm{Var}\,(y_t) - \{[\mathrm{Cov}\,(y_t, X_t)]^2/\mathrm{Var}\,(X_t)\} \qquad (2b)$$

A statistical model is viewed as *a convenient characterization* (*summary*) *of the sample information in a way which enables us to consider the theoretical model in its context.* In this sense the statistical model is data specific and initially devoid of any theoretical meaning. The theoretical meaning is derived by the imposition of theory-induced restrictions. This is necessary in order to reduce the data specificity of the former and thus increase the informational content of the resulting empirical model. Such restrictions induce a *reparameterization* from the statistical to the theoretical parameters of interest and thus change the nature of the estimated model from a purely statistical to an *empirical econometric model* which enjoys both statistical and theoretical interpretations.

The main advantage of this distinction is that by separating the theoretical and statistical aspects of the problem we can test the validity of the assumptions [1]–[5] unimpaired by the theoretical interpretation of the parameters. If the assumptions are not rejected we can proceed to relate the two sets of parameters; in this case the mapping is one to one but in general it doesn't have to be. On the other hand if the assumptions are rejected we cannot use the misspecified statistical model to say anything about the theory in question. In such a case we need to respecify the statistical model in an attempt to find a statistically adequate characterization of the data in hand. This respecification, to take account of statistical information initially ignored, is necessary in order to be able to use valid statistical procedures to consider theoretical questions of interest. The only constraint on the respecified form imposed by the theory, is that it should be possible to relate its parameters to the theoretical parameters of interest.

An important example of statistical respecification arises in the case where for aggregate time series on consumption and income assumption [5] is rejected. In such a case we need to respecify (2) in order to take account of the temporal structure of the data chosen. The situation is analogous to the experimental set up where some omitted variable is highly correlated with the included variables. It is well known that in such circumstances the resulting estimators are both biased and inconsistent (see Leamer (1983)).

In the present case of a non-experimental set up, the omitted variables represent the lags of y_t and X_t. The main difference between the experimental and non-experimental situation is how the relevant information sets are determined. In the former case any variable which has a bearing on the set up is relevant. In the latter case the relevant information is determined by the theory and the probabilistic structure of the data chosen; as described by the joint distribution of the observable random variables involved (chosen by the theory), for the whole of the sample period, say, $D(Z_1, Z_2, \ldots, Z_T; \psi)$, $Z_t \equiv (y_t, X_t)'$. The latter is referred to as the *Haavelmo distribution* (see Spanos (1988b)). In the above case the past history of Z_t is part of the relevant information set. Under certain assumptions (see Spanos (1986)) this respecification gives rise to the dynamic linear regression model:

$$y_t = c_0 + \beta_0 x_t + \sum_{i=1}^{l} [\alpha_i y_{t-i} + \beta_i x_{t-i}] + \epsilon_t \tag{3}$$

which is again viewed purely as a statistical model.

In order to illustrate this argument let us assume that for the data chosen above the statistical model (3), with $l = 1$, turns out to be statistically adequate i.e.

$$C_t = c_0 + \beta_0 Y_t + \beta_1 Y_{t-1} + \alpha_1 C_{t-1} + u_t \tag{4}$$

The question of relating the statistical parameters $\theta \equiv (c_0, \beta_0, \beta_1, \alpha_1, \sigma_0^2)$ to the theoretical parameters $\alpha \equiv (\alpha, \beta)$ is similar to the identification issue in the simultaneous equations model: impose the theory-induced restrictions $\beta_1 = 0$ and $\alpha_1 = 0$. As argued below, these restrictions are likely to be rejected by time series data but the situation is no different from the case of invalid overidentifying restrictions in the simultaneous equations model. If the restrictions are rejected the theoretical model is not accepted on the basis of the data chosen and alternative theories are called for. In this sense the following simple form of the life-cycle hypothesis (Modigliani and Ando (1957)):

$$C_t = a_1 Y_t + a_2 A_{t-1} \tag{5}$$

where A_t refers to non-human wealth determined by $A_t = A_{t-1} + (Y_t - C_t)^3$ can be viewed as an alternative theory to the AIH which is likely to be accepted on the basis of the data in question. Its estimable form:

$$C_t = a_1 Y_t + (a_2 - a_1)Y_{t-1} + (1 - a_2)C_{t-1} \tag{6}$$

gives rise to more reasonable (than $\beta_1 = \alpha_1 = 0$) theory-induced restrictions:

$$c_0 = 0, \qquad \beta_1 = (a_2 - a_1), \qquad \alpha_1 = (1 - a_2) \tag{7}$$

In terms of the theoretical parameters, the empirical econometric model

---

[3] For simplicity we ignore the rate of return on past assets.

takes the form:

$$\Delta C_t = a_1 \Delta Y_t + a_2(Y_{t-1} - C_{t-1}) + \epsilon_t \tag{8}$$

This model is known as the error-correction model (see Hendry (1983), Gilbert (1986b) *inter alia*).

In the following sections the above framework is used to provide a re-appraisal of the early empirical literature on the consumption function with particular emphasis being placed on statistical adequacy.

3. The early empirical consumption functions

In the early 1940s the combination of the newly developed Keynesian macro-theory and the availability of "reliable" data rendered the consumption function a prime target for quantification. The Keynesian revolution posed a very clear problem to the emerging discipline of econometrics. The problem was the measurement of the expenditure multipliers which formed the backbone of Keynesian economic policy. In the context of the income-expenditure model this meant the quantification of the consumption function.

A simplified version of Keynes' theory of the consumption function, known as the Absolute Income Hypothesis (AIH), is commonly summarized by the following four propositions (see Wallis (1979), Thomas (1985) *inter alia*):

(i) Real consumption is a "stable" function of real income, i.e. $C = f(Y)$.

(ii) $0 < \text{MPC} < 1$, where $\text{MPC} \equiv [\partial C / \partial Y]$—The Marginal Propensity to Consume

(iii) $\text{APC} > \text{MPC}$ where $\text{APC} \equiv (Y/C)$—Average Propensity to Consume.

(iv) The proportion of income consumed decreases as income rises, i.e.

$$[\partial(C/Y)/\partial Y] < 0 \tag{9}$$

Since Tinbergen (1939) the task of the econometrician has been considered to be the estimation of α and β and the evaluation of the resulting estimates. Estimating (1) involves two seemingly unrelated steps, the choice of the appropriate data series and the specification of the statistical model whose associated estimation and testing results can be used to quantify the coefficients α and β. In the case of (1) the statistical model is the linear regression. The change from the theoretical model (1) to the statistical model is made by implicitly assuming that the theoretical variables C and Y coincide with the observable variables underlying the data chosen and attaching a white-noise error.

During the 1940s and 50s several data series such as aggregate consumption and income in various forms (constant and current prices, per capita) as well as cross-section data on individual consumption and income have been interchangeably used to estimate the parameters of (1) (see Thomas (this volume)). By the early 1950s there were more than two dozen influential empirical studies of the relationship between consumers' expenditure and income raising a number of interesting methodological "puzzles" (Davis (1952), Ferber (1953)).

A typical estimated form of (10) using annual real consumption and disposable income for the period 1929–40 was reported by Davis (1952):

$$C_t = 10.69 + 0.80Y_t + \hat{\varepsilon}_t, \qquad R^2 = 0.993 \tag{10}$$
$$(\ldots) \quad (0.03)$$

During this period the criteria for judging the "validity" of (10) as a quantification of (1) were a mixture of theoretical and statistical indicators. Theoretical indicators concentrated on the sign, size and the interpretation of the estimated parameters. Initially, the main statistical criterion was "goodness of fit" (the value of the R^2) and later the t-ratios were added. These same criteria with some additional tests such as the Durbin–Watson test are still extensively used in applied econometrics. In terms of these criteria (10) constitutes an impressive quantification of the consumption function (1). The estimated coefficients have the correct signs and magnitudes, the "t-statistic" of the estimated MPC is near 40 and the R^2 was very close to one. The estimated equation appears to "explain" the data very well and at the same time verifies conditions (ii)–(iv) of the AIH.

Despite this apparent confirmation of the AIH, the empirical consumption function (10) ran into various difficulties almost immediately. The *first problem* was that when (10) was used for prediction in the period 1946–50 it underpredicted systematically (see Davis (1952)). This was interpreted as a rejection of the AIH stability proposition (i). The *second problem* for the estimated consumption function (10) was raised by Kuznets (1946a). He argued that when the cyclical changes in consumption and income are ignored their ratio appears to be constant over long periods. Taking averages over overlapping decades between 1869 and 1938 (in order to iron out the cyclical effects) he argued that except for the last decade (the Great Depression) the ratio (C_t/Y_t) appeared to be constant, varying between 0.84 and 0.89 (see Kuznets (1946b)). These findings taken at face value contradicted the AIH underlying (10) in so far as the APC implied by this model is a decreasing function of Y. A *third problem* was raised by studies using cross-section data. The estimates of the MPC based on cross-section data appeared to be invariably lower than the time-series estimates. Moreover, there appeared to be an upward shift of the estimated consumption functions over time (see Brady and Friedman (1947)). In view of Kuznets' findings the cross-section evidence was taken to imply an apparent contradiction between the long-run (time-series over long time) and short-run (cross-section and short time series) empirical results.

By the late 1940s and early 50s the above problems were considered to be "stylized facts" to be explained by further research. In summary these were:

(a) AIH empirical consumption functions were unstable,
(b) the APC was constant over long periods,
(c) short-run consumption functions tended to confirm the AIH but long-run estimates seemed to reject it, and
(d) cross-section estimates of the MPC were systematically lower than time-series estimates, and appeared to shift upwards over time.

The last "stylized fact" raises a number of important issues which cannot be addressed adequately in the present paper because the original data are not available.[4] In view of this we concentrate only on the time series data aspects of the above "stylized facts".

The subsequent literature of the 1950s and 1960s is commonly interpreted as extensions of the AIH which account for the "stylized facts" (see Wallis (1979), Thomas (1985) *inter alia*). Historically such an interpretation appears to provide a useful link between the early literature and subsequent developments. For evaluation purposes, however, this is misleading because as argued in Section 4 the above "stylized facts" on closer examination are found to be wanting. The alternative interpretation proposed in this paper is to view the life-cycle and permanent income hypotheses as theoretical specifications which are acceptable reparameterizations/restrictions of a statistically adequate specification.

4. The early "stylized facts" revisited

To be able to investigate the various problems relating to (10) we need to re-estimate it, especially since the information reported by Davis (1952) is inadequate. Using revised data (see Appendix II) for the same sample period 1929–40 re-estimation of (10) yielded:

$$C_t = 10.287 + 0.790Y_t + \hat{\epsilon}_t, \qquad R^2 = 0.979, \qquad s = 0.931, \qquad T = 12, \quad (11)$$
$$(\ 2.302) \ (0.036)$$

where the standard errors of the coefficient estimates are shown in parentheses. As can be seen this equation is very similar to (10) and can be used to statistically appraise the latter. At this stage we resist the temptation to pronounce this an empirical consumption function, despite the plausibility of the sign and size of the estimated coefficient, the high value of the R^2 and the implied large "t-statistics". This is because arguments that the coefficient of Y_t has the right sign, magnitude and/or is significant constitute informal *specification tests*. As argued in Section 2, the validity of such arguments depends crucially on the validity of the assumptions [1]–[5] underlying the linear regression model.

---

[4] It is important to note that this paradox arose because of the implicit assumption that the form of the statistical model is invariant to the choice of the observed data; a highly questionable assumption (see Spanos 1988b)). For a very interesting discussion on the differences between the cross-section and time-series estimates see Aigner and Simon (1971).

In the case of the early literature on the empirical consumption function it is fair to say that no misspecification tests were applied to the estimated equations simply because apart from the von Neumann ratio (see Brown (1952)) no such tests were available. However, since then numerous misspecification tests, beginning with Durbin and Watson (1950, 1951) have been developed (see Pagan and Hall (1983), Spanos (1986), Pesaran and Pesaran (1987) *inter alia*). Nevertheless these early results have not been reconsidered in view of these developments.

In the case of (11) it is clear from the Durbin–Watson (DW) statistic that the temporal independence assumption [5] is invalid given that the critical value at 5% is 1.06. This is also confirmed by the F-type test proposed by Spanos (1986); its value being $F(2, 7) = 4.94$ with a critical value at 5% $c_\alpha = 4.74$. When this assumption is invalid there is no point in testing for the validity of the other assumptions because none of the statistical inference results routinely used in the context is appropriate (see Spanos (1986)). In particular the quoted t-ratios and the arguments about the sign, size and magnitude of the estimated coefficients are invalid; no statistically valid conclusions can be drawn about the implied MPC of APC on the basis of (11). What is more important for our purposes, the widely adopted interpretation of low value of the DW statistic as suggesting the the error follows a first-order auto-regressive process (AR(1)) is also unwarranted without further statistical investigation. As shown by Hendry and Mizon (1978) before such a "corrective" action is taken the common factor restrictions implicitly imposed by the AR(1) should be tested. If these restrictions are invalid the usual estimators are biased and inconsistent (see Spanos (forthcoming)).

Informally, the *common factor restriction* involved in the present case can be checked by comparing the estimated coefficient of Y_t in (11) and the specification:

$$C_t = 17.129 + 0.687Y_t + \hat{\epsilon}_t, \qquad \hat{\epsilon}_t = 0.872\hat{\epsilon}_{t-1} + \hat{v}_t \qquad (12)$$
$$(3.046)\ (0.042) \qquad\qquad (0.141)$$
$$R^2 = 0.990, \qquad s = 0.6840, \qquad DW = 1.223, \qquad T = 12$$

The sizable change in magnitude in this estimate suggests that the validity of the common factor restriction is doubtful (see Spanos (1986), ch. 22). Formally the validity of the common factor restriction can be tested using a likelihood ratio test (see Hendry and Mizon (1978)) where the unrestricted model is:

$$C_t = 0.106 + 0.689Y_t + 0.863C_{t-1} - 0.557Y_{t-1} + \hat{u}_t \qquad (13)$$
$$(3.52)\ (0.050)\quad (0.284)\qquad (0.200)$$
$$R^2 = 0.992, \qquad s = 0.669, \qquad T = 11$$

For this test to be a proper test, however, we need to ensure that (13) is not statistically misspecified. The *misspecification tests* used yielded:

$$\tau_1(1.6) = 0.205, \qquad \tau_2(1, 6) = 0.009, \qquad \tau_3(1, 6) = 0.051, \qquad \xi(2) = 0.150$$

$\tau_1(.)$—Lagrange multiplier test statistic for 1st order autocorrelation.

$\tau_2(.)$—RESET test for non-linearity, based on the auxiliary regression of the residuals on the original regressors and the square of the fitted values.

$\tau_3(.)$—RESET test for heteroskedasticity based· on the auxiliary regression of the residuals squared on the squared fitted values; all these tests are in F form.

$\xi(.)$—the skewness-kurtosis test for normality. For an extensive discussion of these tests see Spanos (1986), Pesaran and Pesaran (1987).

Looking at the above misspecification test statistics we can see that (13) is reasonably well defined statistically and thus we can proceed to consider the validity of the common factor restriction. Using the likelihood-ratio test this restriction is rejected at the conventional 5% significance level since:

$$-2 \log \lambda = 5.230 \quad \text{and} \quad c_\alpha = 3.841 \quad \text{for} \quad \alpha = 0.05$$

It is important to stress that misspecification testing in the case of a small sample can be particularly hazardous. It is well known that the power of these tests depends crucially on the sample size which in the present case is very small. For this reason care was taken to choose tests which can be used when the degrees of freedom are at a premium. To check the reliability of the estimation and testing for (11)–(13) was repeated for the sample period 1929–1986; the results given in Appendix I. The most striking result to emerge from this is that (11), when estimated for the period 1929–1986, fails all the above misspecification tests.

Before we re-consider the "stylized facts" it is important to stress that the simultaneity argument (see Haavelmo (1947)) based on the identity:

$$Y_t = C_t + I_t \tag{14}$$

does not alleviate the statistical misspecification problem. If anything it makes matters worse since the implied reduced form yielded:

$$C_t = 52.097 + 2.657I_t + \hat{u}_t, \qquad R^2 = 0.637, \qquad s = 3.879, \qquad \text{DW} = 0.426$$
$$(2.157)\ (0.634) \tag{15}$$

In view of the DW value and the F-type test statistic for departures from [5] of $F(2, 7) = 14.746$, the model is clearly misspecified (see Spanos (1988a) for a more extensive discussion).

(3) *Underprediction and stability*

In view of the statistical inadequacy of (11) the question is how does it affect the "stylized facts" (a)–(d). Let us beigin with the underprediction

TABLE 1
Predictions errors

Equat.	(11)	(12)	(13)
1946	0.622	3.642	−2.698
1947	5.114	7.798	0.637
1948	2.999	6.298	−1.436
1949	5.096	8.521	0.099
1950	4.736	9.087	0.031

results. A moment's reflection suggests that underprediction or overprediction are symptomatic of the fact that the temporal independence assumption [5] is invalid. The low value of the DW statistic and the high value of the R^2 in (11) indicates the classic case where the estimated equation "explains" the trend and very little else (see Granger and Newbold (1974)). The short-run dynamics around the trend are left unexplained and as a result systematic underpredictions or overpredictions will be the rule not the exception. In order to illustrate this point let us ignore the fact that (11) and (12) are statistically misspecified and compare their predictions with those of (13) as given in Table 1.

As can be seen the predictions based on (11) and (12) appear very systematic (all positive) and the latter are considerably worse despite the modelling of the error. On the other hand those based on (13) seem non-systematic and apart from the first one the predictions are not significantly different from the residuals and they are well within a 95% prediction interval.

Related to this is the misleadingly high value of the R^2. The problem is not that the trend is unimportant but that the way the R^2 is calculated using:

$$R^2 = 1 - \left[\sum_t \hat{\epsilon}_t^2 \Big/ \sum_t (y_t - \bar{y})^2 \right] \tag{16}$$

is very misleading because the total variation is calculated erroneously around a fixed mean despite the distinct trend. This attributes unduly large weights to the extreme observations on either side of the mean $\bar{y}$. Often the variation around the moving mean (trend) is a small proportion of the variation around a fixed mean. In order to get some idea of the relative magnitudes involved let us consider these two measure of variation for C_t assuming that the changing mean can be approximated by a third order polynomial in t the two measures of variation are:

$$\sum_t (C_t - \bar{C})^2 = 415.195, \qquad \sum_t (C_t - c_0 - c_1 t - c_2 t^2 - c_3 t^3)^2 = 33.327 \tag{17}$$

Using the latter measure of variation the revised goodness of fit value is $\bar{R}^2 = 0.738$.

In view of the above discussion it appears that the interpretation of the predictive failure of (11) as a rejection of the AIH is unwarranted. A more reasonable interpretation seems to be that it is due to the statistical misspecification of the estimated equation. Where does this leave the AIH? At this stage the only reasonably adequate statistical model in the context of which the AIH can be considered is (13). In the context of the methodology summarized in Section 2 the AIH can be viewed as a reparameterization/restriction of (4) with the overidentifying restrictions (see Spanos (1988a)) being:

$$\beta_1 = 0 \quad \text{and} \quad \alpha_1 = 0.$$

On the basis of (13) these restrictions are rejected, for the data chosen, since the F statistic for the overidentifying restrictions takes the value $F(2, 7) = 4.96$.

(b) Kuznets' findings

The most influential of the "stylized facts" was Kuznets' evidence that, over long periods, when the short-run dynamics are "ironed out" by averaging, the APC is relatively constant. This is a purely statistical proposition which can be accepted or rejected for a given set of data. Let us reconsider this argument using the statistical adequacy principle. The constancy of $(\bar{C}_i/\bar{Y}_i)$ can be parameterized in the form of the hypothesis: $H_0: c_0 = 0$, $H_1: c_0 \neq 0$ in the context of:

$$\bar{C}_i = c_0 + c_2 \bar{Y}_i + \epsilon_i, \qquad i = 1, 2, \ldots, n \tag{18}$$

Estimation of (18) using Kuznets' data on 10 year overlapping averages for the period 1869–1938 (excluding the last observation following Kuznets (1946a)) yielded:

$$\bar{C}_i = -1.721 + 0.928 \bar{Y}_i + \hat{\epsilon}_i \tag{19}$$
$$(0.674) \ (0.016)$$

$$R^2 = 0.997, \qquad s = 1.327, \qquad DW = 0.770, \qquad n = 12$$
$$\tau_1(1, 9) = 6.365, \qquad \tau_2(1, 9) = 27.097, \qquad \tau_3(1, 9) = 5.514, \qquad \xi(2) = 3.346$$

These test statistics show most clearly that the estimated model is seriously misspecified and no valid statistical arguments can be based on it to discuss any theoretical questions of interest. The "ironing out" performed by Kuznets failed to eliminate the short-run dynamics and also distorted their dynamic structure.[5]

In view of the way Kuznets derived the overlapping averages one might suspect that this will lead to some complicated Moving Average error. Given the sample size this conjecture could only be tested for a small order Moving Average process (MA). However, re-estimation of (19) with a MA(1) or an AR(1) error were both rejected by the data.

[5] The data series $\bar{C}_i$ and $\bar{Y}_i$ appear to diverge from each other, that is, they are not even co-integrated (see Granger (1986)).

Using the insight offered by the specification of the linear regression given in Section 2 (see Spanos (1986) for more details), the search for a statistically adequate specification, which takes account of the data's temporal structure and non-stationarity (distinct time trends and increasing variance over time), led to the log-linear[6] specification:

$$\ln \bar{C}_i = -0.136 + 0.541 \ln \bar{C}_{i-1} + 0.951 \ln \bar{Y}_i - 0.602 \ln \bar{Y}_{i-1} - 0.026t + \hat{u}_i$$
$$\quad (0.184)\ (0.362) \qquad\quad (0.104) \qquad\quad (0.331) \qquad\qquad (0.017) \quad (20)$$
$$R^2 = 0.9996, \qquad s = 0.0132, \qquad n = 11$$
$$\tau_1(1,5) = 0.620, \qquad \tau_2(1,5) = 0.063, \qquad \tau_3(1,5) = 0.022, \qquad \xi(2) = 1.017$$

where t denotes a simple trend. The misspecification test statistics indicate that (20) can be viewed as an adequate statistical model. The estimated coefficients suggest that if anything the rate of change of $(\bar{C}_i/\bar{Y}_i)$ is increasing with t. This is confirmed by the estimated equation:

$$\Delta \ln (\bar{C}_i/\bar{Y}_i) = -0.024 + 0.004t + \hat{v}_i, \qquad R^2 = 0.605,$$
$$(0.009)\ (0.001)$$
$$s = 0.012, \qquad DW = 1.971, \qquad n = 11 \qquad\qquad (21)$$
$$\tau_1(1,8) = 0.101, \qquad \tau_2(1,8) = 0.137, \qquad \tau_3(1,8) = 0.176, \qquad \xi(2) = 1.263$$

As far as the sample size allows us to draw any inference on the basis of (21), we can deduce that Kuznets' proposition is clearly false.

The main conclusion of the above discussion is that it is dangerous to deduce quantitative relationships from graphs of one series on another because there is no way one can assess the statistical adequacy of the implicit relationship by looking at the plot. In order to illustrate this for more recent data consider the graph of C_t against Y_t for the period 1949–1986 in Fig. 1(a).

As can be seen the implied APC appears to be constant. This, however, is very misleading because the implicit relation turns out to be seriously misspecified, as indicated by the misspecification test statistics:

$$APC_t = 0.909 + \hat{v}_t, \qquad s = 0.0128, \qquad DW = 0.571, \qquad n = 37 \quad (22)$$
$$(0.002)$$
$$\tau_1(1,35) = 17.311, \qquad \tau_2(1,35) = 28.990, \qquad \tau_3(1,35) = 13.410,$$
$$\xi(2) = 4.430$$

This is confirmed by the time plot of the APC shown in Fig. 1(b).

---

[6] The log transformation is used as a variance stabilizing transformation; for more details see Spanos (1986), ch. 21.

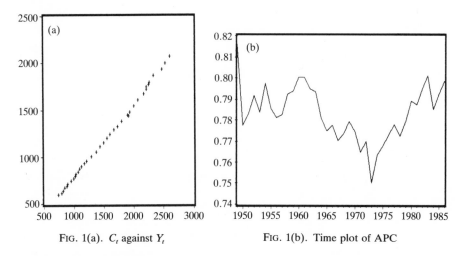

FIG. 1(a). C_t against Y_t FIG. 1(b). Time plot of APC

(c) *Long-run versus short-run*

Kuznets' findings were interpreted at the time as suggesting a linear consumption function of the form:

$$C = 0.865Y \tag{23}$$

This was clearly in conflict with the empirical models based on (1) in four important respects. In terms of (1) and propositions (i)–(iv) (21) implies that the intercept is zero, propositions (iii) and (iv) do not hold and the estimate of the MPC was higher than the ones derived with annual data for the period 1929–1940. These conflicting "evidence" were rationalized by interpreting (23) as referring to the long-run behavior as opposed to the short-run behavior described by (1). The implicit assumption behind this rationalization was that time-series data spanning a 15–20 year period refer to short-run evidence and longer time series averages refer to long-run evidence. This interpretation led to an extensive research effort to reconcile the short and long-run evidence beginning with Smithies (1945) and Duesenberry (1949) (see Ackley (1961), Thomas (1988)).

Apart from the question of statistical adequacy the implicit presupposition on which the above rationalization is based exemplifies a confusion between calendar time and economic-theoretic time. As argued by Suits (1963):

"In the discussion of long-run and short-run effects two things are sometimes confused: the nature of the problem under investigation, and the nature of the data employed. It is possible to use quarterly data and still analyze a very long-run consumption function. The data set a lower limit to the 'length of run' that can be investigated—the Kuznets estimates for decades cannot be used to investigate quarterly variations in consumption—but they do not, of themselves, set an upper limit".

This was brought out most distinctly by Kuznets' data where the ten year averaging did not "iron out" the short-run dynamics. Nowadays, it is well known that the short-term dynamics and long-run effects are closely interrelated and cannot be separated by such transformations of the data. Before any short-run or long-run questions of interest can be asked it is imperative to model the systematic information in the observed data in order to establish an adequate statistical model.

A particularly useful way to relate the theoretical long run with an estimated dynamic empirical model is provided by the LSE tradition (see Gilbert (1986b)) where the former is interpreted as the static solution of the latter. In order to illustrate this let us consider the question of modelling an empirical consumption in the context of the approach discussed in Section 2 using post war data.

Following in the tradition of the post war literature we choose C_t to be real consumers' expenditure on non-durables and services and Y_t to be real disposable income deflated by the overall consumers' expenditure implicit deflator P (see Appendix II for the definitions and sources). With the general form of the estimable model (6) in mind we can proceed to specify the statistical model in the context of which this can be considered. The natural first choice for such a statistical model is:

$$C_t = c_0 + \alpha_1 C_{t-1} + \beta_0 Y_t + \beta_1 Y_{t-1} + \beta_2 P_t + \beta_3 P_{t-1} + u_t \qquad (24)$$

The inclusion of P_t as a separate regressor is based on the general rule of not imposing any unnecessary restrictions on statistical specifications.[7] Estimation of (24) using annual data for the USA for the period 1949–1985 yielded:

$$\hat{C}_t = 0.171 + 0.706 C_{t-1} + 0.364 Y_t - 0.130 Y_{t-1} - 0.373 P_t + 0.420 P_{t-1} \quad (25)$$
$$\phantom{\hat{C}_t =} (6.410)\ (0.130)\qquad (0.056)\quad (0.085)\qquad (0.130)\quad (0.133)$$
$$R^2 = 0.9997, \qquad s = 7.542, \qquad T = 37, \qquad DW = 1.930, \qquad h = 0.346$$
$$\tau_1(1, 30) = 0.0494, \qquad \tau_2(2, 29) = 1.274,[8] \qquad \tau_3(1, 30) = 5.305,$$
$$\xi(2) = 2.017$$

As can be seen the test statistic for heteroskedasticity indicates a certain departure from the assumption (the critical value for 5% is 4.17).

For misspecification purposes the statistical interpretation discussed in Section 2 is particularly useful because the time plots of the data involved can be very informative about possible departures from the underlying assumptions. A look at these plots would have warned us about a number of possible problems. Both the C_t and Y_t series exhibit temporal dependence and non-stationarities in the form of increasing means and variances over

[7] The exclusion of prices requires the inclusion of time trends in order to get a statistically adequate model.
[8] The availability of degrees of freedom enables us to use the cube of the fitted values as well in the auxiliary regression for linearity.

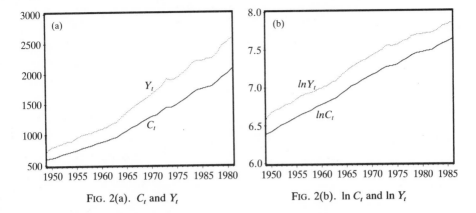

FIG. 2(a). C_t and Y_t FIG. 2(b). ln C_t and ln Y_t

time (See Figs. 2(a) and 3). In view of the relationship between the joint distribution and the conditional in terms of which the assumptions are made, we can see that not just [5] but also [3] and [4] are likely to be invalid in view of the relationships (2(a) and 3) between the parameters and the first two moments.

On the other hand using the log transformation as a variance stabilizing transformation (see Spanos (1986)) we can see in Fig. 4 that no such variance non-stationarity arises. In view of this we proceed to estimate the log-linear form of (25):

$$\ln C_t = -0.079 + 0.513 \ln C_{t-1} + 0.460 \ln Y_t + 0.008 \ln Y_{t-1}$$
$$(0.03) \quad (0.109) \qquad (0.059) \qquad (0.101)$$
$$- 0.242 \ln P_t + 0.262 \ln P_{t-1}$$
$$(0.063) \qquad (0.065)$$

$$R^2 = 0.9998, \quad s = 0.00583, \quad T = 37, \quad DW = 1.761, \quad h = 0.975$$
$$\tau_1(1, 30) = 0.458, \quad \tau_2(2, 29) = 2.485, \quad \tau_3(1, 30) = 0.022,$$
$$\xi(2) = 2.652$$

This estimated statistical model indicates no departures from the underlying assumptions and thus we can proceed to relate it to the estimable model (6). Estimation of (6) in the form given in (8) gives rise to a misspecified empirical model because of the exclusion of the separate price effect. On the other hand extending (8) to include an inflation term yields a statistically adequate empirical econometric model of the form:

$$\Delta \ln C_t = -0.0518 + 0.421 \Delta \ln Y_t + 0.316 \ln (Y_{t-1}/C_{t-1}) - 0.165 \Delta \ln P_t \quad (27)$$
$$(0.018) \quad (0.057) \qquad (0.076) \qquad\qquad (0.050)$$
$$R^2 = 0.710, \quad s = 0.00618, \quad T = 37, \quad DW = 1.757,$$
$$\tau_1(1, 32) = 0.4212, \quad \tau_2(2, 31) = 0.701, \quad \tau_3(1, 32) = 0.147,$$
$$\xi(2) = 2.430$$

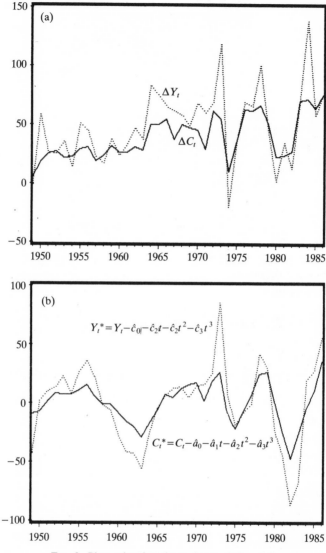

FIG. 3. Plots related to the variance of C_t and Y_t

The restrictions imposed on (26) to derive (27) are accepted at 5% significance level, the test statistic being: $\tau_5(2, 31) = 2.887$, $c_\alpha = 3.32$. This model proved empirically successful for UK data (see Hendry (1983)). On the question of its theoretical underpinnings see Muellbauer and Bover (1986).

A particularly appealing way to relate the empirical econometric model (27) to the long-run is to interpret the consumption function as referring to its static equilibrium solution (see Gilbert (1986b)) where $\ln Z_t = \ln Z_{t-1} =$

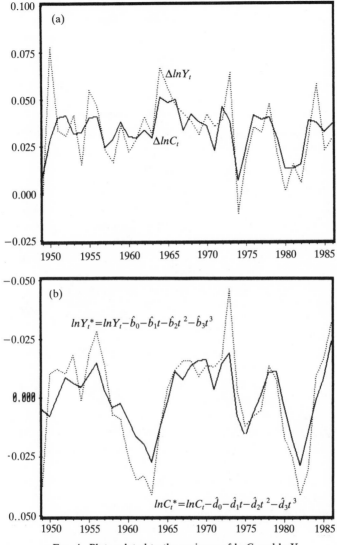

FIG. 4. Plots related to the variance of $\ln C_t$ and $\ln Y_t$

$\ln Z^*$ for all the variables Z_t in the specification. This gives rise to the long-run derived equation:

$$C^* = 0.849Y^* \tag{28}$$

If we interpret this as a quantification of the generic theoretical model underlying the life-cycle and permanent income hypotheses (see Deaton and Muellbauer (1980)) the coefficient value is reasonable.[9]

---

[9] By coincidence the value is close to Kuznets' estimate.

In view of the above questioning of the "stylized facts" the question which arises naturally at this stage is where does this leave the life-cycle (LCH) and permanent income (PIH) hypotheses given that they are commonly viewed as extensions of the AIH which account for these "facts". Although in principle we cannot separate the theoretical from the statistical adequacy of empirical models, the above results suggest that apart from the theoretical advancement over the AIH (because of their explicit modelling of the dynamics), the initial success of the empirical models based on the LCH and PIH can be explained on statistical grounds as being based on more adequate statistical models.

5. Conclusion

The purpose of the above discussion was to consider a re-appraisal of the early empirical work on the consumption function in the light of recent developments in the methodology and practice of econometric modelling. The so-called "stylized facts" associated with the early literature were called into question as being based on seriously misspecified statistical models. The discussion has a number of important implications which can be summarized as follows.

As far as the stylized history of the consumption function is concerned the main implication is that the discussion in macroeconomic and applied econometrics textbooks is rather misleading and needs to be modified (see also Thomas (this volume)).

As far as econometric modelling in general is concerned, the main lesson to be learned is that the principle of statistical adequacy can only be ignored that the modeller's peril. The principle itself is also useful in providing us with a crude but reasonably effective way to narrow down the relevant empirical evidence in a number of different areas in applied econometrics. The approach used in this paper could be employed in a reassessment of current and past empirical models in other areas of applied economics.

VPI and State University, Virginia, USA.

APPENDIX I

Estimation of (11)–(13) for the period 1929–86 (excluding the war years 1941–1945) yielded:

$$C_t = 24.119 + 0.894Y_t + \hat{\epsilon}_t \qquad (11')$$
$$(5.601) \ (0.004)$$

$$R^2 = 0.999, \qquad s = 19.344, \qquad DW = 0.642, \qquad T = 58$$

$$\tau_1(1, 55) = = 36.740, \qquad \tau_2(1, 55) = 33.588, \qquad \tau_3(1, 55) = 21.532, \qquad \xi(2) = 27.713$$

These tests suggest that (13') is seriously misspecified showing strong departures from the assumptions of independence, linearity, homoskedasticity and normality. Note also that the R^2 defined using the variation in C_t around a second degree trend polynomial takes the value

$\bar{R}^2 = 0.670$. Assuming an AR(1) error autocorrelation:

$$C_t = 19.859) + 0.899Y_t + \hat{\epsilon}_t, \qquad \epsilon_t = 0.724\epsilon_{t-1} + \hat{v}_t \qquad (12')$$
$$(13.412) \quad (0.009) \qquad\qquad (0.091)$$
$$R^2 = 0.999, \qquad s = 14.829, \qquad DW = 1.956, \qquad T = 58$$

The validity of this specification is also in question given that:

$$C_t = 8.483 + 0.691Y_t + 0.647C_{t-1} - 0.369Y_{t-1} + \hat{u}_t \qquad (13')$$
$$(5.064) \quad (0.068) \quad (0.106) \qquad (0.096)$$
$$R^2 = 0.999, \qquad s = 14.839, \qquad T = 57$$

and the common factor restrictions test yields:

$$-2\log\lambda = 21.833, \qquad c_\alpha = 3.841, \quad \text{for} \quad \alpha = 0.05.$$

APPENDIX II. DATA DEFINITIONS AND SOURCES

For equations (11)–(15) the data refer to the following annual series for the period 1929–1950 form ERP (1969):

C_t—total consumers' expenditure at 1939 prices, in billions; ERP 1969 table B-16.

Y_t—personal disposable income deflated by total consumers' expenditure implicit deflator, in billions; ERP 1969 table B-16.

For equations (13'), (15') and (18') in Appendix I the data refer to the some variables as the above but the sample period is 1929–1986; from ERP 1987.

For equations (25)–(27) the data refer to the following time series for the period 1949–1985:

C_t—consumers' expenditure on non-durables and services deflected by P_t, in billions; ERP 1987 Tables B-14 and B-26.

Y_t—personal disposable income deflated by total consumers' expenditure implicit deflator P_t, in billions; ERP 1987 Table B-26.

P_t—implicit deflator for total consumers' expenditure; ERP 1987 table B-26.

ERP—Economic Report of the President.

Oxford Economic Papers 41 (1989), 170–188

PHILLIPS' APPROXIMATE REGRESSION*

By NANCY J. WULWICK

I. Phillips' study in context

A. *The engineer-cum-economist*

A. W. H. Phillips received a degree from the London Institute of Electrical Engineers in 1938 and, from the London School of Economics, a B.A. in sociology with economics in 1949 and a Ph.D. in economics in 1953 (Blyth [1975]). His Ph.D. thesis developed a neoclassical dynamic macro-economic model.

Economists recognized that the neoclassical framework, which was a synthesis of Keynesian and Walrasian economics, contained a contradiction. Neoclassical economics acknowledged the Keynesian macroeconomic problem of large scale unemployment, but explained such unemployment using Walrasian microeconomic concepts. According to Keynes' *General Theory* (1936), flexible money-wage rates generally would not secure equilibrium with full employment. In Walrasian economics, persistent unemployment was due solely to inflexible, excessive real-wage rates. The neoclassical synthesis contained flexible money-wage rates and prices which cleared markets in microeconomics, yet a downwardly rigid money-wage- and price-level in macroeconomics (Lipsey [1978] pp. 49–58).

Meanwhile, theorists in microeconomics were working on the dynamics of the price mechanism in markets subject to disturbances. Engineers similarly were studying the properties of dynamic, stable systems. With his background, Phillips saw that economic and engineering dynamics applied the same formal principles. Rejecting the neoclassical fix-price convention, he investigated how a flexible price-level stabilized output given disturbances to the system ([1953] p. i).

As a student Phillips with Walter Newlyn, his contemporary at the LSE, built an analogue machine of the economy which had a flexible price-level (Phillips [1950, 1953]; Newlyn [1950]). The basic model had three transparent tanks—for production, stocks and consumer demand—and tubes through which colored water was pumped. The price-level was determined by the quantity of stocks represented by the quantity of water in the tank and the demand for stocks represented by the capacity of the tank, and was shown inversely by the height of water in the tank. A recorder read off the rate of equilibrating changes in the price-level following upon an autonomous change in production or consumer demand. The hydraulic machine

---

* The author acknowledges the helpful comments of M. Desai, C. L. Gilbert, K. D. Hoover, N. de Marchi, E. H. Phelps Brown, R. J. Wolfson who also gave the title, and an anonymous referee. The author alone is responsible for the views presented in the essay.

was sold as a teaching device to institutions in America, England and Australia, the models sold to the LSE and Cambridge containing a multiplier-accelerator mechanism which made the system wildly unstable for a wide range of values of the system's parameters.

With the analogue machine to clarify his ideas, Phillips [1953, 1954] turned to study government stabilisation measures. He applied the closed-loop control theory of engineering and freed the price-level (Hughes Hallett, this volume). Stabilisation policy required a target and Phillips assumed the target of a constant price-level rather than full employment ([1953] pp. 6–7). The intermediate target, or control variable, was aggregate demand as measured by the unemployment rate.

Phillips' closed-loop block diagram showed that disturbances to aggregate demand caused actual production (Y_a) to deviate from the equilibrium level (Y_e), which in turn induced multiplier-accelerator effects and price-level changes $(\dot{p})$. Phillips represented the relation between $\dot{p}$ and $(Y_a - Y_e)$ by the nonlinear curve in Fig. 1 ([1953] p. 31, [1954] p. 307). The price-level changes triggered changes of the interest rate in the same direction (the Keynes effect) or real balances in the opposite direction (the Pigou effect). Government stabilization measures were required if the degree of price flexibility was small, the time path of the price changes was undesirable, or the price changes induced inflationary expectations. There were three government stabilization measures, measures which were either proportional to, or an integral of, or derivative of the production error $(Y_a - Y_e)$, which became known as the PID model (Allen [1956] pp. 268–69).

B. *A contributor to economic policy*

Phillips' work on stabilization was timely in the first postwar decade of Keynesian demand management. In the House of Commons the moderates of the Conservative and Labour parties were eager to use Keynesian tools

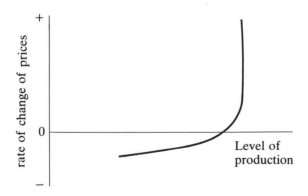

FIG. 1. The first Phillips curve (from Phillips' Ph.D. thesis).

to maintain full employment, or 1.5 percent unemployment, without inflation or exchange rate crises. But after the mild measures of successive Conservative Chancellors failed to eliminate the "creeping inflation" of the early fifties, Mr. Peter Thorneycroft in late 1957 enacted tough monetary measures and proposed a balanced budget. These policies, which put price stability above full employment, were so unpopular that Thorneycroft was forced to resign (Dow [1970] p. 102).

These trials of demand management culminated in two public inquiries, the Radcliffe Committee on the Workings of the Monetary System (1957–59) and the Cohen Council on Prices, Productivity and Incomes (1957–61). Phillips' colleagues from the LSE were actively engaged in the debates. Professors F. Paish and L. C. Robbins testified to the Radcliffe Committee, which included Professor R. S. Sayers as a member. In the summer of 1957 Robbins advised Thorneycroft on economic policy (Robbins [1971]). Sir Dennis Robertson, the external examiner of Phillips' Ph.D. thesis, became the first economist member of the Cohen Council and Professor E. H. Phelps Brown the second.

The difference between these men centered on two issues, whether inflation was caused by demand-pull or cost-push phenomena and to what extent government should intervene to reduce inflation. Paish, the editor of the *Bulletin of the London and Cambridge Economic Service,* was a demand-pull man who proposed that the government maintain unemployment at two percent in order to stabilize the price-level and maximize long run economic growth [1958, 1962]. Sir Dennis Robertson acknowledged that sociological factors affected wage bargaining, but advised that sustained monetary and fiscal restraint which maintained unemployment at two percent would eliminate inflation.[1] The head of the LSE economics department Lionel (later Lord) Robbins, recognized an inverse inflation-unemployment relation but believed statistical problems—of data and forecasting—prevented its reliable quantification. In the main, he blamed an excess money supply generating excess demand in markets for the postwar inflation and feared a wage-price spiral likely to issue in hyperinflation. Robbins counselled that growth of the money supply be fixed at a rate consistent with price-stability which, in his mind, meant unemployment of somewhere over two-and-a-half percent.[2] In contrast to these colleagues Phelps Brown [1958], who held the chair of labor economics, like many an Oxbridge economist was a cost-push man who thought that inflation was caused by institutional factors. Everybody—from Paish to Phelps Brown—admitted that rising import costs had caused much of the early postwar inflation.

---

[1] (Robertson [1955, 1963]; Council on Prices, Productivity and Incomes [1958]).

[2] (Robbins [1932] p. 126, [1947] p. 70, [1954] pp. 69–70; Committee on the Workings of the Monetary System [1960a] pp. 211–19, [1960b] pp. 673–82).

In the context of these debates over inflation, Phillips decided to give his conjecture that there was a causal relation between unemployment and inflation an empirical grounding. The Phelps Brown–Hopkins [1950] money-wage time series was an obvious data source. Drafts of Phillips' empirical study of the wage inflation-unemployment relation during 1861–1957 circulated through the LSE department and Sayers quoted some of the results during the Radcliffe proceedings ([1960b] p. 593).

At this point Sayers was questioning Professor A. J. Brown who had published a statistical study of inflation [1955]. A. J. Brown and Phillips' research was similar, so when Phillips was drafting his findings in the form of a paper, he discussed it with Brown.[3] Using the money-wage time series compiled by Bowley along with data on unemployment and the cost-of-living, Brown set up two statistical scatter diagrams that related wage inflation to unemployment and the cost-of-living respectively. The data scatter, as he testified to the Radcliffe Committee, showed some negative, nonlinear relation between wage inflation and unemployment, but this relation looked unstable from cycle to cycle and in years of low unemployment in the 1914–51 period appeared less important than the relation between wage inflation and costs.[4]

Phillips did more statistical work than his predecessor. He crudely fitted a curve to the scatter diagram relating money-wage inflation to unemployment for 1861–1913, which resulted in a strong, nonlinear inflation-unemployment relation. "It was a rush job", he admitted. He was about to go on sabbatical leave to the University of Melbourne. With the debate continuing, "it was better for understanding to do it (the study) simply and not wait too long". After all, he added modestly, "A. J. Brown had almost got these results earlier".[5]

C. *The transitional era of measurement*

In 1958 Phillips was elected to the Tooke Chair of Economic Science and Statistics because of his publications on a wide range of dynamic problems in economics [1950], control theory [1954, 1957, 1958a], mathematics

---

[3] (Letter to the author from A. J. Brown dated 21 June 1987.)

[4] (Committee on the Workings of the Monetary System [1960b] p. 593).

[5] (Blyth [1975] p. 306). A. J. Brown would have differed with Phillips' statement. As Brown commented to Sayers,

"(some) people claim to be able to see some sort of relation between the pressure of demand measured in some way and the rate of inflation, but I must confess I cannot; perhaps I have not tried hard enough, but I just do not see any clear relation at all".

(Committee on the Workings of the Monetary System [1960b] p. 592–93).

[1959b], and statistics and econometrics [1956]. Phillips, with the famous group of LSE statisticians J. Durbin, M. Kendall and M. H. Quenouille, made important contributions to time-series analysis [1956, 1959b, 1960]. In 1962 Phillips and J. J. Thomas taught the first econometrics course in the economics department and the next year Phillips and Durbin brought J. D. Sargan to the LSE, which consequently became a centre of econometric teaching and research (Gilbert [1986b] p. 39; and this volume).

In this light it appears odd that Phillips' curve, for which he is known to the "non-econometrics" part of the economics profession, should have been constructed by means of a crude curve-fitting technique. No doubt we see in this the willingness of the engineer to use rough-and-ready methods to achieve bold results. Yet why did Phillips assume that the results of the crude technique would be accepted? A likely answer is that this technique did not seem unconventional, for Phillips was working during the transitional period from deterministic to probabilistic techniques of measurement.

Economists since the turn of the century had done statistical studies, but typically rejected the probabilistic basis of statistical theory. To think of economic variables as random and bound by probability distributions required that observations occur under uniform conditions. Yet many economists thought that in economics.

"there is no reason to suppose that uniformities are to be discovered. The 'causes' which bring it about that the ultimate valuations prevailing at any moment are what they are, are heterogeneous in nature; there is no ground for supposing that the resultant effects should exhibit significant uniformity over time and space"

(Robbins [1932] p. 107). For such reasons economists like Robbins either repudiated quantification in economics or assumed that their data were nonstochastic.

Thus for economists, like classical physicists, statistics served to quantify *a priori* causal laws. To deal with the problem of "inconsistent observations" (measurement error), the classical physicist used least squares measures to define the 'true' relationship (e.g. Campbell [1919]. The independent variable was assumed to occur without error, while the dependent variable suffered from measurement error and (in economics) omitted variable error, which however individually were unimportant and on average cancelled out. By common assumption a smooth graph described by a simple analytical function was enough to establish a law, which was just a formalised summary of statistical averages. In economics this deterministic approach prevailed in the quantification of demand curves. If measurements of demand contradicted the theory, economists simply assumed that the data were no good (Morgan [1987a] p. 176). Determinism also marked the development of national income calculations (Horvath [1987] p. 165). The classical idea that least squares measures uncovered "hidden and inner" uniformities in a complex mass of observations prevailed to the 1950s (e.g. Blair [1952] p. 177).

Economists occasionally carried out regression analysis accompanied by some measure of approximation—usually the root mean square error, the standard error or the coefficient of determination (R^2)—but they lacked a statistical basis on which to interpret such measures. Not until after the impact of quantum physics and Haavelmo's (1944) work on probability did economists recognise "error" in a probabilistic perspective, which permitted statistical inference ([Mirowski (this volume); Morgan [1987a]). Even so, it was not till 1960s that econometrics textbooks dealt with stochastic equations, error distributions and hypothesis testing.

The textbook *Statistics for Economists* [1949], by the LSE's R. G. D. Allen, head of the statistics department and a mathematical economist, belonged to the transitional period in economic statistics. Amongst the precursors of econometrics, Allen [1939] discussed regression when both the independent and dependent variables were subject to random errors. Nevertheless, for Allen the point of regression analysis remained to find the "true" relationship between two variables as defined by the least squares lines of averages. As he stated, echoing Galton and Yule,[6]

> "(f) or a continuous frequency distribution of two continuous variables, the regression curve of y on x is defined by the relation of the (arithmetic) mean values of y in x-arrays to the value of x defining the arrays ... (The) regression line( ) gives the true relation ..." (pp. 191, 199).

Allen's textbook (pp. 120–136) listed the steps in this double-averaging procedure:[7] The horizontal axis of a scatter diagram was divided into "convenient" intervals. Given interval i with the lower and upper bounds x_l and x_u respectively, the value of x was defined by the midpoint of the interval,

$$x_i = (x_{li} + x_{ui})/2 \tag{1}$$

on the assumption that the "true" x values (without measurement error) occurred at that point. Given the intervals, vertical arrays were drawn which each contained n observations of $y(y_0)$. Taking the mean value y in vertical array i

$$y_i = \sum_{i=1}^{n_i} y_{0i}/n_i \tag{2}$$

cancelled out the random deviations of y about its "true" values. Least squares estimates were taken on the averaged data x_i, y_i for all intervals i. (In the case of two random variables, these steps were repeated given y as the independent and x as the dependent variable, with the "true" relation

---

[6] (Stigler [1986] pp. 349, 351).
[7] Similar textbooks were Mills [1924b]; Croxton and Cowden [1939]; Charlier [1947]; and Blair [1952].

between x and y lying on an acute angle between the two regression lines). The success of the whole analysis, which shortened the calculations done by hand, depended on whether the mean coordinates fell close to the regression line.

It was this crude technique that Phillips [1958a] exploited in constructing his famous curve.[8]

II. Phillips' approximate regression

A. *The assumption of nonlinearity*

Phillips [1958a] defined money-wage inflation $(\dot{W}/W)$ to be dependent on unemployment (U) and the proportionate change in unemployment $(\dot{U}/U)$,

$$\dot{W}/W = f_1(U) + f_2(\dot{U}/U). \tag{3}$$

To reduce the errors produced by the use of discrete data to represent flow-variables, he approximated $\dot{w}/w$ and $\dot{U}/U$ by taking the first central difference of the indexes, that is

$$(\dot{W}/W)_t \approx (W_{t+1} - W_{t-1})/2W_t \tag{4a}$$

and

$$(\dot{U}/U)_t \approx (U_{t+1} - U_{t-1})/2U_t.\,^9 \tag{4b}$$

Phillips assumed that the relation between $\dot{W}/W$ and U was

"*likely to be highly nonlinear*" (p. 283, emphasis added),

an assumption that dated back to his early work on stabilization policy (see Fig. 1 above).[10] $\dot{U}/U$ was interpreted as a cyclical expectations variable: When $\dot{U}/U$ was negative, $\dot{W}/W$ rose over the rate due to U alone and conversely when $\dot{U}/U$ was positive.

B. *Finding nonlinear data*

Phillips showed the effect of U and $\dot{U}/U$ on $\dot{W}/W$ in seven graphs (his Figures 2–8), each of one of the cycles during 1861–1913. He then commented that

"Figure 3 and Figures 5 to 8 show a very clear relation between the rate of change of wage rates and the level and rate of change of unemployment, but the relation hardly appears at all in the cycle shown in Figure 4" (p. 291),[11]

---

[8] Data grouping has remained in use to maintain confidentiality, remove measurement error and so on (Haitovsky [1973]; Ehrenberg [1975]; Freeman *et al.* [1978]).

[9] (Phillips [1956] p. 107, [1958a] pp. 290–91).

[10] In Phillips' 1958 model, the dependent variable appeared in proportional terms, in the 1953–54 model in differential terms. Stability models of the time took either form, which had the same stationary solution.

[11] Phillips thought that rising import prices influenced inflation in his Fig. 2 (see below, p. 177).

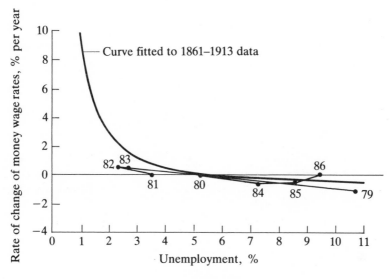

FIG. 2(a). 1879–1886.

(my Figure 2(a)). The Phelps Brown–Hopkins statistics for 1879–1886 were based on an index by G. H. Wood (Phelps Brown [1950] p. 264). There was an alternative index by A. L. Bowley ([1937] p. 6). The two indexes differed in terms of industrial coverage and occupational weights. Neither Wood [1909] nor Bowley [1937] reported that the construction of their index for 1879–1886 involved special problems, except that the data sources were

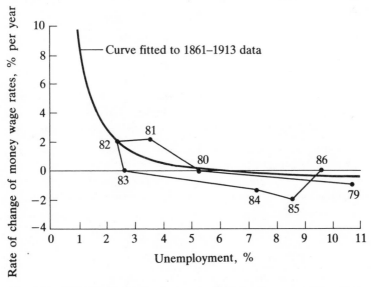

FIG. 2(b). 1879–1886, using Bowley's wage index for the years 1881 to 1886.

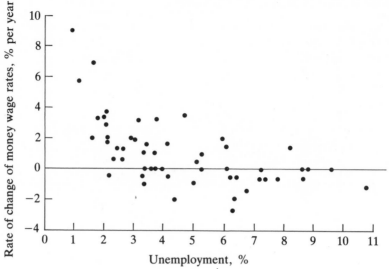

FIG. 3. The scatter-diagram, 1861–1913.

especially scanty for the pre-1884 years (Bowley and Wood [1906] pp. 155, 164). Yet Phillips blamed the inconsistency between his hypothesis and the data on measurement error, stating that

"(*i*)*t* seems possible that some peculiarity may have occurred in the construction of Wood's index for these years"

(Phillips [1958a] p. 291). He then substituted Bowley's index in place of Wood's index for 1881–86 and replaced his Fig. 4 by Fig. 4(a) (my Fig. 2(b)) which showed the

"typical relation between the rate of change of wage rates and the level and rate of change of unemployment" (p. 291).

Phillips kept the Phelps Brown–Hopkins data for 1887–1913 because

"Bowley's index for the remainder of the period up to 1913 gives results which are broadly similar to those shown in Figs. 5–8, but the pattern is rather less regular than that obtained with the index of Phelps Brown and Sheila Hopkins" (pp. 292).

The scatter-diagram below shows Phillips' final data. This diagram could be described by many different curves. A straight line, found in other studies of the $\dot{W}/W - U$ relation,[12] might not have given the best fit, but the 1961–1913 data were so poor that a linear approximation would have sufficed.[13] Alternatively, Fig. 3 could be described by an L-shaped curve

[12] (Dicks–Mireaux and Dow [1959] p. 154; Lipsey [1960] p. 27 n. 2; Griffin [1962] p. 385; Santomero and Seater [1978] pp. 505–06).
[13] (Wulwick [1987] p. 840). Moreover, Phillips was uncertain about lags which "would have the effect of moving each point in the (latter) diagrams horizontally part of the way towards the point of the preceding year . . ." (p. 293).

(with the kink at $U = 5$) as the standard macroeconomics of the time would suggest (Griffin [1962] p. 383). Finally, the scatter-diagram could be estimated as Phillips did, by a nonlinear curve. To this end, Phillips' data-substitution in fact created a noticeable increase in the nonlinearity of the graph (Lipsey [1960] p. 5).

C. *Choosing a nonlinear specification*

Phillips chose a hyperbolic curve to describe the $\dot{W}/W - U$ relation. The basic equation for a rectangular hyperbola would be familiar to an economist or an engineer as the curve of unit elasticity

$$\dot{W}/W = b/U + k\dot{U}/U \qquad \text{(from equation (3)).} \qquad (5)$$

With the hyperbola, $\dot{W}/W$ asymptotically approached infinity as U approach zero, but asymptotically approached a constant small value as U approached infinity. However, when $\dot{W}/W$ took on a zero or negative values equation (5) could not be satisfied. In this case the appropriate form was

$$\dot{W}/W + a = b/U + k\dot{U}/U \qquad a > |\dot{W}/W|. \qquad (6)$$

The result of adding a measure (c) of the speed at which the curve approached its asymptotes and a measure (m) of the rate at which the loops circled about the curve was

$$\dot{W}/W + a = b/U^c + k\dot{U}/U^m \qquad c, m > 0 \qquad (7)$$

(pp. 290–91 n.3).

Unfortunately, it was impossible either to estimate equation (7) which was nonlinear in parameters or to linearize the equation. Phillips dealt with this problem in two steps (Gilbert [1976] p. 52). He omitted $\dot{U}/U$

$$\dot{W}/W + a = b/U^c + e \qquad \leq 0, \qquad (8)$$

arguing on standard statistical grounds that the estimate of b would be consistent

"since it can easily be shown that $\dot{U}/U^m$ is uncorrelated with U or with any power of U provided that U is, as in this case, a trend-free variable" ([1958] p. 291).[14]

Then he log-linearized the equation—

$$\log (\dot{W}/W + a) = \log b + c \log U + e. \qquad (9)$$

D. *Constructing a nonlinear graph of averages*

1. The reason for averaging

At this point Phillips, as a time series analyst recognised another problem. The omission of $\dot{U}/U^m$ gave rise to an additive error term which

---

[14] On the statistical argument see (Phillips [1956] p. 109).

took on negative values during part of the cycle (Gilbert [1976] p. 53). This made it hard to find the appropriate value of the constant a, both to satisfy equation 8 and to permit Phillips to take logarithms. A moving average scheme, given the irregularity of the cycles, would not eliminate $\dot{U}/U^m$.[15] Instead Phillips eliminated the disturbance term by averaging the data. As he explained,

> "the effect of changing unemployment on the rate of change of wage rates tends to be cancelled out by this averaging, so that each cross (or mean coordinate) gives an approximation to the rate of change of wages which would be associated with the indicated level of unemployment if unemployment were held constant at that level" (p. 290).

Phillips divided the U axis of the scatter diagram into six intervals. Six U values were defined by the arithmetic mean of observations within each interval and six $\dot{W}/W$ values were defined by the mean of the observations in each vertical array (see equation (2) above).[16] The interval classes were defined by $U = 0-2$, $2-3$, $3-4$, $4-5$, $5-7$, $7-11$ and contained six, ten, twelve, five, eleven and nine observations respectively.

Why did Phillips choose these intervals? A deceptive answer can be drawn from his statement that

> "each interval includes years in which unemployment was increasing and years in which it was decreasing" (p. 290).[17]

This statement explained why averaging within the groups defined by the six intervals would set $\dot{U}/U$ to zero. It did not explain the choice of the intervals themselves. According to Phillips $\dot{U}$ was a *continuous* variable (as in equation (4b)) which followed a looped path (as in Fig. 2(a)), so that every conceivable interval would include years in which $\dot{U}/U \lessgtr 0$. Even if $\dot{U}/U$ were taken as a discrete variable, a glance at Phillips' data shows that *many* interval sets beside the one that he chose would include $\dot{U}/U \lessgtr 0$.[18] Thus the explanation of Phillips' intervals must lie elsewhere.

Phillips needed a selection of intervals such that the mean points plotted would lie on the presupposed *hyperbolic* curve. Since Phillips left no papers, we do not know if he tried out alternative intervals. We do know that he did his calculations on the LSE electrical desk-calculator rather than the University of London Ferranti mainframe computer, probably because he and his research assistants were unfamiliar with the software.[19] But even though Phillips was in a rush to get this work done, the use of a desk-calculator would have allowed some experimentation with alternative intervals.

---

[15] Phillips used moving averages to reduce the seasonal and random fluctuations in the Australian $\dot{W}/W$ and U data, 1948–58 [1959a].

[16] In averaging their data, statisticians took the midpoint (Allen [1956] p. 122) or the arithmetic mean of the interval (Blair [1952] pp. 184, 243).

[17] The author thanks the anonymous referee for this point.

[18] Phillips' data is available from the author or C. L. Gilbert.

[19] This information was supplied by the anonymous referee.

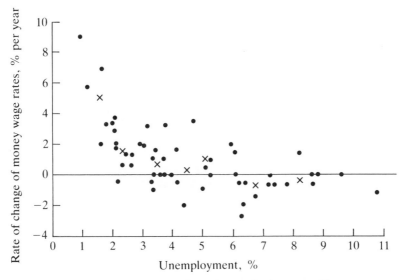

FIG. 4. Constructing an alternative graph of averages (1).

2. An experiment with alternative intervals

For example, consider the seven intervals $U = 0$–2, 2–3, 3–4, 4–5, 5–6, 6–8, 8–11, which are similar to Phillips' intervals. The result, shown in Fig. 4, is an irregular graph of averages with a *positive* $\dot{W}/W - U$ relation at unemployment rates in the 4.5 to 8 percent range.[20] The least squares estimates of Fig. 4 using Phillips' logarithmic specification are

$$\log (\dot{W}/W + 0.90) = 8.267 - 1.190 \log U, \qquad R^2 = 0.92 \qquad (9a)$$

for the U range 0–6, where the value of a is approximated by the absolute mean value of the negative observations of $\dot{W}/W$

$$a = \sum_{j=1}^{n} |(\dot{W}/W)_j/n| = 0.90 \qquad \dot{W}/W < 0. \qquad (10)$$

Alternatively, consider the six intervals $U = 0$–2, 2–3, 3–4, 4–6, 6–8, 8–11, which also are similar to Phillips' intervals. As Fig. 5 shows, the resulting graph of averages is irregular, again with a *positive* relation between $\dot{W}/W$ and U in the high unemployment range.[21] The least squares estimates for the U range 0–6 are

$$\log (\dot{W}/W + 0.90) = 8.326 - 1.185 \log U, \qquad R^2 = 0.92. \qquad (9b)$$

[20] The coordinates are: (1) 1.5167, 5.0585; (2) 2.34; 1.5471; (3) 3.4833, 0.8481; (4) 4.49, 0.3466; (5) 5.31, 0.4952; (6) 6.7, −0.7; (7) 8.2, −0.32. The number of observations are 6, 10, 12, 5, 5, 10 and 5 respectively.
[21] The coordinates are: (1) 1.5167, 5.0585; (2) 2.35, 1.5471; (3) 3.4833, 0.8481; (4) 4.99, 0.5153; (5) 6.7, −0.7; (6) 8.2, −0.32. The intervals contain 6, 10, 12, 10, 10 and 5 observations respectively.

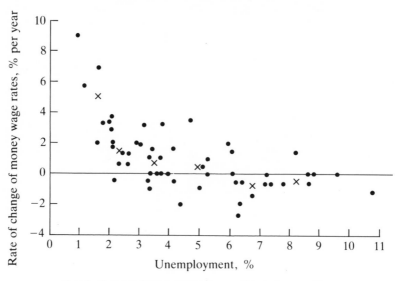

F<small>IG</small>. 5. Constructing an alternative graph of averages (2).

Surprisingly, only Phillips' intervals resulted in the smooth, *hyperbolic* graph of averages, as shown in Fig. 6.[22] Moreover, the least squares estimates for the U range 0–5

$$\log (\dot{W}/W + 0.90) = 9.638 - \log 1.394U, \qquad (R^2 = 0.96), \qquad (9c)$$

involved the least residual error.

Which of the three graphs of averages yielded the most accurate estimates? The nonlinear least square estimates of the complete scatter using Phillips' preferred specification turned out to be

7a. $\dot{W}/W + 1.0035 = 8.7339 + U^{-1.2913} - 0.02529\dot{U}/U^{1.1874}$

s.e.   (0.5154) (0.7466)   (0.2527) (0.01154)   (0.3818)

$$R^2 = 0.8125 \qquad \text{s.e. } e = 1.0374$$

(Gilbert [1976] p. 54). Clearly Phillips' equation (9c) overestimated and the alternative equations (9a, b) underestimated the nonlinearity of the $\dot{W}/W - U$ relation and the responsiveness of $\dot{W}/W$ to U.

E. *A demand-pull relation*

Phillips superimposed his hyperbolic curve for 1861–1913 on the scatter diagrams for 1913–48 and 1948–57, interpreting that the curve represented demand inflation while large deviations represented cost inflation, which he identified with rising import prices.

His explanation went as follows: Prices were set by taking a constant

---

[22] The coordinates were the same as (1)–(4) in note 20 and (5) 6, −0.2; (6) 8.4, −0.35.

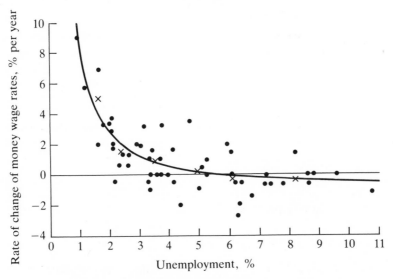

FIG. 6. How Phillips constructed his graph of averages.

percentage mark-up (z) on wage costs, or the money wage rate divided by productivity $(p = z(W/A))$. Therefore price inflation in an open, growing economy was defined by

$$\dot{p}/p \equiv \alpha \dot{W}/W + (1 - \alpha)\hat{p}_m/p_m - \dot{A}/A, \qquad \dot{A}/A > 0, \qquad (11)$$

where $(\dot{p}_m/p_m)$ was the price of imports and $1 - \alpha$ was the share of imports in output. As long as real wages were either rising or constant $(\dot{W}/W \geqslant \dot{p}/p)$, money wage inflation was determined solely by the competitive bidding for labor, for which U was a proxy. The maximum level of import-price inflation consistent with a stable Phillips curve was then

$$\dot{p}_m/p_m = \dot{W}/W + (1/1 - \alpha)\dot{A}/A \qquad \dot{p}/p = \dot{W}/W. \qquad (12)$$

Excessively rapid increases in import prices were able to account for the positive deviations from the Phillips curve in 1947–48 and 1950–51.[23]

In response to this interpretation, Phillips' colleague R. G. Lipsey countered that cost factors affected money-wage bargaining even when real wages were rising (Lipsey [1960] p. 8). Subsequently, Phillips adopted the more familiar explanation of money wage inflation as the sum of demand-pull plus cost-push inflation, while postulating a lag structure that enabled him to eliminate cost inflation for predictive purposes ([1962] p. 11).

F. *The deflationary policy conclusion*

Given this adjustment, it seems clear that Phillips entered the policy debate over inflation on the demand-pull side. He believed his empirical

[23] (Phillips [1958a] pp. 284, 298; Desai [1984] pp. 256–57).

evidence showed that

> "if the average level of unemployment were kept at a little less than $2\frac{1}{2}$ per cent, the average rate of increase in wages over a period of years could be expected to be about 2 per cent per annum so that with the rate of increase of productivity experienced since the war the average level of prices would be almost constant. Also, in the range between $1\frac{1}{2}$ per cent and $2\frac{1}{2}$ per cent unemployment, for every 0.1 per cent that the average level of unemployment was reduced, wages and prices would rise at about 0.3 per cent year faster.... Then we can only reduce inflation, for any given rate of increase of productivity, at the cost of higher unemployment" ([1962] p. 11; [1958] p. 299].

This stabilization policy proposal was premised on a unique and permanent relation between average $\dot{W}/W$ and average U. That indeed was just what the exact curve-fitting procedure implied.

III. A reconstruction of Phillips' curve

Brauchli [1972] and Desai [1975] used trigonometric functions to reconstruct Phillips' curve, which they saw defined a stationary equilibrium relation between $\dot{W}/W$ and U.

Brauchli argued that the loops in Phillips' diagrams (as in Fig. 2(a)) represented a dynamic relation between

$$\dot{W}/W = \dot{W}/W_0 \sin(g_1(t)) + \dot{W}/W_c \qquad t, \text{ time} \qquad (13a)$$

and

$$U = U_0 \cos(g_2(t)) + U_c \qquad (13b)$$

where $\dot{W}/W_c$ (U_c) was the center of gravity of the data and $\dot{W}/W_0$ (U_0) was the average amplitude with respect to the center. These two equations defined the simultaneous, elliptical movement of $\dot{W}/W$ and U over time. The mean locus of states that the dynamical system could realize gave the $\dot{W}/W - U$ relation outside time—or Phillips' curve.

Desai defined Phillips' dynamic system (or loops) by two simultaneous structural nonlinear stochastic differential equations

$$\dot{U}_t = h_1(U_t, (\dot{W}/W)_t) \qquad (14a)$$

and

$$D(\dot{W}/W)_t = h_2((\dot{W}/W)_t, U_t). \qquad (14b)$$

$\dot{U}_t = 0$ $(D(\dot{W}/W)_t = 0)$ gave the equilibrium path of equation (14) on one side of which $\dot{U}_t < 0$ $(D(\dot{W}/W)_t > 0)$ and on the other $\dot{U}_t > 0$ $(D(\dot{W}/W < 0)$. Phillips supposedly set $\dot{U} = 0$ as follows: The $6\frac{1}{2}$ cycles during 1861–1913 (Phillips' Figs. 2–8) were each approximated by a sine wave. The time path of U in each cycle was plotted one on top of another on a graph with t as the horizontal and U as the vertical axis. Next the U axis was divided into Phillips' six intervals $(U = 0\text{-}2, 2\text{-}3 \ldots)$. Horizontal bands were extended across the graph and the average U was calculated in each of the six bands at year five, the median of the cycle.[24] The averaging effectively set $\dot{U} = 0$, which allowed equation (14a) to solve for Phillips' curve. Since this curve was outside the time domain, it was not possible to "slide down" and trade-off $\dot{W}/W$ for U. Setting $D(\dot{W}/W)_t = 0$ by an analogous procedure resulted in an inverse Phillips curve.

Desai's method of defining an equilibrium phase relation was received as "ingenious" and "important" (Gersovitz [1980] p. 439). Nevertheless, as Phillips' [1946] growth model shows, Phillips' curve involved different assumptions than those implied by sinusoidal estimating methods.

Phillips' growth model was based on mark-up pricing and Harrod's growth model. The mark-up price in growth terms for a closed economy was

$$\dot{p}/p \equiv \dot{W}/W - \dot{A}/A, \tag{15}$$

that is, price inflation equalled wage inflation minus the rate of productivity growth. Phillips' curve implied that

$$\dot{p}/p = \dot{w}/w - \dot{A}/A + \beta((Y_a/Y_e) - 1), \tag{16}$$

where $(\dot{w}/w)$ was money-wage inflation at capacity output (Y_e), the same as the rate of productivity growth. Hence price inflation depended only on the ratio of actual to capacity output (Y_a/Y_e), which varied directly with U. The coefficient β rose as U fell since Phillips' curve was nonlinear. In addition,

$$\dot{W}/W - \dot{w}/w = \beta((Y_a/Y_e) - 1), \tag{17}$$

that is, the difference between actual wage inflation and the natural rate of wage inflation depended on capacity utilization. Lastly, the equilibrium rate of economic growth $((\dot{Y}/Y)_e)$ was determined by

$$(\dot{Y}/Y)_e = (S/Y)(Y/K)(Y_a/Y_e) \tag{18}$$

where S/Y was the ratio of savings to income and Y/K the output-capital ratio. The natural rate of equilibrium growth occurred when $Y_a/Y_e = 1$ and actual wage inflation equalled the natural rate of wage inflation.

Capacity utilization (Y_a/Y_e) was regulated by the monetary and fiscal authorities in order to influence inflation, as represented by equations (16)–(17). The value of β in the U range of 1.5–2.5 percent was "a little over unity", a result based on Phillips' curve and Paish's findings on the correlation between changes in U and changes in Y_a/Y_e ([1961] pp.. 361, 365).[25] Lastly, Phillips argued that a small reduction in U within the 1.5 to 2.5 percent range produced offsetting changes in the saving ratio and/or the output-capital ratio, so that the equilibrium growth rate was constant ([1962] p. 14).

In Phillips' model in contrast to the Desai–Brauchli interpretation, U figured as the control, or causal variable. Phillips' model permitted a $\dot{W}/W - U$ trade-off, with the proviso that U be maintained for several years

---

[24] Burns and Mitchell [1946] followed this procedure in their study of business cycles.
[25] On Paish's doctrine see (Wulwick [1987] p. 852).

while economic equilibrium was reestablished ([1962] p. 14). The model, which pertained to historical time, incorporated the Phillips curve on the assumption that it represented the "typical" relation between $\dot{W}/W$ and U ([1958a] pp. 291–95). Phillips himself rejected the total sine-curve analysis because it missed the complexity of economic cycles ([1962] p. 5). Of course, outside the curve-fitting context, Phillips' choice of intervals seemed irrelevant, so the Brauchli–Desai interpretation proffered no explanation.

IV. Phillips' curve 1959–1967

In 1957 R. G. Lipsey initiated a Staff Seminar on Methodology, Measurement and Testing (M^2T) (de Marchi [1988]). M. Steuer (Lipsey and Steuer [1961]), B. Corry (Corry and Laidler [1967]), G. C. Archibald [1969] and M. Peston [1971] amongst others frequented the seminar. The M^2T group vocally advocated econometrics and, as junior faculty and to a large extent LSE graduates, took particular exception to Robbins' traditional views on the subject. Prone as they were to adopt Labour Party views, the group also took offense at Robbins' public warnings of the impending hyperinflation given the postwar levels of unemployment. For these reasons, the M^2T group took a keen interest in an econometric approach to Phillips' curve.[26]

Lipsey was the first member to work on Phillips' curve and the M^2T seminar discussed his paper [1960]. Having recently taught himself econometrics, Lipsey wanted

"to treat (Phillips') data by standard statistical methods" (p. 3).

and specified a multiple regression equation that was linear in parameters

$$\dot{W}/W + a = hU^{-1} + mU^{-2} + v\dot{U}/U. \tag{15}$$

Estimating the complete data for 1862–1913, Lipsey arrived at a curve that virtually coincided with Phillips' curve and had about the same test statistics (Gilbert [1976] p. 55).

This raises the question of why Phillips neglected to specify an equation like Lipsey's to avoid averaging the data. Phillips' preferred specification (equation (7)) was simpler, offering an easily comprehensible indication of the nonlinearity of the data. bU^c was easier to grasp than that of a U series with parameters that could take on different signs and $\dot{U}/U^m$ was a general term, including the case where $m = 1$. Omitting $\dot{U}/U^m$ left

$$(\dot{W}/W)' = bU^c, \qquad (\dot{W}/W)' \equiv \dot{W}/W + a, \tag{8a}$$

the equation for a curve of constant elasticity with which engineers are accustomed to work. When it was impossible to estimate such a nonlinear equation, Phillips the time-series analyst was willing to do some "dirty work" to get an approximation.

In contrast Lipsey, a novice at time-series econometrics, was concerned

[26] (Letter to N. de Marchi from David Laidler dated 26 November 1985).

with standard practice. His equation took on a form derived from time series data. The choice of exponents on U varied with different periods, the additional parameters on U improving the fit. Lipsey experimented with different variables and included measures of correlation and "error". Regressing $\dot{W}/W$ on U, $\dot{U}/U$ and $\dot{p}/p$ for 1923–39 and 1948–57, he found high standard errors on the U coefficients (but did not test for statistical significance) and a partial correlation coefficient of only 0.38 on U ([1960] p. 26).

Lipsey's substitution of his equation for Phillips' reflected the new standard of econometrics. From this perspective, the young LSE economists would see "very serious problems" with Phillips' proposal of an unemployment target to peg inflation given the sizeable "error"—measurement, specification and random error—in the estimates of the $\dot{W}/W - U$ relation.[27]

At the same time, Phillips' curve met with great success in policy circles. Showing a permanent inverse relation between inflation and unemployment, the curve confirmed the prevalent belief that inflation was caused mainly by excess demand. The marked nonlinearity of the curve at low regions of unemployment showed that price-level stability would be consistent with unemployment of $2\frac{1}{4}$ percent, little more than the traditional "full employment" figure of 1.5 percent about the Treasury when Mr. Selwyn Lloyd was the Conservative Chancellor (1960–62).[28] And in 1967, when Phillips left to take a chair in economics at the Australian National University, the Labour Party Chancellor Mr. Jim Callaghan presented a Budget designed to maintain unemployment at $2\frac{1}{4}$ percent according to

"Professor Frank Paish of the LSE . . . the tireless propagandist . . . [and] the original begetter of the theory: Professor A. W. Phillips, also of London University".[29]

V. Summary and conclusion

Phillips initially hypothesised his curve, which made inflation a highly nonlinear function of unemployment, as a stepping-stone in his application of engineering control principles to economic stabilization policy. A national debate over inflation policy, which involved his senior colleagues at the LSE, prompted Phillips to estimate this curve using the Phelps Brown–Hopkins money-wage series along with unemployment data for 1861–1957.

Phillips approached this project with the assurance of a skilled time series analyst and the flourish of a former engineer. When the data did not take a nonlinear form, without compunction he substituted data of an alternative

[27] (Routh [1959], pp. 314–15; Lipsey [1960], p. 30; Lipsey and Steuer [1961] p. 150 n.2). G. Routh, at the National Institute of Economic and Social Research, wrote his Ph.D. thesis under Phelps Brown.
[28] (*Times Review of Industry* [1967] 5 January, p. 14).
[29] (*Spectator* [1967] 4 April, Leader; Blyth [1975] p. 306).

series. To describe the data, he specified a simple estimating equation that was nonlinear in parameters. Since nonlinear least squares were not feasible at the time, Phillips used an approximation to get the necessary practical results. He deftly exploited a crude curve-fitting procedure, which was common in those transitional days between deterministic and probabilistic techniques of measurement, to arrive at the desired hyperbolic curve. In a rush to go off on sabbatical leave, he superimposed the curve on the 1914–1957 data, explained away most instances of cost-push inflation, and found an exact fit for more recent postwar years by the ad hoc lagging of unemployment by a few months.

The resulting Phillips curve supplied economics with a stabilization law, yet one without a basis in either best technique or economic theory. More than twenty years of subsequent research has not confuted this conclusion (Wulwick [1987]).

California State University at Sacramento

Oxford Economic Papers 41 (1989), 189–214

ECONOMETRICS AND THE THEORY OF ECONOMIC POLICY: THE TINBERGEN–THEIL CONTRIBUTIONS 40 YEARS ON*

By A. J. HUGHES HALLETT

1. Introduction

In 1986 we celebrated the 50th anniversary not only of the publication of Keynes' "General Theory", but also of the world's first econometric model. Between them, these two developments have probably had a greater impact on the scope of economic analysis than any other innovation this century. Keynes' contribution was the start of modern macroeconomics and, despite a major challenge from neoclassical economics, it remains the dominant paradigm in macroeconomic thinking. Tinbergen's econometric models of the Dutch and the US economies (Tinbergen 1936, 1939),[1] built up from his business cycle research, started a revolution by opening up the possibility of forecasting analysis and policy evaluation with empirical models. Now there is hardly a government or agency, investment bank or market analyst without access to such models.

At the time Tinbergen was writing a few empirical studies of the demand for agricultural products had been constructed in the US (Schultz, 1938), but the ability to use their results for policy purposes still lay in the future (Waugh, 1944). Tinbergen's models were therefore the first of a whole economy and the first to be aimed specifically at policy analysis (see Klaassen *et al.*, 1959). At that time many countries were faced with major problems of unemployment, inadequate demand and investment. Tinbergen introduced his models to help him formulate corrective policies that were consistent across sectors and expenditure groups.

From all this activity emerged Tinbergen's theory of economic policy. Every student now knows that an equal number of instruments and targets is a necessary condition for the existence of policies capable of reaching specified targets. But more significantly, his theory obliges policy makers to make an efficient, and consistent, use of their policy instruments. The crucial question then was, how should those targets be chosen? To resolve that, Theil introduced the flexible target approach: first you decide where you would like to go, and then you pick policies to steer the economy as

*I am grateful to Professors Tinbergen and Theil for their helpful comments, although neither of them can be held responsible for my interpretation of their work. The comments of Andries Brandsma and two referees were also particularly helpful.

[1] Tinbergen also constructed a business cycle model of the UK, but it was published rather later (Tinbergen, 1951b).

close as possible to that path.[2] But with the development of formal optimal control techniques, interest in the Tinbergen–Theil approach had faded by the 1970's, only to reappear ten years later in the form of algorithms designed to handle nonlinear models. These algorithms are now widely used but, because they are computationally efficient rather than mathematically elegant, and because they are not easily related to standard control theory, they seldom appear in any text.

The value of a historical review is that it can highlight this neglected trade-off between mathematical sophistication and versatility when picking methods which work efficiently for economic policy selection problems. This paper argues that, by setting the policy problem in a more general framework, the Tinbergen–Theil procedure becomes a Newton-type optimisation algorithm. That explains why it is usually so much more efficient computationally than standard control techniques. It also explains why, unlike control techniques, it is so easily extended for the problems which are important to economics (risk, decentralised decisions, expectational effects etc.). This paper therefore reviews the Tinbergen–Theil theory of economic policy principally in relation to modern developments in that area. Obviously both Tinbergen and Theil have made major contributions in many other areas (e.g. development and welfare economics, econometric theory, consumer demand etc.), but this paper will be devoted entirely to econometric models in the theory of economic policy.

2. Historical and political background

(i) *The history*

Ironically it was Keynes himself who dismissed Tinbergen's modelling efforts as misguided (Keynes, 1939). In retrospect, it seems Keynes misjudged the issue. In many problems, policy analysis cannot be conducted without some empirical evidence since policy impacts depend crucially on the signs (and often relative sizes) of the system's underlying parameters. Tinbergen made this point in explaining the poor performance of Haberler's theory of the Business Cycle (Tinbergen 1935, 1937 and 1942a). Forty years later Malinvaud found it necessary to make exactly the same point in an address to the Econometric Society (Malinvaud, 1981).

Tinbergen's contributions to econometric model building, and the use of those models for policy evaluation purposes, fall into two parts—roughly separated by the war. Before the war his contributions were devoted to econometric model building itself, in both the specification and the estimation

---

[2] The first published discussion of the flexible targets approach appeared in Tinbergen (1954) where the idea is attributed to Schouten and Theil of the Central Planning Bureau staff. At that stage the notion of a flexible target had been specified but no-one had developed a method for picking instrument values to steer those targets as close as possible to their desired values. That task fell to Theil who had the technical apparatus from his analysis of consumption behaviour (see Section 5 below).

aspects. Tinbergen himself has made it clear that his ultimate purpose was that those models should be used to improve policy design (Tinbergen, 1987); and his writings of the period draw particular attention to the policy implications of his models. Nevertheless the main effort, and the main intellectual input, was directed at the modelling process itself; the needs of practical policy making and political concerns were important but took second place at that stage. After the war, these priorities became reversed.

However, given the need to improve our understanding of the policy process, his main line of argument and the way in which he got drawn into the model building business have a distinctly modern flavour. The great macroeconomic challenge of the 1930's was to explain how business cycles arose, how they affected the major economic aggregates (output, employment etc.), and what scope policy might have for mitigating the effects of those cycles. Some writers, like Keynes, had set about analysing these problems by identifying the determinants of, and interactions between, individual expenditure categories. Others, among whom Haberler was the leading exponent, analysed the mechanisms of the business cycle itself, linking the main expenditure categories in a dynamic model of the whole economy—see, for example, Haberler (1939). These were all theoretical models, and it was Tinbergen who, on behalf of the new Econometric Society, undertook to test the underlying theories by confronting them with data. The results were not encouraging and that led to a long debate over whether one should accept explanations based on theoretical specifications or whether one should rely on statistical evidence and build a model up from there. To this day that remains a major issue.

Tinbergen's results convinced him that the correct specification depended crucially on empirical evidence. In 1935 he argued that to understand the relations between cycles in the economy one needed econometric estimates of the coefficients; there was, for example, no detectable lag between the production of investment and consumption goods, although that had been hypothesised in the theoretical models (Tinbergen, 1935). In 1938 he proposed a new investment function, which fitted the facts better than the accelerator model used at that time (Tinbergen, 1938b). Later he pointed out that the projection of a cycle's turning points depends crucially on the underlying model's estimated coefficient values (Tinbergen, 1940). In these papers he picked out a number of empirical facts which would have important policy implications: (i) there was no significant lag between investment and consumption demands, but there was one between incomes and outlays and between demand changes and price changes; (ii) stocks fluctuate with interest rates; (iii) the investment cycle came from an income accelerator mechanism; and (iv) the relationship between investment and consumption varied throughout the cycle. It was to put these policy conclusions to the test, and to resolve the issue of whether the existing theoretical models could explain actual events, that brought Tinbergen into the business of macroeconometric model building. That is also why his first published model was entitled "Business Cycles in the US". There had, in fact, been an earlier Dutch business cycle model[3] which showed all the same empirical characteristics, but a greater policy emphasis. But that model attracted little attention outside Holland.

Originally Tinbergen's model building effort had been intended as part of a programme of research carried out by the European branch of the Econometric Society (at that point still independent of its American counterpart) under the intellectual leadership of Ragnar Frisch, together with Jacob Marschak and Tjalling Koopmans as the econometricians. However, because of its policy implications, and because the theoretical business cycle research had been sponsored by the League of Nations, Tinbergen's US model was taken over and published by the League of Nations as a follow up to his Dutch model. It has been planned that Koopmans should build a similar model of the UK economy, but with the threat of war both he and Marschak decided to leave Europe. A rising young econometrician, Laurence Klein, was earmarked to replace Koopmans. However, the outbreak of war in Europe stopped all model building activity and the initiative passed from Northern Europe to the USA. Besides it was already becoming clear that too little was known about the estimation techniques necessary for these macroeconometric models: in particular problems were arising with specification uncertainties, dynamics, and simultaneous equation biases. So when normal research activities resumed after the war, it was in the US that progress was made—both in model building (in the hands of Klein at Pennsylvania) and in estimation theory (in the hands of Koopmans and others at the Cowles Commission).

Thus, at the end of the war, Tinbergen found himself temporarily separated from the main thrust of econometric research, and facing a greater problem in planning the reconstruction of the Dutch economy than even in the 1930's. In 1945 the new Dutch government had created its Central Planning Bureau (CPB), and Tinbergen, who was the leading advocate of quantitative policy analysis and one of the few remaining econometricians from the pre-war model building programme, was appointed as its first director.

(ii) *The politics*

The forces which created the CPB and defined its function, are important for tracking the evolution of Tinbergen's theory of economic policy. As in many European countries at the time, the new Dutch government was an uneasy coalition of socialists and the conservative religious parties, with

---

[3] Tinbergen (1936); republished in English by Klaassen *et al.* (1959).

Social Democrats in between.[4] The Socialist groups contained hardliners who had been excluded from power before the war but who had subsequently played a leading role in the resistance movement. Thus Tinbergen not only found himself at the centre of policy making, but he also had to work with a governing coalition of divergent interests which was held together by the need to set up some framework for repairing the damage of the war years. Initially the government had intended to introduce formalised planning procedures, and there were certainly some who thought (and hoped) that this would lead to detailed compulsory plans in the East European mould. Indeed the CPB could easily have taken over the "command planning" functions of the wartime supply ministries. But Tinbergen, who favoured government intervention but not "command planning", preferred to introduce indicative planning methods in the style of Meade and the United Nations. With Tinbergen effectively taking the Social Democratic position, and with the religious parties opposed to any formalised planning, the result was a compromise in which the Central Planning Bureau adopted indicative planning procedures—see Tinbergen's review of the 1947 economic plan (Tinbergen, 1947).

Under this arrangement, the CPB prepared its advice and policy recommendations to the government by means of a central economic projection made with an econometric model but unchanged policies. Further projections, based on a number of different policies and alternative values for the main noncontrollable variables, would be added to give a series of different scenarios. These scenarios would then be presented to the government and its advisory body (the Central Planning Commission, made up of civil servants, representatives of labour and employer's unions, economists and chaired by the Secretary General of the Ministry of Economic Affairs) for comments, revisions, and further suggestions. Further advice may be prepared in the light of these comments, but it is a characteristic of the CPB's system that the government was always left to make its own choice between a series of policy options and their projected consequences.

This characteristic, which marked the crucial difference between the Dutch indicative planning procedures and the command planning approach, was the result of ideological differences between those who favoured rigid economic plans and those who favoured no more than policy guidelines. These ideological differences ultimately determined the role of the CPB and hence the basis for Tinbergen's theory of economic policy. In fact the CPB

[4] The terms Socialist and Social Democrat have been used here to distinguish, in terms which correspond to modern political alignments, the different political forces which formed the CPB and defined its function. Formally speaking the Social Democratic Labour Party had given up its Marxist charter in 1937, but it provided the government with ministers representing a range of opinion from Socialist to Social Democrat. Thus, in 1945, the Minister for Economic Affairs was a hardliner belonging to a Social Democratic party; he was one of those who argued for centralised "command" planning from an earlier socialist tradition.

had little influence to start with because some wished it to be an arm of government issuing policy directives, while others feared it would come to control *all* aspects of economic and commercial life. However the needs of postwar planning demanded a compromise to balance the immediate concerns of conflicting priorities and relieving specific shortages, with the longer term problems of reconstruction and creating a suitable framework for the future. The only workable compromise was one which made the CPB an independent institution, with free and immediate access to all government departments. That independence requires a theory of policy where planners suggest different policy options to the government, based on an independent choice of model, exogenous information and underlying assumptions. (In practice this independence also meant that the CPB staff had the freedom to develop the econometric techniques they needed for model building and policy analysis; these were the major econometric contributions of the Tinbergen–Theil era.) But, as the CPB's influence grew under this compromise, some institutional structure was needed. The overall direction of economic policy was therefore given to a wider advisory body: the Social and Economic Council. The Planning Commission takes that framework as its guide, and fits in specific policies on the basis of the CPB's technical advice. Then, given the alternatives, the final decision is left to a special cabinet subcommittee (the Council for Economic Affairs) supplemented by the CPB's director, the governor of the Central Bank, and other specialists.

This process obviously closely reflects Tinbergen's own theory of economic policy as it was published over the next few years. His publications of this period were all policy orientated, and explained how planning may be carried out using econometric models to give the same detail as the Soviet planning framework or the French sectoral models, but without any compulsion or refusal to consider alternative scenarios.

3. The Tinbergen theory of economic policy: fixed targets

(i) *Static controllability*

Before evaluating the relative merits of different policy packages, it is important to check that sufficient intervention instruments actually exist for the job in hand. If, given a model of the economy's policy responses and the range of policy instruments at the disposal of the decision makers, the economy can be made to reach any desired set of policy objectives, then the model/economy is said to be *controllable*. Controllability is a property guaranteeing the existence of a sequence of decisions which can achieve arbitrary preassigned values for the target variables within some finite planning interval (Preston, 1974).

The traditional version of Tinbergen's theory of economic policy starts out by classifying the variables of an econometric model into four groups: (a) policy targets; (b) policy instruments; (c) data or noncontrollable variables; and (d) the nontarget or "irrelevant" variables. The targets may be "primary" or "intermediate" depending on whether they have a direct impact on the welfare of the community (such as consumption or unemployment) or whether the impact comes indirectly through changes in monetary conditions (e.g. the balance of trade). In terms of a conventional econometric model:

$$Y_t = \sum_{j=1}^{l} \pi_{1j} Y_{t-j} + \sum_{j=0}^{k} \pi_{2j} x_{t-j} + e_t \tag{1}$$

where Y_t are g endogenous variables, x_t are policy instruments, and e_t are noncontrollable random variables. Y_t itself will contain a subset of m policy targets, y_t. The remaining elements of Y_t are nontargets, and e_t would be composed of variables exogenous to both the policy makers and the model (including the model's disturbance terms). This classification of variables is usually attributed to Tinbergen, but it was first used by Frisch (1949) in his work for the United Nations.

Given (1), a naive policy choice would be to pick x_t so as to reach the desired target values y_t^d in each period $t = 1, \ldots, T$, each time taking all lagged values as fixed and setting the e_t variables at their expected values. Deleting the nontarget equations from (1), the required interventions are then:

$$x_t^* = \tilde{\pi}_{20}^{-1}(y_t^d - a_t) \tag{2}$$

where $a_t = \sum_{j=1}^{k} \pi_{1j} Y_{t-j} + \sum_{j=1}^{k} \pi_{2j} x_{t-j} + E_t(e_t)$ is a known vector at the start of period t, and $\tilde{\pi}_{20}$ contains just m rows from π_{20} in (1). Of course, (2) only exists if $m = n$ and $\tilde{\pi}_{20}$ is nonsingular. Under these conditions, y_t^d will be achieved exactly, period by period, provided $E_t(e_t)$ coincides with the realised values of e_t. This is Tinbergen's theory of economic policy (Tinbergen, 1952).

(ii) Policy effectiveness and policy assignments

In Tinbergen's theory, it is important to distinguish the simple necessary condition that there must be at least as many instruments as targets ($n \geq m$), from the more complicated necessary and sufficient condition that those instruments must also be linearly independent ($\tilde{\pi}_{20}$ nonsingular). The reason is obvious: the instruments may be sufficient in number but unable to generate separate effects.

Consider the model:

$$Y = C + I + G + E - M$$
$$C = a(Y - T) \qquad\qquad 0 < a < 1$$
$$T = t_0 + t_1 Y \qquad\qquad 0 < t_1 < 1 \qquad\qquad (3)$$
$$M = m_1 C + m_2 G \qquad\qquad 0 < m_1, m_2 < 1$$
$$I = bY + z \qquad\qquad 0 < b < 1$$

where C = consumption expenditures, E = exports, M = imports, I = investment expenditures, T = taxes. Suppose Y and M are targets, and t_0 and G the instruments. Then:

$$\begin{pmatrix} \Delta Y \\ \Delta M \end{pmatrix} = d^{-1} \begin{bmatrix} (m_1 - 1)a & (1 - m_2) \\ (m_1 a(b-1)) & m_2(1-b) + a(m_1 - m_2)(1 - t_1) \end{bmatrix} \begin{pmatrix} \Delta t_0 \\ \Delta G \end{pmatrix} \qquad (4)$$

provided that $d = 1 - a(1 - t_1)(1 - m_1) - b \neq 0$. Although the static controllability conditions $(n \geqslant m)$ is satisfied here, one of these instruments becomes redundant if the matrix in (4) is singular. The determinant is $a(m_1 - m_2)(1 - b + a(m_1 - m_2)(1 - t_1))/d^2$, so this happens if $m_1 = m_2$. Consequently the instruments become ineffective as $(m_1 - m_2) \to 0$. A related case of redundant instruments arises when t_1 replaces G as an instrument. It is easy to verify that (4) is now replaced by a system whose matrix is singular for all (rather than particular) values of the model's parameters. One instrument is always redundant in this case because it is not possible to engineer the necessary two separate effects through the single channel of T. It is therefore as important to check the *effectiveness* of policy instruments as it is to check that they are sufficient in number.

Tinbergen however maintains that the most important aspect of his theorem is that, by concentrating on the conditions for $\bar{\pi}_{20}$ to have an inverse, it forces policy makers to distinguish clearly between targets and instruments, and also prevents them from trying to assign instruments to targets on a 1 to 1 basis (Tinbergen, 1956). This is the other side of the policy effectiveness coin. By focusing on the condition that $\bar{\pi}_{20}$ should possess an inverse, rather than replacing $\bar{\pi}_{20}$ by a diagonal assignment matrix, each policy instrument will be given its own level of specialisation while correctly allowing for its interactions with the other instruments. That ensures that the instruments will be used in a way which fully exploits their effectiveness. In planning the Dutch postwar reconstruction, Tinbergen noticed that policy makers had a natural tendency to assign particular instruments to individual targets in their own sector of responsibility. That meant they actually got worse outcomes than they should have done since it is not possible to replace $\bar{\pi}_{20}$ with a diagonal matrix and still satisfy (2) exactly. In modern language, they were denying themselves any Pareto efficiency gains by failing to coordinate their domestic policy instruments properly.

Interestingly this problem was actually analysed twenty years later in an important paper by Cooper (1969)—albeit with a very different motivation. Cooper was interested in the design of policy for interdependent economies. His analysis was concerned with the gains from coordinating policies both internally and between countries, and how those gains vary with the strength of domestic interactions and/or the degree of international dependence. Cooper's conclusion was that, because the side effects of an instrument on the targets to which it is not principally assigned increase with the degree of interdependence, the effectiveness of policy declines with increasing dependence between targets. The coordination of policy changes then becomes more important. In Cooper's analysis, decreasing effectiveness shows up in the size of intervention needed to restore targets to their desired values, and in the speed with which targets approach those values. One to one assignments lead to targets overshooting or oscillating because the side effects of other instruments, which may be small individually but large in sum, are ignored until after they have happened. So you suffer either worse outcomes and the costs of longer periods away from "equilibrium", or the greater cost of restoring the targets to their desired values.

Tinbergen's theory of economic policy was therefore designed to ensure the internal coordination of individual policies. In Tinbergen (1954) he took this a stage further by recognising the existence of multiple policy makers, both domestically and internationally, and examined to what extent the policies of different authorities should be integrated and to what extent they could be left autonomous. Unfortunately he was unable to give that feature much emphasis in his theory because the underdeveloped state of game theory at that time prevented the formalisation of his ideas to the multiple policy makers case (Tinbergen, 1987). As a result, the idea of *efficient* policy selections has vanished from his theory and we are left with just the controllability propositions. Nevertheless the problems of decentralisation and efficient policy selections would be a proper part of this theory, born of the rival claims which were made for central planning and market economics at the formative stage of the Dutch economic planning framework.

(iii) *A critique of Tinbergen's theory*

A number of criticisms can be made of Tinbergen's theory of economic policy. There is nothing in his framework which restrains the cost of intervening, or which ensures that the interventions are politically or administratively feasible.[5] Tinbergen's theory does no more than guarantee the existence of a policy which could reach arbitrary objectives. The other

[5] In fact studies which explicitly restrain the interventions to remain within a set of politically feasible values are still rare. Two examples are De Wolff and Sandee (1959) and Brandsma *et al.* (1983).

problems are:

(a) How should x_t be chosen when there are insufficient instruments?

(b) The theory is obviously myopic because the dynamic impacts of x_t on the outcomes $Y_{t+1} \ldots Y_T$ have been ignored. The "irrelevant" variables are no longer irrelevant in a dynamic problem since they affect future targets via the lags in (1). These dynamic effects will influence the values which will be necessary for $x_{t+1}^* \ldots x_T^*$. Although it is still possible to achieve $y_{t+1}^d \ldots y_T^d$, it may require increasingly large changes in $x_{t+1}^* \ldots x_T^*$ to do so. Policy makers are seldom indifferent to the size of the interventions, and an alternative strategy which takes account of the implications for $x_{t+1} \ldots x_T$ when choosing x_t will almost always be cheaper. For example, budget deficits require financing, so that the best set of interventions would restrict the future financial commitments while attempting to reach each y_t^d.

(c) What should be done when $e_t \neq E_t(e_t)$? Static controllability deals only with expected achievements, not actual outcomes. If there is substantial uncertainty (e.g. if e_t has a large variance) or if $y_t \neq y_t^d$ has serious consequences, it will be cold comfort to know nothing more than y_t^d will be reached *on average*. Risk averse interventions, aiming to stabilise the realisations of y_t, could well be preferable.

Criticisms of Tinbergen's theory have always been that it is incomplete. Theil, writing in 1956, cited four main difficulties: the uncertainty associated with the realisations of noncontrollable variables; the uncertainty in having to operate with estimated, and possibly poorly specified, models; the problem of having to project values for noncontrollables which are actually decision values in the hands of other decision makers; and the suboptimality of picking a solution which aims for arbitrarily chosen y_t^d values. In this context, suboptimality has two aspects: if $n < m$, how should the policies best be chosen; and given any n and m, how should y_t^d be chosen?

In subsequent work Theil offered a solution to most of these difficulties. The problem of model uncertainty was never fully resolved, although risk sensitive rules which react to prediction errors (a combination of information and model errors) are one possible answer.[6] Theil dealt with the suboptimality point by introducing an explicit optimisation approach. Optimisation allowed him to deal with the insufficient instruments problem and, at the same time, to penalise the size of the interventions so that they would remain "acceptable" or politically feasible. By operating this approach with the model in its final rather than reduced form, he was also able to handle dynamic choices and additive uncertainties with a multi-period certainty equivalence theorem and a closed loop control mechanism. But the price paid was that y_t^d would no longer be achieved exactly every period, although the economy might get as close to it as possible.

----

[6] See, for example, Hughes Hallett (1984).

4. Extensions of Tinbergen's theory

(i) *Dynamic controllability*

If Tinbergen ignored uncertainty and dynamics it was because there was no established way of handling them systematically at that time. Frisch had to use a laborious "bunch map analysis" to characterise the reliability of estimated coefficients or disturbance terms. Standard errors, as a measure of parameter or residual uncertainty, had just been introduced by Koopmans in his doctoral thesis but they were not widely accepted until his Cowles Commission work got under way in 1947. Similarly, techniques for estimating distributed lags and dynamics were very primitive—the Koyck lag estimator, for example had not yet been discovered. Nevertheless it is straightforward to demonstrate the existence of fixed target policies in uncertain and dynamic systems. We can, for example, aim to hit desired target values at some pre-assigned date in the future, rather than at each decision period. The targets may now take whatever values they need along the way.

The technical condition for being able to reach ideal values for all the endogenous variables, Y_t^d, from an arbitrary situation t periods earlier, Y_0, is known as *dynamic controllability*. Over an interval of t periods, there should be at least as many independent choices which could be made between now and t as there are elements in Y_t^d. Thus a model containing g equations,

$$Y_t = \pi_1 Y_{t-1} + \pi_2 x_t + e_t, \tag{5}$$

is dynamically controllable over $t \geq g$ if and only if $r(\pi_2, \pi_1\pi_2, ..., \pi_1^{g-1}\pi_2) = g$ where $r(\cdot)$ denotes rank; see Turnovsky (1977). So if we have just one instrument, we could assign it to a different target in each period and give each target exactly that impulse required for the dynamics to carry it along to its ideal value at t. But, if we had more instruments, the lead time needed for all targets to reach their ideal states could be reduced to $t < g$ if and only if[7] $r(\pi_2, \pi_1\pi_2, ..., .\pi_1^{t-1}\pi_2) = g$, because multiple "assignments" are possible in each period. Hence the implication of Tinbergen's nonexclusive "assignments" is that the desired targets can be reached earlier. There is an important tradeoff between using more instruments, or a longer lead time, to achieve one's goals.

What happens if we are interested in a subset of m targets from (5); i.e. y_t from Y_t? Let $y_t^d = SY_t^d$ define the selection matrix S. Backsubstituting Y_{t-1} out of (5), and premultiplying the result by S, shows dynamic controllability holds for the condensed system if $r(R_1 \ldots R_m) = m$ for the chosen t, where

---

[7] Preston and Pagan (1982), p. 235. The point is that, if this condition holds, $\pi_1^g\pi_2$ depends on $\pi_1^i\pi_2$ for $i < g - 1$, so no independent instrument choices are added. Moreover (1) can be rewritten without loss of generality, as a first order system such as (5) in order to apply these results.

$R = S\pi_1^{i-1}\pi_2$, since $r(R_i) \leq \min [r(S), r(\pi_1^{i-1}\pi_2)]$. The necessary condition for this is $nt \geq m$, implying that the minimum lead time reduces to a single period only under the conditions of Tinbergen's original theorem. In addition, we see that it may be significantly easier to control the few targets of economic policy than it is to control the whole economy.

(ii) *Path controllability*

The obvious difficulty with this dynamic version of Tinbergen's theory is that, unless y_t^d happens to be on an equilibrium path, the targets are only sure to pass through the preassigned values; they will not necessarily stay there or follow a specified trajectory thereafter.

Path controllability is a condition which ensures a policy exists which will drive the targets (in expectation) along an arbitrary preassigned path from y_t^d. The necessary and sufficient condition in terms of (5) is difficult to use in practice, but a simple necessary condition is $n \geq m$; i.e. Tinbergen's theorem again.[8]

A less stringent requirement would be *local* path controllability. In this case we seek a policy sequence which drives the expected targets along a preassigned path from y_t^d to y_{T+t}^d; i.e. over the interval $[t, T+t]$ but not necessarily beyond. The necessary condition for this is $m(T+1) \leq n(t+T+1)$; Preston and Pagan (1982). The minimum lead time here is $t \geq (m-n)(T+1)/n$, and the maximum period of local controllability is given by:

$$T+1 \leq \frac{nt}{m-n} \quad \text{if} \quad m > n \text{ (unbounded if } m \leq n\text{).} \tag{6}$$

Thus Tinbergen's theorem may be sufficient for dynamic or local path controllability; but it is only strictly necessary for global path controllability.

(iii) *Stabilisability*

The main difficulty with all these extensions is that they treat the economy as deterministic. It is possible to steer the *expected* target values to their ideal values, but controllability says nothing about being able to hold the targets to a given path in the face of unanticipated shocks. Nothing that we can do will prevent *current* shocks pushing the actual targets away from their ideal values. But we can attempt to damp out the consequence of

---

[8] The full necessary and sufficient condition is

$$r\begin{bmatrix} R_1 & \cdots & R_{2m} \\ & \ddots & \vdots \\ 0 & & R_1 \cdots R_m \end{bmatrix} = m^2$$

when only m targets are of interest. These necessary and sufficient conditions are reviewed in Aoki (1975), Preston and Pagan (1982), and Wohltmann (1984). The necessary condition is proved in Buiter and Gersovitz (1984) and Petit (1987). Wohltmann and Krömer (1984) have provided some simplified sufficient conditions.

those shocks as fast as possible thereafter. Then, whatever shocks strike the system, the economy will tend to return to that ideal with fixed policies.

This *stabilisability* property can be achieved if the policies follow a feedback control rule: $x_t = K_t Y_{t-1} + k_t$ (Phillips, 1954). The economy will then behave as:

$$Y_t = (\pi_1 + \pi_2 K_t) Y_{t-1} + \pi_2 k_t + e_t. \tag{7}$$

What freedom do we now have to impose the characteristics we wish on the economy? The economy's dynamic structure cannot be arbitrarily changed by choice of K_t because to construct an arbitrary dynamic matrix $\pi_1 + \pi_2 K_t$ requires $n = g$ and π_2 nonsingular; i.e. Tinbergen's theorem once again. But we can pick K_t so that $\pi_1 + \pi_2 K_t$ has *any* arbitrary set of eigenvalues, provided (5) is dynamically controllable (Wonham, 1974).[9] Thus we can impose any long term growth characteristics on the economy, but *not* an arbitrary dynamic structure unless Tinbergen's theorem holds. Thus the conditions sufficient to ensure the stability of the system are substantially weaker than those in Tinbergen's theorem.

5. Theil's theory of economic policy: flexible targets

The key difference between Theil's approach and Tinbergen's approach to economic policy is Theil's use of a criterion function. Theil concentrated on policy choice and flexible targets (i.e. y_t^d should be approached as closely as possible, but not necessarily attained exactly) whereas Tinbergen remained with the problem of the existence of policies to reach fixed targets. It was the introduction of an explicit criterion for policy selection which created the distinction.

It was perhaps natural for Theil to introduce an objective function to obtain "the best" policy choices. He was a staff member under Tinbergen's supervision at the Central Planning Bureau in the early 1950's, and soon after that they became colleagues at the Netherlands School of Economics. Theil was therefore well versed in Tinbergen's approach. But he had written his doctoral thesis in consumer demand theory (Theil, 1951). It is quite clear from his early work on policy choice (e.g. Theil, 1954) that he thought of the objective function as a kind of preference function which generates

---

[9] Since we are concerned with the long term stability of the system as a whole here, it makes no sense to look at the stability of a subsystem of targets since they will still be affected by the behaviour of the nontargets. Hence these results focus on $n = g$ rather than $n = m$. A special case of this stabilisability property is Mundell's (1968) assignment of fiscal policy to attaining internal balance and monetary policy to the external balance target. As a 1 to 1 policy assignment this would be inefficient in the sense of Section 3(ii), since monetary policy clearly has internal consequences and fiscal policy external effects. But it certainly is a possible control rule for inducing stability into a system like (7), implying the internal and external targets would be achieved *eventually*. This is the sense in which Mundell's assignment is generally understood today. Note however that this does not provide a general rule of policy assignments when policy makers are uncertain about the precise impacts or side effects their instruments may have on the policy targets. Patrick (1972) shows that no policy assignments would hold under model uncertainty, even if they did when the model is known with certainty.

"utility" for the government (in terms of achieving their aims) and which, more usefully, generates tradeoffs between conflicting but unattainable policy targets just like the indifference curves of demand theory.[10] In fact both his 1954 and 1956 papers draw attention to the close formal relationship between policy choice and consumer demand theory, with analogies appearing between utility and social welfare functions, indifference curves or policy tradeoffs tangent to budget or linear constraints, and so on. The equivalence becomes even more explicit in later work (e.g. Theil 1958, 1964) when most of the major results of demand theory, such as Engel curves, compensated utilities, duality, and substitution effects, also start to appear in his policy framework. Moreover the comparative statics of policy choice takes the same form of that in demand theory complete with homogeneity and a negative definite and symmetric Slutsky matrix.[11] The differences with demand theory are only that the policy maker's "budget constraints" may be nonlinear and may have negative "prices" and "quantities"; and that his "utility" function may be nonmonotonic so that the marginal utilities and indifference curves can switch sign from the usual case (some examples of this appear in Hughes Hallett and Petit, 1988).

Theil's contributions to the theory of economic policy were therefore the result of combining his knowledge of demand theory with the need to produce policy recommendations as a CPB staff member. Indeed, Theil acknowledges that his decision framework was taken from Tinbergen's theory (Theil, 1954). Variables are classified into the same four groups, with both primary and intermediate targets. The model is presented as a set of linear constraints linking targets and instruments via policy multipliers (Theil, 1954, 1956). In the dynamic extension the dynamic multipliers are the same as those appearing in the dynamic controllability matrix (Theil, 1957, 1964). However the question remains, how should the ideal target values be chosen in Tinbergen's theory? Presumably y_t^d in (2) is not picked at random, but corresponds to the unconstrained optimum of some (implicit) welfare function governing the target variables (Holt, 1962). The problem now breaks into two parts; first the choice of ideal paths, y_t^d, and then the choice of policies to get as close as possible to those ideal paths. The result is a greater degree of flexibility in planning.

If the target variables are the sole arguments of the welfare function and there are sufficient instruments, then Theil's optimisation and Tinbergen's controllability approach will obviously coincide.[12] But if there were other

---

[10] For Theil these preferences are those of the government since advisors supply information about the consequences of policy, but do not advise on the desirability of the outcomes. Van Eijk and Sandee (1959) show how this idea translates into specifying the objective function.

[11] Compare Hughes Hallett and Rees (1983) pp. 199–200, with Brown and Deaton (1972) pp. 1161–3.

[12] If $m = n$, R^{-1} exists in (10) below. No instrument penalties implies that A, C, b and a are zero in (8). Hence $x^* = R^{-1}(y^d - s)$, and $y^* = y^d$ follows from both (10) and (12).

arguments of the welfare function—for example policy instruments expressed as deviations from some preferred levels, in order that the interventions should be restrained to some acceptable size—or if there were insufficient independent instruments, then Tinbergen's theory would certainly give suboptimal and arbitrary results as Theil claims. Indeed it is not clear what to do if $n < m$ in (1) since there is an infinite number of generalised left inverses for $\tilde{\pi}_{20}$, and since problems which penalise deviations of the instruments from their preferred values can always be rewritten as a case of insufficient instruments.[13] Theil is quite explicit that the instruments would normally be arguments of the welfare function (Theil, 1954), in the interests of ensuring desirable or acceptable policies (Theil, 1956, 1964) and because instruments usually have ideal levels in their own right (Theil, 1956).

Tinbergen also recognised the need to restrict the interventions to "acceptable" values, but he did this by including extra instrument restrictions in the model and solving it again (Tinbergen, 1952, 1956). Theil's incorporation of instruments into the objective function was therefore just the "flexible target" or *soft constraint* counterpart to Tinbergen's "fixed target" or *hard constraints* on the instruments (Theil, 1965).

Hence it is the introduction of flexible targets, and an explicit criterion function which is the key contribution that allowed Theil to take over and complete Tinbergen's theory of economic policy. Given that this approach was also able to accommodate intertemporal decisions in dynamic systems, information uncertainties, as well as decentralised and risk sensitive decision making, this break with the Tinbergen approach was of major importance for the theory and practice of policy design.

(i) *The decision rule*

In Theil's formulation, the policy maker has a vector of m targets y_t and n instruments x_t in each period $t = 1 \ldots T$. His planning priorities are represented by a (normalised) quadratic function of the deviations of these decision variables from their ideal values, y_t^d and x_t^d respectively. Let $\bar{y}_t = y_t - y_t^d$ and $\bar{x}_t = x_t - x_t^d$ represent those policy "failures". The objective function then is:

$$w = \tfrac{1}{2}(\bar{y}'B\bar{y} + \bar{y}'C'\bar{x} + \bar{x}'C\bar{y} + \bar{x}'A\bar{x}) + b'\bar{y} + a'\bar{x} = \tfrac{1}{2}\bar{z}'Q\bar{z} + q'\bar{z} \qquad (8)$$

where $\bar{y}' = (\bar{y}_1' \ldots \bar{y}_T')$, $\bar{x}' = (\bar{x}_1' \ldots \bar{x}_T')$ and $\bar{z}' = (\bar{y}', \bar{x}')$. Thus

$$Q = \begin{bmatrix} B & C' \\ C & A \end{bmatrix} \quad \text{and} \quad q = \begin{bmatrix} b \\ a \end{bmatrix}.$$

Theil specified A and B are to be positive semi-definite and symmetric matrices because society's true *collective* preferences cannot be known

---

[13] Hughes Hallett (1979).

perfectly a priori. That means one can, at best, specify an implicit performance index: $w = w(\bar{z})$, a convex differentiable function satisfying the usual axioms. Hence (8) is a second order approximation to $w(\bar{z})$ where

$$Q = \left[\frac{\partial^2 w}{\partial z\, \partial z'} \right]$$

has the required properties.

The target values are governed by a dynamic model such as:

$$y_t = f(y_t, y_{t-1}, x_t, e_t) \tag{9}$$

where e_t are exogenous (random) variables. This implies:

$$y = Rx + s \tag{10}$$

where

$$R = \begin{bmatrix} R_{11} & & 0 \\ \vdots & \ddots & \\ R_{T1} & \cdots & R_{TT} \end{bmatrix}$$

contains the dynamic policy multipliers, $R_{tj} = \partial y_t / \partial x_j$ for $t \geq j$, and zeros elsewhere. The noncontrollable elements are represented by $s' = (s'_1 \ldots s'_T)$ where

$$s_t = \sum_{j=1}^{t} (\partial y_t / \partial e_j) e_j + (\partial y_t / \partial y_0) y_0.$$

Equation (10) represents a linearisation of (9) around some trajectory and hence contains time varying policy responses. Theil himself worked with a linear model such as (1), so that (10) simplifies to

$$R = \begin{bmatrix} R_1 & & 0 \\ \vdots & \ddots & \\ R_T & & R_1 \end{bmatrix} \quad \text{where} \quad R_i = \pi_1^{i-1} \pi_2$$

and

$$s_t = \left(\sum_{j=0}^{t-1} \pi_1^j e_{t-j} + \pi_1^t y_0 \right).$$

Deleting the nontarget rows from (10) will produce a small set of constraints from even the largest models.

Now, substituting $\bar{y} = R\bar{x} + c$ into (8), where $c = s - y^d + Rx^d$, yields the constrained objective function:

$$w = \tfrac{1}{2}\bar{x}'K\bar{x} + k'\bar{x} + [b'c + \tfrac{1}{2}c'Bc] \tag{11}$$

where $K = R'BR + R'C' + CR + A$ and $k = a + R'b + (C + R'B)c$. The optimal decisions are therefore:

$$x^* = x^d - K^{-1}k. \tag{12}$$

This decision rule exists provided K is of full rank; i.e. $r(Q) \geq nT$. Hence, unlike most other formulations of the optimal decision rule, (12) can still be used when the specification of the underlying preferences is incomplete. Even when $m > n$, it is possible to compute decisions with no instrument penalties, or no target penalties, or any case in between.

(ii) Multiperiod certainty equivalence and closed loop controls

Theil introduced his certainty equivalence theorem (Theil, 1954, 1957) in order to deal with uncertainty about the noncontrollable elements s. Faced with a stochastic objective w, the policy maker is assumed to optimise the expected value $E_t(w) = E(w \mid \Omega_t)$ conditioned on his current information set Ω_t. But, at $t = 1$,

$$E_1(w(y, x)) - w(E_1(y), x) = \tfrac{1}{2}\{E_1(s'Bs) - E_1(s)'BE_1(s)\} \qquad (13)$$

follows from (8) if R may be taken as fixed. Moreover (13) is invariant to the choice of x so long as the variance–covariance matrix of s is independent of x. Hence the optimal certainty equivalent decisions are given by (12) with $E_1(s)$ replacing s within c and k.

The crucial point here is that, in period 1, only x_1^* can be implemented. Thereafter each decision vector x_t^* is dependent on new information. Each x_t must therefore be updated, before execution, in order to account for the latest information and to maintain certainty equivalence with respect to $E_t(w)$. The information changes may be prediction errors in past variables $(s_t \neq E_{t-1}(s_t))$ or revised expectations of future variables $(E_t(s_{t+1}) \neq E_{t-1}(s_{t+1}))$. The revised decisions can be obtained, at each $t = 2 \ldots T$, by reoptimising $E_t(w)$ subject to (10), $E_t(c)$, and the (by then) fixed values of $x_1^* \ldots x_{t-1}^*$, to give revised values for $x_t^* \ldots x_T^*$.[14] Of these reoptimised values, the leading subvector, x_t^*, gives the decisions to be executed; the remaining subvectors, $x_{t+1}^* \ldots x_T^*$, are updated *forecasts* of the remaining decisions.

In Theil's language, the initial calculation (i.e. (12) with $E_1(s)$) gives first period certainty equivalent decision values; subsequent calculations ((12) with $E_t(s)$) are "first period" certainty equivalent with respect to Ω_t; and the list of implemented decisions x_t^* is multiperiod certainty equivalent. In modern terms, first period certainty equivalence means optimal open loop decisions, while multiperiod certainty equivalence leads to closed loop control (in a discrete time linear model) since the revisions take place as often as data availability and the decision machinery permit.

It is sometimes said that the disadvantage of Theil's approach is that the decisions do not appear in the form of a feedback control rule:

$$x_t^* = \sum_{j=1}^{p} K_{tj} Y_{t-j} + k_t. \qquad (14)$$

---

[14] In practice this means (12) is recomputed sequentially for $t = 1 \ldots T$, cutting down the dimensions of R, Q and q to match the number of decisions still in play, and adjusting s to match the new information set at each point. The details were set out in Theil, 1964.

However the closed loop form of Theil's decision rule (12) can in fact be rewritten as a feedback rule of the form:

$$x_t^* = \sum_{j=1}^{t-1} K_{tj} Y_{t-j} + E_t(k_t) \tag{15}$$

(Hughes Hallett and Rees, 1983, pp. 142–3). Hence x_t^* is computed from a *time-varying* rule of order $t-1$, where the expectations of future noncontrollable events (contained within k_t) are also revised each period. Although this form of decision rule is too complex to be useful for computation, it does illustrate the theoretical properties of Theil's policy regime in relation to others. For example open loop decisions would be:

$$x_t^0 = h_{t,1}(\Omega_1) = K_{t,1}(L) E\left[Y_t \,\Big|\, \sum_{i=1}^{t} R_i x_i, E_1(s_t) \right] + k_{t|1} \tag{16}$$

where $h_{t,1}(\cdot)$ denotes a set of functions determined in the first period, $k_{t|1}$ is a function of $E_1(e_T \ldots e_1)$ and $K_{t,1}(L)$ is a polynomial in the lag operator L. Closed loop decisions, however, would be a function of the latest information (*including* probabilistic information) available on the state of the system:

$$x_t^c = h_{t,t}(\Omega_t) = K_{t,t}(L) E\left[Y_t \,\Big|\, \sum_{i=1}^{t} R_i x_i, E_t(s_t) \right] + k_{t|t}. \tag{17}$$

This closed loop rule is not necessarily the same as a *pure feedback rule* chosen by the same methods:

$$x_t^F = h_{t,1}(\Omega_t) = K_{t,1}(L) E\left[Y_t \,\Big|\, \sum_{i=1}^{t} R_i x_i, E_t(s_t) \right] + k_{t|1}. \tag{18}$$

A closed loop rule reacts to the *currently* expected future events, as well as to the latest information about the past. A pure feedback rule uses the latest measurements of the past, but fails to 'anticipate' future measurements or the closing of the loop implied by recomputing $h_{t,t}(\cdot)$ based on each Ω_t. The decisions will be inferior unless nothing happens to influence our anticipations for the future.

The properties required of any decision rule like (14), if it is to have sufficient power to achieve its objectives, can be analysed by treating it as an error correction mechanism (Salmon, 1982). To eliminate the discrepancy between any state (z_t) and its desired value (z_t^d) requires that state to be determined by a difference equation system at least of the form $(I - L)^p z_t = B(L) z_{t-p}$, where $B(L)$ is a matrix polynomial in the lag operator L and where $p - 1$ equals the order of difference equation system determining z_t^d. If z_t and z_t^d follow difference equation systems of equal order the error $z_t - z_t^d$ will tend to a constant; and if z_t follows a lower-order system the error will eventually explode.

But Theil's decision rule will follow a feedback rule of order $p = t - 1$.

Hence the controlled economy will follow a difference equation system of order max $\{t-1, l\}$, where the underlying system has dynamics of order l. Thus, for t large enough—and assuming sufficient instruments—the optimal control rule always has sufficient power to eliminate the policy 'failures' $y_t - y_t^d$. However, the rule itself is time varying. The big policy adjustments occur in early periods $(t < l)$ because, at that stage, (15) lacks sufficient power to eliminate the 'failure' $\bar{y}_t$ even asymptotically. So the target failures start by tending to increase. Smoother policy adjustments, and decreasing target failures, then follow in later periods $(t > l)$ when the control rule has gained 'sufficient' power.

6. Policy selection and risk

(i) Generalisations of certainty equivalence

There has been some debate about whether Theil can be credited with having introduced the idea of certainty equivalence into the theory of economic policy design. The same idea appears in Simon (1956) as an extension of his version of the flexible target approach.

In fact Theil had first published his Certainty Equivalence Theorem in explicit form in 1954, although it may have been used earlier in his policy work at the Central Planning Bureau. At that stage, certainty equivalence was restricted to multivariate but static decisions. On the other hand Simon's 1956 paper was the first to produce a dynamic certainty equivalence theorem (he used dynamic programming as an optimisation technique), but he was unable to develop a multi-target/multi-instrument decision rule. The multivariate version of Simon's proposal was not put forward as an operational algorithm until fifteen years later (Chow, 1970, Pindyck, 1973). Meanwhile, Theil had managed to extend his 1954 approach, first to a multiperiod formulation (Theil, 1957); and then to the fully-fledged dynamic, innovations dependent, control rule described above (Bogaard and Theil, 1959).

It is of course possible to get Theil's certainty equivalence result by other routes. For example the objective function $E_t(w)$ can be decomposed into two disjoint positive definite quadratic forms; the first dependent on the expectations of the policy variables, and the second on their intertemporal variance–covariance matrix. The composite decision rule which yields optimal values for those expectations, while also minimising the impact of the target variable variances on the objective's stochastic components, actually coincides with the certainty equivalent decision rule.[15] That shows

---

[15] Hughes Hallett (1981). The significance of this result is that comparing the two components of $E_t(w)$ gives an *ex ante* estimate of the importance of stochastic control and the scope for reducing the impact of random shocks by an innovation dependent policy rule. The variance–covariance matrix here contains intertemporal elements since, by (10), the shocks, s_t, follow a moving average scheme. It would not be possible to produce the same results with recursive optimisation techniques.

that the certainty equivalence theorem is primarily useful as a computational short cut. The crucial, and potentially controversial, step—given that w is only implicitly related to collective utility—was to accept $E_t(w)$ as the appropriate decision criterion under uncertainty. The controversial aspect of that step is that it fails to allow for risk aversion, but it is an essential step for certainty equivalence. The risk neutrality of certainty equivalent decisions can be seen in equation (20) below.[16]

Another interesting feature of Theil's early work is that he examines the policy "biases" which occur if certainty equivalence is applied when the objective function is not quadratic or the model is nonlinear. He also stresses the assumption that the noncontrollable variables' covariance matrix (in particular their heteroskedasticity and serial correlations) must be independent of the instruments.[17] To that we must add the assumption that R may be taken as fixed. These are all restrictions which were easily forgotten in later discussions, when solution techniques rather than the problem specification came to hold the centre of the stage. However a local form of certainty equivalence can also be established for nonlinear (nonquadratic) problems, although that entails completing a search for that locality where the linear-quadratic approximations are consistent with the resulting policy choices (see Section 7). Similarly the assumption of independence between the covariance matrix and the instruments is just the strong exogeneity condition which was later emphasised by Engle *et al.* (1983) in the context of regression analysis.

(ii) *Parameter uncertainty and first order certainty equivalence*

If R is stochastic, the decisions which minimise $E_t(w)$ would be:

$$x^* = x^d - [E_t(K)]^{-1}E_t(k) \qquad (19)$$

where $E_t(K) = A + C\bar{R} - \bar{R}'C' + \bar{R}'B\bar{R} + E_t(dR'B\,dR)$ and $E_t(k) = a + \bar{R}'b + (C + \bar{R}'B)E_t(c) + E_t(dR'B\sigma)$, given $\bar{R} = E_t(R)$, $dR = R - \bar{R}$, and $\sigma = c - E_t(c)$. The only difficulty in operating (19) will be the computation of an exact distribution for the dynamic multipliers in R, and hence their means, variances, covariances, and covariances with c.[18] However if the parameter uncertainty is fairly small, the last terms in the expressions for $E_t(K)$ and $E_t(k)$ may be ignored. Hence the strategy of treating the model parameters in (12) as if they were fixed at their mean values is correct up to a first order approximation of $E_t(K)$ and $E_t(k)$ about $\bar{R}$ and $E_t(c)$; Young, 1975. Hence the "first order certainty equivalent" decision rule is $x^* = x^d - \bar{K}^{-1}\bar{k}$ where $E_t(K) = \bar{K} + E_t(dR'B\,dR)$. It doesn't exist if $r(\bar{K}) < nT$. However (19) exists even when $\bar{K}$ is of insufficient rank since it involves

---

[16] These remarks evidently depend on the linear-quadratic nature of the problem—but without that certainty equivalence could not be applied anyway.

[17] These points first appeared in Theil (1954).

[18] This might be done by stochastic simulation. Alternative methods for treating multiplicative uncertainty turn out to be no simpler in practice; see Chow (1976) or Kendrick (1981).

$[\bar{K} + E_t(\mathrm{d}R'B\,\mathrm{d}R)]^{-1}$. In other words, all the instruments will be needed to combat uncertainty even when there are only a few targets compared to the number of instruments.

(iii) Risk sensitive decisions

The reason why $E_t(w)$ might prove undesirable as a decision criterion is that it generates risk neutral decisions: Samuelson (1970). In fact:

$$E_t(w) = \tfrac{1}{2}E_t(\bar{z})'QE_t(\bar{z}) + q'E_t(\bar{z}) + \tfrac{1}{2}\operatorname{tr}QV(z) \qquad (20)$$

where $V(z) = E_t(z - E_t(z))(z - E_t(z))' = (I:O)'V(s)(I:O)$ is the conditional variance of z. Evidently $V(z)$ is independent of x; yet the larger the dispersion of z, for a given mean, the greater the risks about the realised target values. Equation (20) therefore implies that certainty equivalence will generate the same policies whatever the degree of uncertainty.

Theil's decision making framework is easily extended to provide risk-sensitive decisions. A combination of all the moments of w, $E_t(w) + \Sigma \alpha_j \mu_j$ where $\mu_j = E_t(w - E_t(w))^j$, for $\alpha_j \geq 0$ and $j \geq 2$, will approximate the expected value of some general utility function $u(w)$. A straightforward approximation to this is the mean–variance criterion:

$$\min_x \{\alpha E_t(w) + \tfrac{1}{2}(1 - \alpha)V_t(w)\} \qquad (21)$$

where α is a risk aversion parameter; $\alpha = 1$ implies risk neutrality, and $\alpha = 0$ full risk aversion. The solution to (21) can be written as Theil's decision rule (12) but with transformed preference parameters for B, A, b, and a (Hughes Hallett, 1984). This reparameterisation has the effect of penalising the high risk targets more heavily, the instruments less heavily, and of introducing asymmetric penalties to compensate for larger probabilities of getting a shock on one side of the mean than the other. Moreover it is distribution free. But (21) only supplies a second order approximation to $u(w)$. The price of generalising on that is having to impose stochastic separability between periods, and normality on the random variables, irrespective of the characteristics of the true problem (Whittle, 1982).

(iv) Decentralised decision making

The remaining source of uncertainty, in Theil's book, was policy variables in the hands of other decision makers. His framework is also easily extended for that case. Suppose there are two decision makers with their own (private) objective functions:

$$w^{(i)} = \tfrac{1}{2}(\bar{y}^{(i)\prime}B^{(i)}\bar{y}^{(i)} + \bar{y}^{(i)\prime}A\bar{x}^{(i)}) \qquad i = 1, 2 \qquad (22)$$

where $A^{(i)}$ and $B^{(i)}$ are positive definite and symmetric. The constraint set (10) must be partitioned between the targets of the two players:

$$\bar{y}^{(i)} = R^{(i,1)}\bar{x}^{(1)} + R^{(i,2)}\bar{x}^{(2)} + c^{(i)} \qquad i = 1,2. \qquad (23)$$

Thus $R^{(i,i)}$ describes player i's domestic policy responses, and $R^{(i,j)}$ his target's responses to player j's decisions. Player i could substitute (23) into (22) to obtain an optimal reaction function:

$$\bar{x}^{(i)*} = -[R^{(i,i)\prime}B^{(i)}R^{(i,i)} + A^{(i)}]^{-1}R^{(i,i)\prime}B^{(i)}(c^{(i)} + R^{(i,j)}\bar{x}^{(j)}). \qquad (24)$$

Then solving for $x^{(i)}$ and $x^{(j)}$ jointly, using (32) and its counterpart for $x^{(j)}$, yields the Nash equilibrium decisions.

$$\begin{bmatrix} I & -D^{(1)} \\ -D^{(2)} & I \end{bmatrix} \begin{pmatrix} \bar{x}^{(1)} \\ \bar{x}^{(2)} \end{pmatrix} = \begin{pmatrix} F^{(1)}c^{(1)} \\ F^{(2)}c^{(2)} \end{pmatrix}, \qquad (25)$$

where $F^{(i)} = -(R^{(i,i)\prime}B^{(i)}R^{(i,i)} + A^{(i)})^{-1}R^{(i,i)\prime}B^{(i)}$ and $D^{(i)} = F^{(i)}R^{(i,j)}$, for $i, j = 1$ *and* 2. This formulation is extremely easy to use for computation since it uses a condensed model.[19] Moreover the impact of policy threats, $\partial y_t^{(1)}/\partial x_{t+1}^{(2)}$, are represented by (23) and (25) since $D^{(i)}$ is not block triangular. The corresponding recursive optimisation techniques would fail to anticipate such threats (Hughes Hallet, 1986).

Forward looking expectations can also be handled in this framework simply by solving the model numerically to obtain a matrix of dynamic multipliers for (10) which is not block lower triangular. Inserting (10) into (8) in the usual way yields (12) as the optimal decision rule with the modified R matrix. This has been used for policy analysis in speculative markets (Ghosh *et al.*, 1987).

7. Nonlinear models

Most econometric models now used for policy analysis are nonlinear. In view of (10), that poses no problem for Theil's approach to policy design. However there are other problems: (a) how can we ensure the partial derivatives in R are evaluated around a trajectory which matches the policy sequence derived from R; and (b) can certainty equivalence be reconstructed to handle uncertainty with nonlinear models?

(i) *The Newton connection*

A number of nonlinear optimal control algorithms are now available for policy analysis on nonlinear models. They fall into two groups. The most widely used algorithms are derived from nonlinear optimisation theory; see Holbrook (1974), Fair (1974), Rustem and Zarrop (1979, 1981), Brandsma *et al.* (1984). The alternative is to adapt standard optimal control techniques; Athans (1972), Kim *et al.* (1975), Chow (1975). From a historical perspective, the interesting thing is that the algorithms of the first group all turn out to be different implementations of Theil's procedure applied to nonlinear models.

---

[19] Compare the simplicity of (25) with the complications of a recursive approach: e.g. De Bruyne (1979), Chow (1983). As a result, (25) appears to be the only dynamic game procedure which has been used with estimated models (examples in Hughes Hallett, 1986).

To illustrate, consider minimising $w = \frac{1}{2}(\tilde{y}'B\tilde{y} + \tilde{x}'A\tilde{x})$ subject to (9) stacked up over time: $y = f(x, e)$. The constrained objective is therefore:

$$w = \frac{1}{2}\{(f(x, e) - y^d)'B(f(x, e) - y^d) + \tilde{x}'A\tilde{x}\}. \tag{26}$$

The Newton–Raphson method, with α_k chosen such that $w(x_{k+1}) \leqslant w(x_k)$, is

$$x_{k+1} = x_k - \alpha_k G_k^{-1} g_k \tag{27}$$

where[20] $G_k = R_k'BR_k + A$ and $R_k = [\partial f / \partial x]_{x_k}$, and the gradient vector is:

$$g_k = R_k'B(f(x_k, e) - y^d) + A\tilde{x}_k. \tag{28}$$

Thus, given an x_0, the iteration (27) will generate the optimal policy values. Alternatively, we could linearise the model itself at x_k and e, and substitute the result $y = y_k + R_k(x - x_k)$ into w. Differentiating that constrained objective with respect to x implies:

$$x_{k+1} = x_k - (R_k'BR_k + A)^{-1}(R_k'B\tilde{y}_k + A\tilde{x}_k). \tag{29}$$

That is Holbrook's algorithm. It is identical to (27) if step length α_k is used, since g_k is an exact gradient evaluation. A third possibility is to note that, at the minimum of (26), $g_k = 0$. That implies:

$$x_{k+1} = x^d - (R_k'BR_k + A)^{-1}R_k'Bc_k \tag{30}$$

since $f(x_k, e) = R_k x_k + s_k$, where $s_k = [\partial f / \partial e]_{x_k}$ and $c_k = s_k - y^d + R_k x^d$.

Equation (30) is of course just Theil's method applied to a linearisation of the model about x_k and e. It is also exactly what you get with repeated applications of Theil's method, where the model is linearised at the latest policy trajectory x_k and that linearisation is inserted into (12). The new policy x_{k+1} then implies a new linearisation, and so on iteratively until convergence in R_k. If convergence difficulties arise, (30) may be accelerated as:

$$\tilde{x}_{k+1} = -\alpha_k(R_k'BR_k + A)^{-1}R_k'Bc_k + (1 - \alpha_k)\tilde{x}_k. \tag{31}$$

But that is the same as the Newton and the Holbrook algorithms. Since s_k would actually be computed as $y_k - R_k x_k$, a simple reorganisation of (30) gives (29). Similarly substituting the expressions for G_k and g_k into (27) yields (31).

(ii) *Convergence analysis*

Thus the Theil approach, extended to ensure the policies are consistent with the linearisations used to generate them, actually is the same Newton-type algorithm as recommended in the recent literature for the control of nonlinear models. Various simplifications can be introduced for

---

[20] By convention, all these control algorithms ignore the second order derivatives in the Hessian. No extra convergence difficulties arise, and superlinear convergence is retained, since G_k is automatically positive definite at each k (Rustem and Zarrop, 1979).

calculating R_k (see Rustem and Zarrop (1979, 1981) or Preston et al. (1976)).

But the important point here is that Theil's framework gives greater insight into how these algorithms work. The two part iteration splits the problem into a "prediction" phase (where $R_k = \partial y/\partial x$ is evaluated by solving the model for small changes in x about x_k) alternating with a "control" phase (where x_{k+1} is evaluated by (12) at R_k and s_k). Convergence now follows by analysing roots of $[\partial R_k/\partial x] \cdot [\partial x_k/\partial R]$ along the iteration path; i.e. in terms of the sensitivity of the multipliers to policy changes *and* the sensitivity of the policies to multiplier changes (Brandsma et al., 1984). The first component depends only on the model, but the second depends also on the priorities in (8). That means a low degree of nonlinearity in the model may be necessary, but is certainly *not* sufficient, for justifying the use of linear policy evaluation methods. For example the highly nonlinear responses of a target will not matter if that target carries a low priority. But the slightly nonlinear responses of a high priority target will certainly invalidate linear evaluation techniques.

(iii) *The feedback approach*

The alternative to all this is to adapt standard optimal control techniques in feedback form. Chow (1975) describes an algorithm in which the model is linearised, in each period separately, around some base trajectory. Given that sequence of linearisations, conventional dynamic programming or Pontryagin techniques can be employed to generate a conditionally optimal feedback control rule. However, as before, the policies implied by that control and a given information set will not generally match those used to make the linearisations. It is shown that if the relative priorities on reducing the gap between the new policies and the previous linearisation path are the same as in (8), then the new linearisation path should be computed from $\Delta x_t = K_t \Delta y_{t-1}$ where K_t is the feedback matrix used in the optimal control rule. So, once again, we get into alternating phases of linearisation and optimisation. The crucial difference is that the entire model has to be re-linearised at each period separately. Moreover, if there are several lags in the model, it must then be transformed into a first order difference equation system (Chow, 1975) or a state space system (Aoki, 1976). In either case the dimensions of that entire model will be substantially increased. The Theil approach, in contrast, requires a linearisation of only the target-instrument linkages at the "prediction" phase since we need only multipliers for the target variables for the decision rule of the "control" phase. That means, all nontargets and lagged variables may be deleted in the model's condensed form. This is particularly important for the large econometric models used in economic policy analysis. There may well be 100 or more endogenous variables and several lags, but there are typically only 5 or 6 policy targets. As a result, the computational burden is much lower in the Theil approach. For example, in a typical macroeconomic exercise involving the Dutch

Central Planning Bureau's model with 7 targets, 5 instruments, and 5 periods, the number of calculations was reduced by a factor of 1000; in a conventional market stabilisation exercise involving 2 targets, 1 instrument, and 40 periods, it was reduced by a factor of 550 (Hughes Hallett and Rees, 1983). With these model reductions, systematic policy searches over alternative problem specifications become a routine matter (Brandsma *et al.*, 1983).

(iv) *Local certainty equivalence*

This discussion has ignored the certainty equivalence issue. One advantage of using a sequence of explicit linearisations is that certainty equivalence can be applied at each step, inserting $E(s_k)$ for s_k in (30). The same argument applies to replacing y_k with $E(y_k)$ in (29). But it is not clear that the corresponding substitution of $E(e)$ for e in (28) is correct for the Newton method, and to use that approach may affect convergence and conceivably the final solution. All that we can say for sure is that $f(x_k, e)$ can be replaced by $R_k x_k + E(s_k)$ at convergence. Hence, strictly speaking, certainty equivalence applies only locally—that is, within a neighbourhood defined by the current linearisation of the model.

The latter remark highlights the fact that certainty equivalence actually has *two* aspects. Current policies must be predicated on the currently expected future optimal policy values *and* on the currently expected future model. Since the latter contains a linearisation dependent on the former, certainty equivalence cannot finally be applied until the linearisation iterations are complete. Similarly to obtain proper closed loop control, in the manner described in Section 5, the alternating linearisation-policy calculation sequence has to be repeated at each period to produce the currently expected model multipliers; R_k is a function of Ω_t, but the R_k appropriate for the policy revisions cannot be determined in advance since it depends on Ω_{t+1}. This difficulty does not arise with linear models since R is independent of the information set.

(v) *Traditional control theory techniques*

One would imagine that the conflict between the mathematically sophisticated methods of control theory and the computationally efficient methods of the Theil/Newton approach would have generated considerable controversy. In practice that debate has not surfaced in the literature, largely because economists have "voted with their feet". Control theory methods continue to be used to formally describe the decision problem and its characteristics, while calculations and policy experiments on large empirical models are nevertheless performed using software based on Theil/Newton type algorithms (continuous time problems excepted). Controversy only starts to emerge with those topics which standard control theory methods find hard to handle systematically—dynamic games, expectational effects, intertemporal preferences, risk elements etc. Here controversy can be seen in the debate over how to treat reputation, time-consistency, the sensistivity of the results to model uncertainty, or the application of equilibrium growth solutions to short run problems, etc. On the other hand, one might expect control engineering problems to be solved with traditional control theory techniques, because they usually involve small, dense, nonlinear systems rather than the large, sparse, near-linear systems typical of economics. But in fact control engineering applications are being solved increasingly by sequential Theil-type quadratic programming techniques for reasons of computational efficiency. Even in continuous time problems, control engineers often prefer to use a discrete time approach and then fit continuous time adjustments by interpolation (see Pierson, 1988).

8. Conclusion

It has taken some time for economists to recognise the advantages of the Tinbergen–Theil approach to policy analysis. The main advantage is clearly its versatility and its computational simplicity. The latter is important because without it the "experimental" calculations (e.g. on alternative priorities or target values, robustness to model/information errors etc.) necessary in economic policy design become impossible. The former is important because the major policy problems of economics (decentralisation, coordination, expectations, risk management) can be incorporated. The main disadvantage appears to be that the difficulty of analysing the dynamic properties of different control rules and problems in continuous time, although even control engineers now prefer to use discrete time techniques and then fit continuous time dynamic adjustments by interpolation.

Finally, can econometric policy evaluations of this type ever be justified given imperfect models? The alternative is of course to use some less formal and less checkable technique. The advantage of the econometric approach is accountability for the mutual consistency and the assumptions underlying the policy projections. The policy problem contains four elements: a model, an objective function, an information set, and a risk aversion measure. It is the fact that the specification of these components is forced to be explicit, open to criticism, and hence accountable to informed opinion, which is the real achievement of the Tinbergen–Theil framework.

University of Newcastle upon Tyne and CEPR, London

SECTION 4

Critical Histories

Oxford Economic Papers 41 (1989), 217-235

THE PROBABILISTIC COUNTER-REVOLUTION, OR HOW STOCHASTIC CONCEPTS CAME TO NEOCLASSICAL ECONOMIC THEORY

By PHILIP MIROWSKI*

THE EARLIEST historiography of the rise of econometrics, such as that found in Schumpeter (1954, p. 962) served to conflate the rise of econometrics with the development of empirical measurement in economics; and it is true many contemporaries did tend to regard the elaboration of mathematical economic theory and that of statistical estimation as aspects of the same research program, at least until circa 1950. The timing of the introduction of procedures such as least squares estimation was regarded by many as a simple process of diffusion of technique across disciplinary boundaries, with historians such as Schumpter asserting that, "The majority of theorists, including some of the greatest, were completely unaware of the possibility of a theory that might eventually achieve numerical results."

Some familiarity with recent discussions in the history and philosophy of science would suggest that an understanding of the "Econometrics Revolution" demands a broader scope than that which presumes a simple model of diffusion of techniques, or one which tries to explain the rise of econometrics solely from such "internalist" considerations as the "demands of the data" or the "logic of the economic problem". Briefly, in our alternative reading the timing and structure of what subsequently became known as "econometrics" was due in large part of a crisis within neoclassical economic theory, ultimately deriving from an advocacy of a strong determinist model of explanation copied directly from physics, just as physics seemed to be repudiating such a model. The genesis of a probabalistic quantum mechanics in 1925–6 exacerbated the crisis, but also provided neoclassical economists with certain resources to rebuff the criticisms and to forge a rapprochement between stochastic principles and their theory.

* This paper is part of a larger project on the history and interpretations of stochastic concepts in the history of economic thought entitled "Uncertain Wavering", which itself draws upon my forthcoming history of the influence of physics upon economics, *More Heat Than Light*. I would like to thank Neil de Marchi, Mary Morgan, David Garman and Nancy Wulwick for discussions on these issues, and Nancy Cartwright and Martin Klein for suggestions regarding the history of physics. Those who know me will find the conventional disclaimer that none of the above should be held accountable for what follows indispensable. I would also like to acknowledge the support of a grant from the National Endowment for the Humanities, which made much of this research possible.

I. Determinism vs. indeterminism

To understand the history of econometrics, one must first consider the history of neoclassical economics; and, to understand neoclassical economics, one must first have some understanding of the history of physics. Most economists understand instinctively that the neoclassical research program has striven to attain the status of a science, and not just any science, but that most respected of the modern sciences, physics. Yet few realize the extent to which the progenitors of neoclassicism acted to secure that status. Indeed, I have argued elsewhere that the so-called Marginalist Revolution in the 1870s consisted largely of engineers directly appropriating the newly developed formalisms of nineteenth century energy physics, changing the names of the variables, and renaming the result "mathematical economics" (Mirowski, 1984a; forthcoming a). Precisely because this claim may appear controversial, I shall not attempt a full elaboration here, but merely take this thesis as a point of departure.

When economists such as Jevons, Walras, Edgeworth, Pareto and Fisher transmuted the physics of energy into the social mechanics of utility, it was with some ambivalence that they enlisted in the determinist program. On the one hand, it seems fairly clear that they conflated the notion of classical determinism with scientific explanation as a whole. However, when it came to the actual mathematics, the bulk of the work of these protagonists displayed much more fascination with the variational principles than with the conservation principles, to the detriment of the development of an analogous dynamics (Mirowski, forthcoming, chap. 5). Whatever the motivation, this tergiversation over conservation principles had severe consequences for the goal of a neoclassical dynamics which could claim to parallel the classical determinist doctrine (Northrop, 1941). Recourse to the formalisms of Hamiltonian dynamics would have explicitly required that something be conserved through time. Since neoclassical economists were unwilling or unable to specify what that was, their prognostications were effectively confined to static theory. This conflict between the physics ideal of classical determinism and the retreat to a purely static theory was a blight on the neoclassical research program, a canker that could not be ignored by the first decades of the twentieth century.[1]

If this deficiency with respect to a legitimate dynamics were not sufficiently distressing, the neoclassical research program was further buffeted by some bad news from the physicists' camp. Just as the economists had come to pay homage to the physicists' belief in determinism, the

---

[1] Published examples can be found in Frisch (1933a, p. 156 in 1965 edition; Roos, 1934, p. 8) as well as in Mirowski forthcoming, chap. 5. As for unpublished evidence, the collection of unpublished papers of Harold T. Davis held in the Cowles Foundation Archives contain numerous explicit references to this problem. For instance, see "The Perturbation Problem for Economic Series", a paper presented to the June 1932 Econometric society meetings; or, "The Econometric Problem", paper presented to the third annual Research Conference of the Cowles Commission, Colorado Springs, June 28, 1937.

physicists themselves were contriving to distance themselves from it, and in some cases, even to express doubts concerning its intellectual validity (Hacking, 1983b; Brush, 1983). These doubts began with the observation that it was humanly impossible to know all of the ititial conditions for any moderately complicated Hamiltonian, and therefore it was simpler to treat an aggregate of mass points such as, say, an ideal gas, by statistical averages (Porter, 1985). Statistical gas theory then led to an explanation of the second law of thermodynamics using stochastic constructs (Brush, 1983). By 1919, some physicists were suggesting that, "statistical law must be regarded as the comprehensive genus, a concept of higher order than that of dynamic laws and including them as a special case" (Cassirer, 1956, p. 81). But the most devastating jolt came in 1926 with Max Born's interpretation of the formalisms of the new quantum mechanics as explicitly and irreducably stochastic. It prompted physicists in the 1920s to openly worry about a "crisis in the foundations of physics" (Brush, 1983, p. 128) and to speculate that classical determinism had become untenable. Whatever one's opinions on the wayward course of classical physics, most agreed that the future of physics lay in statistical concepts (Brush, 1983, p. 102; Brush, 1980).

It is difficult now to evoke the extent to which this was regarded as an epoch-making departure in Western physics and philosophy in the 1930s (similar to the reactions to "chaos theory" in the 1980s). Not only was it the topic of arcane disquisitions amongst physicists, but was also widely bandied about in more popular venues. Heisenberg's "Uncertainty Principle" was thought to support all sorts of outlandish philosophical positions, from solipsism to the necessity of the existence of free will (Born, 1949). It became briefly fashionable in certain quarters to maintain that the very concept of causality had been undermined (Forman, 1971). By the 1930s, any culturally literate layperson could not turn around without bumping into some denunciation of determinism and praise of stochastical concepts:

> "[classical determinism] was the gold standard in the vaults; [statistical laws were] the paper currency actually used. But everyone still adhered to the traditional view that paper currency needs to be backed by gold. As physics progressed the occasions when the gold was actually produced became rarer until they ceased altogether. Then it occurred to some of us to question whether there still was a hoard of gold in the vaults or whether its existence was a mythical tradition. The dramatic ending of the story would be that the vaults were opened and found to be empty. The actual ending is not quite so simple. It turns out that the key has been lost, and no one can say for certain whether there is any gold in the vaults or not. But I think it is clear that, with either termination, present-day physics is *off the gold standard.*" (Eddington, 1935, p. 81).

Thus the neoclassical research program confronted a serious dilemma in the first few decades of the twentieth century. The adoption of the mathematical metaphor of utility as potential energy was intertwined with the classical determinist posture, one which equated scientific causal explanation with mechanical prediction. Yet the allegiance to classical determinism was not paying off, as a plausible dynamics still appeared beyond reach, no closer than it had been in the 1870s (Mirowski, forthcoming, chaps 5–6). Moreover, a quantitative empirical program was stymied by the rigors of classical determinism, since anything less than exact conformity of data to a mechanistic model meant the rejection of that model. Time series of economic data were beyond the pale of neoclassical explanation, since the static model could not legitimately be extended through time, due to the perennial complaint that the very structure of the fundamental determinants of the economy had changed in the interim.

Hence, the neoclassical research program at the turn of the century faced an unpleasant choice: either persist in a determinism bereft of the kind of results one associated with physics, or else throw over the entire program of copying physics. In retrospect, it seems that neoclassicals might have remained satisfied with their flawed science, perhaps papered over by various Marshallian devices like the "long run" and the "short run", had it not been for the further bad tidings from the physicists' camp. It slowly dawned upon some neoclassicals that the physicists were changing the rules of the game when it came to "natural law", and it was this cohort which were identified with the rise of "econometrics": Ragnar Frisch, Harold T. Davis, Tjalling Koopmans, Henry Schultz, Trygve Haavelmo, Gerhard Tintner, Harold Hotelling, Charles Roos, Jacob Marschak and others loosely affiliated with the Cowles Commission.

The first neoclassicals such as Jevons, Walras, Fisher and Edgeworth had appropriated the earlier vintage of physics metaphor in order to arrogate the legitimacy of a "science"; and now their legacy risked being downgraded to a "non-scientific" status as their deterministic conception of explanation was being rendered obsolete. The ideal resolution from the neoclassical point of view would be to admit just a 'little bit' of indeterminism into neoclassical models; just enough to resonate with the evolution of physics, but not enough to relinquish the original commitment to deterministic explanation and utility maximization. Something very much like this ideal package was put together by a new generation of neoclassicals mentioned above in the 1930s and 1940s, and the label on the package read "Econometrics". It is the purpose of this paper to investigate how one might begin to document this thesis.

The struggle to establish econometrics has frequently been misrepresented as a battle between the misguided partisans of "measurement without theory" versus the level-headed exponents of a judicious and balanced empiricism. The canonical text in this interpretation was the famous debate in the 1940s between Tjalling Koopmans and Rutledge Vining (Koopmans, 1947; Vining, 1949a). The problem with this interpretation is that it willfully disregards the fact that the main point of contention between the disputants was the validity of *neoclassical* economic theory, and not all theory *tout court*. The real battle was over what neoclassical economists were willing to "see" in the world: more precisely, what was the extent and meaning of the relative proportions of "order" and "chaos" in the economy? One disputant summed it up like this:

> "I simply do not believe that any set of econometric models . . . will ever suffice for reliable economic forecasting over any great length of time. The element of novel social conception is always breaking in. The social process, I submit, is peculiarly unfitted for description in terms either of simple positivism or mechanically imposed law. Such approaches result from the naive application of 'scientific' notions already out of date in their own field. Koopmans should realize that things have happened since the publication of Newton's *Scholium*. There is relativity, evolution and the quantum theory. Economics today is striving to become more mechanical and determinate at the very time physical science is loosening its bonds" (Wright, 1951, p. 147).

II. Stochastic economics as an anti-neoclassical movement

Upon reading the pioneering works of the earliest economic statisticians, one is immediately struck by the frequency and insistence with which they all appeal to physics for legitimacy. The very earliest economists who used least squares in order to empirically estimate what they called demand curves, namely Mackeprang, Benini and Moore, all felt compelled to defend their curious activities from a multitude of detractors by invoking the name and power of science. The earliest instance of what was to become a litany is reported in (Moore, 1908, p. 24):

> "Upon the occasion of the meeting of the Italian economists at Parma in 1907, Professor Benini, stimulated by the fact that economists were holding their sessions as one section of a general association of physical and natural scientists, urged that economists should adopt in their investigations the methods of research employed by the natural sciences. In particular, he advised the use of methods of interpolation for the discovery of empirical laws from statistical data, and instanced the utility of the evaluation of the laws of demand and supply."

The next thing which impresses the modern reader is the extent to which these appeals to science were unsuccessful in the first two decades of the twentieth century.[2] Strangely enough, none of those appeals struck a sympathetic chord with any prominent neoclassical economist, even though they were prone to make their own appeals to "science" in other contexts. In many instances Walras, Marshall and others made extremely disparaging

---

[2] One particularly poignant example comes from the Henry Schultz diary in the Cowles Foundation archives. In an entry dated 26 March 1934, one finds:

> "Called on Prof. Benini, who was the first to derive the demand for sugar as a function of the price of sugar and the price of coffee. . . B., like all the other professors, has a fascist button on his lapel. He is no longer interested in statistical or mathematical economics."

comments about this sort of work, and used their influence to discourage interest in those directions.[3] The fact that both the advocates and the detractors of statistical/probabilistic work could invoke the mantle of Science of indicative of the conflicting and confused images of science in the period. Recourse to explicit stochastic models was regarded in some quarters as a backsliding repudiation of scientific determinism, whereas in other quarters the mere fact a technique was used by astronomers was good enough to earn it the scientific stamp of approval.

One of the most curious aspects of the rise of *neoclassical* theory is that many of the leading lights of marginalism were also instrumental in the development of probability theory and statistics: Jevons, Edgeworth, Bowley, Keynes, Slutsky and Wald, only to name the most illustrious. And yet in the period roughly 1870–1925 *none* of these polymath theoreticians saw fit to forge direct explicit links between stochastic theory and neoclassical economic theory. This point is subtle, and deserves some careful attention (Menard, 1987). This is not to claim that none of the above ever prosecuted any empirical research program in economics broadly speaking: Jevons obviously used graphical techniques to discuss the price level, and his sunspot theory had some recourse to notions of correlation (Mirowski, 1984c). Edgeworth did work in the theory of index numbers; Bowley published empirical work on wages and the distribution of income;

---

[3] For Walras' attitudes, see (Menard, 1980). In the case of Marshall, there exists a revealing letter written to Moore dated Jan. 16, 1912, from the Moore archives at Columbia University:

"I will be frank. I have had your book Laws of Wages... For what dips I have made into the book make me believe that it proceeds on lines which I had deliberately decided not to follow years ago; even before mathematics had ceased to be a familiar language to me. My reasons for it are mainly two.

(1) No important economic chain of events seems likely to be associated with any one cause so predominantly that a study of the concomitant variation of the two elements with a large number of other causes representing the other operative causes: the 'caeteris paribus' clause—though formally adequate seems to me impracticable.

(2) Nearly a half of the whole operative economic causes have refused as yet to be established statistically."

"...each of the last 40 years has confirmed me in the belief that your method is not likely to have practical fruit for a long time."

As if this were not enough of a crushing blow, Marshall then had what he himself called the "rash, or even impudent audacity" to enclose with the letter a personal note from Edgeworth to Marshall giving his own impression of Moore's work. The language makes it clear it was not meant for Moore's eyes:

"Moore is a nightmare to me. I know I must write to him and I am afraid...

"So you will bear in mind that all these pictures and decimals and learned terms are introduced to prepare the way for a future generation of workers, who can put all the faith I have just mentioned into a group of mathematical machines and turn the handles. But neither our statistics nor our mathematics is ready for this work. We are like the first assailants of a fortified position: our corpses will fill the trenches so that Moore can get on...

"He seems to me to have only proved that there was *some sort* of causal connection in cases in which no one would doubt there was one: and to have reached results not really as helpful *practically* as those which I could have got by looking at the world with wide open eyes for a few minutes."

and so on. Rather, the point is that none of the first two generations of innovators of neoclassical price theory such as Jevons, Walras, Marshall, Edgeworth, Bowley and so forth felt compelled to link that particular theory to explicit empirical evidence or to pollute their value theory with stochastic concepts.

For instance, Bowley thought statistics could merely serve as a source of facts, and not as a means of testing functional forms (Darnell, 1981, p. 148). Edgeworth dashed any hopes of obtaining demand curves by means of statistical observation as "chimerical" (Edgeworth, 1894, p. 473; see also Edgeworth, 1925, vol. I, p. 8), and wrote that, "There is really only one theorem in the higher part of the calculus [of probabilities], but it is a very difficult one, the theory of errors, or deviations from an average. The direct applications of this theory to human affairs are not very considerable" (Edgeworth, 1925, vol. II, p. 287). Indeed, Edgeworth could write an entire paper entitled "Applications of Probability to Economics" (Edgeworth, 1925, vol. II) which had no statistical theory or applications in it!

The irony was that, prior to 1930, it was mainly (but not entirely) economists who distanced themselves from the neoclassical research program and were openly skeptical about neoclassical price theory who pioneered the explicit connection between a stochastically informed empiricism and some sort of economic theory. (The primary exception to this generalization were the agricultural economists, who deserve, but have not yet received, separate attention from historians.)

In the United States, the center of the heterodox movement to construct a stochastic economics was located at Columbia University, and included in its ranks Wesley Clair Mitchell, Frederick Mills and Henry Moore. Mitchell was a student of Thorstein Veblen and a leading partisan of the American Institutionalist school of economics. Anyone who reads Mitchell's lecture notes on *Types of Economic Theory* will attest to his profoundly skeptical posture with regard to neoclassical economic theory (Mitchell, 1969). A formidable academic entrepreneur, Mitchell helped found the NBER in 1920, a research organization whose task in its early years was to implement an empirically grounded economics and encourage the development of a modern 'scientific' economics. In his Presidential Address to the American Economics Association Mitchell decried the similarity of orthodox economics to the older Lagrangean mechanics, and suggested economic theory be reconstructed in the pattern of more modern physics (Mitchell, 1925).

One of the first members of the NBER staff was Frederick Mills, another Columbia economist. In a manifesto proclaiming the arrival of a "New Economics" in 1924, Mills denounced the mechanical ambitions of neoclassical theory, and quoted James Clerk Maxwell to the effect that, "The scientific view of nature is thus. . . neither purely historical nor purely mechanical, it is statistical" (Mills, 1924a, p. 39). Amongst other ringing phrases, he proclaimed that, "In dealing with social and economic phenomena the existence of variation and the consequent inapplicability of the mechanical method must be realized", that "the concept of law is quite inconsistent with the statistical view of nature", and that, "Of contemporary writers, Henry L. Moore has not only clearly described the essential characteristics of statistical laws, but has demonstrated the fruitfulness of the concept when applied to economic problems" (Mills, 1924a, pp. 41, 42, 45).

The opposition of Mitchell and Mills to neoclassical theory and its predispositions went well beyond empty appeals to statistical mechanics or evolutionary biology: it also involved opposition to the conceptualization of stochastic phenomena as "errors" superimposed upon a deterministic structure. It is a little-known fact that doubts about the dependence upon Gaussian distributions and central limit theorems were broached as early as 1915 by, among others, Wesley Clair Mitchell, and that there have been subsequently a parade of empirically inclined economic researchers who have arrayed themselves against the notion of a normally distributed perturbations impressed upon a lawlike neoclassical model.[4] In the 1920s people at NBER who looked at distributions of price changes noted that they had "tails" that were much too fat to qualify as Gaussian; (Mills, 1927, p. 336) was perceptive enough to notice that this phenomenon might imply "infinite probable error".[5] These observations were persistently ignored by neoclassical critics, who instead excoriated Mills and the NBER for abjuring the guidance of neoclassical theory in their inquiries (Bye, 1940; Marschak, 1941; Koopmans, 1947).

But the person most responsible for prodding the neoclassicals and forcing them to sit up and take notice in the first few decades of the century was Henry Ludwell Moore. It was he whom Henry Schultz declared was single-handedly responsible for the creation of the new field of the statistical study of demand (Schultz, 1938, p. 63). This statement has irked later generations of econometricians, and indeed, is false from a number of points of view: first, others had fitted things which looked like demand curves before Moore; but second, a careful reading reveals that Moore was *not* engaged in simply trying to implement the work of Marshall in the empirical sphere; rather, he considered himself to have embarked upon the creation of an alternative and highly novel "synthetic economics". Moore has been ill-served by historians such as (Stigler, 1962) who try to portray

---

[4] The original caveat by Mitchell appeared in his "Index-numbers of Wholesale prices in the U.S. and in foreign countries", *Bulletin of the U.S. Bureau of Labor Statistics*, no. 173. It was seconded by (Flux, 1921) and (Gini, 1924) and the massive study by (Mills, 1927). Curiously enough, Edgeworth came to the defence of the "normal law" in 1918 on the grounds that it was convenient for purposes of calculation and the circular argument that "the law is the outcome of numerous independent causes... it is unlikely that independent phenomena should vary concurrently" (Edgeworth, 1925, vol. I, pp. 390–393).

[5] These early observations could be regarded as the precursors of the profound critique of neoclassical econometrics developed in Mandelbrot (1963a, b), especially concerning the ubiquity of "stable Paretian" distributions in economic phenomena. This critique is discussed in Mirowski (forthcoming, b).

him as a fledgling neoclassical econometrician, but then find they must suppress or explain away his numerous eccentricities. What is most essential for our present thesis is to observe that as his empirical concerns ripened, Moore evolved into a sharp critic of neoclassical theory.

In his earliest writings, such as (Moore, 1908), he assumed the mantle of a proselytizer within the neoclassical camp for an explicitly statistical economics, praising Cournot, Edgeworth and Pareto, and hinting that economic laws might be initially discovered by empirical statistical methods, and then later rationalized using the principles of "pure economics".[6] Yet in 1912 Moore's hopes had been rudely discounted by Marshall; and further, his request of 1908 to Walras concerning his attitude towards statistics was never answered (Jaffé, 1965, vol. III, letter 1685). It seems that by 1914, Moore's view of neoclassicals, and perhaps of neoclassical theory, had grown a little jaundiced. After noting, quite correctly, that the statistical requirement of a large quantity of observations would dictate the collection of data over time, and deducing that it was inevitable that this practice would violate the orthodox *ceteris paribus* conditions and the static framework of neoclassical price theory, he gave vent to a barrage calculated to provoke even the most thick-skinned of his colleagues:

"In the closing quarter of the last century great hopes were entertained by economists with regard to the capacity of economics to be made an 'exact science'. According to the view of the foremost theorists, the development of the doctrines of utility and value had laid the foundations of scientific economics in exact concepts, and it would be possible to erect upon the new foundation a firm structure of interrelated parts which, in definiteness and cogency, would be suggestive of the severe beauty of the mathematico-physical sciences. But this expectation has not been realized... The explanation is found in the prejudiced point of view from which economists regarded the possibilities of science and in the radically wrong method which they pursued. It was assumed gratuitously that economics was to be modeled on the simpler mathematical, physical sciences, and this assumption created a prejudice at the outset both in selecting the data to be investigated and in conceiving the types of laws that were to be the object of research. Economics was to be a 'calculus of pleasure and pain', a 'mechanics of utility', a 'social mechanics', a *'physique sociale'*... The biased point of view implied in these descriptions led to an undue stressing of those aspects of the science which seemed to bear out the pretentious metaphors. One would naturally suppose from this manner of conceiving the science that the economic theorists would have at once entered upon their task with the methods that had proved

[6] "Professor Pareto's law of income is a purely empirical law for whose origin Pareto has not offered an explanation. His procedure has been similar to the procedure in physical science in which such laws as those of Boyle, Gay-Lussac, and Lavogardo were at first established as purely empirical results. But just as one of the most fertile and characteristic developments of physics since the early work of Clerk–Maxwell has been the rational deduction of these and similar empirical laws from molecular theory, so likewise has a movement appeared in economics in which an attempt is made to devise from the principles of pure economics the laws established by empirical methods." (Moore, 1908, p. 28).

themselves useful in the physical sciences. But this they did not do. They seemed to identify the method of the physical sciences with experimentation, and since, as they held, scientific experimentation is impossible in social life, a special method has to be devised. This invention was a disguised form of the classical *cetaris paribus,* the method of the static state" (Moore, 1914, pp. 84–86).

Moore coupled this attack with his own preferred method, the ordinary least squares estimation of a brace of curves relating agricultural crop harvests to their prices, as well as pig iron production to its price. In the latter case, he claimed to have discovered an upward sloping "demand curve". Subsequent commentators went to great lengths discounting this finding by elaborating Moore's "mistakes" (e.g., Ezekiel, 1928; Wright, 1930; Stigler, 1962; Epstein, 1987), especially with regard to what was later dubbed "the identification problem" and the conflict with Marshallian theory. Yet all these commentators start from the mistaken premise that Moore intended to empirically implement Marshallian concepts, a practice that he later explicitly renounced[7] (Moore, 1929, p. 8). If Moore had a precursor, it was more nearly Cournot: both searched for phenomenological regularities cast in the form of a mathematical function; for Moore, these were to be linked in a chain to develop an explicitly *macroeconomic* theory of business cycles. In Moore's opinion, this was a 'scientific' theory because it linked business fluctuations to exogenous 'physical' determinants, or as he put it, "The law of the cycles of rainfall is the law of the cycles of the crops and the law of Economic Cycles" (Moore, 1914, p. 135).

In short, by the 1930s some new lines were being drawn. On the one side were many of the neoclassicals, holding tight to a incorrigibly deterministic physical metaphor from the mid-nineteenth century and the mathematics of constrained optimization, wary of any hint of indeterminist or historicist arguments and skeptical of the possibility of any theoretically informed precise empiricism; and on the other side, there were those who had started down the road of co-opting the methphors of the newer sciences, be it statistical mechanics or some version of Darwinian evolutionary theory, stressing the mathematics of probability and dispersion, flirting with a mixture of historicism and institutionalism. Both were intent on occupying the higher ground of 'science' in the debate; but the latter group had a leg up, since they could make reference to a more recent vintage of physics or biology, as well as trumpeting their greater respect for the practice of "scientific empiricism". To once again quote Henry Moore (for he is so eminently quotable):

"But what is the source of the sense of unreality so many experience after having

---

[7] In the Moore Papers at Columbia University, Box 47, there is an unpublished book-length manuscript entitled "The Good Life in a Progressive Democracy" which discusses in detail a system of general economic equilibrium, including *both* empirical demand and supply functions, but with no reference to utility. It seems this manuscript was completed by 1940 at the latest.

heroically struggled through the writings of Walras and Pareto? . . . Foremost among the causes of the sense of unreality are these: the method of proceeding by successive approximations in the approach to a theory of general equilibrium, which give a feeling of indefinitely postponed real solution; the use of the hypothesis of perfect competition with a meaning that does not accord with reality; the limitation of all conclusions to the static state, when, as a matter of fact, all economic phenomena are in perpetual flux; the assumption of an immediate adjustment of changes, when in reality there are always leads and lags; the complexity of the functions which must be derived from reality and the absence of any known method of making the derivation; the assumption that the simultaneous equations may never be solved, first, because their empirical forms can never be known. . ." (Moore, 1929, p. 29).

Perhaps this situation would never have evolved beyond such guerrilla warfare had there not been an incursion of a third destabilizing force into the battlefield in the mid-1920s. The new quantum mechanics of Heisenberg, Born and Jordan irreversibly changed the ontological position of stochastic concepts in science. As (Eddington, 1935, pp. 77–78) put it, "The formulae given in modern textbooks on quantum theory. . . are explicitly concerned with probabilities and averages. . . But further it is now recognized that the classical laws of mechanics and electromagnetism. . . are simply the limiting form assumed by the formulae of quantum theory when the number of individual quanta or particles is very large. This connection is known as Bohr's Correspondence Principle. The classical laws are not a fresh set of laws, but a particular adaptation of the quantum laws."

It is simply not feasible to provide a summary in this venue of quantum mechanics for the uninitiated, although Eddington is as good as a guide as any to what was widely believed in the mid-1930s. For a more modern and accessible primer one might consult (Davies, 1980; Jordan 1986; Cropper, 1970; Landshoff & Metherell, 1979). Nevertheless, even a superficial acquaintance with quantum mechanics would reveal that it clearly tipped the balance in favor of the challengers to neoclassical price theory because it suggested that all deterministic laws were merely limiting cases of a more fundamental stochastic substratum. In such an altered environment, neoclassical economists had two choices. Either they could withdraw deep within the obscurity of the Walrasian ramparts, or else they could try and strike some sort of accomodation with the new stochastic worldview. The Ostrich Option was advocated by many such as (Robbins, 1932, p. 101) who asserted without any justification that statistical laws discovered by the partisans of a stochastic economics could not possess the same status as statistical laws generated by the natural sciences. The Munich Option was the essential strategy of the partisans of the Econometrics Revolution.

III. How quantum mechanics influenced early econometrics

In this reading of the events of the 1930s–1960s, the rise of econometrics as a distinct subfield of economics was not a unified evolutionary process, but rather the multifaceted reaction to a *logical* crisis in the evolution of the conception of scientific explanation in the research program. Not everyone saw the potential set of problems being linked in the same manner, nor did everyone see the potential set of solutions (or indeed, "econometrics" itself) as comprising an identical set of practices; but it is a fact that the entire discourse was conducted by continuous reference to images of "science". Only in retrospect can be observed that the problems of determinism vs. indeterminism, abstract theory vs. empiricism, statics vs. dynamics, and subjectivity vs. objectivity, and individualism vs. macroscopic laws were all bound up together as problems created by the original physics metaphor which prompted neoclassical theory in the 1870s, and therefore it was neoclassical theorists who were most concerned to find a potential solution under the rubric of "econometrics".

While the advent of quantum mechanics precipitated "econometrics" out of the turbulent cross-currents of early 20th century economics, it did not *determine* its final structure in anything near the same way that 19th century energy physics determined the structure and formalisms of neoclassical price theory. The early econometricians did not copy, say, the wave equation term for term; for among other reasons, their prime objective was to preserve their 19th century price theory, not to supersede it. Hence the dowry bequeathed to economics by quantum mechanics is rather subtle, and historical evidence will not generally take the format of some key figure blithely asserting they were nothing more than an imitator of Heisenberg or Schrödinger or Born. Instead, historical inquiry will uncover two classes of evidence: suggestions as to the ways in which quantum mechanics focused attention on certain formalisms or structures of explanation (because there was as yet no such thing as a single "correct" stochastic formulation of an economic problem); and evidence as to the personal influences of quantum mechanics on some of the primary actors. Let us first make a brief list of possible paths of influence, starting from the broadly philosophical and ending with the narrowly technical; and then indicate some relevant biographical particulars.

[1] First and foremost, the success of quantum mechanics fostered the impression that stochastic explanation was eminently scientific, giving it sanction as being grounded in Nature, as indicated in the first section of this paper. Hence the neoclassical school was now willing to co-opt much of the language of the appeals to science of their opponents, saying that, ". . .each of the so-called laws of nature is essentially statistical" (Roos, 1934, p. 9); or "The class of scientific statements that can be expressed in probability theory is enormous. In fact, this class contains all the 'laws' that have, so far, been formulated" (Haavelmo, 1944, p. iv); or, "The analysis of time series has also revealed the present status of economics as a science" (Davis, 1941a, p. 579). But beyond that, it also changed the rules as to what level of analysis was appropriate for the introduction of stochastic considerations. Prior to quantum mechanics, statistical considerations in

thermodynamics entered in at the macro level, purportedly due to the inability to track every single individual particle. Now atoms themselves had stochastic aspects, and this encouraged neoclassical economists to likewise allow their appearance at the level of individual behavior (Morgan, 1987a, p. 186). As Roos (1934, p. 8) observed:

"There is necessarily little use made of the static theory of utility and its relation to demand. This does not mean that utility has *nothing* to do with the determination of demand... As long as physicists dealt with composites of molecules and atoms they were able to discover useful laws. When they attempted the problem of analyzing the atom, they soon came upon the problem of indeterminacy. In economics the individual occupies a role closely analogous to that of the atom in physics."

[2] However, the vintage of quantum mechanics most familiar to the partisans of the econometrics revolution was the sort that favored classical interpretations of quantum relationships. It took quite a while after the genesis of the quantum formalism for physicists to come round to a concensus that it fundamentally ruled out determinism; and by and large the early econometricians were not students of those who advocated such a drastic renunciation. For instance, Tinberger's familiarity with Ehrenfest (see below) may have included familiarity with the "Ehrenfest theorem" of 1927 (Ehrenfest, 1959, pp. 556–558), which stated that the mean of electron states follows a classical trajectory. Likewise, Koopmans' tutelage under Hendrik Kramers may have caused him to share Kramers' "unwillingness, or inability, to detatch himself from classical visualizable physics or to make a decisive, irreversible break with classical concepts" (Dresden, 1987, p. 429). This would have translated into a belief that one could ultimately reconcile the deterministic neoclassical model with stochastic considerations in the economic context as well.

[3] Quantum mechanics also suggested a way out of the impasse of importing Fisherian-style maximum liklihood techniques from a context of sampling designs in controlled experiments into a context where such samples were impossible. As Haavelmo (1944, p. 15) insisted in his famous manifesto, "If every theory should be accompanied by a carefully described design of experiments, much confusion on the subject of constant versus changing economic 'laws' would be cleared up"; a dictum seconded by Koopmans (1937, p. 7): "it is clear that the expression 'repeated sampling' required an interpretation somewhat different from that prevailing in the agricultural and biological field". Haavelmo's proposal was to redefine the meaning of "population" and "sample" in economics: the population could be conceptualized as all possible economic decisions (or, what is equivalent, all virtual "economies"), whereas the sample would be the actual observed realizations (Haavelmo, 1944, pp. 51–52). This is, of course, a metaphor: there is no distribution of ghostly 1988 GNP growth rates from which the actual experience is drawn. Nevertheless, the metaphor was rendered more

plausible by its resemblance to the new doctrines in quantum mechanics, in particular the concept of superposition of states. It is no accident that many supposed descriptions of underlying stochastic processes in later econometrics resemble the "many worlds" interpretation in later quantum mechanics.

[4] It is well known that quantum mechanics began with explicit condsideration of some simple models of oscillators, such as Planck's work on black-body radiation. Heisenberg's first matrix exercise was written for a simple oscillator (Jordan, 1986, chap. 18). Familiarity with such models may have seemed to suggest connections with simple oscillators in economic models, and thence to possible explanations of time series movements and the "business cycle". This process began with the work of Davis (1941a, pp. 35–37) Tinbergen, and Roos, but was best represented by Frisch's conception of "propagation and impluse problems". As he wrote, "I believe that this idea will give an interesting synthesis between the stochastical point of view and the point of view of rigidly determined dynamical laws" (Frisch, 1933b, p. 198 in 1965 edition). Frisch compared to the economy to a pendulum, claiming that the configuration of its swings could be accounted for by an abstract theory of dynamics, but the actual energy of motion would be tracable to "shocks" impinging upon the pendulum from outside the system. These shocks were then identified with stochastic phenomena. The use of linear operators and Fourier decompositions by Frisch (1933b, p. 181 in 1965 edition) and Davis (1941a, pp. 61 *et seq.*) were unusual for that time, and probably indicated a familiarity with quantum mechanics, or at least the physics of vibrations of elastic solids (Epstein, 1987, p. 62).

Neoclassical economists rapidly became enamoured of this metaphor, irrespective of the fact that they still were bereft of any legitimate dynamic theory, because they could place all the technical emphasis upon stochastic shocks as the ultimate cause of the movement of the economy (Koopmans, 1947, p. 171). Hence, econometrics bequeathed to neoclassicism an *ersatz* dynamics, or as Samuelson (1965, p. 147) put it:

"Why should a person interested in economics... spend time considering conservative oscillations of mechanics? Experience suggests that our dynamic problems in economics have something in common with those of the physical and biological sciences... Just as Ehrenfest and other physicists had to add probability to the causal systems of physics in order to get around the time-irreversibility feature of classical mechanics that was so inconsistent with the second law of thermodynamics, so we must, in the interests of realism, add stochastic probability distributions to our economic and biological causal systems."

This problem was misconstrued by early econometricians such as Haavelmo (1944, p. 20), who actually claimed that irreversible phenomena could be simply reduced to a mechanical (i.e., reversible) format by the mere addition of more relevant independent variables.

[5] Quantum mechanics may also have inadvertently focused attention

upon a particular conception of "structure" which then become the rallying cry of the Cowles Commission's program of "structural estimation". Tjalling Koopmans' mentor, Hendrik Kramers, developed a particular program of explanation in quantum electrodynamics in the early 1930s (Dresden, 1987, p. 341) which consisted of the following steps: (1) start from the classical model of the extended electron; (2) construct a Hamiltonian for the system consisting of electrons and radiation; (3) separate the analytical description of the system into structure-dependent and structure-independent parts; and (4) eliminate structure-dependent features by canonical transformations. As Dresden (1987, p. 343) put it, "To Kramers, 'the elimination of the structure' almost became a slogan". There would appear to be strong resemblances to the Cowles program for econometrics in the 1940s, with its stress on adherence to the neoclassical model, deriving behavioral structural equations from constrained optimization, and isolating the "structure" from stochastic components by means of the process of "identification". Indeed, the whole purpose of canonical transformations is the production of ignorable variables by means of transformations of the original set of coordinates (Lanczos, 1949, chap. 7), which is very similar to the problem of identification.

[5] With respect to the actual formalisms of econometrics, the progenitors did not actually *copy* quantum mechanics so much as they imitated some of the mathematical formalisms which were characteristic of quantum mechanics. Although matrix algebra was formulated by Cayley and others in the nineteenth century, it was first extensively introduced into physics with the Born–Jordan–Heisenberg formalization of matrix mechanics in the mid-1920s (Mehra & Rechenberg, vol. III, 1982, pp. 65–71). In matrix mechanics, which was a precursor to the full-blown quantum mechanics, the concern was to manipulate matricies of position and momentum coordinates of electrons. In the elaboration of matrix mechanics, one primarily has recourse to Hermetian matricies: that is, matrix transposes result in a symmetric matrix of complex conjugates. One advantage of a familiarity with Hermetian matricies is that if one arbitrarily restricts the elements of the matrix to be real numbers, then the Hermetian matrix is simply a symmetric matrix, and all analytical results automatically carry over for such matricies. One significant aspect of Hermetian matricies for Born and Jordan was their natural link to the mathematics of quadratic forms, and the reduction of finitely many complex variables to a sum of squares (Mehra & Rechenberg, 1982, vol. III, pp. 120–123).

Potential applications in the formalization of multivariate least squares estimation of this matrix framework by someone schooled in quantum mechanics must have seemed plentiful and obvious. Indeed, it was Frisch and Koopmans who introduced matrix algebra, quadratic forms, the eigenvalue problem and symmetric matricies into econometrics (Koopmans, 1937, pp. 10–13; Frisch, 1934, ch. 1). Koopmans was referring to just this phenomenon in a 1977 unpublished lecture to the Operations Research Society:

> "There is the precedent in physics of the 30's when matricies and wave equations came in with quantum mechanics, causing a great deal of distress to physicists who did not have previous exposure to these tools. Similar things happened in statistics in the 30's and 40's, and in econometrics and mathematical economics in the 40's and 50's; in both cases an upward jump in what you might call the intensity of the mathematics used."[8]

[7] The concern of early quantum mechanics with quasi-classical Gaussian states (Holevo, 1982, Ch. 5) may help account for the focus of attention of the early econometricians upon Gaussian distributions to the exclusion of those considerations raised by Mitchell, Mills and others that economic variates generally did not conform to normal distributions.

And now for some brief biographical evidence. The connections of the early Cowles/Econometric Society group with contemporary physics has not received the attention which it deserves. Here we shall just restrict ourselves to a subset of the relevant cast of characters.

Jan Tinbergen, one of the earliest advocates of econometric model building, actually received his Doctoraat in 1929 from the University of Leiden in physics. According to (Klein, 1970, pp. 305–306). He was encouraged to venture into economics by his advisor, the renowned physicist Paul Ehrenfest, one of the pre-eminent authorities on statistical mechanics of the early twentieth century. His thesis (Tinbergen, 1929) was concerned with the connection between variational principles and conservation principles—the critical issue in Hamiltonian dynamics—and their implications for Lorentz's classical model of the electron. In a retrospective interview he suggested he undertook his physics studies because he "hoped to get sufficient capability to handle things with mathematics and perhaps take physics as an expample of a more developed science than economics" (in Magnus & Morgan, 1987, p. 118), but it seems clear that his respect for the physics paradigm waned over the course of his career. His earliest work, true to the format of our hypothesis, began with the application of complex functions in order to render neoclassical theory "dynamic" (Tinbergen, 1933), and to estimate oscillatory solutions to aggregative difference equations using least squares. Yet he revealed an early disinclination to defend the neoclassical theory of pricing and allocation, as well as a lack of

---

[8] "Some Early Origins of OR/MS", opening remarks by Tjalling Koopmans at joint national ORSA/TIMS meeting, Atlanta, Ga., November 8, 1977; typescript in Koopmans Papers, Box 22, folder 445. These mathematical techniques served to identify those with the appropriate scientific backgrounds: "It is good to find another mathematical statistician able to use matrix theory in connection with correlation and regression problems... The theory of the roots of various determinental equations, and of symmetric functions of these roots, is surely destined to play a large part in statistics" Harold Hotelling to Tjalling Koopmans, 30 August 1937, Koopmans papers.

interest in segregating deterministic "laws" from stochastic "errors" (Tinbergen and Polak, 1950, p. 78—Dutch edition 1942). He was too early to be a student of Kramers; and throughout his life showed little interest in problems of "identification" and simultaneous equations estimation. Perhaps this reproduces the classical stance of his advisor Ehrenfest towards quantum mechanics, and goes some distance in explaining his later withdrawal from "econometrics" and his gravitation towards work of a more conventional political character (Epstein, 1987, pp. 127–8).

An econometrician closer to our model was Ragnar Frisch. Frisch took a Ph.D. in mathematical statistics from the University of Oslo in 1926; biographical material on his life is somewhat scarce because of the language barrier (ours, not his) and the inaccessability of his papers at the University of Oslo. Nevertheless, numerous comments in his published writings suggest a familiarity with the physics of his time. Frisch's earliest work explicitly discussed the analogies between neoclassical price theory and rational mechanics, and proposed the use of least squares models to explain errors or divergences from that model (Frisch, 1926, p. 19). By 1929 he was troubled by the possibility of "fictitious determinateness created by random errors" (Frisch, 1933a, p. 9; 1934, p. 6), and proposed his method of "confluence analysis" to uncover the "true determinate" system from the data, using the aforementioned matrix analysis to initiate the discussion of what was later called the identification problem. In 1937, Frisch was lecturing the Cowles researchers on physical analogies with oscillatory equations in economics, and in 1933 he produced the "solution" to the problem of neoclassical dynamics mentioned above. Although Frisch served as the earliest editor of *Econometrica*, it seems he also grew disenchanted with the program in later life, effectively renouncing econometrics as defined by the Cowles Commission by the early 1960s (Epstein, 1987, pp. 127–8).

Another important Leiden alumnus was Tjalling Koopmans, who earned a Ph.D. in mathematical statistics in 1936, following an M.A. in physics at Utrecht in 1933. Koopmans' advisor was the pre-eminent quantum physicist outside of Copenhagen, Hendrik Kramers; and indeed, Koopmans' first academic publication was in quantum physics. The title of (Koopmans, 1934) could be roughly translated as "On the Relationship of Wavefunctions and Characteristic Values to Individual Electrons".[9] His subsequent move to economics is best described in his own words:

"Why did I leave physics at the end of 1933? In the depth of the worldwide economc depression I felt that the physical sciences were far ahead of the social and economic sciences. What held me back was the completely different, mostly verbal, and to me almost indigestible style of writing in the social sciences. Then I

[9] A translation of this article into English was prepared, but apparently never published. A copy may be found in the Koopmans papers, box 14, folder 479.

learned from a friend that there was a field called mathematical economics, and that Jan Tinbergen, a former student of Paul Ehrenfest, had left physics to devote himself to economics. Tinbergen received me cordially and guided me into the field in his own inimitable way. I moved to Amsterdam which had a faculty of economics. The transition was not easy... Also, because of my reading block, I chose problems that, by their nature, or because of the mathematical tools required, have similarity with physics."[10]

The areas of similarity with quantum mechanics, such as Kramers' program, the use of matrix methods, and the general stance towards stochastic phenomena have been mentioned above. Koopmans became Research Associate at Cowles from 1944–48, and Director of Research from 1948–54, the periods in which the Cowles approach to econometrics was promulgated.

Some of the economists affiliated with the early Cowles Commission also came to economics from backgrounds in mathematical physics. Charles Roos was a 1926 mathematics Ph.D. from Rice University with a minor in physics. In 1931, Roos was one of the founding members of the Econometrics Society. One of the most prolific and sophisticated, Harold T. Davis, was a 1926 mathematics Ph.D. from Wisconsin who wrote extensively on physics (Davis, 1931). Davis made repeated references to physical analogies in his published works, especially (Davis, 1941a; 1941b), where among other analogies, he developed a formal comparison of the variance of a timeseries to the physical concept of energy (Davis, 1941a, p. 178). But more importantly, Davis' frequent talks and memorandums to both the Cowles Commission and to the Econometrics Society in the 1930s make even more explicit reference to the issues discussed in this paper. Quoting a paper read to a Cowles conference in 1937: "The physicist in his study of microphysics, that is to say, the phenomena of the electron and the quantum, has encountered difficulties similar to our own. Heisenberg was led to postulate the existence of a rectangle of indeterminacy, within which complete statistical chaos existed. Perhaps the main difference between our problem and theirs, statistically considered, is merely in the size of the price-time or production-time rectangle."[11]

Hence, many of the new generation of neoclassicals associated with the Cowles Commission and the Econometrics Society were eminently well-equipped to attempt to effect a reconciliation between neoclassical economics and the new physics. This new cohort recognized that neoclassical theory was an imitation of nineteenth century energetics, and they openly said so (Davis, 1941, pp. 49, 577; Koopmans, 1957, p. 176; Tintner & Sengupta,

[10] "Experiences in Moving From Physics to Economics", unpublished talk delivered to the American Physical Association, New York, Jan. 29, 1979; copy in Koopmans papers, box 18, folder 333.

[11] P. 7–8 of draft manuscript "The Econometric Problem", presented to the Third Annual Research Conference of the Cowles Commission, Colorado Springs, June 28, 1937; Cowles Archives, Davis manuscripts.

1972; p. 9; Henry Schultz to Harold Hotelling, letter, May 11, 1932, Hotelling papers). They were trained in universities in Holland and the U.S. where quantum mechanics was regarded as the vanguard of the new physics, and which were *avant garde* in their reception of the new doctrines (Cobden, 1971). Even though many of their approaches were ultimately different, in the very early stages of the reconciliation of neoclassical theory and stochastic concepts they recognized one another as comrades in arms, engaged in essentially the same research project.

The point here is not that all the protagonists wanted to copy quantum mechanics: rather, it is that some common vocabulary was needed to accomodate the economic orthodoxy with the novel cultural currents. The real underlying issue was order versus chaos: any old advocacy of stochastic descriptions of economic phenomena would not do, because the conception of the market as a natural organizing force was at risk. The subtle shading came, not with the mathematics *per se,* but rather with the accompanying assertions that a rational stochastic economics was *not* irreducably random: it simply reconciled stochastic disturbance and deterministic law into a tidy package. As (Koopmans, 1937, pp. 5–6) insisted, "Following Frisch, each of the variables may be conceived as the sum of two components, a 'systematic component' or 'true value' and an 'erratic component' or 'disturbance' or 'accidental error'. The systematic components are assumed to satisfy the regression equation exactly. . . the erratic component is taken as error in the literal sense of the word."

Might it be possible to suggest that, just as in the case of the history of physics, once stochastic concepts are admitted into the fold, one progressively discovers that the damage to the deterministic world view is not so easily localized? And that, just perhaps, the more that we find out, the more meaningless the paradigm of constrained optimization becomes?

Yale University and Tufts University

Oxford Economic Papers 41 (1989), 236–258

REALISM AND INSTRUMENTALISM IN THE DEVELOPMENT OF ECONOMETRICS*

By TONY LAWSON

I. Introduction

WHEN, in the early decades of this century, various economists took a critical stance towards the application of formal probabilistic methods to the material of economic time-series, the proponents of these methods, whatever their intentions, apparently conveyed the view that all legitimate concerns were being attended to. In fact, this impression seems to have been so pervasive amongst the econometrics community that a somewhat dismissive attitude came to be adopted towards those economists, including Keynes, who continued to display any reservations about the soundness and relevance of the project (See e.g. Koopmans, 1941; Haavelmo, 1943a; Schumpeter, 1946). As Vining (1949b) observes economists came to regard Keynes' concerns about econometrics as the "conclusions of a sadly misinformed and misguided man" (p. 93). In truth, however, it is not clear that such concerns have ever been adequately met in practice. Indeed, today, as economists find themselves reluctantly still puzzling over the essential nature of, and the claims that can legitimately be made for, econometric analysis, the sort of concerns put forward by Keynes and others are generally accepted as being as relevant and pressing as ever (see e.g. Meeks, 1978; Hendry, 1980; Lawson, 1985; Pesaran and Smith, 1985a, 1985b; Epstein, 1987; Gilbert, 1987; Rowley and Hamouda, 1987; Rowley and Jain, 1987; and Gillies, 1988). A relevant question, then, is what lies behind this state of affairs? Why are the sort of worries expressed by Keynes still being resurrected? And how were these concerns allayed in the first place?

In what follows I want to address these sorts of issues from an explicit philosophy of science vantage point. A general neglect of philosophical considerations in this area has often been noted, (e.g. Caldwell, 1982, p. 216) and what is proposed can best be considered as an exploratory first step. Specifically I want to delineate two largely oppositional positions, *realism* and *instrumentalism* (defined below), and to indicate their bearing on the development of the subject in general and particularly on the issues referred to above. This philosophical opposition has often been found to provide a leverage to a better understanding of developments in the 'natural sciences' and in what follows I want to suggest that its explanatory potential with regard to econometric analysis may be no less significant.

* For helpful comments on a previous draft of this paper I am very grateful to Nancy Cartwright, Geoff Hodgson, Clive Lawson, Gabriel Palma, William Peterson, Jo Runde, Steve Satchell, Paul Seabright and Arnis Vilks.

Now in distinguishing realism from instrumentalism I do not want to suggest that the opposed parties in the early econometric debates divide neatly and unproblematically behind one or other of these philosophical/methodological banners. But then nor can these philosophical/methodological doctrines be seen as irrelevant to an adequate understanding of the different positions taken. I do want to argue, in fact, that the more prominent critics of the 'probability approach in econometrics' reveal an implicit realist position on relevant issues; but I want to suggest that this is also true to some extent of the proponents and practitioners of the approach. However, I shall also argue that, because of certain premisses that must be accepted if econometrics is to be advanced, then, whatever their philosophical inclinations might otherwise be, the early proponents of the econometric approach—and the same is generally true of current day practitioners[1]—appear to turn ultimately, to a form of instrumentalist reasoning.

If this observation is correct then certain implications follow. To the extent that *both* critics such as Keynes as well as proponents of the econometric approach are indeed *inclined* to an implicit realist position (especially in presentation) then the account being proposed is suggestive of why an impression was generally gained that all relevant concerns were being attended to. But to the extent that, at the end of the day, the proponents of the econometric approach feel bound to rely on a non-realist form of reasoning, it is possible to suggest why Keynes' concerns have been resurrected as incompletely or inadequately attended to—and why it may even follow that a 'satisfactory' (i.e. a comprehensively realist) response may not be forthcoming at all. And to the extent that the sort of philosophical issues raised here are indeed relevant to the econometrics issue but seem rarely if ever to be explicitly addressed in the econometrics context, then it may also be possible to suggest why disparities between what econometric text-book theory presupposes and what practicing econometricians find actually has to be the case—disparities which have apparently motivated much of the re-examining of Keynes—continue to exist.

It is thus an aim of this paper to argue that a focus upon the traditional philosophy of science opposition of realism and instrumentalism in the context of econometric analysis may indeed be fruitful for an adequate understanding of the subject matter's essential nature and path of development, as well as ambiguities that continue to exist.

II. Realism, instrumentalism and scientific analysis

At a very general level the version of (scientific) realism considered here asserts the existence of the objects of analysis independent of the enquiry in

---

[1] It is unfortunately not possible here to explore the arguments of this paper in the context of more recent innovations to the econometric literature. The sort of conclusions drawn, however, seem just as relevant with regard to these more recent contributions.

which they are the objects.[2] According to this doctrine there exist a material and social world independent of (any individual) consciousness but which is knowable by consciousness—it is accepted that true theories can be obtained.[3] And a methodological doctrine that is subsumed under the general heading of realism here is that such knowledge—or true theories—should be pursued. The version of instrumentalism to be considered is the largely oppositional methodological doctrine that predictively successful theories is all that is required. Adherence to this latter doctrine usually reflects an idealist position wherebye theories can never be considered as true or false but merely as instruments of prediction. In the context of economic analysis, however, it is not uncommon to find an effective attachment to instrumentalism combined with an implicit acceptance of the view both that there is an independently existing real world *and* that it is possible to judge whether or not our theories of it are false (or true). Economists adhering to this position thus often assert that theories acknowledged as false or fictitious can serve as useful tools of prediction.[4] For purposes of the discussion which follows, then, instrumentalism will be taken as the methodological doctrine that all that is required of analysis (whether or not it is all that is considered to be possible) is a theory that is consistent with the given set of empirical data in question. These distinctions in the economics context clearly require some further elaborating; and in doing so I shall draw significantly on some recent contributions to the philosophy of science, and particularly on Bhaskar (1978).[5]

It is helpful to start out by schematizing a conceptual research programme into three stages. The first stage[6] of the analysis is a controlled experimental situation in which a particular regularity amongst events (under some description) is found persistently to hold. In other words, it is found that whenever certain (types of) 'conditions' hold then the same (type of) 'effect'

[2] I focus below on an (essentially Aristotelean) account of the doctrine of realism that seems to me to be the most suited to a discussion of econometrics. I do not wish to imply by this emphasis, of course, that all versions of realism are equivalent to, or encompassed by, the account developed. The same sort of qualificatory comments also apply to the version of instrumentalism considered below.

[3] For discussions bearing on the 'truth' of theories as interpreted here see Bradley, 1914; S. Sayers, 1985; and Lawson, 1987.

[4] It is because economists often presuppose that acknowledged false theories, or theories about fictions, can be useful as tools of prediction, that the releveant oppositional position to realism to consider here is the methodological doctrine of instrumentalism. Outside of economics, however, it seems less common to find the view that the construction of acknowledged false theories is an adequate objective combined with an acknowledgement that true theories of real mechanisms can be found. Consequently, outside of economics the usual oppositional position to realism is the epistemologically doctrine of idealism. For example, Bhaskar's account of transcendental realism in the natural sciences—which the following account is similar, and owes much, to—is, in the main, counterpoised to transcendental idealism.

[5] Other recent Philosophy of Science accounts which have a significant bearing, and have been very influential, upon what follows include Cartwright, 1983; Chalmers, 1978; Hacking, 1983a, b; Levy, 1981; A. Sayer, 1984; S. Sayers, 1985; and Van Fraassen, 1980.

[6] These stages need not be understood as necessarily taking place in any fixed order.

seems always to 'follow'. The second stage of analysis is the construction of a model that can entail this regularity. And the third stage involves subjecting the entities postulated at the modelling stage to further/continuous scrutiny. Positivists, including those who accept instrumentalism, tend to be content with the first two stages only. In fact, for the instrumentalist there is no necessary requirement that the model even be plausible, for all that is required is a model that is consistent with the relevant data—data consistency is a sufficient condition of model adequacy (although not necessarily of model choice—there may be numerous 'adequate' models). A model can be accepted as adequate by the instrumentalist if the empirical 'data' are *merely* 'as if' they had been generated in accordance with it. The hope then is that the model will continue to be successful with respect to predicting data that, as yet, are unavailable. In contrast, for the realist committed to the view that the entities and mechanisms postulated at the modelling stage are (or may be) real, the third stage is essential. The objective on this realist view is to identify and understand enduring causal structures of mechanisms that lie behind the flux of observable phenomena; to understand the real mechanisms that actually give rise to the (equally real) events in question.

Now all forms of analysis implicitly take some object of knowledge to be relatively fixed or enduring. And in order to identify ways in which realism and instrumentalism have substantively different consequences in the context of econometrics it is useful to focus upon what it is, in the differing accounts, that is taken to so endure. For the instrumentalist, as with numerous other conceptions of science, it is a regularity amongst events (or 'variables') under some description that is taken to be stable. And it is a statement of an event-regularity that is the usual interpretation of a law. For the realist, in contrast, it is real things and their powers or ways of acting that are considered to be knowable and are taken to endure. Specific kinds of things have powers to act in definite ways in appropriate circumstances by virtue of certain relatively constant intrinsic structures or constitutions or, more generally, natures—which are discerned *a posteriori* in the process of science and general experience. It is these essential natures that designate what things are. And once we know what a thing is then, if certain 'activating' or 'triggering' conditions hold, we know how it will behave. Once we understand the nature of private enterprises, trade unions, multi-nationals and copper, for example, then we can deduce their respective powers or dispositions to seek profits, defend conditions of workers, operate in different national markets and conduct electricity well.[8] Realists, then, attempt to understand causal things and the ways in which they act; to analyse causal structures at their own level of being. And in

---

[8] Of course, complex entities may have numerous constant intrinsic structures or natures. The one focussed upon in any analysis will be that which is essential to explaining a given empirical phenomenon of interest (see Lawson, 1988).

this, clearly, realists adopt a non-reductionist, rather than a persistently atomist/individualist, outlook.

For the instrumentalist, to reiterate, it is a conjunction of events that is taken to be constant while for the realist is is a relation between the conditions which activate a causal structure and its way of acting. The latter relationship is not the same thing as, and will not usually coincide with, an event regularity, because the action of any causal mechanism will, in general, be offset by the countervailing actions of juxtaposed mechanisms. In recent realist literature, in fact, this notion of a power that may be exercised without being realised in manifest phenomena is designated a tendency. And (in a similar sort of fashion to Marshall (1890, p. 27), amongst others) it is this ascription of a tendency to a certain kind of thing that is the usual understanding of a statement of a law. Thus, because a leaf departing from a branch of a tree is subject to influences other than gravity, it does not usually fall with constant acceleration or land on the ground directly below the point of fall. In other words the law of gravity (as a statement of a tendency) may still be accepted as operative in this case,[9] but the *actual* motion of the leaf does not follow any regular empirical pattern—the leaf is also dependent upon thermal, aerodynamic and numerous other tendencies.

It follows from this reasoning that, for the realist, a constant conjunction of events can be expected to occur only under certain special conditions— those in which the operating of some enduring causal mechanism is effectively isolated from the effects of other mechanisms.[10] It is only in such a case that there may be a one-to-one correspondence between the acting of some causal entity and actual events. It is thus clear that the hypothesised first stage of the conceptual research program outlined above—an experimental situation in which a constant conjunction of events is repeatedly observed—represents a very special situation. I started with this conception, in part, because it facilitates the discussion set out; but also because so many economists seem to presuppose that the sort of conditions that obtain in experimental set-ups represent the general situation. In fact, for many realists a situation or system in which a constant conjunction of events holds—which I shall henceforth refer to as a *closed system*—is considered instead to be the exceptional case rather than the general rule (see e.g. Bhaskar, 1978; Hacking, 1983a, b). This observations, if correct, however, does not undermine the efficacy of realist analysis. Indeed the advantage of realism is that it allows the possibility of useful analysis even when the world is *open*. Thus in a non-experimental realm—or more generally where a closed system does not obtain—a realist can still explain, and even predict

---

[9] The main realist criterion of theory adequacy is depth of explanatory power rather than predictive accuracy—its ability to illuminate a range of empirical phenomena. (See Lawson, 1988.)

[10] Such an 'isolation' may include the engineering of a situation wherein the effects of other mechanisms are constant or orthogonal to those so far included or at least analytically tractable.

the operation of identified tendencies (although the juxtapositioning of different causal mechanisms may prevent the prediction of actual events). For the instrumentalist, however, these options are not available, and the only recourse in a non-experimental science is to continually seek out a naturally occuring closure.

It is in this respect, then, that the forms of realism and instrumentalism that I believe to be relevant in the current context, bear substantively different consequences for analysis. In short, for the realist relative endurability lies at the level of causal structures and the ways in which they act, and knowledge of such things is considered to be possible. On this view successful science is comprehensible even in an *open* world—explanation and the prediction of identified tendencies (although not actual outcomes) can occur. For the instrumentalist it is presumed that the only knowable endurable item (or the only one that we need necessarily consider) is an empirical regularity—a conjunction of events. Successful analysis is thus centred on the notion of event-predictability, and its possibility requires a continuous seeking out of effective closures.

Clearly much depends here on the general availability of closed systems—those in which constant conjunctions of events necessarily hold. Just as instrumentalism presupposes a closed system so too does econometrics. And the distinctiveness of realism and its comparative advantage over instrumentalism clearly increase to the extent that the world is not closed but open. As such, the conditions under which a closure can obtain seem to warrant examining further.

Conditions for closure

A closed system is one in which a constant conjunction of event holds.[11] In the context of econometrics at least, such a closure seems to necessitate the satisfaction of two fundamental conditions. If we refer to one sort of event (or set of events) as 'effects' (say y) and label the remaining (set of) events 'causes'[12] (say $x_1, x_2, \ldots, x_n$), then the necessary conditions are, first, that each cause has the same effect, and second, that each effect has the same cause or set of causes. The former stipulation (that each cause has the same effect) is the *intrinsic condition* for a closure, and the latter stipulation (that each effect has the same set of causes) is the *extrinsic condition* for a closure.[13]

How, then, might these conditions be satisfied? The intrinsic condition for

---

[11] The open/closed systems differentiation owes much to the contributions of Von Bertalanffy (See e.g. Von Bertalanffy, 1950).

[12] The notion of 'cause' can be understood in many ways here depending upon the philosophical doctrine being adhered to. For example it may be a set of conditions that regularly preceeds or accompanies the event y; or it may be merely something that renders some event intelligible; or it may be real causes or the conditions that trigger real causal mechanisms and so forth.

[13] Notice that the intrinsic condition for a closure corresponds to what is often referred to as the assumption of uniformity of nature, while the extrinsic condition is stronger than the assumption of universal causality—that each effect has *some* cause.

a closure is clearly satisfied by the realist through the identification of enduring real causal things or structures. As noted above, the possibility that something can be understood as a certain kind of thing means that it has a praticular constant intrinsic structure or essential nature. And tendencies possessed by virtue of this constant intrinsic structure will themselves be relatively enduring. Thus copper is understood and so defined according to its (constant) atomic structure; and it is by virtue of this (constant) intrinsic structure that copper has an enduring tendency to conduct electricity well.

Now the instrumentalist has no obvious coherent approach to satisfying the intrinsic condition for closure. In fact, if the intrinsic condition is deemed not to be satisfied—if, for example, an empirical relationship breaks down even when events or structures external to the system do not change—the only recourse appears to be to search out relationships described as more 'autonomous' or some such, in the hope that increased stability can be found. It is not clear that such a search can be structured in any sensible manner—although Bhaskar (1978, p. 75) has suggested that such a situation may result in analyses being couched in ever more simple or 'atomic' descriptions; and ultimately in terms of units or 'individuals' that have an absence of, and therefore cannot have a varying, internal or intrinsic structure. And to the extent that the latter occurs, of course, and to the extent that prediction at the level of complexes is called for, some extra assumption of 'atomic uniformity' will then be required guaranteeing that behaviour at the level of complexes can be determined from behaviour at the more autonomous or atomic level.

But there is nothing in all this that necessitates that the econometrician be realist or instrumentalist in approaching the satisfaction of the intrinsic condition for closure. It may be true that some current econometricians— perhaps even a majority—are content to posit acknowledged fictions or false theories at the outset—globally optimising individuals with perfect foresight or rational expectations being an obvious example. And in practice it may often be found that, in the context of the analysis that the econometrician wishes to consider, the intrinsic condition is difficult to satisfy. For example, the econometrician who wishes, say, to study the relationship between 'employment demand' and 'output conditions' will find it difficult to satisfy the intrinsic condition for a closure if, over the time-period or region in question, the firm or industry whose supposedly stable internal structure grounds the analysis, switches production from, say, manufacturing to services, or significantly changes its process technology in general. But in what follows I want to suggest that, at least at the theoretical level at which their contributions are pitched, the early proponents of the probability approach in econometrics do, by and large, appear to adopt a realist attitude in their discussion bearing upon the intrinsic condition for closure. Indeed I suggest that it is in this sense, or in connection with this issue of intrinsic constancy, that they might have appeared to be sharing various concerns with Keynes. (Even if Keynes was more sceptical about the prospects of success in the general economic time-series context).

It is the presumption of a satisfaction of the extrinsic condition for closure, however, that seems much more difficult to justify—even at a theoretical level. To the extent that economics is an essentially non-experimental science the realist may just rest content with the ability to explain and predict the tendencies of identified causal structures. For the instrumentalist, as for the econometrician, this option is clearly not open. If the extrinsic condition is deemed to be not satisfied in any piece of econometric analysis the general strategy must be to keep on searching—to include, or to somehow account for, or to isolate the system from the action of, the so far excluded, but relevant, causal factors. But a significant problem in the context of economic analysis is that it almost always appears to be possible to conceive of further causal factors capable of impinging on the event in question but not yet explicitly accounted for in the context of a given econometric analysis. Of course, even in a well controlled experimental situation it will still be logically conceivable that, no matter what the experimental design, there remain some excluded causal factors whose effects are not orthogonal, etc, to those explicitly considered. The knowledge of the experimenter, however, will typically be such as to be satisfied that this is not the case.[14] The opposite, however, is true in the sort of non-experimental situation that the economist is typically dealing with. In otherwords the econometrician will usually have positive knowledge of numerous—perhaps of an almost unlimited number of—potentially relevant causal factors that it is not possible to explicitly consider. In such situations, I want to suggest, econometricians who have acknowledged this problem—including those whose contributions to the development of the probability approach in econometrics are considered below—appear to have been unable, or unprepared, to develop any option other than that of introducing, or recommending others to introduce, some acknowledged convenient fiction, some relatively arbitrary if creative (set of) assumptions(s), in the hope that (typically amongst many other things) it serves analytically to account for the combined action of the multitude of excluded (as well as included) factors; in the hope that the model so constructed turns out to be data consistent. Now to the extent that this recourse is indeed followed by the econometrician then it is at this point that econometric analyses appear to become, in effect, instrumentalist—whatever the implicit philosophical inclinations of the econometrician might otherwise be. And any basis for using models so constructed for forecasting 'future' events is then largely a matter of convention.

---

[14] It is easy both to idealize and also to under estimate the role of controlled experiment in those sciences in which it is possible. Were it to be held that any comparative benefit obtained from an experimental as against a non-experimental situation was just an insignificant matter of degree then the conclusion would seem to follow that all science is essentially explanatory rather than predictive.

The next step, then, is to indicate the relevance of this outline to an understanding of the early contributions to the development of the probability approach in econometrics, and specifically to justify the historical claims made above concerning the positions of both early sceptics as well as proponents of the probability approach. I am suggesting that the realist/instrumentalist opposition helps us to pinpoint aspects of the different accounts which are essentially similar and which are essentially distinct. I have characterized Keynes, a notable sceptic, as implicitly realist, and noteworthy proponents of the econometric approach as, to some extent, also realist—at least in as far as they could be. I am now also suggesting that it is when faced with difficulties of providing grounds for satisfying the extrinsic condition for a closure that, as econometricians, the second group turned ultimately to a form of instrumentalist reasoning. To substantiate such claims it is thus to a consideration of the positions of both noteworthy sceptics as well as noteworthy proponents of the econometric approach that I now turn, beginning with the former, the more prominent of whom appears to have been Keynes.[15]

III. Keynes and realism

In *A Treatise on Probability* (CW VIII)[16] Keynes addresses numerous issues but a consistent underlying theme is that any justification of methods of analysis must be grounded in our understanding of the natures of the objects of study.

Thus, for example, scientists are viewed as acting upon the assumption that the world is composed of atomic entities which exercise their own separate and invariable causal tendencies or 'effects'—a view which Keynes refers to as an assumption of "the *atomic* character of natural law":[17]

---

[15] It should be noted that in the category of sceptics, Keynes was by no means alone. Others who publicly expressed critical reservations include Ezekiel, (1928); Persons, (1924); and initially at least even Frisch (1938), as well as Robbins (1932). [Despite being usually characterized as a 'subjectivist' it is interesting to note that Robbins' criticisms of econometrics can be interpreted as revealing a realist inclination *on such matters*. Thus Robbins asserts that it "is a characteristic of scientific generalisations that they refer to reality"; that ". . . their reference is to that which exists, or that which may exist, rather than to purely formal relations" (p. 104). And he argues, for example, that "there is no ground for supposing that the resultant effect [of economic 'causes'] should exhibit significant uniformity over time and space" (p. 107, 109), nor reason to suppose that the theory of probability is relevant in an economic time-series context. (p. 112)]. Perhaps because of the prominence of his debate with Tinbergen in the Economic Journal in 1939, Keynes, however, appears to have been the more influential of this group. Certainly others, (for example Persons, 1924) acknowledge that their reasoning is explicitly influenced by Keynes' *A Treatise on Probability*.

[16] 'CW VIII' refers to the Royal Economic Society's Collected Works of J. M. Keynes, Volume VIII, published in 1973. In what follows the notation CW followed by the respective volume will be used throughout. Unattributed references to Keynes' writings, however, refer to CV VIII, *A Treatise in Probability*.

[17] Keynes explicitly observes that this assumption is more powerful than the supposition of "laws of universal causation and the uniformity of nature, namely, that all events have *some* cause and that the same total cause always produces the same effect" (p. 276)—attributed by Keynes to logicians in their attempts to validate methods of induction and analogy.

The system of the material universe must consist, if this kind of assumption is warranted, of bodies which we may term (without any implication as to their size being conveyed thereby) *legal atoms,* such that each of them exercises its own separate, independent, and invariable effect, a change of the total state being compounded of a number of separate changes each of which is solely due to a separate portion of the preceding state. We do not have an invariable relation between particular bodies, but nevertheless each has on the others its own separate and invariable effect, which does not change with changing circumstances, although, of course, the total effect may be changed to almost any extent if all the other accompanying causes are different. Each atom can, according to this theory, be treated as a separate cause and does not enter into different organic combinations in each of which it is regulated by different laws (p. 276).

Thus, according to Keynes, scientists appear to presuppose a world consisting of material entities referred to as atoms; that the ways of acting (or causal tendencies) of these atoms are invariable in that they do not change with changing circumstances (satisfying the intrinsic condition for closure); and that the total effect of any such causal bodies may be changed 'to almost any extent' when juxtaposed against different causes (thus creating a problem in satisfying the extrinsic condition for a closure). Moreover the atomic view, Keynes observes, is not necessitated by the assumption of uniformity of nature. Thus, to the extent that such an atomic view is maintained, and to the extent that the actions of complexes are also to be explained, then some assumption of 'atomic uniformity' is also required guaranteeing that the actions of complexes can be reduced to, or inferred from a knowledge of, a combination of these of individual components[18] (p. 277).

Keynes himself, however, is concerned to develop a wider or more general account of conditions that validate the use of inductive methods; one which is not restricted in scope to material causation.[19] And he is also concerned that the conditions thus specified are such that the probability calculus can be legitimately employed. Now in this endeavour Keynes essentially focuses upon the assumption of a system of *limitation of independent variety.* This assumption amounts to the restriction that the number of *ultimate constituents* or *indefinables* of the system (on the basis of which other members are 'generated') together with the *laws of necessary connection* must be finite (p. 279–288). As such, the correspondence of such a system with one of material causation seems clear: the laws of necessary connection correlate with necessary relations between triggering conditions and causal tendencies; the presumption that such laws are constant and enable all members of a system to be generated from a (finite) number of

[18] And if the assumption of atomic uniformity is invalid, Keynes points out, then natural law would not be "as generally supposed atomic". Yet "nature might still be uniform, causation soverign and laws timeless and absolute" (p. 277).

[19] Keynes suggests that the reason that scientists often hold "that we ought to limit inductive methods to the content of the particular material universe in which we live, is, most probably, the fact that we can easily imagine a universe so constructed that such methods would be useless" (p. 272).

ultimate constituents entails the satisfaction of the intrinsic condition for closure; and the finiteness of independent variety allows that a finite probability derivation is feasible (see esp pp. 290, 302, 319). Once again, however, the question of satisfying the extrinsic condition for closure is raised by Keynes but is found not to be guaranteed by his specification. Indeed Keynes is explicit that any assumption ruling out the possibility of a 'plurality of generators' would be difficult if not impossible to justify (pp. 286, 287). In short, whatever the merits or general applicability[20] of such a system of a limited independent variety it is clear that in considering it, and in considering its relevance or correspondence to ways of acting of things as well as properties of systems of numbers (p. 190), Keynes is continually seeking to ground a justification of various methods of analysis in the nature of the objects under study.

And it is a similar attitude or approach that Keynes brings to bear in the final part of *A Treatise on Probability* on the question of how *statistical* induction in particular might be justified. The main points relevant to the current discussion are that Keynes is first very critical of accounts such as Pearson's which presuppose that unknown factors can be accounted for by the analytically-convenient fiction of an "equal distribution of ignorance" (pp. 413, 419); and second, Keynes' main conclusion is that the use of statistical induction is only justified when there are grounds available for supposing that the nature and conditions of things under consideration are of a particular type—specifically when their conditions can be likened to a game of chance (p. 419).[21]

Keynes and econometrics

To what extent then are the realist type concerns which appear to underpin much of Keynes' analysis in *A Treatise on Probability,* carried over into his contribution to the debate on econometrics? It is clear from his biographical note on Edgeworth published in 1926 that by this time Keynes is of the view that the materials of the social sciences are such that the atomic hypothesis is not considered appropraite; that we "are faced at every turn with . . . problems of organic unity, . . ." (CW, X, p. 262). And, in his later writings on economics, references can be found to such things as 'persistent tendencies' in an economy which contribute to the establishment

---

[20] And in general Keynes realises the difficulties involved in providing grounds for supposing a limitation of independent variety in any situation; and in any case acknowledges that the finite character of all available systems cannto be supposed (p. 291).

[21] On the last point, for example, Keynes observes that "the more closely we find the conditions in scientific examples assimilated to those of games of chance, the more confidently does common sense recommend [the statistical] method" (p. 458). In taking leave of *A Treatise on Probability* Keynes notes that the contemporary doctrines of Mendelian biology and physics, in fact, did make claims about the nature of matter that were analogous to games of chance. To the extent that such claims remained tenable Keynes concludes that statistical inference might, in such cases, be legitimately applied. However, Keynes certainly held the view that there were many situations where the procedures of statistical inference were illegitimately applied.

of mean positions or outcomes, without such outcomes being thereby regarded as necessary. Thus, in discussing the determinants of unemployment Keynes observes:

". . . we must not conclude that the mean position thus determined by 'natural' tendencies, namely, by those tendencies which are likely to persist, failing measures expressly designed to correct them, is, therefore, established by laws of necessity" (CW, VII, p. 254).

Thus, amongst other things, Keynes brings to the issue of econometrics a view of the nature of the material of economics such that the atomic hypothesis is not relevant to satisfying the intrinsic condition for closure, while the satisfaction of the extrinsic condition is apparently undermined by an ever present real possibility either of effecting new causal mechanisms which can, or of transforming existing ones which do, influence the actual position of the economy. In short Keynes is of the view that the economic process is non-atomistic and open. Now if this is so, and to the extent that well controlled experimentation is rarely if ever possible in economics, a question that obviously arises from this vantage point is what justification can there be for accepting the methods of econometrics—which clearly presuppose a closure? This is indeed Keynes' concern as revealed, in particular, in his comments upon Tinbergen's work on business cycles:[22] In this, for example, Keynes stresses the centrality of questions of methodology to econometrics (CW, XIV, p. 285); notes that, amongst other things,[23] there are grounds for supposing the atomic hypothesis to be inappropriate in the economic context (p. 286), and questions whether there are not serious problems due to the fact that the list of significant causes will typically be incomplete (CW, XIV, pp. 287, 308). Consequently, for example, he concludes that the sort of coefficients that time series econometricians were assuming to be constant could not in general be taken as so: "The coefficients arrived at are apparently assumed to be constant for ten years or for a longer period. Yet, surely we know they are not constant. There is no reason at all why they should not be different every year" (CW, XIV, p. 285).

In sum, it seems clearly to be the case that the sort of views expressed by Keynes, both in his attempt to justify methods of induction as well as in his particular criticisms of econometrics, can be understood as reflecting an

[22] Keynes wrote numerous comments and letters concerning Tinbergen's work to his associates at the time. These can be found in CW XIV. An analysis of Keynes' position as revealed by these comments, can be found in Meeks, 1978; Lawson 1985; Pesaran and Smith, 1985a.

[23] Note that present day econometricians may consider that many of Keynes' concerns relating to the heterogeneous, interdependent and evolutionary nature of economic materials do not *per se* prevent economic processes from being open to analysis. Modern probability theory involving generalized martingale differences, for example, seems capable of meeting such concerns. Practical problems of satisfying the conditions for a closure, however, remain.

implicit orientation to the sort of realist concerns (focusing upon real things and their ways of acting) that I have outlined at length above.[24] And, in the context of the sort of economic time-series relationships that econometricians were attempting to deal with, this orientation leads Keynes to observe that there are reasonable grounds for supposing that the conditions for a closure will generally be violated. As such, Keynes requests that, at the very least, proponents of the econometric approach should provide some grounds for believing otherwise (CW, XIV, p. 306).

The next question to ask, then, is to what extent were the issues raised by Keynes attended to by the early proponents of the probability approach in econometrics? How was it, in fact, that the early proponents were so successful in alleviating most economists' concerns about the rationale and general viability of the approach? Perhaps the two most significant contributors to public discussion and general advancement of this approach were Trygve Haavelmo and Tjalling Koopmans, and their accounts are considered below.[25] It seems, in fact, to have been Haavelmo's 1944 Econometrica paper that most stimulated what is sometimes dubbed the 'probability revolution' in econometrics and it is this which is considered first.[26]

---

[24] It is clearly not possible here to address the issue as to whether Keynes is necessarily a thorough going realist on all matters. However, such a view does seem to be held by some. Thus O'Donnell (1982) surveys Keynes' entire writings and observes that for Keynes, the object of general or 'abstract' thought is to "generate theories which lay bare 'fundamental things' (XIII 3), uncover the 'essential mechanism' (V 274), capture the 'essential features' (XXIX 87), disclose 'the causal forces behind the apparent facts' (XVII 427), penetrate to the 'the true process of causation lying behind current events" (XVIII 67)..." and so on. (O'Donnell, 1982, p. 166). See Pheby (1985) for a discussion of Keynes' attitude to instrumentalism. See Carabelli (1985) for an account that deals explicitly with Keynes' views on cause, chance and possibility. And for an interesting account which touches on the issues mentioned above, but which may support some different conclusions to the extent that it attributes to Keynes a conception of probability that changed over his lifetime, see Bateman (1987).

[25] By adopting this (necessarily restricted) focus I by no means wish to understate the important contributions to the subject made elsewhere—both to the development of the probability approach in particular and of econometrics in general. Many of the significant early contributions were produced by numerous co-workers at institutions like the Cowles Commission in the US and the Department of Applied Economics in the UK. Historical accounts of these organisations can be found in Christ (1952, 1983) and in Stone (1978) respectively. A general overview of the development of econometrics can be found in Pesaran (1987) and for a recent history of econometrics see Epstein (1987).

[26] A first draft of Haavelmo's Econometrica paper was written in 1941, two years after Keynes' debate with Tinbergen had been published in the Economic Journal. Originally entitled *On The Theory and Measurement of Economic Relations* it was eventually published in 1944 under the title *The Probability Approach is Econometrics*. Although the published version does not make reference to Keynes, it seems clear that it was stimulated in large part by Keynes' criticisms (and doubtless also by the reservations of Frisch amongst others); while in a shorter piece published one year earlier in the Review of Economic Studies, Haavelmo (1943a) acknowledges explicitly his awareness of, and general frustration with, Keynes critical concerns.

IV. The Advocacy of the 'Probability Approach in Econometrics'

Haavelmo and econometrics

Now it could be argued that, in fact, Haavelmo brings a prior instrumentalist orientation to bear upon his analysis of econometrics. Certainly this can be read into his introductory, rather detached, overview of the nature of theories, models and explanations in science. Thus explanations, for Haavelmo, "are all our own artificial inventions in a search for an understanding of real life; they are not hidden truths to be 'discovered'" (p. 3). And it appears to be the case that models do not represent processes whereby relevant data are generated. Instead it is merely as if the relevant data were generated by them.

> The idea behind this is, one could say, that Nature has a way of selecting joint value-systems of the 'true' variables such that these systems are as if the selection had been made by the rule defining our theoretical model (p. 9).

Nevertheless, behind such apparently instrumentalist assertions, it will be seen, a more complicated and subtle approach to the subject-matter is to be found. As noted above, the success or usefulness of econometrics presupposes a closure. Keynes' concerns with regards to econometrics amount to the belief that such a closure cannot be expected in this context. The obvious issue to consider, then, is how, according to Haavelmo, an effective closure is to be achieved? What are Haavelmo's arguments for ensuring that the intrinsic and extrinsic conditions for a closure are satisfied?

The intrinsic condition for closure

The intrinsic condition for closure—that each 'cause' has the same 'effect' (whatever changes might be occurring elsewhere in the system)—is essentially dealt with by Haavelmo under the heading of *autonomy*. Here the recommendation is made to "dig down to such relationships as actually might be expected to have a great degree of invariance with respect to certain changes in structure that are 'reasonable'"[27] (p. 29). Haavelmo

---

[27] The notion of autonomy here refers to relationships amongst events (rather than to causal things or structures). A set of automonous relations—amongst, say, a set of variables or measurable quantities $x_1, x_2, \ldots, x_n$—is a system such that if one constituent relation undergoes a change in functional form then the remaining autonomous relations need not. Now the problem that Haavelmo raises here has nothing to do with the potential effects of variables not included among the $x_1, x_2, \ldots, x_n$ (which relates to the extrinsic condition for closure.) The problem arises from the fact that even if all the relevant variables or measurable quantities can in principle be incorporated, there can typically be numerous systems of constructed relations connecting them. Thus for any set of (relatively) autonomous relations, other systems of *confluent* relations can conceivably be derived by combining two or more such autonomous relations. The problem with any such system of derived equations is that if one of the original autonomous relations changes, then all relationships in the 'derived' system that are, in part, composed of this underlying (relatively) autonomous relation, are liable to change also. For a useful, more extensive, discussion of autonomy see Aldrich (this volume).

illustrates the idea with a motoring analogy (p. 27) arguing that any relationship between "pressure on the gas throttle" and the "corresponding maximum speed of the car" will be less autonomous than the "general laws of thermodynamics, the dynamics of friction, etc." Haavelmo's reasoning here is that the former (pressure/speed) relation is thought to be less autonomous because it depends upon the assumption that the complex internal structure of a car will remain constant; an assumption that Haavelmo appears to reject or at least regard as unsubstantiated: the pressure/speed "relation leaves the whole inner mechanism of a car in complete mystery, and . . . such a relation might break down at any time, as soon as there is some disorder or change in the working part of the car" (p. 27).[28] Haavelmo thus appears to effectively acknowledge that in order for the intrinsic condition for closure—or the assumption of relative autonomy—to be satisfied, it is necessary that real entities with known enduring internal structures be identified. He does not, however, really address the issue of what the relatively enduring entities might be in the economics context—other than including a passing reference to 'individuals' decisions to produce and to consume 'giving rise to' 'certain fundamental behavioristic relations' (p. 28). And it must also be emphasised that Haavelmo always seeks the expression of invariance or autonomy at the level of regularities amongst events. Nevertheless, this search is conceived not as a *purely* logical (p. 29) or analytical (p. 31) activity, but one that, in general, will depend essentially upon the nature of the reality in question: "to *find* such a basic system of highly autonomous relations in an actual case is not an analytical process, it is a task of making fruitful hypothesis as to how reality actually is" (p. 31). In actual econometric practice, of course, it may often prove difficult to satisfy this criterion in the context of interest. Nevertheless, the point of relevance here is that, at a theoretical level at least, Haavelmo's emphasis is to ground analyses in our knowledge of causal things—and at this point, at least, he may seem to be addressing the same concerns as Keynes.

Now, if Haavelmo's discussion on autonomy—relating to the satisfaction of the intrinsic condition for closure—appears to be essentially realist, it seems to be counterposed to a discussion bearing upon the extrinsic condition for closure that is ultimately instrumentalist.

The extrinsic condition for closure

The question, then, in considering the extrinsic condition for a closure, is how to effectively isolate a system from the effect of (or how to make analytically tractable) any external causes not explicitly allowed for; how to avoid having to employ *ceteris paribus* assumptions that will knowingly not

---

[28] In comparison, the laws of thermodynamics, etc. are thought to be "highly autonomous relations with respect to the automobile mechanism, because these relations describe the functioning of some parts of the mechanism *irrespective* of what happens in some *other* parts" (p. 28).

be satisfied, Haavelmo writes:

> Here we should, first of all, think of the difficulties that arise from the fact that series of passive observations are influenced by a great many factors not accounted for in theory; in other words, the difficulties of fulfilling the condition "Other things being equal". But this is a problem common to all practical observations and measurements; it is, in point of principle, not a particular defect of economic time series. If we cannot clear the data of such "other influences" we have to try to introduce these influences in the theory, in order to bring about more agreement between theory and facts (p. 18).

This is indeed a problem situation common to all sciences;—although on the realist view, of course, satisfaction of the extrinsic condition for closure is necessary *neither* for the stating of a law as a tendency *nor* for the activity of explanation. However, in the context of economic time-series analysis the problem is complicated by the fact that reliable data-sets are rarely particularly large.[29] Certainly, the option is not open to economists to endlessly include further variables in the equation. The usual recourse in this situation appears to be for econometricians to embark upon prolonged searches for simple stable laws involving a relatively small number of conditions, events or variables. The obvious question which follows, then, is what grounds are there for supposing that simple empirical laws exist to be discovered? Now it seems clear from Haavelmo's discussion that we must merely "hope that, for each variable, y, to be 'explained', there is a relatively small number of explaining factors the variations of which are practically decisive in determining the variations of y" (p. 23). Haavelmo acknowledges that the nature of the economic process is such that "there is, in general, no limit to the number of such factors that might have a *potential* influence on y" (p. 24), but recommends proceeding 'as if' this were not the case; adopting "the assumption that we may proceed as if such natural limitations of the number of relevant factors exist" (p. 24).

To repeat, then, Haavelmo provides no grounds for supposing the extrinsic condition for closure to be satisfied. His strategy, instead, is to emphasise the logical point that even if there are grounds for supposing an infinity of potential influences in any situation, it may conceivably still turn out to be the case that, under some configuration at least, the effects of excluded (and included) events or factors, taken as a whole, may prove to be analytically tractable. And having emphasised that such an eventuality is logically conceivable, the invocation is to carry on in the hope that this, in fact, will turn out to be the case. In this, of course, Haavelmo takes the specific course of supposing that the effects of the excluded factors be modelled "as a random variable with a certain probability distribution for each fixed set of values of the variable x..." (p. 51) or some such. A question that clearly arises, then, is what grounds are there for this line of

---

[29] Leamer (1983, p. 34) observes that the number of annual observations used in econometric analyses can be less than thirty.

approach? Under what conditions might such probabilities be meaningfully said to exist? Is there something known about the nature of the excluded (and included) factors or underlying mechanisms that provides grounds for the supposition of a stable probability law, and one typically taking a convenient form at that? Keynes, it has been noted, argues that there must be positive grounds for supposing that the material, or conditions, in question be analogous to games of chance, or some such, before the probability calculus can be invoked. Haavelmo, instead, reveals a somewhat more instrumentalist orientation in addressing these issues. He argues, in fact, that much "futile discussion has taken place in regard to the questions of what probabilities actually are, the type of events for which probabilities 'exist', and so forth" (p. 48). And he asserts:

> The question is not whether probabilities *exist* or not, but whether—if we proceed *as if* they existed—we are able to make statements about real phenomena that are "correct for practical purposes" (p. 43).

In fact, Haavelmo goes on to suggest that the assignment of probability laws represents nothing more than a trick or invention of our own, and that such 'laws' serve merely as useful tools for deriving practical statements; that any notion of a "true" probability law must be seen merely as a matter of convention, and so on:

> The rigorous notions of probabilities and probability distributions "exist" only in our rational mind, serving us only as a tool for deriving practical statements of the type described above.
>
> When we state that a certain number of observable variables have a certain joint probability law we may consider this as a construction of a rational *mechanism*, capable of producing (or reproducing) the observable values of the variables considered. . . . .
>
> Since the assignment of a certain probability law to a system of observable variables is a trick of our own, invented for analytical purposes, and since the same observable results may be produced under a great variety of different probability schemes, the question arises as to which probability law should be chosen, in any given case, to represent the "true" mechanism under which the data considered are being produced. To make this a rational problem of statistical inference we have to start out by an axiom, postulating that every set of observable variables has associated with it one particular "true", but unknown, probability law (p. 48).

This passage taken as a whole, then, seems to convey the message that a model, serving merely as an instrument or tool for deriving practical statements, is all that is required or can be hoped for. It should be emphasised that the situation being considered by Haavelmo is not one in which the status of some empirically successful model is being disputed. Rather it is one in which successful empirical generalisations have yet to be discovered in economics, (p. 15) while there exist good theoretical reasons to suppose that simple empirical relationships may not be there to be found. In this situation it is being suggested that simple probability laws or models which "are all are own artificial inventions" (p. 3) be continually examined just in case one turns out to be practically useful.[30]

The next issue to consider is whether Koopman's position is essentially very different.

The Koopmans/Vining debate

Koopmans' arguments bearing on the issues under consideration are most clearly revealed in his debate with Vining (Koopmans, 1947, 1949a, 1949b; Vining, 1949a, 1949b).[31] This debate was sparked off by Koopmans' 1947 paper, entitled 'Measurement Without Theory', which is itself a critical review of a further contribution, by Burns and Mitchell (1946), on *Measuring Business Cycles*. In this Koopmans levels three specific arguments against the account of Burns and Mitchell, which deal with issues of the sort that I have been considering throughout—namely the role of theories and models, the conditions of prediction, and the grounds for adopting a probability approach in econometrics. As such, Koopmans' contribution, and the critical response it eventually provoked by Vining, bear examining on these matters. And in doing so it proves useful once again to focus upon arguments made that relate, if implicitly, to the satisfaction of the two identified conditions for closure.

The role of theory and the intrinsic conditions for closure

Koopmans presents his position as an argument for a theoretical framework in opposition to an argument for a non-theoretidal framework. As Vining (1949a) subsequently points out, however, Koopmans is really stating a preference for a *specific* theoretical framework—one that focuses on the nature of the individual in the economy (the consumer, worker, entrepreneur, dealer, etc, p. 164) rather than one, such as that attributed to Burns and Mitchell, which takes cyclical behaviour *per se* as a unit of analysis.[32]

---

[30] Or rather, given that any set of values of n variables can be shown to be consistent with *some* set of n-dimensional probability laws, the invocation is to choose one such data-consistent probability law in the hope that it continues to be consistent with data yet to be observed.

[31] Now it is true that it is Koopmans' 1941 paper that is explicitly set up as a response to Keynes' request (as formulated in the latter's debate with Tinbergen) for the logic of econometrics to be more clearly stated. But, in fact, this earlier contribution of Koopmans essentially concerns itself with a few of Keynes' technical criticisms without revealing much, if any, awareness of the more deep seated criticisms stemming from Keynes' philosophical position.

[32] It is interesting to note that this debate is thus a precursor to one that is currently taking place concerning the relative advantages of so called old and new institutionalism. Burns and Mitchell, of course, are very much part of the 'old' institutionalist camp. (See e.g. Hodgson, 1988; Mayhew, 1988).

Now it seems clear that in drawing attention to theoretical entities here, Koopmans is taking a fairly straightforward realist position. In apparent contrast to Burns and Mitchell's 'empiricism' Koopmans wishes to ground analyses in the natures of individuals or agents whose "modes of action and response ... are the ultimate determinants of the levels of economic variables as well as their fluctuations" (1947, p. 164). In this, however, Koopmans reveals an *a priori* belief that 'persistance' or 'autonomy' will be found only at the level of the 'individual' (1947, pp. 166, 167).

Despite this concern with causal entities of some kind Koopmans also reveals an attachment to the view that persistancy or stability is to be found at the level of relationships amongst variables or events. The emphasis is thus placed on the need to search out structural relationships—underlying behavioural relationships of consumers, workers, entrepreneurs etc.—which are considered to be the most autonomous form of such event-regularities. Any observed regularity not so traced to underlying behavioural patterns etc, is considered to be "an instrument of unknown reliability" (p. 167).

In his response to Koopmans, Vining (1949a) draws attention to each of these points. He notes that Koopmans' criticisms of the approach of Burns and Mitchell "turn not so much upon assertions of the existence or absence of a hypothetical framework as upon the nature of the entity the behaviour of which is to be accounted for" (p. 79). And Vining takes issue with Koopmans' exclusive concern with the 'individual economising agent', emphasising, with Keynes, a more organicist view of the nature of economic material:

> "It is conceivable. . . that the aggregate has an existence apart from its constituent particles and behaviour characteristics of its own not deducible from the behaviour characteristics of the particles. We should work towards an explicit delineation of the entity itself—its structure and functioning—and the role that hypothesis and formal theory play in the earlier stages of this growth of understanding is subtle and irregular (p. 79).

Vining also questions whether there is any basis to the claim that invariant or autonomous equations—even so called behavioural relationships—are there to be found (1949a, p. 82).

In his subsequent reply to Vining, Koopmans (1949a) makes two further points bearing on these issues. First he observes that "we economists have the good luck of being some of the 'molecules' of economic life ourselves, and of having the possibility through human contacts to study the behaviour of other 'molecules'" (p. 87). And it is this observation that appears to inform his 'basic assumption' that "the numerically measurable effects of the implementation of individual decisions have a relatively persistent relationship to the principal numerically measurable aspects of the information that has gone into the making of these decisions—persistent, if not for a given individual, then in some average or aggregate sense for a group of individuals." (p. 88). Second, Koopmans suggests that there "has been a good deal of experience (Harvard barometer, etc.) to show that relationships between economic variables observed over a period of time but not traced to underlying behaviour equations are unreliable as instruments for prediction" (p. 89).

Vining's (1949b) reply to these points is again consistent with a more thorough going realism. He does not deny that the possibility of 'persistance' at the level of the individual but stresses that there may also be complex enduring structures whose ways of acting are irreducable to those of individuals. Thus Vining is of the view that it is "gratuitous for anyone to specify any particular entity as necessarily the ultimate unit for the whole range of enquiry within some general and essentially unexplored field of study . . ." (p. 92); adding that Koopman's position leaves no room "for the possibility of structural features and dynamic behavioural characteristics that are invariant with respect to human decisions" (p. 92). And in response to Koopmans second point Vining essentially emphasises that the failure of empirical relationships not traced to 'underlying behaviour equations' does not in itself entail that relationships that apparently are so traced must necessarily fare any better:

> The point of the discussion, of course, has to do with where Koopmans thinks we should look for "autonomous behaviour relations". He appeals to experience but in a somewhat oblique manner. He refers to the Harvard barometer "to show that relationships between economic variables . . . not traced to underlying behaviour equations are unreliable as instruments for prediction" . . . His argument would have been more effectively put had he been able to give instances of relationships that *have been* "traced to underlying behaviour equations" *and* that have been reliable instruments for prediction. He did not do this, and I know of no conclusive case that he could draw upon. There are of course cases of economic models that he could have mentioned as having been *unreliable* predictors. But these latter instances demonstrate no more than the failure of Harvard barometer: all were presumably built upon relations that were more or less unstable in time. The meaning conveyed, we may suppose, by the term "fundamental autonomous relation" is a relation stable in time and not drawn as an inference from combinations of other relations. The discovery of such relations suitable for the prediction procedure that Koopmans has in mind has yet to be publicly presented, and the phrase "underlying behaviour equation" is left utterly devoid of content (p. 93).

In short, Koopmans, like Haavelmo, seems to go some way towards addressing Keynes' concerns when he effectively argues for the satisfaction of the intrinsic condition for closure through a grounding of analysis in the nature of causal entities—albeit, and in contrast to Vining and Keynes apparently always at the 'molecular' or individual level even in the context of economic analysis. But Koopmans also shares with Haavelmo the view that regularities amongst variables or events can be found. He thus recommends that searches be carried out for autonomous empirical relationships at the level of individual behaviour. What then are Koopmans arguments bearing on the extrinsic condition for closure?

Extrinsic closure and the justification of the probability approach

A satisfaction of the extrinsic condition for closure requires that the system in question be somehow effectively isolated from the causal influences of structures not explicitly considered. It requires either that there are no extraneous influences, or that their effects are constant or at least capable of being accounted for in some analytically tractable fashion. Koopmans sees the presumption of probabilistic or stochastic processes as capable of overcoming the fact that there will almost always be causal influences involved other than those that are directly or explicitly identified:

> In dynamic economics, the phenomenon itself is either essentially a stochastic process or needs to be treated as such because of the great number of factors at work. Hence the analysis and interpretation of economic data call for the application of the methods of statistical inference . . . .

> Most theories of this kind recently constructed have in common the attempt to describe the fluctuating economy by a complete system of structural equations which, as to their form, are stochastic difference equations. They are difference equations (embodying dynamic theory), in that they describe responses subject to time lags: past values of economic variables affect current actions of individuals. They are stochastic equations in that the behaviour of any group of individuals, and the outcome of any production process, is determined in part by many minor factors, further scrutiny of which is either impossible or unrewarding. Such further scrutiny is not necessary provided that the analysis of each structural equation be pushed to the point where the joint effect of unanalysed factors can indeed be regarded as random (if not necessarily independent) drawings from a reasonably stable probability distribution (p. 169).

But what reason is there to suppose that the analysis can be pushed to, or even that there exists, such a point where the joint effect of unanalysed factors can be "regarded as random drawings from a reasonably stable probability distribution"? In truth, Koopmans makes no real attempt to address this question, or indeed to justify the probability approach on other than pragmatic criteria.[33] He merely expresses a preference for it on grounds of the "greater wealth, definiteness, rigor, and relevance to specific questions of such conditional information" (p. 170). As Vining notes Koopmans' "insistence upon a 'distributional hypothesis' is based upon estimation considerations rather than upon a primary interest in the distribution itself." (1949a, p. 85).

In short, although Koopmans adopts a particular realist position with

---

[33] He observes that the distributional assumptions are made merely in order to extract more information from the data, and often "are not themselves subject to statistical testing from the same data" (p. 170); and he acknowledges that "the validity of information so obtained is logically conditional upon the validity of the statistically unverifiable aspects of these basic hypotheses" (p. 170). But he provides no substantive justification for this framework.

regards to the satisfaction of the intrinsic condition for closure, his arguments relating to the extrinsic condition, like those of Haavelmo, appear to rest upon a form of essentially instrumentalist reasoning. Vining, in contrast, brings an apparently more thoroughgoing realist orientation to bear, essentially arguing that the nature of the subject matter of economics in such that a less reductionist approach is required; and that the nature of economic interaction is such that fundamental 'autonomous' relations amongst economic events are unlikely to be found. In this, Vining appears to adopt a similar philosophical/methodological position to Keynes. Consequently it is perhaps not surprising that he ends up sympathising with Keynes remarks on econometrics, suggesting that the latter's criticisms have yet to be adequately addressed:

> Econometricians have in general held that [Keynes'] criticisms [of Tinbergen] were the conclusions of a sadly misinformed and misguided man. But I judge that with the arguments simply put, many economists today would agree with most of what Keynes had to say; and those points upon which he was misinformed they would regard as among the less important. Moreover, in my judgement, many economists, given a full account in simple terms of the theoretical and technical developments since Tinbergen's models of 1939, would find the present models as intellectually unsatisfying as the models of Tinbergen, and for the same basic cosmological reason. Many would simply remain unconvinced that the real thing is put together in any such fashion as is implied. They could be readily convinced of the validity of these procedures through empirical demonstrations. But many economists remain unimpressed by what has been made available (Vining, 1949b, p. 93).

V. Summary and conclusion

This paper has considered a version of the traditional realist/instrumentalist opposition and questioned whether it bears at all upon recurring themes in econometric analysis. This emphasis, in turn, has led to a focus upon the open system/closed system differentiation that bears on the possibility of simple empirical regularities and prediction. To the extent that a realist/open system view is held then the conclusion would seem to follow that science is possible but must, in general, be explanatory rather than predictive. To the extent that, in contrast, the world can always be considered as effectively closed in relevant contexts—an apparent presupposition of econometricians—then it would seem instead to follow that science *can* reasonably aim at event prediction, and can support both realist and instrumentalist reasoning. It is these rough differentiations then, and their possible, and some historical, econometric implications, that have been explored in the course of the discussion. Specifically, I have examined possible reasons for the continual resurrection of the worries expressed by various sceptics, including Keynes. In this I have interpreted the concerns of Keynes and others as reflecting a realist/open system view. Clearly, if this characterization is correct, then, to the extent that econometrics necessarily presupposes an effective closure in any chosen context and/or relies at some stage, and specifically when faced with apparent system openness, on a form of instrumentalist reasoning, such worries (which may indeed be tempered by a particular 'empirical demonstration') seem unlikely ever to be generally allayed.

University of Cambridge

Oxford Economic Papers 41 (1989), 259–282

CONSOLIDATED REFERENCES

ACKLEY, G. (1961) *Macroeconomic Theory*, New York, Macmillan.

AIGNER, D. J. and SIMON, J. L. (1971) 'A Specification Bias Interpretation of Cross-Section Versus Time-Series', *Western Economic Journal*, 9, 144–61.

AKAIKE, H. (1985) 'Prediction and Entropy', in A. A. Atkinson and S. E. Fienberg eds. *A Celebration of Statistics*, 1–24, New York, Springer-Verlag.

ALLEN, R. G. D. (1935) 'Review of Frisch (1934)', *Economic Journal*, 45, 741–42.

ALLEN, R. G. D. (1939) 'The Assumptions of Linear Regression', *Economica*, 6, 191–204.

ALLEN, R. G. D. (1949) *Statistics for Economists*, London, Hutchinson.

ALLEN, R. G. D. (1956) *Mathematical Economics*, London, Macmillan.

ANDERSON, O. A. (1980) *Forecasting Public Utilities*, Amsterdam, North Holland.

ANDERSON, T. W. (1958) *An Introduction to Multivariate Statistical Analysis*, New York, Wiley.

ANDERSON, T. W. (1971) *The Statistical Analysis of Time Series*, New York, Wiley.

ANDERSON, T. W. and HURWICZ, L. (1948) 'Errors and Shocks in Economic Relationships', abstract, *Econometrica*, 15, 36–37.

ANDERSON, T. W. and RUBIN, H. (1949) 'Estimation of the Parameters of a Single Equation in a Complete System of Stochastic Equations' *Econometrica*, 55, 251–76.

ANDVIG, J. C. (1985) *Ragnar Frisch and the Great Depression: A Study in the History of Macroeconomic Theory and Policy*, Oslo, Norsk Utenrikspolitisk Institutt.

AOKI, M. (1975) 'On a Generalisation of Tinbergen's Condition in the Theory of Policy to Dynamic Models', *Review of Economic Studies*, 42, 293–6.

AOKI, M. (1976) *Optimal Control and System Theory in Dynamic Economic Analysis*, Amsterdam, North Holland.

ARCHIBALD, G. C. (1969) 'Wage-Price Dynamics, Inflation and Unemployment: the Phillips Curve and the Distribution of Unemployment', *American Economic Review*, 59, 124–34.

ATHANS, M. (1972) 'The Discrete Time Linear-Quadratic-Gaussian Stochastic Control Problem', *Annals of Economic and Social Measurement*, 3, 49–64.

BANGS, R. B., (1942) 'The Changing Relation of Consumer Income and Expenditure' *Survey of Current Business*, 22, 4, 8–12.

BASSIE, V. L. (1948) 'Consumption-Saving Function Again', *Review of Economics and Statistics*, 30, 298–300.

BATEMAN, B. W. (1987) 'Keynes' Changing Conception of Probability', *Economics and Philosophy*, 3, 98–120.

BEACH, E. F. (1957) *Economic Models*, New York, Wiley.

BEAN, L. H. (1929) 'A Simplied Method of Graphic Curvilinear Correlation', *Journal of the American Statistical Association*, 24, 386–97.

BEAN, L. H., BOLLINGER, P. H. and WELLS, O. V. (1937) *Nonagricultural Income as a Measure of Domestic Demand*, Program Planning Division, Agricultural Adjustment Administration, USDA, Washington DC, Government Printing Office.

BENNION, E. G. (1946) 'The Consumption Function: Cyclically Variable?', *Review of Economic Statistics*, 28, 219–24.

BERGSTROM, A. R., CATT, A. J. L., PESTON, M. H. and SILVERSTONE, D. D. J. eds. (1978) *Stability and Inflation*, Chichester, Wiley.

BERTALANFFY VON, L. (1950) 'The Theory of Open Systems in Physics and Biology', *Science*, III, 23–29.

BHASKAR, R. (1978) *A Realist Theory of Science*, Brighton, Harvester Press.

BLAIR, M. M. (1952) *Elementary Statistics*, New York, Henry Holt.

BLYTH, C. A. (1960) *The Use of Economic Statistics*, London, Allen and Unwin.

BLYTH, C. A. (1975) 'A. W. H. Phillips, MBE', *Economic Record*, 50, 303–7.

BLYTH, C. A. (1978) 'Biographical Note: A. W. H. Phillips, MBE: 1914–1975', in Bergstrom *et al.*, eds. (1978), xiii–xvii.

BOGAARD VAN DEN, P. and THEIL, H., (1959) 'Macro-dynamic policy making: an application of strategy and certainty equivalence concepts to the economy of the United States 1933–6' *Metroeconomica*, 11, 149–67.

BORN, M., (1949) *Natural Philosophy of Cause and Chance*, Oxford, Clarendon Press.

BOWLEY, A. L. (1934) 'Francis Ysidro Edgeworth', *Econometrica*, 2, 113–124.

BOWLEY, A. L. (1937) *Wages and Income in the United Kingdom Since* 1869, London, Cambridge University Press.

BOWLEY, A. L. and WOOD, G. H. (1906) 'The Statistics of Wages in the United Kingdom During the Nineteenth Century, Part XIV', *Journal of the Royal Statistical Society*, 69, 148–92.

BOX, G. E. P. and JENKINS, G. M., (1970) *Time Series Analysis: Forecasting and Control*, San Francisco, Holden-Day.

BRADLEY, F. H. (1914) *Essays on Truth and Reality*, Clarendon Press, Oxford and New York.

BRADY, D. S. (1938) 'Variations in Family Living Expenditures', *Journal of the American Statistical Association*, 33, 385–9.

BRADY, D. S. (1951) 'Research on the Size Distribution of Income', NBER *Studies in Income and Wealth*, 13, 2–55, New York, NBER.

BRADY, D. S. and FRIEDMAN, R. D. (1947) 'Savings and Income Distribution', *Studies in Income and Wealth*, 10, 247–65, New York. NBER.

BRADY, D. S. and WILLIAMS, F. M. (1945) 'Advances in the Techniques of Measuring and Estimating Consumer Expenditures', *Journal of Farm Economics*, 27, 315–44.

BRANDSMA, A. S., HUGHES HALLETT, A. J. and WINDT VAN DER, N. (1983) 'Optimal Control of Large Nonlinear Models: An Efficient Method of Policy Search Applied to the Dutch Economy', *Journal of Policy Modeling*, 5, 253–70.

BRANDSMA, A. S., HUGHES HALLETT, A. J. and WINDT VAN DER, N. (1984) 'Optimal Economic Policies and Uncertainty: The Case Against Policy Selection by Nonlinear Programming', *Computers and Operations Research*, 11, 179–97.

BRAUCHLI, H. (1972) 'A Theoretical Comment on the Phillips Curve', *Schweizerische Zeitschrift für Volkswirtschaft und Statistik*, 104, 177–82.

BRONFENBRENNER, M. (1948) 'The Consumption Function Controversy', *Southern Economic Journal*, 14, 305–20.

BRONFENBRENNER, M. and DOUGLAS, P. H. (1939) 'Cross-Section Studies in the Cobb–Douglas Function', *Journal of Political Economy*, 47, 761–85.

BROWN, A. J., (1955) *The Great Inflation*, 1939–1951, London, Oxford.

BROWN, J. A. C. and DEATON, A. S. (1972) 'Models of Consumer Behaviour: A Survey', *Economic Journal*, 82, 1145–236.

BROWN, T. M. (1952) 'Habit Persistence and Lags in Consumer Behavior', *Econometrica*, 20, 355–71.

BRUSH, S. (1976) 'Irreversibility and Indeterminism', *Journal of the History of Ideas*, 37, 603–30.

BRUSH, S. (1980) 'The Chimerical Cat: Philosophy of Quantum Mechanics in Historical Perspective,', *Social Studies of Science*, 10, 393–447.

BRUSH, S. (1983) *Statistical Physics and the Atomic Theory of Matter*, Princeton, Princeton University Press.

BUITER, W. H. and GERSOVITZ, M. (1984) 'Controllability and the Theory of Economic Policy: A Further Note', *Journal of Public Economics*, 24, 127–9.

BULMER, M. (1984) *The Chicago School of Sociology*, Chicago, University of Chicago Press.

BURNS, A. F. and MITCHELL, W. C. (1946) *Measuring Business Cycles*, New York, NBER.

BUTLER, E. (1985) *Milton Friedman: A Guide to his Economic Thought*, London, Gower.

BYE, R. T. (1940) *Critiques of Research in the Social Sciences: An Appraisal of F. C. Mills' The Behavior of Prices*, New York, SSRC.

CALDWELL, B. (1982) *Beyond Positivism: Economic Methodology in the Twentieth Century*, London, Allen & Unwin.

CAMPBELL, N. R. (1919) *Foundations of Science*, New York, Dover.

CARABELLI, A. (1985) 'Keynes on Cause, Chance and Possibility' in Lawson and Pesaran, (1985), 151–80.

CARTWRIGHT, N. (1983) *How the Laws of Physics Lie,* Oxford, Clarendon Press.

CASSIRER, E. (1956) *Determinism and Indeterminism in Modern Physics,* New Haven, Yale University Press.

CHALMERS, A. F (1978) *What is This Thing Called Science?* Milton Keynes, Open University Press.

CHAMPERNOWNE, D. G. (1945) 'Discussion of Mr Stone's Paper', *Journal of the Royal Statistical Society,* A, 108, 385–7.

CHARLIER, C. V. L. (1947) *Elements of Mathematical Statistics,* New York, Harper.

CHOW, G. C. (1960) 'Tests of Equality Between Sets of Coefficients in Two Linear Regressions', *Econometrica,* 28, 591–605.

CHOW, G. C. (1970) 'Optimal Stochastic Control of Linear Economic Systems', *Journal of Money, Credit and Banking,* 2, 291–302.

CHOW, G. C. (1975) *Analysis and Control of Dynamic Economic Systems,* New York, Wiley.

CHOW, G. C., (1976) 'The Control of Nonlinear Econometric Systems with Unknown Parameters', *Econometrica,* 44, 685–95.

CHOW, G. C. (1983) *Econometrics,* New York, McGraw-Hill.

CHRIST, C. F. (1952) 'A History of the Cowles Commission, 1932–1952' in Cowles Commission (1952).

CHRIST, C. F. (1966) *Econometric Models and Methods,* New York, Wiley.

CHRIST, C. F. (1983) 'The Founding of The Econometric Society and Econometrica', *Econometrica,* 51, 3–6.

CHRIST, C. F. (1985) 'Early Progress in Estimating Quantitative Economic Relationships in America.' *American Economic Review,* 75, 39–52.

CLARK, C. (1938) 'Determination of the Multiplier from National Income Statistics', *Economic Journal,* 48, 435–48.

CLARK, C., (1948) *A System of Equations Explaining the US Trade Cycle 1921 to 1941,* Brisbane, Bureau of Industry.

CLARK, C. (1985) 'Development Economics: The Early Years', in G. M. Meier and D. Seers (eds), *Pioneers in Development,* Oxford, Oxford University Press.

COBDEN, S. (1971) 'The Scientific Establishment and the Transmission of Quantum Mechanics to the United States, 1919–32', *American Historical Review,* 76, 442–66.

COCHRANE, D. and ORCUTT, G. H. (1949) 'Application of Least Squares Regression to Relationships Containing Auto-Correlated Error Terms', *Journal of the American Statistical Association,* 44, 32–61.

Committee on the Working of the Monetary System (1960a) *Principal Memoranda of Evidence,* Cmnd 827, 3, London, HMSO.

Committee on the Working of the Monetary System (1960b) *Minutes,* Cmnd 827, London, HMSO.

COOK, T. D. and CAMPBELL, D. T. (1979) *Quasi-Experimentation: Design and Analysis Issues for Field Settings,* Chicago, Chicago University Press.

COOKINGHAM, M. E. (1987) 'Social Economics and Reform: Berkeley, 1906–1961', *History of Political Economy,* 19, 47–65.

COOLEY, T. F. and LEROY, S. F. (1985) 'Atheoretical Macroeconometrics: a Critique.' *Journal of Monetary Economics,* 16, 283–308.

COOPER, R. L. (1972) 'The Predictive Performance of Quarterly Econometric Models of the United States', in Hickman, B. ed., *Econometric Models of Cyclical Behavior,* NBE Studies in Income and Wealth, 36, 813–926, New York, Columbia University Press.

COOPER, R. N. (1969) 'Macroeconomic Policy Adjustment in Interdependent Economies', *Quarterly Journal of Economics,* 83, 1–24.

CORRY, B. and LAIDLER, D. (1967) 'The Phillips Relation: A Theoretical Explanation', *Economica,* 34, 189–97.

Council on Prices, Productivity and Incomes (1958) *First Report,* London, HMSO.

Cowles Commission, (1940) *Report of Sixth Annual Research Conference on Economics and Statistics at Colorado Springs,* Cowles Commission, University of Chicago.

Cowles Commission, (1952) *Economic Theory and Measurement: A Twenty Year Research Report 1932–1952,* Cowles Commission, University of Chicago.

Cox, D. R. (1961) 'Tests of Separate Families of Hypotheses', *Proceedings of the Fourth Berkeley Symposium on Mathematical Statistics and Probability,* 1, 105–123, Berkeley, University of California Press.

Cox, D. R. (1962) 'Further Results on Tests of Separate Families of Hypotheses', *Journal of the Royal Statistical Society,* B, 24, 406–24.

Cropper, W., (1970) *The Quantum Physicists,* New York, Oxford University Press.

Croxton, F. E. and Cowden, D. J. (1939) *Applied General Statistics,* New York, Prentice Hall.

Crum, W. L. (1935) 'Individual Shares in the national income', *Review of Economic Statistics* **17**, 116–30.

Darnell, A. (1981) 'Bowley' in O'Brien, D. & Presley, J. eds. *Pioneers of Modern Economics in Britain,* London, Macmillan, 140–74.

Darnell, A., (1984) 'Economic Statistics and Econometrics', in, Creedy, J. and O'Brien, D., eds. *Economic Analysis in Historical Perspective,* London, Butterworths, 152–85.

Davidson, J. E. H. (1987) 'Error Correction Systems', Paper presented to the European Meeting of the Econometric Society, Copenhagen.

Davidson, J. E. H., Hendry, D. F., Srba, F. and Yeo, S., (1978), 'Econometric modelling of the aggregate time-series relationship between consumers' expenditure and income in the United Kingdom', *Economic Journal,* 88, 661–92.

Davies, P. (1980) *Other Worlds,* New York, Simon and Schuster.

Davis, H. T. (1931) *Philosophy and Modern Science,* Bloomington, Principia Press.

Davis, H. T. (1941a) *The Analysis of Economic Time Series,* Bloomington, Principia Press (Cowles Commission Monograph, 6).

Davis, H. T. (1941b) *The Theory of Econometrics,* Bloomington, Principia Press.

Davis, J. S. (1945) 'Standards and Content of Living', *American Economic Review,* 35, 1–15.

Davis, T. E. (1952) 'The Consumption Function as a Tool for Prediction', *Review of Economics and Statistics,* 34, 270–7.

De Bruyne, G. (1979) 'Pareto Optimality of Non-Cooperative Equilibrium in a Time Dependent Multiperiod Game', *European Economic Review,* 12, 243–60.

de Marchi, N. (1988) 'Popper and the LSE Economists', in de Marchi, N. ed, *The Popperian Legacy in Economics,* London, Cambridge University Press.

De Wolff, P. and Sandee, J. (1959) 'Recent Experience in the Application of Econometric Policy Models in the Netherlands', Paper Presented to the Econometric Policy, Amsterdam.

Deaton, A. S. and Muellbauer, J. (1980) *Economics and Consumer Behavior,* Cambridge, Cambridge University Press.

Desai, M. (1975) 'The Phillips Curve: a Revisionist Interpretation', *Economica,* 42, 1–19.

Desai, M. (1984) 'Wages, Prices and Unemployment a Quarter Century After the Phillips Curve' in Hendry and Wallis, (1984), 253–73.

Dicks-Mireaux, L. A. and Dow, J. C. R. (1959) 'The Determinants of Wage Inflation: United Kingdom, 1946–56', *Journal of the Royal Statistical Society,* A, 122, 145–84.

Dirks, F. C. (1938) 'Retail Sales and Labor Income', *Review of Economic Statistics,* 20, 128–34.

Dornbusch, R. and Fischer, S. (1987) *Macroeconomics,* 4th Edition, New York, McGraw-Hill.

Douglas, P. H. (1948) 'Are There Laws of Production?', *American Economic Review,* 38, 1–41.

Douglas, P. H. (1976) 'The Cobb–Douglas Production Function Once Again: Its History, its Testing, and Some New Empirical Values', *Journal of Political Economy,* 84, 903–15.

Dow, J. C. R. (1970) *The Management of the British Economy 1944–60,* Cambridge, Cambridge University Press.

DRESDEN, M. (1987) *H. A. Kramers,* New York, Springer-Verlag.

DUESENBERRY, J. S., (1949) *Income, Saving and the Theory of Consumer Behavior,* Cambridge, Mass., Harvard University Press.

DUNCAN, O. D. (1964) 'Introduction', in O. D. Duncan ed, *William F. Ogburn, On Culture and Social Change: Selected Papers,* Chicago, University of Chicago Press.

DURBIN, J. (1954) 'Errors in Variables', *Revue de l'Institut International de Statistique,* 22, 23–54.

DURBIN, J. (1960a) 'The Estimation of Parameters in Time-Series Regression Models', *Journal of the Royal Statistical Society,* B, 22, 139–53.

DURBIN, J. (1960b) 'The Fitting of Time-Series Models', *Revue de l'Institut International de Statistique,* 28, 233–43.

DURBIN, J. and WATSON, G. S. (1950) 'Testing for Serial Correlation in Least Squares Regression I', *Biometrika,* 37, 409–28.

DURBIN, J. and WATSON, G. S. (1951), 'Testing for Serial Correlation in Least-Squares Regression II', *Biometrika,* 38, 159–78.

EATWELL, J., MILGATE, M. and NEWMAN, P. eds, (1987) *The New Palgrave: A Dictionary of Economics,* London, Macmillan.

Econometrica (1937) 'Report of the Oxford Meeting, September 25–29 1936.' *Econometrica,* 5, 361–83.

Economic Report of the President, (1969, 1987) Washington DC, United States Printing Office.

EDDINGTON, A. (1935) *New Pathways in Science,* New York, Macmillan.

EDGEWORTH, F. Y. (1894) 'Curves', in R. H. I. Palgrave ed. *Palgrave's Dictionary of Political Economy,* London, Macmillan.

EDGEWORTH, F. Y. (1922) 'The Philosophy of Chance', *Mind,* 31, 257–83.

EDGEWORTH, F. Y. (1925) *Papers Relating to Political Economy,* 3 vols., London, Macmillan.

EHRENBERG, A. S. C. (1975) *Data Reduction,* London, Wiley.

EHRENFEST, P. (1959) In Klein, M. ed. *Collected Scientific Papers,* Amsterdam, North Holland.

ENGLE, R. F. and GRANGER, C. W. J. (1987) 'Dynamic Model Specification and Equilibrium Constraints: Co-integration and Error Correction', *Econometrica,* 55, 251–76.

ENGLE, R. F. HENDRY, D. F. and RICHARD, F. J.-F. (1983) 'Exogeneity', *Econometrica,* 51, 277–304.

EPSTEIN, R. J. (1987) *A History of Econometrics,* Amsterdam, North Holland.

EVANS, M. K. (1969) *Macroeconomic Activity,* New York, Harper & Row.

EVANS, R. A. (1984) 'The Aggregate Consumption Function', in van der Ploeg, F. ed. *Mathematical Methods in Economics,* Chichester, Wiley, 95–120.

EZEKIEL, M. (1924) 'A Method of Handling Curvilinear Correlation for any Number of Variables', *Journal of the American Statistical Association.* 19, 431–453.

EZEKIEL, M. (1927) 'A Statistical Examination of Factors Related to Lamb Prices', *Journal of Political Economy,* 35, 233–60.

EZEKIEL, M. (1928) 'Statistical Analysis and the "Laws" of Price', *Quarterly Journal of Economics,* 42, 199–227.

EZEKIEL, M. (1930) *Methods of Correlation Analysis,* New York, Wiley.

EZEKIEL, M. (1938) 'The Cobweb Theorem', *Quarterly Journal of Economics,* 52, 255–80.

EZEKIEL, M. (1942) 'Statistical Investigations of Saving, Consumption, and Investment, (I) Saving, Consumption and National Income', *American Economic Review,* 32, 22–49.

EZEKIEL, M. (1944) 'The Statistical Determination of the Investment Schedule', *Econometrica,* 12, 89–90.

EZEKIEL, M. and BEAN, L. H. (1933) *Economic Bases for the Agricultural Adjustment Act,* Washington DC, Government Printing Office.

EZEKIEL, M. and FOX, K. A. (1959) *Methods of Correlation and Regression Analysis: Linear and Curvilinear,* 3rd ed., New York, Wiley.

FAIR, R. E. (1974) 'On the Solution of Control Problems as Maximisation Problems', *Annals of Economic and Social Measurement,* 3, 135–54.

FERBER, R. (1953) *A Study of Aggregate Consumption Functions,* New York, NBER.

FERBER, R. (1973) 'Consumer Economics: A Survey', *Journal of Economic Literature*, 11, 1303–42.

FISHER, F. M. (1966) *The Identification Problem in Econometrics*, New York, McGraw-Hill.

FISHER, I. (1941) 'Mathematical Method in the Social Sciences', *Econometrica*, 9, 185–97.

FISHER, R. A. (1925) *Statistical Methods for Research Workers*, Edinburgh, Oliver and Boyd.

FLUX, A. (1921) 'The Measurement of Price Changes', *Journal of the Royal Statistical Society*, 84, 190.

FOOTE, R. J. (1955) 'A Comparison of Single and Simultaneous Equation Techniques', *Journal of Farm Economics*, 37, 975–90.

FOOTE, R. J. and FOX, K. A. (1954) *Analytical Tools for Measuring Demand*. Agriculture Handbook No. 64, Agricultural Marketing Service, USDA, Washington DC, Government Printing Office.

FORMAN, P. (1971) 'Weimar Culture, Causality and Quantum Theory', *Historical Studies in the Physical Sciences*, 3, 1–116.

FOX, K. A. (1951) 'Factors Affecting Farm Income, Farm Prices, and Food Consumption', *Agricultural Economics Research*, 3, 65–82.

FOX, K. A. (1953) *The Analysis of Demand for Farm Products*, USDA Technical Bulletin 1081, Washington DC, Government Printing Office.

FOX, K. A. (1954) 'Structural Analysis and the Measurement of Demand for Farm Products', *Review of Economics and Statistics*, 36, 57–66.

FOX, K. A. (1956) 'Econometric Models of the United States', *Journal of Political Economy*, 64, 128–42.

FOX, K. A. (1958) *Econometric analysis for Public Policy*. Ames, IA, Iowa State University Press.

FOX, K. A. (1986) 'Agricultural Economists as World Leaders in Applied Econometrics, 1917–33', *American Journal of Agricultural Economics*, 68, 381–386.

FOX, K. A. (1987) 'Agricultural Economics' in Eatwell et al., (1987) 1, 55–62.

FOX, K. A. (1988) 'Econometrics Needs a History: Two Cases of Conspicuous Neglect', in Kadekodi, G. and Sengupta, J. K. eds., *Econometrics of Planning and Efficiency Models: Essays in Memory of Gerhard Tintner*, Amsterdam, Nijhoff.

FOX, K., SENGUPTA, J. and NARASIMHAM, G. (1969) *Economic Models, Estimation and Risk Programming*, New York, Springer-Verlag.

FREEMAN, D., PISANI, R. and PURVES, R. (1978), *Statistics*, New York, Norton.

FRIEDMAN, M. (1957) *A Theory of the Consumption Function*, Princeton, Princeton University Press.

FRIEDMAN, J. and FOOTE, R. J. (1955) *Computational Methods for Handling Systems of Simultaneous Equations*, Agriculture Handbook No. 94, Agricultural Marketing Service, USDA, Washington DC, Government Printing Office.

FRIEDMAN, M. and KUZNETS, S. (1945) *Income from Independent Professional Practice*, New York, NBER.

FRIEND, I. (1946) 'Relationship Between Consumers' Expenditures, Saving, and Disposable Income, *Review of Economic Statistics*, 28, 208–15.

FRISCH, R. (1926) 'Sur une Problème d'Economie Pure', *Nordic Statistical Journal*, 16, 1–40.

FRISCH, R. (1929) 'Correlation and Scatter in Statistical Variables', *Nordic Statistical Journal*, 8, 36–102.

FRISCH, R. (1932) *New Methods of Measuring Marginal Utility*, Tubingen, Mohr.

FRISCH, R. (1933a) *Pitfalls in the Statistical Construction of Demand and Supply Curves*, Leipzig, Hans Buske Verlag.

FRISCH, R. (1933b) 'Propagation Problems and Impulse Problems in Dynamic Economics', in *Economic Essays in Honour of Gustav Cassel*, London, Allen and Unwin, Reprinted in Gordon, R. and Klein, L., (1965) *Readings in Business Cycles*, Homewood, Il, Irwin.

FRISCH, R. (1934) *Statistical Confluence Analysis by Means of Complete Regression Systems*, Oslo, Universitets Økonomiske Institutt.

FRISCH, R. (1938) 'Statistical Versus Theoretical Relations in Economic Macrodynamics',

Mimeograph Dated 17 July 1938, Contained in Memorandum 'Autonomy of Economic Relations', Dated 6 November 1948, Oslo, Universitets Økonomiske Institutt.

FRISCH, R. ed. (1948a) *Autonomy of Economic Relations*, A Collection of Mimeo Articles Issued by the University of Oslo.

FRISCH, R. (1948b) 'Repercussion Studies at Oslo', *American Economic Review*, 39, 367–72.

FRISCH, R. (1949) 'A Memorandum on Price-Wage-Tax-Subsidy Policies as Instruments in Maintaining Optimal Employment', UN Document E(CN1/Sub2/13, April), New York, United Nations.

FRISCH, R. and MUDGETT, B. D. (1931) 'Statistical Correlation and the Theory of Cluster Types', *Journal of the American Statistical Association*, 26, 375–92.

FRISCH, R. and WAUGH, F. V. (1933) 'Partial Time Regressions as Compared with Individual Trends', *Econometrica*, 1, 387–401.

GEARY, R. C. (1943) 'Relations Between Statistics: The General and the Damping Problem when the Samples are Large', *Proceedings of the Royal Irish Academy*, A, 49, 177–96.

GEARY, R. C. (1949) 'Determination of Linear Relations between Systematic Parts of Variables with Errors of Observation the Variances of Which are Unknown', *Econometrica*, 17, 30–58.

GERSOVITZ, M. (1980) 'Mis-Specification and Cyclical Models: the Real Wage and the Phillips Curve', *Economica*, 433–41.

GHOSH, S., GILBERT, C. L. and HUGHES HALLETT A. J. (1987) 'Stabilizing Speculative Commodity Markets', Oxford, *Oxford University Press*.

GILBERT, C. L. (1976) 'The Original Phillips Curve Estimates', *Economica*, 43, 51–57.

GILBERT, C. L. (1986a) 'Professor Hendry's Econometric Methodology', *Oxford Bulletin of Economics and Statistics*, 48, 283–307.

GILBERT, C. L. (1986b) 'The Development of British Econometrics 1945–85', Institute of Economics and Statistics, Oxford, Applied Economics Discussions Paper, 8.

GILBERT, C. L. (1987) 'Extreme Bounds, Vector Autoregressions and Dynamic Structural Models: Alternative Approaches to Econometric Methodology', Institute of Economics and Statistics, Oxford, Applied Economics Discussion Paper 23.

GILBOY, E. W. (1931) 'The Leontief and Schultz Methods of Deriving "Demand" Curves', *Quarterly Journal of Economics*, 45, 218–61.

GILBOY, E. W. (1932a) 'Demand Curves by Personal Estimate', *Quarterly Journal of Economics*, 46, 376–84.

GILBOY, E. W. (1932b) 'Studies in Demand: Milk and Butter', *Quarterly Journal of Economics*, 671–97.

GILBOY, E. W. (1934) 'Time Series and the Derivation of Demand and Supply Curves: A Study of Coffee and Tea, 1850–1930', *Quarterly Journal of Economics*, 48, 667–85.

GILBOY, E. W. (1937) 'The Unemployed: Their Income and Expenditure', *American Economic Review*, **27**, 309–23.

GILBOY, E. W. (1938a), 'The Propensity to Consume', *Quarterly Journal of Economics*, 53, 120–40.

GILBOY, E. W. (1938b) 'The Expenditure of the Unemployed', *American Sociological Review*, 3, 801–14.

GILBOY, E. W. (1939) 'Methods of Measuring Demand or Consumption', *Review of Economic Statistics*, 21, 69–74.

GILBOY, E. W. (1940) 'Income-Expenditure Relations', *Review of Economic Statistics*, 22, 115–21.

GILBOY, E. W. (1941) 'Changes in Consumption Expenditures and the Defence Program', *Review of Economic Statistics*, 23, 155–64.

GILLIES, D. (1988) 'Keynes as a Methodologist', *British Journal for the Philosophy of Science*, 39, 117–29.

GINI, C. (1924) 'Quelques Considerations au Sujet de la Construction des Nombres Indices des Prix et des Questions Analogues', *Metron*, 4, 3–162.

GIRSHICK, M. A. and HAAVELMO, T. (1947) 'Statistical Analysis of the Demand for Food:

Examples of Simultaneous Estimation of Structural Equations', *Econometrica*, 15, 79–110, Reprinted in Hood & Koopmans (1953), 92–111.

GODFREY, L. G. (1978) 'Testing Against General Autoregressive and Moving Average Models when the Regressors Contain Lagged Dependent Variables', *Econometrica*, 46, 1293–1301.

GODFREY, L. G. and WICKENS, M. R. (1981) 'Testing Linear and Log-Linear Regressions for Functional Form', *Review of Economic Studies*, 48, 487–96.

GOLDBERGER, A. S. (1964) *Econometric Theory*, New York, Wiley.

GOLDBERGER, A. S. (1972) 'Structural Equation Methods in the Social Sciences', *Econometrica*, 40, 979–1001.

GOODMAN, N. (1954) *Fact, Fiction and Forecast*, New York.

GOTTMAN, J. M. (1981) *Time Series Analysis*, Cambridge, Cambridge University Press.

GRANGER, C. W. J. (1986) 'Developments in the Study of Co-Integrated Economic Variables', *Oxford Bulletin of Economics and Statistics*, 48, 213–28.

GRANGER, C. W. J. and NEWBOLD, P. (1974) 'Spurious Regressions in Econometrics', *Journal of Econometrics*, 2, 111–20.

GRANGER, C. W. J. and WEISS, A. A. (1983) 'Time Series Analysis of Error-Correction Models' in Karlin, S., Amemiya, T. and Goodman, L. A. eds. *Studies in Econometrics, Time Series and Multivariate Statistics*, New York, Academic Press, 255–78.

GRIFFIN, K. B. (1962) 'A Note on Wages, Prices and Employment', *Bulletin of the Oxford University Institute of Economics and Statistics*, 24, 379–85.

GRILICHES, Z. (1974) 'Errors in Variables and Other Unobservables', *Econometrica*, 42, 971–98.

GRUNBERG, E. and MODIGLIANI, F. (1954) 'The Predictability of Social Events', *Journal of Political Economy*, 42, 465–78.

HAAS, G. C. and EZEKIEL, M., (1926) *Factors Affecting the Price of Hogs*. USDA Bulletin 1440, Washington DC, Government Printing Office.

HAAVELMO, T. (1938) 'The Method of Supplementary Confluent Relations, Illustrated by a Study of Stock Prices', *Econometrica*, 6, 203–218.

HAAVELMO, T. (1943a) 'Statistical Testing of Business Cycle Theories', *Review of Economic Statistics*, 25, 13–18.

HAAVELMO, T. (1943b) 'The Statistical Implications of a System of Simultaneous Equations', *Econometrica*, 11, 1–12.

HAAVELMO, T. (1944) 'The Probability Approach in Econometrics', *Econometrica*, 12, Supplement, 1–118.

HAAVELMO, T. (1947) 'Methods of Measuring the Marginal Propensity to Consume', *Journal of the American Statistical Association*, 42, 105–22, in Hood & Koopmans (1953), 75–91.

HAAVELMO, T. (1950) 'Remarks on Frisch's Confluence Analysis and Its Use in Econometrics', in Koopmans (1950) 258–65.

HABERLER VON, G. (1939) *Prosperity and Depression*, Geneva, League of Nations.

HACKING, I. (1983a) *Representing and Intervening: Introductory Topics in the Philosophy of Natural Science*, Cambridge, Cambridge University Press.

HACKING, I. (1983b) 'Nineteenth Century Cracks in the Concept of Determinism', *Journal of the History of Ideas*, 44, 455–475.

HADJIMATHEOU, G. (1987) *Consumer Economics After Keynes: Theory and Evidence of the Consumption Function*, Brighton, Wheatsheaf.

HAGSTROEM, K. (1938) 'Pure Economics as a Stochastical Theory', *Econometrica*, 6, 40–47.

HAITOVSKY, Y. (1973) *Regression Estimates from Grouped Observations*, New York, Hafner.

HALL, A. D. (1987) 'Worldwide Rankings of Research Activity in Econometrics: 1980–85', *Econometric Theory*, 3, 171–94.

HALL, R. E. and TAYLOR, J. B. (1986) *Macroeconomics: Theory, Performance and Policy*, New York, Norton.

HANSEN, B. (1969) 'Jan Tinbergen: An Appraisal of His Contribution to Economics', *Swedish Journal of Economics*, 71, 325–36.

HARVEY, A. C. (1981a) *The Econometric Analysis of Time Series*, Deddington, Philip Allan.

HARVEY, A. C. (1981b) *Time Series Models*, Deddington, Philip Allen.

HARVEY, A. C. and DURBIN, J. (1986) 'The Effects of Seat Belt Legislation on British Road Casualties: A Case Study in Structural Time Series Modelling', *Journal of the Royal Statistical Society*, A, 149, 187–227.

HARDING, S. (1976) *Can Theories Be Refuted?* Boston, Reidel.

HASTAY, M. (1951) 'Review of Koopmans', *Journal of the American Statistical Association*, 46, 388–90.

HENDRY, D. F. (1974) 'Stochastic Specification in an Aggregate Demand Model of the UK', *Econometrica*, 42, 559–78.

HENDRY, D. F. (1976) 'Discussion of "Estimation of Linear Functional Relationships: Approximate Distributions and Connections with Simultaneous Equations in Econometrics", by T. W. Anderson', *Journal of the Royal Statistical Society* B, 38, 24–5.

HENDRY, D. F. (1980) 'Econometrics—Alchemy or Science?', *Economica*, 47, 387–406.

HENDRY, D. F. (1983) 'Econometric Modelling: The Consumption Function in Retrospect', *Scottish Journal of Political Economy*, 30, 193–220.

HENDRY, D. F. (1986) 'Econometric Modelling with Cointegrated Variables: An Overview', *Oxford Bulletin of Economics and Statistics*, 48, 201–212.

HENDRY, D. F. and ANDERSON, G. J. (1977) 'Testing Dynamic Specification in Small Simultaneous Systems: An Application to a Model of Building Society Behavior in the United Kingdom', in M. D. Intrilogator Ed., *Frontiers of Quantitative Economics*, IIIA, Amsterdam, North Holland.

HENDRY, F. F. and MIZON, G. E. (1978) 'Serial Correlation as a Conventient Simplication, Not a Nuisance: A Comment on a Study of the Demand for Money by the Bank of England', *Economic Journal*, 88, 549–63.

HENDRY, D. F. and WALLIS, K. F. eds., (1984) *Econometrics and Quantitative Economics*, Oxford, Blackwell.

HILDRETH, C. (1986) *The Cowles Commission in Chicago*, 1935–55, Berlin, Springer-Verlag.

HILL, N. M. (1988) 'Some Subjective Bayesian Considerations in the Selection of Models', *Econometric Reviews*, 4, 191–246.

HINKLEY, D. V. (1984) 'A Hitchhiker's Guide to the Galaxy of Theoretical Statistics', in David, H. A. and David, H. T. eds. *Statistics: an Appraisal*, Iowa, The Iowa State University Press.

HODGSON, G. M. (1988) 'Institutional Economic Theory: The Old Versus the New', *Review of Political Economy*, 437–53.

HOLBROOK, R. S. (1974) 'A Practical Method for Controlling a Large Nonlinear Stochastic System', *Annals of Economic and Social Measurement*, 3, 155–76.

HOLEVO, A. S. (1982) *Probabilistic and Statistical Aspects of Quantum Theory*, Amsterdam, North Holland.

HOLT, C. C. (1962) 'Linear Decision Rules for Economic Stabilisation and Growth', *Quarterly Journal of Economics*, 76, 20–45.

HOOD, W. C. and KOOPMANS, T. C., eds. (1953) *Studies in Econometric Method*, Cowles Commission Monograph 14, New York, Wiley.

HORVATH, R. A. (1967) 'The Rise of Macroeconomic Calculations in Economic Science', in Krüger et al. (1987) 2, 147–69.

HOYT, E. E. (1938) *Consumption in Our Society*, New York, McGraw-Hill.

HOYT, E. E. and MEINTS, V. C. (1932) 'Academic Incomes and Planes of Living', *American Economic Review*, 22, 78–81.

HUGHES HALLETT, A. J. (1979) 'On Methods for Avoiding the *a priori* Numerical Specification of Preferences in Policy Selection, *Economics Letters*, 3, 221–8.

HUGHES HALLETT, A. J. (1981) 'Measuring the Importance of Stochastic Control in the Design of Economic Policies', *Economics Letters*, 8, 341–7.

HUGHES HALLETT, A. J. (1984) 'Optimal Stockpiling in a High Risk Commodity Market: The Case of Copper', *Journal of Economic Dynamics and Control*, 8, 211–38.

HUGHES HALLETT, A. J. (1986) 'Autonomy and the Choice of Policy in Asymmetrically Dependent Economies', *Oxford Economic Papers*, 38, 516–44.

HUGHES HALLETT, A. J. and PETIT, M. L. (1988) 'Trade-Off Reversals, in Macroeconomic Policy', *Journal of Economic Dynamics and Control*, 12, 85–91.

HUGHES HALLETT, A. J. and REES, H. J. B. (1983) *Quantitative Economic Policies and Interactive Planning*, Cambridge, Cambridge University Press.

HURWICZ, L. (1950) 'Generalization of the Concept of Identification' in Koopmans (1950) 245–57.

HURWICZ, L. (1962) 'On the Structural Form of Interdependent Systems', in *Logic Methodology, and the Philosophy of Science*, Nagel, E. *et al.* ed., Stanford, Stanford University Press.

INTRILGATOR, M. D. (1978) *Econometric Models, Techniques and Applications*, Amsterdam, North Holland.

JAFFE, W. (1965) *The Correspondence of Leon Walras and Related Papers*, Amsterdam, North Holland.

JOHANSEN, S. (1987) 'Statistical Analysis of Cointegrating Vectors', Mimeo, University of Copenhagen.

JOHNSTON, J. (1963) *Econometric Methods*, Maidenhead, McGraw Hill.

JORDAN, T. (1986) *Quantum Mechanics in Simple Matrix Form*, New York, Wiley.

JORGENSON, D. W. (1966) 'Rational Distributed Lag Functions', *Econometrica*, 34, 135–49.

JUDGE, G. G., GRIFFITHS, W. E., HILL, R. C. and LEE, T.-C. (1980) *The Theory and Practice of Econometrics*, New York, Wiley.

KALMAN, R. (1982a) 'Identifiability and Modeling in Econometrics' in Krishnaiah P. ed. *Developments in Statistics*, New York, Academic Press, 97–136.

KALMAN, R. (1982b) 'Identification from Real Data', in Hazewinkel, M. and Rinrooy Kan, A. H. G. eds. *Current Developments in the Interface*: *Economics, Econometrics, Mathematics*, Dordrecht, Reidel, 161–96.

KAPLAN, A. D. H. (1938) 'Expenditure Patterns of Urban Families', *Journal of the American Statistical Association*, 33, 81–100.

KENDALL, M. (1945) 'Discussion of Mr Stone's Paper', *Journal of the Royal Statistical Society*, A, 108, 384–85.

KENDRICK, D. A. (1981) *Stochastic Control for Economic Models*, New York, McGraw Hill.

KEYNES, J. M. (1939) 'Professor Tinbergen's Method', *Economic Journal*, 44, 558–68.

KEYNES, J. M. (1971) *The Collected Writings of John Maynard Keynes*, V, VII, VIII, X, XIII, XIV, XVII, XVIII, XXIX, Royal Economic Society, London, Macmillan.

KIM, H. K., GOREUX, L. M. and KENDRICK, D. A. (1975) 'Feedback Control Rules for Cocoa Market Stabilisation' in Labys W. C. ed., *Quantitative Models of Commodity Markets*, Cambridge, Mass., Ballinger, 233–63.

KIRKPATRICK, E. L. (1934) *The Life Cycle of the Farm Family*, Madison, Wisconsin Agricultural Experimental Station Research Bulletin 121.

KLAASSEN, L., KOYCK, L. M. and WITTEVEEN, H. (1959) *Jan Tinbergen: Selected Papers*, Amsterdam, North Holland.

KLEIN, L. R. (1943) 'Pitfalls in the Statistical Determination of the Investment Schedule', *Econometrica*, 11, 246–58.

KLEIN, L. R. (1944) 'The Statistical Determination of the Investment Schedule: A Reply', *Econometrica*, 12, 91–92.

KLEIN, L. R. (1946) 'A Macroeconomic System, USA, 1921–41', *Econometrica*, 14, 159–62.

KLEIN L. R. (1947a) 'The Use of Econometric Models as a Guide to Economic Policy', *Econometrica*, 111–51.

KLEIN, L. R. (1947b) 'Economic Fluctuations in the United States 1921–41, Chicago, Cowles Commission Working Paper.

KLEIN, L. R. (1950) Economic Fluctuations in the United States 1921–41, Cowles Commission Monograph No 11, Wiley.

KLEIN, L. R. (1953) A Textbook of Econometrics, Evanston, Row Peterson.

KLEIN, L. R. (1962) Introduction to Econometrics, Englewood Cliffs, Prentice Hall.

KLEIN, L. R. (1987) 'The History of Computation in Econometrics', University of Pennsylvania, Mimeo.

KLEIN, L. R. BALL, R., J., HAZLEWOOD, A. and VANDOME, P., (1961) An Econometric Model of the United Kingdom, Oxford, Blackwell.

KLEIN, M. (1970) Paul Ehrenfest, I, Amsterdam, North Holland.

KLEPPER, S. and LEAMER, E. E. (1982) 'Consistent Sets of Estimates for Regressions with Errors in all Variables', Econometrica, 52, 163–84.

KNEELAND, H., SCHOENBERG, E. H. and FRIEMAN, M. (1936) 'Plans for a Study of the Consumption of Goods and Services by American Families', Journal of the American Statistical Association, 31, 135–40.

KOFFSKY, N. (1948) 'An Additional View on the Consumption Function', Review of Economics and Statistics, 30, 55–6.

KOOPMANS, T. C. (1934) 'Uber die Zuordnung von Wellenfunktionen und Eigenwerten zu den einzelnen Elektronen eines Atoms', Physica, 1, 104–113.

KOOPMANS, T. C. (1937) Linear Regression Analysis of Economic Time Series, Haarlem, De Erven F. Bohn.

KOOPMANS, T. C. (1941) 'The Logic of Econometric Business-Cycle Research', Journal of Political Economy, 49, 157–81.

KOOPMANS, T. C. (1942) 'Serial Correlation and Quadratic Forms in Normal Variables', Annals of Mathematical Statistics, 13, 14–33.

KOOPMAN, T. C. (1945) 'Statistical Estimation of Simultaneous Economic Relations', Journal of the American Statistical Association, 40, 448–66.

KOOPMANS, T. C. (1947) 'Measurement Without Theory', Review of Economic Statistics, 29, 161–72.

KOOPMANS, T. C. (1949a) 'Methodological Issues in Quantitative Economics: A Reply', Review of Economics and Statistics, 31, 36–91.

KOOPMANS, T. C. (1949b) 'Identification Problems in Economic Model Construction', Econometrica, 17, 125–44.

KOOPMANS, T. C. ed., (1950), Statistical Inference in Dynamic Economic Models, Cowles Commission Monograph 10, New York, Wiley.

KOOPMANS, T. C. (1953) 'Identification Problems in Economic Model Construction', Econometrica, 17, 125–44.

KOOPMANS, T. C. (1957) Three Essays on the State of Economic Science, New York, McGraw Hill.

KOOPMANS, T. C. (1970), Scientific Papers of Tjalling Koopmans, I, New York, Springer Verlag.

KOOPMANS, T. C. and REIERSØL, O. (1950) 'The Identification of Structural Characteristics', The Annals of Mathematical Statistics, 21, 165–81.

KOOPMANS, T., RUBIN, H. and LEIPNIK, R. (1950) 'Measuring the Equation systems of Dynamic Economics', in Hood and Koopmans ed. (1950), 53–237.

KRÜGER, L., GIGERENZER, G. and MORGAN, M. eds. (1987) The Probabilistic Revolution, Vol. 2, Cambridge, MIT Press.

KUZNETS, S. (1942) Uses of National Income in Peace and War, NBER, Occasional Paper 6.

KUZNETS, S. (1946a) National Product Since 1869, New York, NBER.

KUZNETS, S. (1946b), National Income: A Summary of Findings, New York, NBER.

KYRK, H. (1923) A Theory of Consumption, Boston, Houghton Mifflin.

KYRK, H. (1929) 'Discussion', *Journal of Farm Economics*, 11, 575–77.

LAKATOS, I. (1970) 'Falsification and the Methodology of Scientific Research Programmes', in I. Lakatos and A. Musgrave eds., *Criticism and the Growth of Knowledge*, Cambridge, Cambridge University Press.

LANCZOS, C. (1949) *The Variational Principles of Mechanics*, Toronto, University of Toronto Press.

LANDSHOFF, P. and METHERELL, A. (1979) *Simple Quantum Physics*, Cambridge, Cambridge University Press.

LAWSON, T. (1985) 'Keynes, Prediction and Econometrics', in Lawson and Pesaran (1985), 116–133.

LAWSON, T. (1987) 'The Relative/Absolute Nature of Knowledge', *Economic Journal*, 97, 951–70.

LAWSON, T. (1988) 'Abstraction, Tendencies and Stylized Facts: A Realist Approach to Economic Analysis', Mimeo, Cambridge.

LAWSON, T. and PESARAN, M. H. eds. (1985) *Keynes Economics: Methodological Issues*, London, Croom Helm.

LEAMER, E. E. (1974) 'False Models and Post-Data Model Construction', *Journal of the American Statistical Association*, 69, 122–31.

LEAMER, E. E. (1975) 'Explaining Your Results as Access-Biased Memory', *Journal of the American Statistical Association*, 70, 88–93.

LEAMER, E. E. (1978) *Specification Searches: Ad Hoc Inference with Non-Experimental Data*, New York, Wiley.

LEAMER, E. E. (1983) 'Let's Take the Con Out of Econometrics', *American Economic Review*, 79, 31–43.

LEAMER, E. E. (1985) 'Vector Autoregressions for Causal Inference?' in Brunner, K. and Meltzer, A. eds. *Understanding Monetary Regimes, Journal of Monetary Economics*, Supplement, 22, 255–304.

LEIGHTON THOMAS, R., (1984) 'The Consumption Function', in Demery D., Duck, N. W., Sumner, M. T., Thomas, R. L. and Thompson, W. N. *Surveys in Economics: Macroeconomics*, London, Longman, 53–99.

LEIGHTON THOMAS, R. (1985) *Introductory Econometrics: Theory and Applications*, London, Longman.

LEVEN, M., MOULTON, H. G. and WARBURTON, C. (1934) *America's Capacity to Consume*, Brookings Institute.

LEVY, D. J. (1981) *Realism: An Essay in Interpretation and Social Reality*, Manchester, Carcanet New Press.

LEWIS, H. G. and DOUGLAS, P. H. (1947) 'Studies in Consumer Expenditures, 1901, 1918–19, 1922–24', *Journal of Business of the University of Chicago*, 20, 1–75.

LIPSEY, R. G. (1960) 'The Relation Between Unemployment and the Rate of Change of Money Wage Rates in the United Kingdom 1862–1957', *Economica*, 27, 1–31.

LIPSEY, R. G. (1978) 'The Place of the Phillips Curve in Macroeconomic Models', in Bergstrom, *et al.* eds., (1978), 29–75.

LIPSEY, R. G. and PARKIN, J. M. (1970) 'Incomes Policy: A Re-Appraisal', *Economica*, 37, 115–38.

LIPSEY, R. G. and STEUER, M. (1961) 'The Relation between Profits and Wages', *Economica*, 28, 137–55.

LIU, T. C. (1960) 'Underidentification, Structural Estimation, and Forecasting', *Econometrica*, 38, 855–65.

LIVINGSTONE, S. M. (1945) 'Forecasting Postwar Demand: II', *Econometrica*, 13, 15–24.

LOOMIS, C. P. and BEEGLE, J. A. (1950) *Rural Social Systems: A Textbook in Rural Sociology and Anthropology*, Englewood Cliffs, Prentice Hall.

LOS, C. A. (1986) 'Collinearity Analysis of Simple Money Demand Equation', Federal Reserve Bank of New York Research Paper 8604.

LOWITT, R. ed. (1980) *Journal of a Tamed Bureaucrat: Nils A. Olsen and the BAE*, 1925–35, Ames, Iowa State University Press.

LUCAS, R. E. (1976) 'Econometric Policy Evaluation: A Critique', in Brunner, K. and Meltzer, A. eds. *The Phillips Curve and Labor Markets, Journal of Monetary Economics*, Supplement, 1, 19–46.

MACK, R. P. (1948) 'The Direction of Change in Income and the Consumption Function', *Review of Economics and Statistics*, 30, 239–58.

MACK, R. P. (1952) 'Economics of consumption', in Haley, B. F. ed. *A Survey of Contemporary Economics*, Holmewood, Il., Irwin, 39–82.

MAGNUS, J. and MORGAN, M. (1987) 'The ET Interview: Professor J. Tinbergen', *Econometric Theory*, 3, 117–42.

MALINVAUD, E. (1964) '*Methodes Statistiques de l'Econometrie*, Paris, Dunod.

MALINVAUD, E. (1981) 'Econometrics Faced with the Needs of Macroeconomic Policy', *Econometrica*, 49, 1363–75.

MALINVAUD, E. (1983) 'Econometric Methodology: Rise and Maturity', Paper Presented at the 50th Anniversary of the Cowles Commission for Research in Economics, 3 June 1983, Yale University.

MALLOWS, C. L. (1973), 'Some Comments on C_p', *Technometrics*, 15, 661–75.

MANDELBROT, B. (1963a) 'New Methods in Statistical Economics', *Journal of Political Economy*, 71, 421–40.

MANDELBROT, B. (1963b) 'The Variation of Certain Speculative Prices', *Journal of Business*, 36, 394–419.

MANDELBROT, B. (1964) 'On the Derivation of Statistical Thermodynamics from Purely Phenomenological Principles', *Journal of Mathematical Physics*.

MANN, H. and WALD, A. (1943) 'On the Statistical Treatment of Linear Stochastic Difference Equations', *Econometrica*, 11, 173–220.

MARGET, A. (1929) 'Morgenstern on the Methodology of Economic Forecasting', *Journal of Political Economy*, 37, 312–39.

MARSCHAK, J. (1939) 'Personal and Collective Budget Functions', *Review of Economic Statistics*, 21, 69–74.

MARSCHAK, J. (1941) 'A Discussion on Methods in Economics', *Journal of Political Economy*, 49, 441–48.

MARSCHAK, J. (1942) 'Economic Interdependence and Statistical Analysis', in Lange, O., McIntyre, F. & Yntema, T. O. eds. *Studies in Mathematical Economics and Econometrics*, Chicago, University of Chicago Press, 135–50.

MARSCHAK, J. (1950) 'Statistical Inference in Economics: An Introduction', in Koopmans (1950), 1–50.

MARSCHAK, J. (1953) 'Economic Measurements for Policy and Prediction', in Hood & Koopmans eds. (1953), 1–26.

MARSHALL, A. (1890) *Principles of Economics*, London, Macmillan.

MAYER, J. (1933) 'Pseudo-Scientific Method in Economics', *Econometrica*, 1, 418–28.

MAYHEW, A. (1988) 'Contrasting Origins of the Two Institutionalisms: The Social Science Context', Mimeograph, University of Tennessee.

MCALEER, M., PAGAN, A. R. and VOLKER, P. A. (1985) 'What Will Take the Con Out of Econometrics?', *American Economic Review*, 75, 293–307.

MCINTYRE, F. (1936) 'Review of Frisch (1934)', *Journal of the American Statistical Association*, 31, 619–20.

MEEKS, J. G. T. (1978) 'Bray on Keynes on Scientific Method: A Comment', *Journal of Economic Studies*, 5, 146–8.

MEHRA, J. and RECHENBERG, H. (1982) *Historical Development of the Quantum Theory*, 5 vols., Berlin, Springer-Verlag.

MENARD, C. (1980) 'Three Forms of Resistance to Statistics: Say, Cournot, Walras', *History of Political Economy*, 12, 524–41.

MENARD, C. (1987) 'Why was there no Probabilistic Revolution in Economic Thought?', in Krüger *et al* (1987), 139–48.

MENDERSHAUSEN, H. (1939) 'The Relationship Between Income and Savings of American Metropolitan Families', *American Economic Review*, 29, 521–37.

MENDERSHAUSEN, H. (1940) 'Differences in Family Savings Between Cities of Different Size and Location, Whites and Negroes', *Review of Economic Statistics*, 22, 122–35.

MENDERSHAUSEN, H. (1946) *Changes in Income Distribution During the Great Depression*, New York, NBER.

MILL, J. S. (1844) 'On the Definition of Political Economy; and on the Method of Investigation Proper to it', in *Essays on Some Unsettled Questions of Political Economy*. Reprinted in ROBSON, J. M. ed. (1967) *J. S. Mill, Collected Works*, IV, Toronto, Toronto University Press.

MILLS, F. (1924a) 'On Measurement in Economics', in Tugwell, R. ed. *The Trend of Economics*, New York, Knopf, 38–71.

MILLS, F. (1924b) *Statistical Methods*, New York, Henry Holt.

MILLS, F. (1927) *The Behavior of Prices*, New York, NBER.

MIROWSKI, P. (1984a) 'Physics and the Marginalist Revolution', *Cambridge Journal of Economics*, 8, 361–79.

MIROWSKI, P. (1984b) 'The Role of Conservation Principles in 20th Century Economic Theory', *Philosophy of the Social Sciences*, 14, 461–73.

MIROWSKI, P. (1984c) 'Macroeconomic Instability and "Natural" Fluctuations in Early Neoclassical Economics', *Journal of Economic History*, 69, 345–54.

MIROWSKI, P. ed. (1986) *The Reconstruction of Economic Theory*, Hingham, Nijhoff.

MIROWSKI, P. (forthcoming a), *More Heat Than Light: Economics as Social Physics*, New York, Cambridge University Press.

MIROWSKI, P. (forthcoming b), ''Tis a Pity Econometrics Isn't an Empirical Endeavour: Mandelbrot and the Infinite Variance Hypothesis', *Richerche Economiche*.

MITCHELL, W. C. (1925) 'Quantitative Analysis in Economic Theory', *American Economic Review*, 15, 1–12.

MITCHELL, W. C. (1969) *Types of Economic Theory*, 2, New York, Kelley.

MIZON, G. E. (1977) 'Inferential Procedures in Nonlinear Models: An Application in a UK Industrial Cross Section Study of Factor Substitution and Returns to Scale', *Econometrica*, 45, 1221–42.

MIZON, G. E. (1984) 'The Encompassing Principle in Econometrics', in Hendry and Wallis, (1984), 135–72.

MIZON, G. E. and HENDRY, D. F. (1980) 'An Empirical Application and Monte Carlo Analysis of Tests of Dynamic Specification', *Review of Economic Studies*, 47, 21–46.

MIZON, G. E. and RICHARD, J.-F. (1986) 'The Encompassing Principle and its Application to Non-Nested Hypotheses', *Econometrica*, 54, 657–78.

MODIGLIANI, F. (1947) 'Fluctuations in the Saving Ratio: A Problem in Economic Forecasting', *Social Research*, 14, 413–20.

MODIGLIANI, F. (1949) 'Fluctuations in the Saving-Income Ratio: A Problem in Economic Forecasting', in *Studies in Income and Wealth*, 11, New York, NBER, 371–441.

MODIGLIANI, F. (1975) 'The Life Cycle Hypothesis of Saving Twenty Years Later', In M. Parkin and A. R. Nobay (eds), *Contemporary Issues in Economics*, Manchester University Press.

MODIGLIANI, F. and ANDO, A. (1957) 'Tests of the Life-Cycle Hypothesis of Savings', *Bulletin of the Oxford Institue of Economics and Statistics*, 19, 99–124.

MODIGLIANI, F. and BRUMBERG, R. (1954) 'Utility Analysis and the Consumption Function: An Interpretation of Cross-Section Data', in Kurihara, K. K. ed., *Post-Keynesian Economics*, London, Allen & Unwin.

MONROE, D. (1937) 'Analyzing Families by Composition Type with Respect to Consumption', *Journal of the American Statistical Association*, 32, 35–39.

MOORE, H. L. (1908) 'The Statistical Complement of Pure Economics', *Quarterly Journal of Economics*, 23, 1–33.

MOORE, H. L. (1914) *Economic Cycles: Their Law and Cause,* New York, Macmillan.

MOORE, H. L. (1917) *Forecasting the Yield and the Price of Cotton,* New York, Macmillan.

MOORE, H. L. (1929) *Synthetic Economics,* New York, Macmillan.

MORGAN, M. S. (1984) 'The History of Econometric Thought: Analysis of the Main Problems of Relating Economic Theory to Data in the First Half of the Twentieth Century', Ph.D. Thesis, London School of Economics.

MORGAN, M. S. (1987a) 'Statistics Without Probability and Haavelmo's Revolution in Econometrics', in Krüger *et al.* (1987), 2, 171–200.

MORGAN, M. S. (1987b) 'The Stamping Out of Process Analysis from Econometrics', paper prepared for a Symposium on the History and Philosophy of Econometrics, Duke University, November 1987.

MORGAN, M. S. (1989) *The History of Econometric Ideas,* Cambridge, Cambridge University Press.

MOSAK, J. L. (1945) 'Forecasting Postwar Demand: III', *Econometrica,* 13, 25–53.

MUELLBAUER, J. and BOVER, O. (1986) 'Liquidity Constraints and Aggregation in Consumption Function under Uncertainty', Applied Economics Discussion Paper 12, Institute of Economics and Statistics, Oxford.

MUNDELL, R. A. (1968) 'International Economics', New York, Macmillan.

NELSON, C. R. (1972) 'The Prediction Performance of the FRB–MIT–PENN Model of the US Economy', *American Economic Review,* 62, 902–17.

NEWLYN, W. T. (1950) 'The Phillips/Newlyn Hydraulic Model', *Yorkshire Bulletin of Economic and Social Research,* 2, 111–127.

NICKELL, S. J. (1985) 'Error Correction, Partial Adjustment and all that: An Expository Note', *Oxford Bulletin of Economics and Statistics,* 47, 119–31.

NORTHROP, F. (1941) 'The Impossibility of a Theoretical Science of Economic Dynamics', *Quarterly Journal of Economics,* 55, 1–17.

O'DONNELL, R. M. (1982) 'Keynes: Philosophy and Economics (An Approach to Rationality and Uncertainty)', Ph.D. Thesis, Cambridge University

OGBURN, W. F. (1919a) 'Measurement of the Cost of Living and Wages', *Annals of the American Academy of Political and Social Science,* 81, 110–22.

OGBURN, W. F. (1919b) 'Analysis of the Standard of Living in the District of Columbia in 1916', *Journal of the American Statistical Association,* 16, 374–94.

OGBURN, W. F. (1919c) 'A Study of Food Costs in Various Cities', *Monthly Labor Review,* August, 1–25.

OGBURN, W. F. (1919d) 'A Study of Rents in Various Cities', *Monthly Labor Review,* September, 1–22.

OGBURN, W. F. (1923) 'The Standard-of-Living Factor in Wages', *American Economic Review,* 13, 118–28.

OLIVIER, M. (1926) 'Les Nombres Indices de la Variation des Prix', Ph.D Thesis, University of Paris.

ORCUTT, G. H. and ROY, A. D. (1949) *A Bibliography of the Consumption Function,* Cambridge, Department of Applied Economics, Mimeo.

PAGAN, A. R. and HALL, A. D. (1983) 'Diagnostic Tests as Residual Analysis', *Econometric Reviews,* 2, 159–218.

PAINLEVE, P. (1960) 'The Place of Mathematical Reasoning in Economics', in Sommer, L. ed. *Essays in European Economic Thought,* Princeton, Van Nostrand.

PAISH, F. (1958) 'Progress, Prices and the Pound', *District Bank Review,* 1–29.

PAISH, F. (1962) *Studies in an Inflationary Economy: The United Kingdom 1948–61,* London, Macmillan.

PARADISO, L. (1945) *National Budgets for Full Employment,* Washington DC, National Planning Board.

PARKIN, M. and BADE, R. (1982) *Modern Macroeconomics,* Deddington, Philip Allan.

PARETO, V. (1966) *Statistique et Economie Mathématique,* Oeuvres Complètes, VIII, Geneva, Droz.

PATINKIN, D. (1976) 'Keynes and Econometrics: On the Interaction Between the Macroeconomic Revolutions of the Interwar Period', *Econometrica,* 44, 1091–123.

PATRICK, J. D. (1972) 'Establishing Convergent Decentralised Policy Assignments', *Journal of International Economics,* 3, 37–52.

PEIXOTTO, J. B. (1927) *Getting and Spending at the Professional Standard of Living: A Study of the Costs of an Academic Life,* New York, Macmillan.

PEIXOTTO, J. B. (1929) 'How Workers Spend a Living Wage: A Study of the Incomes and Expenditures of Eighty-Two Typographers' Families in San Francisco', University of California Publications in Economics, 5.

PERSONS, W. M. (1924) 'The Problem of Business Forecasting; in Persons, Foster and Hettinger eds., *The Problem of Business Forecasting,* Cambridge, Mass., Riverside Press.

PESARAN, M. H. (1974) 'On the General Problem of Model Selection', *Review of Economic Studies,* 41, 153–71.

PESARAN, M. H. (1987) 'Econometrics', in Eatwell *et al.* eds. (1987), 2, 8–19.

PESARAN, M. H. and DEATON, A. S. (1978) 'Testing Non-Nested Non-Linear Regression Models', *Econometrica,* 46, 677–94.

PESARAN, H. M. and PESARAN, B. (1987) *Data FIT, Econometric Computer Package,* Oxford, Oxford University Press.

PESARAN, M. H. and SMITH, R. P. (1985a) 'Keynes on Econometrics' in Lawson and Pesaran eds., (1985), 134–50.

PESARAN, M. H. and SMITH, R. P. (1985b) 'Evaluation of Macroeconometric Models', *Economics Modelling,* 2, 125–34.

PESTON, M. (1981) 'Lionel Robbins', in J. R. Shackleton and G. Locksley eds., *Twelve Contemporary Economists,* London, Macmillan.

PESTON, M. (1971) 'The Microeconomics of the Phillips Curve', in Johnson, H. G. and Nobay, A. R. eds. *The Current Inflation,* London, Macmillan, 125–42.

PETIT, M. L. (1987) 'A System Theoretical Approach to the Theory of Economic Policy' in Carraro, C. and Sartore, D. eds., *Development on Control Theory for Economic Analysis,* Boston, Kluwer, 31–45.

PHEBY, J. (1985) 'Are Popperian Criticisms of Keynes Justified?', in Lawson and Pesaran (1985), 99–115.

PHELPS BROWN, E. H. (1958) 'The Conditions for the Avoidance of the Spiral', *Scottish Journal of Political Economy,* 5, 145–48.

PHELPS BROWN, E. H. and HOPKINS, S. (1950) 'The Course of Wage-Rages in Five Countries, 1860–1939', *Oxford Economic Papers,* 2, 226–67.

PHILLIPS, A. W. (1950) 'Mechanical Models in Economic Dynamics', *Economica,* 17, 283–305.

PHILLIPS, A. W. (1953) Dynamic Models in Economics, Ph.D. Thesis, University of London.

PHILLIPS, A. W. (1954) 'Stabilisation Policy in a Closed Economy', *Economic Journal,* 64, 290–323.

PHILLIPS, A. W. (1956) 'Some Notes on the Estimation of Time-Forms', *Economica,* 23, 99–113.

PHILLIPS, A. W. (1957) 'Stabilization Policy and the Time Form of Lagged Responses', *Economic Journal,* 67, 265–77.

PHILLIPS, A. W. (1958a) 'The Relationship Between Unemployment and the Rate of Change of Money Wage Rates in the United Kingdom, 1861–1857', *Economica,* 25, 283–99.

PHILLIPS, A. W. (1958b) 'La Cybernétique et le Contrôle des Systèmes Economiques', *Etudes Sur la Cybernetique et l'Economie,* N, 21, 41–50.

PHILLIPS, A. W. (1959a) 'Wage Change and Unemployment in Australia, 1947–58', Economic Society of Australia and New Zealand (Victoria Branch) Monograph 14.

PHILLIPS, A. W. (1959b) 'The Estimation of Parameters in Systems of Stochastic Differential Equations', *Biometrika,* 46, 67–76.

PHILLIPS, A. W. (1961) 'A Simple Model of Employment, Money and Prices in a Growing Economy', *Economica*, 28, 360–70.

PHILLIPS, A. W. (1962) 'Employment, Inflation and Growth, An Inaugural Address', *Economica*, 29, 1–16.

PHILLIPS, A. W. (1978) 'Estimates of Systems of Difference Equations with Moving Average Disturbances', 1966 Walras-Bowley Lecture, San Francisco, in Bergstron *et al.* (1978), 181–99.

PHILLIPS, A. W. and QUENOUILLE, M. H. (1960) 'Estimation, Regulation, and Prediction in Interdependent Dynamic Systems', *Bulletin de l'Institut International Statistique*, 335–43.

PHILLIPS, P. C. B. (1985) 'Interview with Denis Sargan, *Econometric Theory*, 1, 119–39.

PHILLIPS, P. C. B. (1986a) 'Regression Theory for Near-Integrated Time Series', Cowles Foundation Discussion Paper, 781, Yale University.

PHILLIPS, P. C. B. (1986b) 'The ET Interview: Professor T. W. Anderson', *Econometric Theory*, 2, 249–88.

PHILLIPS, P. C. B. and PARK, J. Y. (1986) 'Statistical Inference in Regressions with Integrated Processes: Part I' Cowles Foundation Discussion Paper 811, Yale University.

PIERSON, B. L. (1988) 'Sequential Quadratic Programming and its use in Optimal Control Model Comparisons', in Feichtinger, G., ed. *Optimal Control Theory and Economic Analysis*, 3, Amsterdam, North Holland, 173–93.

PIGOU, A. C. (1956) *Memorials of Alfred Marshall*, New York, Kelley and Millman.

PINDYCK, R. S. (1973) 'Optimal Policies for Economic Stabilisation', *Econometrica*, 41, 529–59.

PINDYCK, R. S. and RUBINFELD, D. L. (1981) *Econometric Models and Economic Forecasts*, 2nd ed. New York, MacGraw Hill.

PITMAN, E. J. G. (1979) *Some Basic Theory for Statistical Inference*, London, Chapman and Hall.

POLAK, J. J. (1939) 'Fluctuations in United States Consumption, 1919–32', *Review of Economic Statistics*, 21, 1–12.

PORTER, T. (1985) 'The Mathematics of Society', *British Journal of the History of Science*, 18, 51–69.

PORTER, T. (1986) *The Rise of Statistical Thinking*, Princeton, Princeton University Press.

PRATT, J. W. and SCHLAIFER, R. (1984) 'On the Nature and Discovery of Structure', *Journal of the American Statistical Association*, 79, 9–21.

PRESTON, A. J. (1974) 'A Dynamic Generalisation of Tinbergen's Theory of Policy', *Review of Economic Studies*, 41, 65–74.

PRESTON, A. J. and PAGAN, A. R. (1982) *The Theory of Economic Policy*, Cambridge, Cambridge University Press.

PRESTON, R. S., KLEIN, L. R., O'BRIEN, Y. C. and BROWN, B. W. (1976) *Control Theory Simulations Using the Wharton Long Term Annual and Industry Forecasting Model*, Philadelphia, Wharton EFA Inc.

PROTHERO, D. L. and WALLIS, K. F. (1976) 'Modelling Macroeconomic Time Series', *Journal of the Royal Statistical Society*, A. 139, 486–500.

QUENOUILLE, M. H. (1957) *The Analysis of Multiple Time Series*, London, Griffin.

RADICE, E. A. (1939) 'A Dynamic Scheme for the British Trade Cycle, 1929–37', *Econometrica*, 7, 47–56.

RASMUSSEN, W. D. and BAKER, L. G. (1972) *The Department of Agriculture*, New York, Praeger.

RAYNER, J. and ALDRICH, J. (1988) 'Identification Issues in Specification Searching', Mimeo. University of Southampton.

REID, M. G. (1934) *Economics of Household Production*, New York, Wiley.

REID, M. G. (1938) *Consumers and the Market*, New York, Croft.

REID, M. G. (1952) 'Effect of Income Concept Upon Expenditure Curves of Farm Families', in *Studies in Income and Wealth*, 14, New York, NBER.

REIERSØL, O. (1941) 'Confluence Analysis by Means of Lag Moments and Other Methods of Confluence Analysis', *Econometrica*, 9, 1–24.

REIERSØL, O. (1945) 'Confluence Analysis by Means of Instrumental Sets of Variables', *Arkiv for Matematik, Astronomi och Fysik*, 32, 1–119.

REIERSØL, O. (1950) 'Identifiability of a Linear Relationship Between Variables Which are Subject to Error', *Econometrica*, 18, 375–89.

ROBBINS, L. (1932) *An Essay on the Nature and Significance of Economic Science*, London, Macmillan.

ROBBINS, L. (1947) *The Economic Problem in Peace and War*, London, Macmillan.

ROBBINS, L. (1954) *The Economist in the Twentieth Century*, London, Macmillan.

ROBBINS, L. (1959) 'The Present Position of Economics', *Rivista di Politica Economica*, 49, 1347–63.

ROBBINS, L. (1971) *Autobiography of an Economist*, London, Macmillan.

ROBERTSON, D. H. (1955) 'Creeping Inflation', *Bulletin of the London and Cambridge Economic Service*.

ROBSERTSON, D. H. (1963) 'Thoughts on Inflation', in Robertson, D. H. *Lectures on Economics Principles*, London, Fontana, 472–80.

ROOS, C. (1934) *Dynamic Economics*, Cowles Commission Monograph 1, Bloomington, Principia Press.

ROSA, R. V. (1948) 'Use of the Consumption Function in Short Run Forecasting', *Review of Economics and Statistics*, 30, 91–105.

ROTHENBERG, T. J. (1971) 'Identification in Parametric Models', *Econometrica*, 39, 577–92.

ROUTH, G. (1959) 'The Relation between Unemployment and the Rate of Change of Money Wages: A Comment', *Economica*, 26, 299–315.

ROWLEY, J. C. R. (1973), *Econometric Estimation*, London, Weidenfield and Nicholson.

ROWLEY, J. C. R. and HAMOUDA, I. (1987) 'Troublesome Probability and Economics', Mimeo, McGill University.

ROWLEY, J. C. R. and JAIN, R. (1987) 'The Way the Cook Chooses: A Modern Reassessment of the Keynes–Tinbergen Exchange, Mimeo, McGill Univerity.

ROWNTREE, B. S. (1902) *Poverty: A Study of Town Life*, London, Macmillan.

RUSTEM, B. and ZARROP, M. B. (1979) 'A Newton Type Method for the Optimisation and Control of Nonlinear Econometric Models', *Journal of Economic Dynamics and Control*, 1, 283–300.

RUSTEM, B. and ZARROP, M. B. (1981) 'A Quasi-Newton Algorithm for the Control of Large Nonlinear Econometric Models', *Large Scale Systems*, 2, 105–111.

SALMON, M. (1982) 'Error Correction Mechanisms', *Economic Journal*, 92, 615–29.

SAMUELSON, P. A. (1941) 'Appendix to Chapter 11: A Statistical Analysis of the Consumption Function', in Hansen, A. H. *Fiscal Policy and Business Cycles*, Allen & Unwin, 250–61.

SAMUELSON, P. A. (1943) 'Full Employment After the War', in Harris, S. E. ed., *Postwar Economic Problems*, New York, McGraw Hill, 27–53.

SAMUELSON, P. A. (1947) *Foundations of Economic Analysis*, Cambridge, Ma., Harvard University Press.

SAMUELSON, P. A. (1965) 'Some Notions of Causality and Teleology in Economics', in Lerner, D. ed *Cause and Effect*, Glencoe Ill., Free Press.

SAMUELSON, P. A. (1970) 'The Fundamental Approximation Theorem of Portfolio Analysis in Terms of Means, Variances, and Higher Moments', *Review of Economics and Statistics*, 37, 537–42.

SAMUELSON, P. A. (1977) *Collected Scientific Papers*, 4, Cambridge, Mass., MIT Press.

SAMUELSON, P. A. (1979) 'Paul Douglas's Measurement of Production Functions and Marginal Productivities', *Journal of Political Economy*, 87, 923–39.

SAMUELSON, P. A., KOOPMANS, T. C. and STONE, J. R. N. (1954) 'Report of the Evaluative Committee for Econometrica', *Econometrica*, 22, 141–6.

SANTOMERO, A. and SEATER, J. (1978) 'The Inflation Unemployment Trade Off: A Critique of the Literature', *Journal of Economic Literature*, 16, 499–544.

SARGAN, J. D. (1959) 'The Estimation of Relationships with Autocorrelated Residuals by the Use of Instrumental Variables', *Journal of the Royal Statistical Society*, B, 21, 91–105.

SARGAN, J. D. (1964) 'Wages and Prices in the United Kingdom: A Study in Econometric Methodology', in Hart, R. E., Mills, G. and Whittaker, J. K. eds. *Econometric Analysis for National Economic Planning*, London, Butterworth, 25–54; Reprinted in Hendry and Wallis (1984), 275–314.

SARGAN, J. D. (1980) 'Some Tests of Dynamic Specification', *Econometrica*, 48, 879–97.

SARGENT, T. (1976) 'The Observational Equivalence of Natural and Unnatural Rate Theories of Macroeconomics', *Journal of Political Economy*, 84, 631–40.

SARGENT, T. (1979) *Macroeconomic Theory*, New York, Academic Press.

SARLE, C. F. (1927) *Reliability and Adequacy of Farm-Price Data*, USDA Bulletin 1480, Washington DC, Government Printing Office.

SARLE, C. F. (1932) *Adequacy and Reliability of Crop-Yield Estimates*, USDA Bulletin 311, Washington DC, Government Printing Office.

SAYER, A. (1984) *Method in Social Science: A Realist Approach*, London, Hutchinson.

SAYERS, S. (1985) *Reality and Reason*, Oxford, Blackwell.

SCHULTZ, H. (1925) 'The Statistical Law of Demand as Illustrated by the Demand for Sugar', *Journal of Political Economy*, 33, 481–504 and 477–637.

SCHULTZ, H. (1931) 'Review of G. Evans', Mathematical Introduction to Economics', *Journal of the American Statistical Association*, 26, 484–91.

SCHULTZ, H. (1938) *Theory and Measurement of Demand*, Chicago, University of Chicago Press.

SCHUMPETER, J. A. (1933) 'The Common Sense of Econometrics', *Econometrica*, 1, 5–12.

SCHUMPETER, J. A. (1946) 'Keynes and Statistics', *Review of Economics and Statistics*, 27, 194–96.

SCHUMPETER, J. A. (1954) *A History of Economic Analysis*, New York, Oxford University Press.

SHORES, L. N. (1946) 'A System of Structural Equations Explaining the Demand for Food in the United States', University of Chicago, Mimeo.

SIMON, H. A. (1953) 'Causal Ordering and Identifiability', in Hood & Koopmans eds. (1953), 49–74.

SIMON, H. A. (1956) 'Dynamic Programming Under Uncertainty with a Quadratic Criterion Function', *Econometrica*, 24, 74–81.

SIMON, H. A. (1977) *Models of Discovery*, Dordrecht, Reidel.

SIMS, C. A. (1980) 'Macroeconomics and Reality', *Econometrica*, 48, 1–49.

SIMS, C. A. (1982) 'Policy Analysis with Econometric Models', *Brookings Papers on Economic Activity*, 1982 (1), 107–163.

SLUTSKY, E. (1937) 'The Summation of Random Causes as the Source of Cyclic Processes', *Econometrica*, 5, 105–46.

SMITHIES, A. (1945) 'Forecasting Postwar Demand I', *Econometrica*, 13, 1–14.

SPANOS, A. (1986) *Statistical Foundations of Econometric Modelling*, Cambridge, Cambridge University Press.

SPANOS, A. (1987) 'Error Autocorrelation Revisited: The AR(1) Case', *Econometric Reviews*, 6, 285–94.

SPANOS, A. (1988a) 'Towards a Unifying Methodological Framework for Econometric Modelling', *Economic Notes*, 1–28.

SPANOS, A. (1988b) 'On re-reading Haavelmo', Birbeck College Discussion Paper.

SPANOS, A. (forthcoming) 'The Simultaneous Equations Model Revisited: Statistical Adequacy and Empirical Modeling', *Journal of Econometrics*.

Spectator, (1967) 'Put Not They Trust in Paish', Leading Article, 14/4/67.

STAEHLE, H. (1934a) 'The Reaction of Consumers to Changes in Prices and Income: A Quantitative Study in Immigrants' Behavior', *Econometrica*, 2, 59–72.

STAEHLE, H. (1934b) 'Annual Survey of Statistical Information: Family Budgets', *Econometrica*, 2, 349–62.

STAEHLE, H. (1937a) 'A General Method for the Comparison of the Price of Living', *Review of Economic Studies*, 4, 205–14.

STAEHLE, H. (1937b) 'Short-Period Variations in the Distribution of Incomes', *Review of Economic Statistics*, 19, 133–43.

STAEHLE, H. (1938) 'New Considerations on the Distribution of Incomes and the Propensity to Consume (Partly in Reply to Mr Dirks)' *Review of Economic Statistics*, 20, 134–41.

STAEHLE, H. and HAAVELMO, T. (1941) *The Elements of Frisch's Confluence Analysis*, Mimeo.

STEINDL, J. (1944) 'Postwar Employment in the USA', *Bulletin of the Oxford Institute of Statistics*, 6, 193–202.

STIGLER, G. J. (1954) 'The Early History of Empirical Studies of Consumer Behavior', *Journal of Political Economy*, 42, 95–113.

STIGLER, G. J. (1962) 'Henry L. Moore and Statistical Economics', *Econometrica*, 30, 1–21.

STIGLER, S. (1986) *The History of Statistics*, Cambridge, Mass., Harvard University Press.

STONE, J. R. N. (1942) 'National Income in the United Kingdom and the United States of America', *Review of Economic Studies*, 10, 1–27.

STONE, J. R. N. (1945) 'The analysis of Market Demand', *Journal of the Royal Statistical Society*, A, 108, 1–98.

STONE, J. R. N. (1951) 'The Demand for Food in the United Kingdom Before the War', *Metroeconomica*, 3, 8–27.

STONE, J. R. N. (1954) *The Measurement of Consumers' Expenditure and Behaviour in the United Kingdom*, 1920–38, Vol. 1, Cambridge, Cambridge University Press.

STONE, J. R. N. (1978) 'Keynes, Political Arithmetic and Econometrics', British Academy, Seventh Keynes Lecture in Economics.

STONE, J. R. N. and STONE, W. M. (1938) 'The Marginal Propensity to Consume and the Multiplier: A Statistical Investigation', *Review of Economic Studies*, 6, 1–24.

SUITS, D. B. (1963) 'The Determinants of Consumer Expenditure: A Review of Present Knowledge', in *Impacts of Monetary Policy*, Englewood Cliffs, Prentice Hall.

SWANN, G. M. P. (1982) 'Multicollinearity and Measurement Error', University of Bristol, Mimeo.

SWANN, G. M. P. (1985) 'Uncertainty in Regression Estimates: The Relative Importance of Sampling and Non-Sampling Uncertainty', *Oxford Bulletin of Economics and Statistics*, 47, 303–310.

SYDENSTRICKER, E., KING, W. I. and WIEHL, D. (1924) *The Income Cycle in the Life of the Wage Earner*, Washington DC, U.S. Public Health Service.

TAYLOR, H. C. (1905) *Agricultural Economics*, New York, Macmillan.

TEBBUTT, A. R. (1933) *The Behavior of Consumption in Business Depression*, Harvard Graduate School of Business Administration, Business Research Studies, 3.

THEIL, H. (1951) 'De Invleod van de Vooraden op het Consumentengedrag', Amsterdam, Poortpers.

THEIL, H. (1954) 'Econometric Models and Welfare Maximisation', *Weltwirtschaftliches Archiv*. 72, 60–83.

THEIL, H. (1956) 'On the Theory of Economic Policy', *American Economic Review, Papers and Proceedings*, 46, 360–66.

THEIL, H. (1957) 'A Note on Certainty Equivalence in Dynamic Planning', *Econometrica*, 25, 246–49.

THEIL, H. (1958) *Economic Forecasts and Policy*, Amsterdam, North Holland.

THEIL, H. (1964) *Optimal Decision Rules for Government and Industry*, Amsterdam, North Holland.

THEIL, H. (1965) 'Linear Decision Rules for Macrodynamic Policy Problems', in Hickman, B. ed. *Quantitative Planning for Economic Policy*, Washington DC, Brookings, 18–42.

THOMAS, J. J. (1985), 'Keynes, Income Distribution and Early Empirical Studies of the Consumption Function', Mimeo, London, School of Economics.

THOMSEN, F. L. and FOOTE, R. J. (1952) *Agricultural Prices*, 2nd ed., New York, McGraw Hill.

THURSTONE, L. L. (1935) *The Vectors of Mind*, Chicago, University of Chicago Press.

TIMBRELL, M. C. (1976) 'Consumption Functions'. In Heathfield, D. ed. *Topics in Applied Macroeconomics*, London, Macmillan.

Times Review of Industry (1967) 'Exit Neild: Re-Enter Paish', 4/1/67, 14.

TINBERGEN, J. (1929) *Minimumproblemen in de Natuurkunde en de Ekonomie*, Amsterdam, Paris.

TINBERGEN, J. (1930) 'Bestimmung und Deutung von Angebotskurven: Ein Beispiel', *Zeitschrift Für Nationalökonomie*, 1, 669–79.

TINBERGEN, J. (1933) 'L'Utilisation des Equations Fonctionnelles et des Nombres Complexes dans les Recherches Economiques', *Econometrica*, 1, 36–51.

TINBERGEN, J. (1935) 'Suggestions on Quantitative Business Cycle Theory', *Econometrica*, 3, 241–54.

TINBERGEN, J. (1936) 'Preadvies voor de Vereniging voor Staathuishoudkunde', The Hague.

TINBERGEN, J. (1937) *An Econometric Approach to Business Cycle Problems*, Paris, Herman.

TINBERGEN, J. (1938a) 'Mr Tinbergen's Reply to Professor Frisch's Note on Statistical Versus Theoretical Relations in Economic Macrodynamics', Geneva, League of Nations, reprinted in Frisch (1948a).

TINBERGEN, J. (1938b) 'Statistical Evidence on the Acceleration Principle', *Economica*, 5, 164–76.

TINBERGEN, J. (1939) *Statistical Testing of Business Cycle Theories*, 2 vols., Geneva, League of Nations.

TINBERGEN, J. (1940) 'Econometric Business Cycle Research, *Review of Economic Studies*, 7, 83.

TINBERGEN, J. (1942a) 'Critical Remarks on Some Business Cycle Theories', *Econometrica*, 10, 129.

TINBERGEN, J. (1942b) 'Does Consumption Lag Behind Incomes?', *Review of Economic Statistics*, 24, 1–8.

TINBERGEN, J. (1947) 'The Netherlands Central Economic Plan for 1947', *Schweizerische Zeitschrift fuer Volkswirtschaft und Statistik*. 83, 19–29.

TINBERGEN, J. (1951a) *Econometrics*, London, Allen & Unwin.

TINBERGEN, J. (1951b) *Business Cycles in the United Kingdom* 1870–1914, Amsterdam, North Holland.

TINBERGEN, J. (1952) *On the Theory of Economic Policy*, Amsterdam, North Holland.

TINBERGEN, J. (1954) *Centralisation and Decentralisation in Economic Policy*, Amsterdam, North-Holland.

TINBERGEN, J. (1956) *Economic Policy: Principles and Design*, Amsterdam, North Holland.

TINBERGEN, J. (1959) 'An Economic Policy for 1936', in Klassen *et al.* (1959), 37–84.

TINBERGEN, J. (1987) 'Over Modellen', Paper Presented at the 50th Anniversary Meeting of de Vereniging voor Staathuishoudkunde.

TINBERGEN, J. and POLAK, J. J. (1950) *Dynamics of Business Cycles*, Chicago, University of Chicago Press.

TINTNER, G. (1944) 'An Application of the Variate Difference Method to Multiple Regression', *Econometrica*, 12, 97–113.

TINTNER, G. (1950) 'Static Econometric Models and Their Empirical Verification: Illustrated by a Study of the American Meat Market', *Metroeconomica*, 2, 172–81.

TINTNER, G. (1952) *Econometrics*, New York, Wiley.

TINTNER, G. (1953) 'The Definition of Econometrics', *Econometrica*, 21, 31–9.

TINTNER, G. and SENGUPTA, J. (1972) *Stochastic Economics*, New York, Academic Press.

TOBIN, J. (1951) 'Relative Income, Absolute Income, and Saving', in Dupriez, L. H. *et al. Money, Trade, and Economic Growth*, London, Macmillan, 135–56.

TOBIN, J. (1968) 'Consumption Function', in *International Encyclopaedia of the Social Sciences*, London, Macmillan, 3, 358–69.

TOLLEY, H. R. and EZEKIEL, M. (1923), 'A Method of Handling Multiple Correlation Problems', *Journal of the American Statistical Association*, 18, 994–1003.

TOLLEY, HOWARD R., BLACK, J. D. and EZEKIEL, M. (1924) *Input as Related to Output in Farm Organization and Cost of Production Studies*, USDA Bulletin 1277, Washington DC, Government Printing Office.

TURNOVSKY, S., (1977) *Macroeconomic Analysis and Stabilisation Policy*, Cambridge, Cambridge University Press.

VALAVANIS, S. (1959) *Econometrics*, New York, McGraw Hill.

VAN EIJK, C. and SANDEE, J. (1959) 'Quantitative Determination of an Optimum Economic Policy', *Econometrica*, 27, 1–13.

VAN FRAASSEN, B. C. (1980), *The Scientific Image*, Oxford, Clarendon Press.

VINING, R. (1949a) 'Koopmans on the Choice of Variables', *Review of Economics and Statistics*, 31, 77–86.

VINING, R. (1949b) 'Methodological Issues in Quantitative Economics: A Rejoinder', *The Review of Economics and Statistics*, 31, 91–94.

WAITE, W. C. (1929) 'The Economics of Consumption as a Field for Research in Agricultural Economics', *Journal of Farm Economics*, 11, 565–73.

WALD, A. (1940) 'The Fitting of Straight Lines if Both Variables are Subject to Error', *Annals of Mathematical Statistics*, 11, 284–300.

WALD, A. (1943) Tests of Statistical Hypotheses Concerning Several Parameters when the Number of Observations is Large', *Transactions of the American Mathematical Society*, 4, 464–482.

WALD, A. (1950) 'Note on the Identification of Economic Relations', in Koopmans ed. (1950), 238–44.

WALLIS, K. F. (1971) 'Wages, Prices and Incomes Policies: Some Comments', *Economica*, 38, 304–10.

WALLIS, K. F. (1977) 'Multiple Time Series Analysis and the Final Form of Econometric Models', *Econometrica*, 45, 1481–97.

WALLIS, K. F. (1979) *Topics in Applied Econometrics*, Oxford, Blackwell.

WALLIS, W. A. (1942) The Temporal Stability of Consumption Patterns', *Review of Economic Statistics*, 24, 177–83.

WAUGH, F. V. (1923) *Factors Influencing the Price of New Jersey Potatoes on the New York Market*, New Jersey Department of Agriculture Circular 66.

WAUGH, F. V. (1929) *Quality as a Determinant of Vegetable Prices*, New York, Columbia University Press.

WAUGH, F. V. (1935a) 'A Simplified Method of Determining Multiple Regression Constants', *Journal of the American Statistical Association*, 30, 694–700.

WAUGH, F. V. (1935b) 'The Marginal Utility of Money in the United States from 1917 to 1921 and from 1922 to 1932', *Econometrica*, 3, 376–399.

WAUGH, F. V. (1938) 'Market Prorates and Social Welfare', *Journal of Farm Economics*, 20, 403–16.

WAUGH, F. V. (1942) 'Regressions Between Sets of Variables', *Econometrica*, 10, 290–310.

WAUGH, F. V. (1944) 'Does the Consumer Benefit from Instability?', *Quarterly Journal of Economics*, 58, 602–14.

WAUGH, F. V. (1950) 'Inversion of the Leontief Matrix by Power Series', *Econometrica*, 18, 142–54.

WAUGH, F. V. (1951) 'The Minimum-Cost Dairy Feed: (An Application of "Linear Programing")', *Journal of Farm Economics*, 33, 299–310.

WAUGH, F. V. (1956) 'A Partial Indifference Surface for Beef and Pork', *Journal of Farm Economics*, 38, 102–12.

WAUGH, F. V. (1964a) 'Cobweb Models', *Journal of Farm Economics*, 46, 732–50.

WAUGH, F. V. (1964b) *Demand and Price Analysis: Some Examples from Agriculture*, USDA Bulletin 1316, Washington DC, Government Printing Office.

WAUGH, F. V. (1984) *Selected Writings on Agricultural Policy and Economic Analysis*, Houck, J. P. and Abel, M. E. eds., Minneapolis, University of Minnesota Press,

WEINTRAUB, E. R. (1985) *General Equilibrium Analysis, Studies in Appraisal*, Cambridge, Cambridge University Press.

WHITTLE, P. (1982) *Optimisation Over Time*, New York, Wiley.

WILLIAMS, F. M. (1937) 'Methods of Measuring Variations in Family Expenditures', *Journal of the American Statistical Association*, 32, 40–6.

WINSTON, C. and SMITH, M. A. (1948) 'Retail Sales and Consumer Income', *Survey of Current Business*, 28, 12–9.

WOHLTMANN, H. W. (1984) 'A Note on Aoki's Conditions for Path Controllability of Continuous Time Dynamic Economic Systems', *Review of Economic Studies*, 51, 343–9.

WOHLTMANN, H. W. and KRÖMER, W. (1984) 'Sufficient Conditions for Dynamic Path Controllability of Economic Systems', *Journal of Economic Dynamics and Control*, 7, 314–30.

WOLD, H. O. A. (1938) *A Study in the Analysis of Stationary Time Series*, Stockholm, Almqvist and Wiksell.

WONHAM, W. H. (1974) 'Linear Multivariate Control: a Geometric Approach', *Lecture Notes in Economics and Mathematical Systems*, 101, Berlin, Springer-Verlag.

WOOD, H. (1909) 'Real Wages and the Standard of Comfort since 1850', *Journal of the Royal Statistical Society*, 72, 91–103.

WORKING, E. J. (1927) 'What do Statistical Demand Curves Show', *Quarterly Journal of Economics*, 41, 212–235.

WORKING, H. (1922) 'Factors Determining the Price of Potatoes in St Paul and Minneapolis', University of Minnesota Agricultural Experiment Station Technical Bulletin 10, St Paul.

WORKING, H. (1925) 'The Statistical Determination of Demand Curves', *Quarterly Journal of Economics*, 39, 503–543.

WOYTINSKY, W. S. (1943) 'Income cycle in the life of Families and Individuals', *Social Security Bulletin*, 6, 8–17.

WOYTINSKY, W. S. (1946) 'Relationship Between Consumers' Expenditures, Savings, and Disposable Income', *Review of Economic Statistics*, 28, 1–12.

WOYTINSKY, W. S. (1948) 'Consumption-Saving Function: Its Algebra and Philosophy', *Review of Economic Statistics*, 30, 45–55.

WRIGHT, D. M. (1951) 'Comment' in *NBER Conference on Business Cycles*, New York, NBER, 125–67.

WRIGHT, P. (1915) 'Moore's Economic Cycles', *Quarterly Journal of Economics*, 29, 631–641.

WRIGHT, P. (1928) *The Tariff on Animal and Vegetable Oils*, New York, Macmillan.

WRIGHT, P. (1930) 'Moore's Synthetic Economics', *Journal of Political Economy*, 38, 328–44.

WRIGHT, S. (1934) 'The Method of Path Coefficients', *Annals of Mathematical Statistics*, 5, 161–215.

WULWICK, N. J., (1987) 'The Phillips Curve: Which? Whose? To do what?, How?', *Southern Economic Journal*, 53, 834–57.

YOUNG, R. M. (1975) 'Certainty Equivalence, First Order Certainty Equivalence, Stochastic Control, and the Covariance Structure', *Econometrica*, 43, 421–30.

YULE, G. U. (1921) 'On the Time-Correlation Problem, with Especial Reference to the

YULE, G. U. (1927) 'On a Method of Investigating Periodicities in Disturbed Series, with Special Reference to Wolfer's Sunspot Numbers', *Philosophical Transactions of the Royal Society*, A, 226, 267–98.

ZELLNER, A. (1988) 'Bayesian Analysis in Econometrics', *Journal of Econometrics*, 37, 27–50. Variate-Difference Correlation Method', *Journal of the Royal Statistical Society*, 84, 497–526.

ZELLNER, A. and PALM, F. (1974) 'Time Series Analysis and Simultaneous Equation Econometric Models, *Journal of Econometrics,* 2, 17–54.

ZIMMERMAN, C. C. (1927) 'Objectives and Methods in Rural Living Studies', *Journal of Farm Economics,* 9, 223–37.

ZIMMERMAN, C. C. (1936) *Consumption and Standards of Living,* London, Williams and Norgate.

INDEX